REA's Test Prep Books Are The Best!

(a sample of the <u>hundreds of letters</u> REA receives each year)

" I did well because of your wonderful prep books... I just wanted to thank you for helping me prepare for these tests. "
Student, San Diego, CA

" My students report your chapters of review as the most valuable single resource they used for review and preparation. "
Teacher, American Fork, UT

" Your book was such a better value and was so much more complete than anything your competition has produced — and I have them all! "
Teacher, Virginia Beach, VA

" Compared to the other books that my fellow students had, your book was the most useful in helping me get a great score. "
Student, North Hollywood, CA

" Your book was responsible for my success on the exam, which helped me get into the college of my choice... I will look for REA the next time I need help. "
Student, Chesterfield, MO

" Just a short note to say thanks for the great support your book gave me in helping me pass the test... I'm on my way to a B.S. degree because of you! "
Student, Orlando, FL

(more on next page)

(continued from front page)

" I just wanted to thank you for helping me get a great score on the AP U.S. History exam... Thank you for making great test preps! "
Student, Los Angeles, CA

" Your *Fundamentals of Engineering Exam* book was the absolute best preparation I could have had for the exam, and it is one of the major reasons I did so well and passed the FE on my first try. "
Student, Sweetwater, TN

" I used your book to prepare for the test and found that the advice and the sample tests were highly relevant... Without using any other material, I earned very high scores and will be going to the graduate school of my choice. "
Student, New Orleans, LA

" What I found in your book was a wealth of information sufficient to shore up my basic skills in math and verbal... The section on analytical ability was excellent. The practice tests were challenging and the answer explanations most helpful. It certainly is the *Best Test Prep for the GRE!* "
Student, Pullman, WA

" I really appreciate the help from your excellent book. Please keep up the great work. "
Student, Albuquerque, NM

" I am writing to thank you for your test preparation... your book helped me immeasurably and I have nothing but praise for your *GRE* preparation."
Student, Benton Harbor, MI

(more on front page)

The Best Test Preparation for the
AP
Art History
Exam

With CD-ROM for Windows®

Frank Chmiel
AP Art History Instructor
Montgomery High School
Skillman, New Jersey

Larry Krieger
Former AP Art History Instructor
Montgomery High School
Skillman, New Jersey

Research & Education Association
Visit our website at
www.rea.com

Research & Education Association
61 Ethel Road West
Piscataway, New Jersey 08854
E-mail: info@rea.com

The Best Test Preparation for the
AP ART HISTORY EXAM
With TEST*ware*® on CD-ROM

Printed in the United States of America

Library of Congress Control Number 2006933743

International Standard Book Number 0-7386-0292-2

Windows® is a registered trademark of Microsoft Corporation.

 REA® and TEST*ware*® are registered trademarks of
Research & Education Association, Inc.

CONTENTS

ABOUT OUR AUTHORS

The co-authors of this book, Larry Krieger and Frank Chmiel, have invested in these pages the wisdom and experience they have gained as developers of an AP Art History program that, according to the College Board, has led the world three years running "in helping the widest segment of their total school population achieve an exam grade of 3 or higher." That program, which has produced hundreds of individual success stories, is based at Montgomery High School in Skillman, New Jersey. Together, Mr. Krieger and Mr. Chmiel now give you access to the same materials that provided the platform for their students' achievement at Montgomery High.

Larry Krieger earned his B.A. and M.A.T. from the University of North Carolina at Chapel Hill and his M.A. from Wake Forest. In a career spanning three decades, in North Carolina and later in New Jersey, Mr. Krieger taught sociology, American history, world history, and European history, retiring in 2004. It was Mr. Krieger who established Montgomery High School's AP Art History program and later team-taught with Frank Chmiel. Mr. Krieger is also the author of numerous United States history and world history textbooks. Currently, Mr. Krieger presents SAT workshops in Atlanta, Minneapolis, Denver, and Charles County, Maryland.

Over the past four years, **Frank Chmiel,** a 1998 graduate of Princeton University, has taught more than 400 students in AP Art History, and a number of them have been motivated to continue their study in art history at the college level, including study abroad. Mr. Chmiel has also taught a lecture series entitled "Christian Art from the Catacombs to the Cathedrals," as well as "Christian Art from the 14th through 16th Centuries" at Nassau Christian Center Church in Princeton. In 2005 he participated in the "Teachers as Scholars Program" through Princeton University, focusing on 19th-century French painting. Mr. Chmiel's nine-year teaching career has also included classes in 20th-century U.S. history, world history, and criminal justice.

ABOUT RESEARCH & EDUCATION ASSOCIATION

Founded in 1959, Research & Education Association (REA) is dedicated to publishing the finest and most effective educational materials—including software, study guides, and test preps—for students in middle school, high school, college, graduate school, and beyond.

Today, REA's wide-ranging catalog is a leading resource for teachers, students, and professionals.

We invite you to visit us at *www.rea.com* to find out how "REA is making the world smarter."

STAFF ACKNOWLEDGMENTS

In addition to our authors, we would like to thank Larry B. Kling, Vice President, Editorial, for his overall guidance, which brought this publication to completion; Pam Weston, Vice President, Publishing, for setting the quality standards for production integrity and managing the publication to completion; John Cording, Vice President, Technology, for coordinating the design and development of REA's TEST*ware*®; Diane Goldschmidt, Senior Editor, for editorial project management; Anne Winthrop Esposito, Senior Editor, and Molly Solanki, Associate Editor, for preflight editorial review; Heena Patel and Michelle Boykins-Smith, Technology Project Managers, for their design contributions and software testing efforts; Jeff LoBalbo, Senior Graphic Designer, for page design and art acquisition; Christine Saul, Senior Graphic Designer, for our cover design; and Tim Schoch for researching the images used throughout this publication.

We also gratefully acknowledge Barbara McGowran for copyediting the manuscript and the team at Aquent Publishing Services for typesetting this edition.

STUDY SCHEDULE
AP Art History

The following study schedule allows for thorough preparation for the AP Art History Examination. Although it is designed for six weeks, it can be condensed into a three-week review by collapsing each two-week period into a single week. Be sure to set aside at least two hours each day to study. Bear in mind that the more time you spend studying, the more prepared and relaxed you will feel on the day of the exam.

Week	Activity
1	Read and study Chapter 1 of this book, which will introduce you to the AP Art History Examination. Then take Practice Exam 1 on CD-ROM. This will familiarize you with the test while also enabling you to evaluate your strengths and weaknesses. After taking Practice Exam 1, study Chapters 2, 3, and 11. These chapters will provide examples for the long essay question on the exam that requires you to write an essay on art beyond the European tradition.
2	Carefully read and study Chapters 4 through 8 in Part 1, Ancient Art and Chapters 9 through 14 in Part 2, Medieval Art. Familiarize yourself with key terms and key artistic styles. Study and review terms 1 through 31 in Chapter 36.
3	Carefully read and study Chapters 15 through 19 in Part 3, Renaissance Art. Familiarize yourself with the key terms, styles and artists. In Chapter 36, study and review terms 32 through 35.
4	Carefully read and study Chapters 20 through 22 in Part 4, Baroque Art, and Chapters 23 and 24 in Part 5, Nineteenth-Century Art. Familiarize yourself with key terms, styles, and artists. Then review the first 15 key female artists and patrons listed in Chapter 33.
5	Carefully read and study Chapters 25 through 28 in Part 5, Nineteenth-Century Art, and Chapters 29 through 32 in Part 6, Twentieth-Century Art. Familiarize yourself with key terms, styles, and artists. Review key terms 36 through 50 listed in Chapter 36 and also the female artists and patrons numbered 16 through 32 in Chapter 33.
6	Carefully read and study Chapters 34, 35, and 37 in Part 7, Key Points You Absolutely, Positively Have to Know. Take Practice Exam 2 on CD-ROM. Use this exam as a guide to help you focus your final review on topics requiring additional study. If time allows, enhance your feel for the rhythm and flow of the exam by taking the printed version of practice exams 1 and 2 in this book.

INTRODUCTION

AP Art History

A NOTE FROM THE AUTHORS

AP ART HISTORY: THE ULTIMATE COURSE

Congratulations and welcome! Congratulations because you are studying AP Art History, and welcome because you are reading this book. We begin by admitting that we have a strong bias in favor of the AP Art History course. AP Art History is the ultimate course because it encompasses so much, beginning with prehistoric art and concluding with pop art.

In addition, as you learn about the great civilizations of the past, you will meet an incredible number of key artists and study their masterpieces. You will learn a great deal about Greek mythology as you study the gods, goddesses, and heroes who inspired so much Western art.

Beyond the great civilizations and Greek mythology, you will also learn a great deal about religion. For a millennium, the Catholic Church was the most important patron of the arts. It commissioned works of art designed to illustrate the Bible for its worshippers, who were predominantly illiterate. You will also learn about the Protestant Reformation and how it affected Western art, as well as the distinctive characteristics of Islamic art.

Finally, you will learn how artists look at and interpret the world around them. You'll see how this artistic vision is expressed in paintings, sculptures, and architectural treasures. We're confident that this exposure to great works of art will teach you about the aesthetics of beauty. We are also confident that as a result of this exposure, you will acquire great insights into the human mind and soul—insights that we hope last a lifetime.

— Larry Krieger and Frank Chmiel

Chapter 1

Excelling on the AP Art History Exam

About This Book and TEST*ware*® CD-ROM with Full-Color Art Browser

This book, along with the companion TEST*ware*® software, provides a thorough review for the Advanced Placement Art History Examination and is intended to make test preparation as easy and effective as possible. Cited throughout the book are art images that can be found on the accompanying CD-ROM. The image numbers in the book's review section correspond to those on the CD for simultaneous reference as you study. The practice tests, for which images are also presented on the CD in color, feature detailed answer explanations, giving you the context you need to excel on the AP Art History Exam.

The two full-length practice exams are included in two formats: in printed format in this book and in TEST*ware*® format on the enclosed CD. We strongly recommend that you begin your preparation with the TEST*ware*® practice exams. The software provides the added benefits of automatic, accurate scoring and enforced time conditions. To best utilize your study time, follow our Study Schedule, which you will find in the front of this book. The schedule is based on a six-week program, but if necessary can be condensed to three weeks by collapsing each two-week period into one week.

SSD accommodations for students with disabilities

Many students qualify for extra time to take the AP exams, and our TEST*ware*® can be adapted to accommodate your time extension. This allows you to practice under the same extended-time accommodations that you will receive on the actual test day. To customize your TEST*ware*® to suit the most common extensions, visit our website at *www.rea.com/ssd*.

About the Advanced Placement Program

The Advanced Placement Program is designed to provide high school students with the opportunity to pursue college-level studies. The program consists of two components: a course and an exam. Students are expected to gain college-level skills and acquire college-level knowledge of art history through the AP course. When they complete the course, students take the AP Art History exam. Test results are used to grant course credit and/or determine placement level in the subject when students enter college.

The AP Art History exam, along with the other AP exams, is administered each May at participating schools and multischool centers throughout the world.

About the Exam

The AP Art History exam is 3 hours long and contains 115 multiple-choice questions, 7 short essay questions, and 2 long essay questions. The questions are designed to provide a comprehensive evaluation of your knowledge of art history.

Content of the Exam

The following table shows the key content areas and the percentage of questions typically asked in each area:

	Content	Approximate Percentages	Total
I.	**Ancient Through Medieval**		30%
	A. Greece and Rome	10–15%	
	B. Early Christian, Byzantine, Early Medieval	5–10%	
	C. Romanesque	3–7%	
	D. Gothic	7–10%	
II.	**Beyond the European Artistic Traditions**		20%
	Africa (including Egypt), the Americas, Asia, Near East, Oceania, and Global Islamic Traditions		
III.	**Renaissance to Present**		50%
	A. 14th through 16th Centuries	12–17%	
	B. 17th and 18th Centuries	10–15%	
	C. 19th Century	10–15%	
	D. 20th and 21st Centuries	10–15%	

As you can see, the course is both comprehensive and flexible—comprehensive because it covers many topics and flexible because it gives teachers a great deal of freedom to choose what to teach. This freedom encourages teachers to be creative, but it can also pose problems for students preparing for the AP exam. For example, a number of questions about twentieth-century German Expressionists and American

Abstract Expressionists appeared on a recent administration of the exam. In contrast, an administration of the exam a few years later contained no questions on either style.

The course's broad scope—combined with the fact that different topics are emphasized each year—means that both teachers and students must make choices. It is impossible for art history teachers to cover everything because the course is too vast. It is also impossible for students to study everything. This book will help you decide which topics to study in depth and which topics to briefly review. Each chapter contains an introduction explaining why the topic is important and how it has been tested in the past.

Take another look at the course content outline. It distinguishes between topics within the European tradition and topics beyond the European artistic tradition. Topics beyond the European artistic tradition include art from the Americas, Asia, Africa, and Oceania. Although these topics could easily generate their own course, very few questions are devoted to them. Instead, most such questions are devoted to the ancient Near East, ancient Egypt, and the global Islamic tradition.

Format of the Exam

The AP Art History exam includes various types of questions. The best way to familiarize you with the test format is to walk you through it from beginning to end.

Section I

Part A: Slide-Based Multiple-Choice Questions (0.69 point per question)

When your test begins, your proctor will dim the lights and then use slide projectors to project images onto one or (usually) two screens. The two images are related. For example, a recent exam began with slides of cathedrals in Florence and Siena. The churches were built at about the same time and have many similarities and differences. Questions relating to the slides will focus on issues such as functions of works of art, patronage, period styles, chronology, and technique.

Four sets of these slide-based multiple-choice questions will be presented. Each set contains from seven to nine questions, each with four answer choices. You are allotted 4 minutes to answer each set of questions.

Part B: Multiple-Choice Questions (0.69 point per question)

After you complete the slide-based multiple-choice questions, your proctor will turn off the slide projectors and ask you to turn to Part B in your test booklet. Part B contains from 85 to 87 multiple-choice questions, each with four answer choices. About half of the questions refer to pictures of specific works of art, which are illustrated in the test booklet. A specific picture can be accompanied by one to four questions. The remaining multiple-choice questions will test your knowledge of artists and artistic styles. The questions are not arranged in chronological order.

You will have 1 hour to complete the 115 multiple-choice questions in Section I, Parts A and B. This section of the exam will be followed by a brief break.

Section II: Free-Response Questions

Long Essay Question (25 points)

After the break, you will given 30 minutes to write a long essay. This essay will require you to incorporate at least one example of art from beyond the European artistic tradition.

Short Essay Questions (10 points per question)

This part of the exam, which is 60 minutes long, consists of seven timed essay questions. The amount of time you are allotted for each question varies: you will be given 5 minutes to answer each of two questions and 10 minutes to answer each of the other five questions. Each question is based on one or two slides, and one question will include a primary source quotation. The short essay questions ask you to discuss specific works of art selected from at least seven periods in art history. A recent exam included short questions on an early Christian mosaic, a Greek sculpture, and a department store in Chicago designed by Louis Sullivan.

Long Essay Question (25 points)

Your test will conclude with a second 30-minute essay question. The question asks you to address significant art history themes and problems. Your essay must include a discussion of specific works of art. The topics for this essay are very broad. Recently students were asked to "select and identify two works of art that include symbolic or allegorical images."

Scoring the Exam

A Perfect Score

Each of the questions on your exam has a point value, but not all questions or types of questions are equal. Here is how the points are distributed:

1. Multiple-Choice Questions—80 points

The 115 multiple-choice questions are worth 0.69 point each, so a perfect score on the multiple-choice sections is 80. Remember, random guessing will not help your score. The College Board calculates the number of multiple-choice questions you answered incorrectly and multiplies that total by 1/3. This number is subtracted from the total number of questions you answered correctly to calculate your raw score. For example, 100 correctly answered questions and 15 incorrectly answered questions would be calculated as follows:

100 (Number correct) − [15 (Number wrong) × 1/3] = 95 (Raw score)

The raw score (95 in the example) is then multiplied by 0.69 to show the multiple-choice score (66 in the example).

2. Short Essay Questions—70 points

Each of the seven short essay questions is worth 10 points, but the AP exam readers will grade them on a 4-point scale. Each point is therefore worth 2.5 points. If your essay receives a 2, for example, you will earn 5 points for that essay.

3. Long Essay Questions—50 points

Each of the two long essay questions is worth 25 points. Each essay is scored on a scale of 0 to 9. Your scaled number is then multiplied by 2.77. It is important to remember that your first long essay is divided into two parts. One part will discuss an example from the European tradition, and one part will discuss an example from outside the European tradition. So each part of this essay is worth 12.5 points.

The College Board's 5-Point Scale

Although the questions on the AP Art History exam total 200 points, the score report you receive from the College Board will show your score as a number between 1 and 5. According to the College Board, 5 means "extremely well qualified," 4 means "well qualified," 3 means "qualified," 2 means "possibly qualified," and 1 means "no recommendation."

A score of 5 or 4 will enhance your academic résumé and impress college admission committees, and most colleges will award you academic credit for either score. It is not easy to score a 5 or 4. AP exams are designed to produce average scores of approximately 50 percent of the maximum possible score for the multiple-choice and essay sections. You should not expect to attain a perfect or even near-perfect score.

In a recent administration of the AP Art History exam, 13.5 percent of the students scored a 5 and 14.2 percent scored a 1. These percentages are very stable and vary only by a small amount from year to year.

The All-Important Score Range

You do not have to score a perfect 200 to achieve a 5. Instead, statisticians determine a score range for each test. Here is the score range for the 2004 exam:

Score Range	AP Grade	Percent Correct
135–200	5	67.5%
102–134	4	51.0%
72–101	3	36.0%
52–71	2	26.0%
0–51	1	<25.5%

Many students are surprised when they see this chart. Scoring a 5 or a 4 is not impossible. You need to answer only two-thirds of the questions correctly to score a 5 and answer just over one-half to score a 4.

Strategic Reviewing for the Exam

You should begin your review about three weeks before the exam. Here are some important dos and don'ts.

1. *DO* read and study this book.

If you are reading this book, you have already taken your first and most important step. Read and study it! Each chapter is carefully designed to review the artists, styles, and works of art you need to know. The two practice exams will give you a chance to test your knowledge and evaluate your progress. Use the tests and the answer guides to determine your strengths and weaknesses. Then refine your strengths and address your weaknesses.

2. *DO* go to AP Central.

The College Board maintains a comprehensive Web site called AP Central at *http://apcentral.collegeboard.com/*. The site contains a wealth of information about each AP exam, including a booklet titled "Art History Course Description," which is the authoritative guide to the course and to the types of questions found on the exam. The information related to the AP Art History exam includes essay questions, sample essays, and all the slide-based multiple-choice questions since 1999. You should examine a number of the sample essays and multiple-choice questions.

3. *DO NOT* skip twentieth-century art.

Your art history teacher may not reach the twentieth century, because covering everything is a challenge. Do *not* skip it when you prepare for the AP Art History exam. Between 10 and 15 percent of your test will be devoted to this topic, including a number of multiple-choice questions and at least one short essay question. In addition, using twentieth-century examples on your long essays can be very useful. The test writers know that teachers typically do not have enough time to cover this topic in depth. As a result, questions tend to focus on very specific information. This is especially true of the topics since 1950.

4. *DO* study the ancient Near East and ancient Egypt.

Art works from the ancient Near East and ancient Egypt are categorized as art beyond the European tradition, and the two topics usually account for multiple-choice and short essay questions worth about 20 points, or 10 percent of your total test score. In addition, you can use examples from either the ancient Near East or ancient Egypt for the long essay question requiring at least one example of art beyond the European tradition. That example is worth another 12.5 points.

5. *DO NOT* spend too much time on African, Asian, pre-Columbian, and Oceanic art.

Although these topics are important, interesting, and exciting to study, the reality is that the AP Art History exam contains few questions on them.

6. *DO* study female artists.

Even though the AP Art History Committee has a wide range of topics, artists, and artistic styles to cover, in recent years emphasis has been placed on the important role and contributions of female artists. Carefully study and review Chapter 32 in this book, which provides a review of key female artists.

7. *DO* build a coalition of points.

Your goal is not to score a perfect 200. You do not need 200 points to score a 5. You need 135 points to score a 5 and 102 points to score a 4. Set a score of 4 or 5 as your goal. With the help of this book, you can do it!

The key to scoring a 5 or a 4 is to build a winning coalition of points. Your coalition should begin with the ancient Near East and ancient Egypt. These two topics can be worth between 20 and 30 of the points you need to reach a 102, the minimum needed for a 4. The next topics in your coalition depend on you. You need another 80 to 90 points. What are your favorite artistic styles and eras? For example, a combination of Greece and Rome, Gothic art, the Renaissance, and the twentieth century will usually be worth between 80 and 90 points.

Another successful strategy is based on the proportions of the exam devoted to various art media. According to the course description booklet, 40 percent to 50 percent of the test questions will be devoted to painting and drawing, 25 percent to architecture, 25 percent to sculpture, and 5 percent to 10 percent to other media. Painting is a vast topic that includes a huge number of artists and works of art, but sculpture is very compact. You might consider a strategy of focusing on great sculptors and the works they created. Successfully implemented, this strategy would be worth as much as 50 points.

Keep in mind that you do not have to be an expert on every topic to achieve a high score. The best strategy is to have a good general feel for each period and then concentrate on building a winning coalition of the artists and styles of art you enjoy studying.

Strategic Thinking During the Exam

The AP Art History exam is long and challenging. Here are key dos and don'ts to keep in mind as you are taking the exam:

1. *DO NOT* make random, wild guesses on the multiple-choice questions.

If you can eliminate one or two answer choices, make an educated guess. However, if you do not know the answer and cannot eliminate any of the answer choices, leave the question blank and move on.

2. *DO* remember that readers score each short essay on a 4-point scale.

Each short essay question typically begins with a question asking you to identify and date an artist, an architect, or a work of art. This part of the question is worth 1 of the 4 points. For example, one of the short essay questions on a recent exam asked students to identify the architect of the Carson, Pirie, Scott Building in Chicago. Stating that the architect was Louis Sullivan was worth 1 point. Students were then asked, "How did the innovations in this building lead to the development of the modern skyscraper?" Although the question did not *ask* for three innovations, that was *implied:* the question was worth 4 points and students earned 1 point by naming the architect, so discussing three innovations in the short essay earned students the full 4 points.

3. *DO* carefully examine the pictures and describe what you see.

Many short essay questions ask you to discuss characteristics of a specific work. For example, a recent short essay asked students to discuss the characteristics that revealed the classical sources of the *Christ as Good Shepherd* mosaic from the early Christian period. By carefully examining the slide, students saw that Christ was wearing a gold and purple robe. Because the Roman emperors wore purple, the color showed that Christ was a regal figure. Describing this feature was worth 1 point. If you are not sure what to answer, always begin by describing what you see.

4. *DO* write a brief outline before beginning your long essays.

Always think before you begin your long essays. Take a few minutes to brainstorm possible examples to use. If you have a mental block, try reviewing key works of art from your favorite artistic style or period. Remember, the questions are always broad and can be answered with a large number of examples. Take your time and you will soon find an example you can write about.

Contacting the AP Program

For more information on the AP Art History exam, contact the College Board at:

AP Services
P.O. Box 6671
Princeton, NJ 08541-6671
Phone: (609) 771-7300 or (888) 225-5427
Fax: (609) 530-0482
E-mail: apexams@info.collegeboard.org
Website: www.collegeboard.com

Part 1
Ancient Art

Chapter 2

Prehistoric Art

Introduction and Exam Strategy Overview

Which art historical period lasted the longest and has sparked the most controversy? The Ancient Egyptians created works of art for almost three thousand years, changing relatively little during that period. Modern artists have certainly generated a great deal of controversy. But neither Ancient Egyptian nor Modern artists can compare in terms of duration and controversy with the prehistoric artists.

Prehistoric art first appeared about thirty thousand years ago during the Old Stone Age or Paleolithic period. From its first discovery in 1879, Prehistoric art has aroused intense speculation. Who created the "Venus" statuettes and the wall paintings found in more than two hundred caves? These images are both impressive and tantalizing. Why were they created and what do they mean? Because Prehistoric artists and sculptors left no written records, the meanings of these works have been lost forever.

Although prehistory is much longer than any other art historical period, it generates the fewest questions of any artistic era covered on the AP Art History exam. The official *Art History Course Description* booklet relegates Prehistoric art to a brief footnote, stating that "the exam may occasionally include questions about Prehistoric art."

The word *occasionally* should be taken literally. Of the 115 multiple-choice questions on the exam, no more than 2 have been devoted to Prehistoric art. Several recent exams have had no multiple-choice questions on the topic. No exam has ever included a slide-based multiple-choice question on Prehistoric art, and only one essay question on the topic has appeared. Given this lack of coverage, the pragmatic student should save Prehistoric art for last and then review this chapter.

Paleolithic Sculpture

The most famous Paleolithic sculptures are statuettes of women that archaeologists have named after the Greco-Roman goddess of beauty and love, Venus. The name is almost certainly erroneous. There is no evidence that Old Stone Age people worshipped gods and goddesses that took human form.

The oldest and most famous prehistoric statue is now known as the *Venus of Willendorf* (**CD Fig. 2-1**). The limestone figure is nude and just 4 inches high. The artist emphasizes the woman's head, breasts, torso, and thighs, while her facial features, neck, arms, and lower legs are disproportionally small. Interestingly, this early portrayal of a nude female is a distinctive aspect of Paleolithic art that began a long-standing tradition in art. The purpose of prehistoric figures like the *Venus of Willendorf* has never been determined. The 1985 AP test asked students to "suggest a possible purpose" for the *Venus of Willendorf*. This was the first and thus far only essay question devoted to Prehistoric art.

Paleolithic Cave Paintings

The first Paleolithic cave paintings were discovered in 1879 at Altamira in northwest Spain. Since then, Paleolithic paintings have been found at more than two hundred sites. The most famous of these sites are Lascaux and the recently discovered Chauvet Cave in France (**CD Fig. 2-2**).

Figure 2-2. Hall of Bulls, Lascaux Cave, Dordogne, France

Cave artists primarily depicted animals such as bison, horses, and deer. As they charge across the cave wall, the animals convey a sense of vitality and movement. The artists used strong outlines and vivid naturalistic colors while demonstrating an intimate knowledge of the physical characteristics of the creatures being portrayed. Although they clearly possessed great artistic skills, cave artists never drew landscapes and rarely portrayed human figures. Like much of Paleolithic art, the reasons for these omissions are unknown.

Neolithic Art

The Neolithic period began about ten thousand years ago. During this period, humans gradually made the transition from nomadic hunters and gatherers to farmers living in stable villages. Modern archaeologists have made exciting discoveries in several Neolithic villages. For example, the biblical town of Jericho really did have thick walls and a great circular tower that may have been almost 30 feet high. The walls of Jericho thus mark the beginning of monumental architecture.

Although Jericho's farmers built protective walls, artists in another Neolithic village now known as Çatal Höyük created wall paintings. Unlike the Paleolithic cave paintings, clearly drawn humans dominate the Neolithic scenes. Even more remarkable, one of the rooms at Çatal Höyük contains a painting that has been acclaimed as the world's first landscape.

Stonehenge

Stonehenge is one of the most remarkable and certainly the best-known Neolithic monument (**CD Fig. 2-3**). A **henge** is a circle of huge stones. With enormous stones rising as high as 17 feet and weighing as much as 50 tons, Stonehenge is indeed a massive henge.

Stonehenge has amazed and fascinated people for centuries. During the Middle Ages, baffled writers concluded that the mysterious structure was built by the legendary magician Merlin. Today, archaeologists believe that Stonehenge is a remarkably accurate solar calendar constructed in phases beginning about four thousand years ago.

Stonehenge has inspired modern environmental artists. In the mid-1970s, Nancy Holt used four large concrete tubes to create a work of art she named *Sun Tunnels* (**CD Fig. 2-4**). Located in the Utah desert, the *Sun Tunnels* mark the sun at the summer and winter solstices. A multiple-choice question on the 2004 AP test asked students to note that Holt's *Sun Tunnels* recall prehistoric works like Stonehenge.

Conclusion

Prehistoric art is a fascinating topic that has generated heated and even passionate debate. However, the AP Art History exam has few if any questions on this topic. As a result, it is best to briefly review this topic.

Chapter 3

Art of the Ancient Near East

Introduction and Exam Strategy Overview

Who built the first urban communities, developed the earliest known writing system, and invented the wheel? A people now known as the Sumerians are credited with making all these innovations. The Sumerians lived in a dozen independent city-states located in a flat valley between the Tigris and Euphrates rivers. This region is known as Mesopotamia, which in Greek means "land between the rivers."

Numerous peoples competed for power and control over Mesopotamia. History texts make careful distinctions among the Sumerians, Akkadians, Neo-Sumerians, Babylonians, Assyrians, and Persians. In contrast, the AP Art History committee looks broadly at the works of art created by all these peoples of the Ancient Near East. This chapter focuses on key works of art that have repeatedly appeared on AP Art History exams.

Ancient Near Eastern art occupies a strategically important place on the exam. You can expect to have three or four multiple-choice questions on this period. Since 1989, test writers have included three sets of slide-based multiple-choice questions and four essay questions. The most recent essay question appeared on the 2005 test. As you know, one of the two 25-point essay questions must include an example from a non-European source. It is important to remember that Ancient Near Eastern art is part of the non-European tradition. As a result, Ancient Near Eastern art can be worth an additional 12.5 points of your total test score.

Ziggurats

The Sumerians and other Mesopotamians believed that each city-state was under the special protection of a god or goddess. Where should these gods be worshipped? Like other ancient peoples, the Sumerians believed that their deities resided in the heavens above humanity. To reach up to their gods and goddesses, the Sumerians used mud bricks to construct stepped platforms called **ziggurats**, or "mountains of the gods" (**CD Figs. 3-1** and **3-2**). The first ziggurats rose at least 40 feet above the city center. The tallest ziggurat was built in Babylon. Known to the Hebrews as the Tower of Babel, it soared an astonishing 270 feet high.

The ziggurats were the center of a temple complex that formed a city within a city. Each day, priests with shaved heads climbed the ziggurat's mud-brick stairs, often dragging a plump goat or sheep to sacrifice to their gods. Although the priests could devote their full attention to serving their gods, everyday citizens had to work in the fields or sell goods in small shops. How could these people demonstrate their reverence toward the gods? Sumerians devised an ingenious solution to solve this problem. Archeologists have discovered dozens of small statuettes hidden beneath temple floors. These statuettes represented local citizens. Their folded hands clasp libation cups used in religious ceremonies. Their eyes are wide open to demonstrate that they are eternally alert and reverent. Ironically, many of these statuettes have survived while the images of the gods and goddesses they worshipped have vanished.

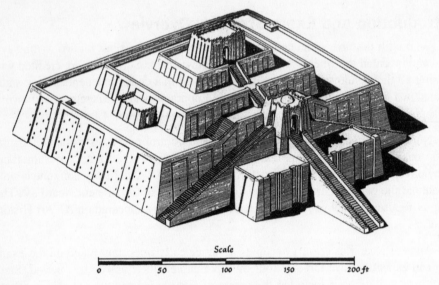

Scale

| 0 | 50 | 100 | 150 | 200 ft |

Figure 3-2. Diagram of a ziggurat from Ur in Sumer

Standard of Ur

During the 1920s, a British archaeologist named Leonard Woolley excavated a large cemetery in the Sumerian city of Ur. Some of the tombs were very humble, but others contained rich treasures like gold helmets, jewelry, musical instruments, and statues covered with gold leaf. While the golden treasures of Ur impress thousands of museum visitors, art historians and AP test writers have focused their attention on an object Woolley called the *Standard of Ur*.

The *Standard of Ur* is a four-sided rectangular box. Its 18-inch-wide side panels are inlaid in shell and lapis lazuli depicting a panorama of figures from all classes of Sumerian society. Art historians refer to the long side panels as the war panel and the peace panel. The artist who created the *Standard of Ur* wanted to tell a narrative story about how the Sumerians won and celebrated a great military victory. The artist divided each side panel into three horizontal bands called **registers**. This technique of using registers to organize a story can still be seen in modern comic strips.

The *Standard of Ur* reads from bottom to top and from left to right. The war panel (**CD Fig. 3-3**) begins with a row of wooden-wheeled chariots trampling enemy soldiers. In the middle register, a row of well-disciplined infantrymen equipped with heavy protective cloaks and short spears march confidently before the viewer. In the top register, the soldiers present captives to a tall ruler. The artist uses size to indicate the ruler's high status. Known as **hierarchical scale**, this technique would be used by artists throughout history.

The peace panel also uses registers and hierarchical scale to help tell its narrative story. In the lower register, a row of porters carry sacks of grain, strips of fish, and packages of wool. In the center, the porters lead animals to a banquet already under way in the top register. The ruler of Ur, clad in a sheepskin skirt and holding a beaker of wine, sits on a throne and listens to a court harpist and singer. The ruler faces a row of smaller officials who are clearly his obedient subordinates.

The *Standard of Ur* can be a very useful work of art on your AP exam. For example, the 2005 exam asked students to "select and fully identify two works of art that visually convey a narrative." One of the choices had to be outside the European tradition. As an example of Ancient Near Eastern art, which is by definition non-European, the *Standard of Ur* would have been an excellent choice for this 25-point essay.

Victory Stele of Naram-Sin

Sometime between 2254 and 2218 BCE, an Akkadian king named Naram-Sin won a great victory over the Lullubi, a rebellious mountain people from Zagros. Naram-Sin commissioned skilled sculptors to create a **stele**, an upright stone slab or pillar to commemorate his victory. The surviving portion of the stele is 6 feet 6 inches high. The imagery clearly proclaims Naram-Sin's military and religious authority. Naram-Sin is by far the largest and most prominent figure. Armed with a short spear, he is seen triumphantly trampling on the bodies of fallen enemies, some of whom futilely beg for mercy (**CD Fig. 3-4**).

The stele shows Naram-Sin to be more than a victorious military commander. He conspicuously wears a horned helmet. In Mesopotamia, a horned helmet symbolized divinity and had previously only been worn by gods. This stele uses the horned helmet to announce that Naram-Sin was also a god. Three stars symbolizing gods shine on his glorious triumph.

The *Victory Stele of Naram-Sin* is more than just an impressive monument to a ruler's power. Although the anonymous sculptor used hierarchical scale to denote Naram-Sin's elevated status, the sculptor abandoned the use of registers to tell a narrative story. Instead, the troops are shown marching up the slope of a steep mountain. In contrast, the defeated Lullubi fall down the mountainside in a chaotic route.

Hammurabi's Code

In about 1780 BCE, a highly successful general named Hammurabi conquered all of Mesopotamia. As the capital of a great empire, Babylon quickly became a thriving commercial center. But its rapid growth soon caused problems. Merchants, farmers, and workers all needed written laws to help resolve disputes. Although individual cities had developed codes of laws, Hammurabi recognized that a single, uniform code would help unify the diverse groups within his empire. He therefore compiled a collection of laws known as *Hammurabi's Code* or the *Stele of Hammurabi*. Scribes carved these laws onto a black basalt stele. The nearly 8-foot stele contained more than thirty-five hundred lines of cuneiform characters (**CD Fig. 3-5**).

Although legal scholars and historians focus on the code's 282 laws, art historians carefully study the upper part of the stele. Sculptors depicted Hammurabi and the god Shamash in **bas** or low relief. The patron god of justice, Shamash, is shown seated on a throne wearing a horned helmet to signify his divinity. Shamash extends to Hammurabi a rod and ring, symbolizing authority. Although standing upright, Hammurabi is clearly smaller than Shamash. The images powerfully convey the close link between the human and divine rulers. Hammurabi literally had the god-given authority to enforce the laws inscribed on the stele.

Assyrian Lamassu

More than a thousand years after Hammurabi's reign, a ruthless people who called themselves the Assyrians conquered Mesopotamia. Assyrian rulers built vast palaces to express their power and impress conquered peoples. One ruler boasted that he ordered sculptors to carve "beasts of the mountains fashioned out of limestone and fittingly imposing." Known as **lamassu**, the limestone beasts were indeed imposing. Reaching a height of nearly 14 feet, the lamassu were winged five-legged bulls with human heads. Assyrian kings considered the lamassu divine guardians who protected them from both human enemies and evil spirits. The Assyrian sculptors gave the lamassu five legs so that each guardian stands firmly in place when viewed from the front but appears to stride forward when viewed from the side (**CD Fig. 3-6**).

Figure 3-6. Lamassu

Assyrian Low-Relief Panels

The Assyrians dominated Mesopotamia from the ninth to the seventh centuries BCE. Warrior-kings such as Sargon II and Ashurnasirpal II decorated their palace rooms with large alabaster panels. The panels feature scenes chronicling the king's military exploits and displaying his valor while hunting lions. One particularly poignant panel is known as the Dying Lioness **(CD Fig. 3-7)**. Its legs pierced by three arrows, the mortally wounded lion defiantly raises its powerful head and roars one final time at its royal tormentor. Modern viewers sympathize with the lion. But this was not the sculptor's intent. Like all Assyrian art, the panel was intended to glorify the ruler's skill and bravery.

Ishtar Gate

Despite, or perhaps because of, its cruelty, the Assyrian Empire collapsed in 612 BCE. A new ruler named Nebuchadnezzar II quickly transformed Babylon into the greatest city in Mesopotamia. Nebuchadnezzar is credited with building Babylon's famous Hanging Gardens, celebrated as one of the Seven Wonders of the Ancient World.

The city's wonders also included the Ishtar Gate (**CD Fig. 3-8**). As a result of the meticulous work of German archaeologists, the restored Ishtar Gate can be seen in the Staatliche Museum in Berlin. Named in honor of Ishtar, the goddess of love, fertility, and war, the gate spanned a processional route that led to the city's towering ziggurat incorporated into the biblical legend as the Tower of Babel.

The double-arched Ishtar Gate was made of dark blue-glazed bricks. Rows of horned dragons sacred to Marduk (the patron god of Babylon) and yellow bulls with blue hair sacred to Adad (the storm god) stride proudly across the walls. Regal lions, symbols of the goddess Ishtar, served as divine signs pointing the way to Marduk's great ziggurat.

Triumphant Persians

The long history of Mesopotamia culminated with the rise of the Persians. At its height under Darius I (521–486 BCE), the Persian Empire extended from the Indus River to the Nile River. Darius I and his son Xerxes built a magnificent royal citadel in Persepolis (**CD Fig. 3-9**). The citadel included an enormous audience hall, or **apadama**, supported by 36 colossal columns, each of which was surmounted by bull's heads of gray limestone.

Conclusion

The Ancient Near East is an important component of the AP Art History exam. Test writers frequently ask questions about the function of ziggurats, the use of registers and hierarchical scale to tell narrative stories, the subject of *Hammurabi's Code* and how it is conveyed, the purpose of lamassu, and the design of the Ishtar Gate. Always remember that the Ancient Near East is considered to be outside the Western artistic tradition. It is therefore an excellent source of examples for the long essay requiring an example from the non-European tradition.

Chapter 4

Ancient Egyptian Art

Introduction and Exam Strategy Overview

What thoughts come to your mind when you think of Ancient Egypt? If you are like most people, you immediately think of the pyramids, the Great Sphinx, and the golden treasures of King Tutankhamen. In contrast, AP Art History test writers have an entirely different set of artistic priorities. They are far more interested in the Stepped Pyramid than the Great Pyramid, the *Statue of Khafre* than the Great Sphinx, and the artistic revolution of Akhenaton than the treasures of King Tutankhamen. This chapter focuses on the artistic styles and works of art and architecture that have the greatest likelihood of appearing on the AP Art History exam.

Ancient Egypt has always occupied an important place on the AP Art History exam. You can expect to have 10 points, or 5 percent of the total test, devoted to Ancient Egypt. Slide-based multiple-choice questions are relatively infrequent; only three have appeared on tests since 1983. Because the most recent slide-based multiple-choice question on Ancient Egypt was on the 2005 test, it is unlikely your test will have any. In contrast, essay questions on Ancient Egypt are far more common, with 11 appearing on tests since 1983. Because the last essay question devoted to Ancient Egyptian art was on the 2003 test, it is very likely that your test will have one.

Ancient Egypt is important for another reason: it is considered part of the non-European artistic tradition. As you know, one of the two 25-point essay questions must include an example from outside the European tradition. As a result, Ancient Egyptian art can be worth as much as 20 points, or 10 percent of your test. Because you need approximately 135 points to earn a test score of 5, ancient Egypt is a vital and easily mastered building block in your drive for a 5.

Ancient Egyptian Religion

History texts almost always begin their chapters on Ancient Egypt by using Herodotus's famous quote that "Egypt is the gift of the Nile." Herodotus also noted that the Egyptians were the most religious people he had encountered.

Herodotus was both succinct and accurate. The Nile River made civilization in Ancient Egypt possible. The Nile's annual flood symbolized rebirth and this concept was central to Egyptian religious beliefs.

The Ancient Egyptians were polytheists who believed that gods were manifest in every aspect of nature. A god could appear in human or animal form or as a combination of both. Regardless of how they appeared, the gods influenced human lives and gave order to the world.

The Ancient Egyptians did not view death as the end of life. The Nile's annual flood and the daily rising of the sun suggested a cycle of continual rebirth. The Ancient Egyptians believed that a dead person's **ka**, or soul, could enjoy an afterlife. To ensure a comfortable afterlife, the deceased had to be physically preserved along with his or her earthly possessions and other reminders of daily activities. As a result, much of Ancient Egypt's surviving artistic heritage is funerary.

Position of the Pharaohs

The pharaoh, or king, played a crucial role in Egyptian life. As a son of the sun god, Ra, a pharaoh was a god-king who had absolute power. The pharaoh's power did not end when he died. Egyptians believed that the pharaoh rejoined his solar father and continued to influence life along the Nile. Egypt's monumental works of art were built to ensure the pharaohs' continuing goodwill.

Palette of Narmer

The *Palette of Narmer* (**CD Fig. 4-1**) occupies an important place in Ancient Egyptian art. Created in approximately 3100 BCE, the palette is one of the world's first historical works of art. Taken together, the palette's two sides commemorate Narmer's victorious unification of Upper and Lower Egypt. Every image on the palette is designed to convey Narmer's invincible power. Each side is divided into **registers**, or horizontal bands. In an excellent example of **hierarchical scale**, Narmer towers above his defeated enemies.

Representation of the Human Figure

Take a close look at the way Narmer is portrayed. Notice that his head, legs, and arms are shown in profile, while his eye and torso are shown in frontal view. This pose became the standard way that Ancient Egyptian artists represented the human figure. Two other excellent examples of this conventional pose are the images of Hesire and Ti.

Periods in Ancient Egyptian History

Ancient Egyptian history began when Narmer unified Egypt in approximately 3100 BCE and ended with the Roman conquest in 30 BCE. Scholars have traditionally divided Egyptian history into periods called the Old Kingdom, the Middle Kingdom, and the New Kingdom. Although the AP Art History test writers do not expect you to know the dates of each period, they do expect you to know the distinctive artistic achievements of each period.

Old Kingdom Architecture

Old Kingdom rulers and architects focused most of their attention on building tombs that would protect the royal ka for all eternity. The first tombs were flat-topped, single-story, trapezoidal structures called **mastabas** (**CD Fig. 4-2**). Each mastaba was erected above an underground burial chamber that contained a **sarcophagus**, or stone coffin. The sarcophagus protected the deceased ruler's mummy.

During the Third Dynasty, an innovative royal architect named Imhotep had a bold new idea. He created a pyramid with a stepped construction by placing six mastaba-like structures of decreasing size on top of each other. Although the Stepped Pyramid resembles Sumerian ziggurats, its purpose is very different. The ziggurats were temples made out of mud bricks. The Stepped Pyramid is a limestone tomb designed to protect King Djoser's mummy and symbolize his godlike power. It is important to note that Imhotep has the honor of being the first known artist in recorded history.

The stepped-pyramid design (**CD Fig. 4-3**) soon evolved into a true geometric pyramid. Ancient Egyptian rulers built at least eighty pyramids. The best-known and largest are the three pyramids located at Giza. Each of these pyramids was part of a vast funerary complex that included temples and mastabas for lesser officials. Although they are world famous, the pyramids have never been the subjects of questions on an AP Art History exam.

Figure 4-3. Stepped Pyramid of Djoser, Saqqara, Egypt

Old Kingdom Sculpture

What would happen if a ruler's mummy was damaged or destroyed? What would the royal ka do? Fortunately, sculptors had an ingenuous alternative. If anything happened to the mummy, a statue could serve as an abode for the ka. The Egyptian sculptures now on display in museums throughout the world were originally created for tombs and temples.

The artistic principle that "form follows function" provides a key to understanding Old Kingdom sculpture. For example, carefully examine the famous seated statue of Khafre (**CD Figs. 4-4 and 4-5**). The statue is designed to last for eternity. It is made out of diorite, one of the hardest and most durable stones a sculptor can use. Khafre's body is regal and compact, with no exposed limbs that could break. Khafre is portrayed as having a muscular, flawless body that befits an all-powerful god-king. The falcon god, Horus, who enfolds the king's head with his wings, protects him. The *Statue of Khafre* projects dignity, power, and above all, permanence.

Figure 4-4. Statue of Khafre, Giza, Egypt

Now look at the standing statue of Khafre's son, King Menkaura, and Menkaura's wife, Queen Khamerernebty (**CD Fig. 4-6**). Portrayed with idealized youthful bodies, the royal couple gaze confidently and serenely into the future. They stand proudly erect facing straight ahead. Menkaura's arms are frozen at his sides, while his wife touches him in a formalized gesture of "belonging together." Notice that their left legs are slightly advanced. As you will see, this upright rigid pose influenced early Greek sculptors.

Kings and queens were not the only figures portrayed in sculpture. The famous *Seated Scribe* from Saqqara (**CD Fig. 4-7**) is an especially important example of a statue portraying a nonroyal official. Notice that the scribe is less monumental than the statues of Khafre and Menkaura. Whereas the kings are shown with idealized proportions, the scribe has sagging chest muscles and a protruding belly. During most of art history, formality is relaxed and realism is increased as a human subject's importance decreases.

Middle Kingdom

As you have seen, Old Kingdom rulers were buried in mastabas and pyramids. In contrast, Middle Kingdom rulers and high-level officials chose to be buried in rock-cut tombs hollowed out of the faces of cliffs. Paintings depicting scenes from daily life often decorated the chamber walls.

Middle Kingdom rulers faced a number of difficult political and military challenges. Portraits of Middle Kingdom pharaohs often reveal a sense of brooding anxiety. For example, statues of Senusret III depict a grimly determined ruler with a deeply lined face.

New Kingdom Rulers: Hatshepsut

The New Kingdom (1550–1070 BCE) marked the zenith of Ancient Egypt's power and prosperity. Warrior-kings conquered vast new territories, built impressive temples, and carved elaborate tombs in the Valley of the Kings.

The long line of warrior-kings was interrupted by the reign of a remarkable female ruler named Hatshepsut. When Thutmose II died, his rightful heir, Thutmose III, was still a child. As a result, Hatshepsut, the late king's consort and the stepmother of Thutmose III, became regent. Within a few years, Hatshepsut contrived to have herself crowned king with full pharaonic powers. Hatshepsut thus became history's first great female monarch.

Hatshepsut's most important artistic achievement was the construction of a funerary temple at Deir el-Bahri (**CD Fig. 4-8**). Designed by a royal architect named Senenmut, the temple rises from the valley floor in three colonnaded terraces connected by ramps. High cliffs form a dramatic backdrop. The long horizontal and vertical lines of the colonnades repeat the pattern of the limestone cliffs.

More than two hundred statues of Hatshepsut lined the temple corridors. Because the sculptors were unsure how to portray the female monarch, many of the carved statues displayed a mix of male and female attributes. For example, some statutes showed Hatshepsut with a ceremonial beard and breasts, while others represent her femininity. The temple's interior walls were decorated with painted reliefs depicting Hatshepsut's accomplishments. They represented the first tribute to a woman's achievements in the history of art (**CD Fig. 4-9**).

New Kingdom Rulers: Akhenaton

Akhenaton is the most controversial and intriguing pharaoh in Egypt's long history. He simultaneously launched religious and artistic revolutions that challenged entrenched religious cults and aesthetic conventions.

For reasons that are still unclear, Akhenaton began his seventeen-year reign by disavowing Egypt's traditional gods. He then founded a new religion based on a single all-powerful god called Aton. To escape the influence of the priests, he moved his capital from Thebes to a new site now known as Tellel-Amarna.

Akhenaton also overturned artistic traditions dating back to the *Palette of Narmer*. His new **Amarna style** emphasized naturalistic representations, refined sensuality, and unprecedented intimacy. These qualities can be seen in the *Statue of Akhenaton* (**CD Fig. 4-10**), the famous *Bust of Nefertiti* (**CD Fig. 4-11**), and a limestone relief portraying Akhenaton, Nefertiti, and three of their children (**CD Fig. 4-12**).

Carefully examine the *Statue of Akhenaton*. In striking contrast to the rigid poses and idealized figures of Old Kingdom pharaohs, Akhenaton is shown with a long face, thick lips, a protruding belly and effeminate curving hips. Elongated figures and curvilinear lines are the hallmarks of the Amarna style.

These qualities can be seen in the painted *Bust of Nefertiti*. The bust illustrates why the queen was named Nefertiti, which means "the beautiful one is here." The sculpture is life size. The queen wears a deep blue crown and a large necklace. Her refined features and long graceful neck convey a sensuality that is unprecedented in Egyptian art.

Figure 4-11. Bust of Nefertiti

The Amarna style also encouraged intimate scenes of the royal couple and their children. A small limestone stele portrays the family playing together while basking in Aton's life-giving rays. This sculpture provides an excellent example of **sunken relief**. In this technique, outlines are carved into the surface and the figure is modeled within them, from the surface down.

New Kingdom Rulers: Tutankhamen

Akhenaton's revolutionary reforms proved to be short lived. After his death, Tutankhamen revived the worship of Amen and returned the capital to Thebes. Tutankhamen died when he was just eighteen years old.

Although Tutankhamen's reign was brief and undistinguished, he is by far the best-known ruler in Egyptian history. In 1922, an English Egyptologist, Howard Carter, discovered Tutankhamen's tomb in the Valley of the Kings. The tomb contained a treasure trove of more than five thousand works of art. Tutankhamen's gold burial mask is one of the most recognized works of art in the world.

Pylon Temples

As you have seen, pyramids and rock-cut tombs were the most distinctive and enduring structures built during the Old and Middle Kingdoms. New Kingdom pharaohs commanded their architects to build enormous pylon temples to honor the gods and emphasize their own power.

Pylon temples all had a similar design. Two massive **pylons**, or gateways with sloping walls, flanked the entrance (**CD Fig. 4-13**). A long axial corridor led to an enormous hypostyle hall. In a **hypostyle hall**, a large number of columns supported the roof (**CD Fig. 4-14**). At Karnak, the hypostyle hall has central columns that are 66 feet high and 22 feet in diameter. The corridor ultimately led to an inner sanctuary containing images of the gods. Only the pharaoh and high priests could enter this sanctuary.

Conclusion

Ancient Egypt is an important part of each AP Art History exam. Test writers rarely ask questions about popular topics such as the pyramids and Pharaoh Tutankhamen. Instead, make sure you study the *Palette of Narmer*, the Stepped Pyramid, the *Statue of Khafre*, Hatshepsut's mortuary temple, and the Amarna style of art. Always remember that Ancient Egypt is considered to be outside the European artistic tradition. It is therefore an excellent source of examples for the long essay requiring an example of non-European art.

Chapter 5

Aegean Art

Introduction and Exam Strategy Overview

Would an AP Art History exam written in 1870 have had any questions on ancient Aegean art? The topic almost certainly would not have generated any questions. In the mid-nineteenth century, Aegean culture was remembered only in myths, legends, and the epic poems of Homer. Although Homer's epics were regarded as great literature, they were considered fictional stories with little or no basis in historic reality.

The situation today is very different. Art history textbooks now devote a full chapter to ancient Aegean art. The AP Art History exam typically asks three to five multiple-choice questions on the topic. Thus far, the test writers have not written a slide-based multiple-choice question or an essay question on Aegean art.

During the third and second millennia BCE, three distinct cultures emerged in the Aegean: the Cycladic on the small islands north of Crete, the Minoan on Crete, and the Helladic on the mainland of Greece. Painstaking archaeological excavations have yielded an impressive amount of information about these cultures and the art they created. However, much work remains and many questions are still unanswered.

Cycladic Art

The Cyclades is a group of islands forming a circle around the island of Delos. Although the Cycladic islands are small, they contain quarries that produce brilliant, crystalline white marble. Between 2700 and 2200 BCE, Cycladic sculptors used this superb marble to carve statuettes ranging in height from a few inches to 4 feet (**CD Fig. 5-1**).

Archaeologists found these Cycladic statuettes in modest stone tombs scattered among the islands. Most of the statuettes depict nude women. When men are depicted, they are often musicians playing harplike instruments. The purpose of these marble figurines remains a mystery. Some scholars think each piece was intended for use in the owner's lifetime, but others see the statuary as objects made exclusively for the grave.

Figure 5-1. Cycladic female figure

Although the function of Cycladic sculpture remains unknown, their extraordinary artistic qualities are not in dispute. Pure line and extreme abstraction are the hallmarks of these surprisingly modern-looking statuettes. As you will see, early twentieth-century artists had a passion for abstraction (see Chapter 27). Although they were carved 4,500 years ago, the Cycladic statuary bears a striking resemblance to the works of Brancusi and Modigliani (**CD Figs. 5-2 and 5-3**).

Minoan Civilization

Crete is the largest island in the eastern Mediterranean Sea. Until 1900, its history was shrouded in mythical stories about a legendary King Minos who ruled from a vast palace where the half-bull, half-man Minotaur lived in a labyrinthine maze. Inspired by these legends, the English archaeologist Arthur Evans began to excavate at Knossos on the northern coast of Crete.

Evans soon announced a series of discoveries that stunned art historians. Knossos was the center of an elegant civilization that flourished from about 2000 to 1400 BCE. It contained a palace complex that included rectangular courts, workshops, storerooms, and even mansions and villas (**CD Fig. 5-4**). Evans proudly called the culture he discovered Minoan after the legendary King Minos.

Minoan Frescoes

The discovery of a vast palace complex at Knossos revolutionized the study of Aegean history. From an art history perspective, Evans made an even more remarkable discovery. The palaces at Knossos and other Minoan cities contained a rich collection of fresco paintings. **Fresco** is a technique in which the artist paints on the plaster surface of a wall or ceiling while it is still damp. As a result, the pigments become fused with the plaster as it dries.

The Minoan frescoes (**CD Figs. 5-5 and 5-6**) portray a lively people with a zest for athletic contests, festivals, and stylish dress. Clad in ruffled gowns, women of the court wore delicate gold jewelry and styled their hair into long graceful coils. They took part in activities ranging from dancing to strenuous sports. This evidence suggests that Minoan women enjoyed a level of social equality rarely found in the ancient world. The Minoans also enjoyed a close relationship with their natural environment. The many flowers, fish, and animals in Minoan paintings reveal a people who delighted in observing and recording the beauty of nature. Interestingly, Minoan artists did not paint soldiers or battles.

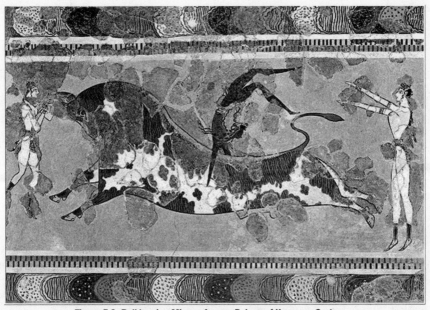

Figure 5-6. Bull-leaping Minoan fresco, Palace of Knossos, Crete

Minoan wall paintings are distinctive and easy to recognize. The 2004 AP Art History test included a picture of a stylish Minoan woman and a landscape with rocks and flowers. Students were asked to recognize that the style was Minoan and to remember that the medium used to decorate the walls of Minoan palaces was fresco (**CD Fig. 5-7**).

Minoan Pottery and Sculpture

In the past century, archaeologists have recovered a significant collection of Minoan pottery and sculpture. Like the fresco artists, Minoan ceramic artists were inspired by the sea and the creatures that inhabit it. For example, one jar features a smiling octopus with tentacles that wrap around the entire vessel. It is very difficult to imagine the war-like Assyrians creating such a vase.

Minoan sculptors carved impressive but sometimes perplexing works of art. For example, a statuette known as the *Snake Goddess* (**CD Fig. 5-8**) depicts a woman with exposed breasts holding a snake in each hand. A leopardlike feline is peacefully perched on her head. Art historians believe the statuette represents a goddess.

Discovery of Mycenae

By the sixteenth century BCE, Knossos was a sophisticated cultural center that may have been home to as many as 80,000 people. But the joys of Minoan civilization ended abruptly. A combination of natural disasters and conquest by the warlike Mycenaeans ended Knossos's golden age.

In the *Iliad*, Homer refers to "the great stronghold of Mycenae" and to powerful kings like Agamemnon who were "rich in gold." These descriptions were dismissed as typical examples of Homer's vivid imagination. However, a German businessman named Heinrich Schliemann believed that the stories in the *Iliad* were based on real people and places.

After teaching himself the rudiments of archaeology, Schliemann set out to find and excavate Mycenae. While scholars scoffed, Schliemann followed Homer to the golden treasures of Mycenae.

Cyclopean Walls and a Lion's Gate

Whereas Knossos lacked protective walls, Mycenae was built to withstand almost any attack. The citadel was located on a steep, rocky ridge and was surrounded by protective walls up to 20 feet thick. Believing that humans could not possibly have built such massive walls, the ancient Greeks attributed their construction to a race of one-eyed giants called Cyclops. Modern historians still refer to the enormous stone blocks as **cyclopean stones**.

In 1876, Schliemann and other archaeologists uncovered more than just massive walls. Mycenaean architects constructed a sophisticated entrance now called the Lion's Gate (**CD Fig. 5-9**). Two massive stone posts support a lintel weighing 25 tons. Above the lintel, a corbel arch directs the weight of the heavy wall to the stone posts below. **Corbelling** is a technique in which stones are laid so that each course of masonry projects slightly beyond the course below it. The span thus created forms an irregular arch.

Figure 5-9. Lion's Gate and cyclopean stones, Mycenae

The space above the lintel is called a **relieving triangle** because it reduces or relieves the weight pressing down on the horizontal lintel. Mycenaean sculptors filled this space with two limestone lions, each measuring almost 10 feet tall. Much like the Assyrian lamassu, the lions are meant to be protective guardians.

Treasury of Atreus

The nobles who lived within Mycenae's fortress walls enjoyed a life of surprising splendor. They feasted in great halls 35 feet wide and 50 feet long. During banquets, the light glittered from a dazzling variety of gold and silver pitchers, bowls, and cups.

When a member of Mycenaean royalty died, he or she was laid to rest outside the citadel walls in a structure called a **tholos**—a beehive-shaped tomb covered by an enormous earthen mound. The largest surviving structure at Mycenae is a tholos (**CD Fig. 5-10**) that has been mistakenly called the Treasury of Atreus. Atreus was the father of Agamemnon and the Spartan king Menelaus. The 43-foot high tomb was clearly built for an important person. However, it is not known if Atreus was in fact buried in this tomb.

Although it is an architectural masterpiece, the so-called Treasury of Atreus had been thoroughly looted centuries before its modern rediscovery. Undaunted by his failure to find any golden objects in Atreus's tomb, Schliemann continued digging just inside the Lion's Gate. Within a short time, he discovered graves filled with treasures that included solid gold funerary masks. Flushed with excitement, Schliemann tele-graphed the king of Greece: "I have gazed on the face of Agamemnon!"

Art historians no longer believe that the death mask belonged to Agamemnon. How-ever, the golden mask was a spectacular find. Although AP Art History exam writers will not ask you whom the death mask portrays, they will ask you to identify the technique used to create it. Both Pharaoh Tutankhamen's death mask and the Mycenaean death mask were created by a technique called **repoussé**. In this technique, artists hammer a metal plate from the back, leaving raised features on the front (**CD Fig. 5-11**).

Conclusion

Aegean art is a compact and thus easily studied topic. Here are the key points to remember: Cycladic statuettes are abstract and usually portray nude women. Knossos was discovered by Arthur Evans. Knossos and other Minoan palaces and towns contain a rich collection of fresco paintings. The Minoans portray themselves as a peaceful people who appreciated natural beauty. In contrast, the Mycenaeans were warlike and surrounded their citadels with walls 20 feet thick. The Lion's Gate features a corbelled arch and includes a relieving triangle containing statues of guardian lions. Finally, the Treasury of Atreus is actually a tomb discovered by Heinrich Schliemann in the late nineteenth century. The famous Mycenaean burial masks in the Treasury of Atreus were made using a technique called repoussé.

Chapter 6

Art of Ancient Greece

Introduction and Exam Strategy Overview

What do you think the ideal male and female bodies should look like? At first glance, this question may appear superficial. After all, frivolous celebrity magazines frequently feature pictures of Hollywood stars who have "six-pack abs," "perfect pecs," or "legs that go on for miles." Yet the question can be traced back to ancient Greece. Greek sculptors strove to create ideal images of beauty for both men and women. The statues they carved created "classic" models of beauty that link ancient Greece to Renaissance Italy (see Chapter 16) and even to contemporary celebrity magazines.

The importance of the art of the ancient Greeks is not limited to their quest to define ideal male and female proportions. Greek architecture, sculpture, and vase paintings have all had a far-reaching influence on subsequent Western art and culture.

The AP Art History exam reflects the significant contribution of ancient Greek art. Most exams contain five to six multiple-choice questions and either one slide-based multiple-choice question or one short essay question. In many years, ancient Greek examples can be used to answer at least one of the long essay questions. Given its importance, ancient Greek art can be worth between 15 and 20 points on the exam.

Ancient Greek art is a complex topic. Unlike the art of the ancient Egyptians, Greek art did not remain static. As a result, art historians have traditionally divided ancient Greek art into at four stylistic periods: Geometric, Archaic, Classical, and Hellenistic. This chapter follows that approach.

Geometric Art

Mycenaean civilization (see Chapter 5) collapsed around 1200 BCE. As population declined and the arts of reading and writing were lost, Greece plunged into a four-hundred-year period known as the Dark Ages of Greece. After four long centuries of decline, Greece slowly began to recover. Farmers settled in city-states, writers preserved Homer's epics, and artists created a new Geometric style of art.

As its name implies, the Geometric style featured triangles, concentric circles, and "checkerboard" shapes that were used for both ornamental and human figures. The

Geometric style can clearly be seen in a huge **krater**, or mixing bowl, that served as a grave marker for an Athenian leader buried around 740 BCE (**CD Fig. 6-1**).

Figure 6-1. Geometric Funerary Vase

The 3½-foot-tall vase is divided into three large registers. The top register contains an intricate rectilinear design. The middle register shows the deceased lying on a funerary couch. Surrounding him are his distraught wife, his children, and a long row of mourners. The human figures have tiny circular heads attached to triangular torsos. Their long, thin rectangular arms are raised in a gesture expressing anguished grief. The bottom register features a procession of horse-drawn foot soldiers carrying figure-eight-shaped shields.

Archaic Statuary: Kouros and Kore

As the Greeks gradually recovered from the Dark Ages, they took to the sea and established trading and agricultural communities throughout the Mediterranean. This expansion brought the Greeks into contact with the culture and the artistic achievements of ancient Egypt, sparking a new archaic style of art. The archaic style stretches from approximately 650 to 480 BCE. Two types of archaic statuary appeared simultaneously: a young, standing nude male called the **kouros** (plural is **kouroi**) and a draped young woman known as the **kore** (plural is **korai**).

The *New York Kouros* (so called because it is displayed at the Metropolitan Museum of Art in New York) (**CD Fig. 6-2**) provides an excellent example of an early Archaic statue. Sculpted around 600 BCE, the 6-foot-4-inch statue probably stood on the tomb of a young man. The statue was clearly inspired by Egyptian works such as the funerary statue of the pharaoh Menkaure (see Chapter 4). Both the *New York Kouros* and Menkaure stand erect with arms rigidly at their sides, fists clenched, and left legs slightly advanced.

Although influenced by Egyptian statues, the Archaic sculptors were bold innovators. First, note that the *New York Kouros* is free of the back slab that supports Egyptian stone statues. The Archaic statues are thus the first sculpted human figures that stand freely on their own. Second, the *New York Kouros* and all other kouroi are nude. No other ancient civilization created nude figures. The Greeks were proud of the human body. Greek youths trained and competed in athletic contests in the nude. The Greeks believed that everything, including the human figure, has an ideal beauty. The *New York Kouros* thus marks the beginning of the Greek quest to create the ideal human form.

The **kore** is the second type of Archaic statuary. A kore is a freestanding, draped female figure. The *Peplos Kore* (**CD Fig. 6-3**) is a particularly well-known example. Like her male counterparts, the *Peplos Kore* is freestanding and frontal. However, unlike the *New York Kouros*, she is clothed. Her **peplos** is a long, woolen garment that gives her figure a columnar appearance.

Although the *Peplos Kore* is conventionally clothed, she does present two bold innovations. The statue's missing left arm was extended, marking a clear attempt to represent motion. Also, take a close look at the woman's face. She is smiling. This **Archaic smile** (**CD Fig. 6-4**) was designed to make the statue appear more lifelike.

Archaic Architecture: Doric and Ionic Temples

All the ancient peoples mentioned in this book so far built temples to worship their gods and goddesses. During the Archaic Age, Greek architects designed and built two orders or styles of stone temples. The Doric order was developed on the Greek mainland and in southern Italy, and the Ionic order was developed on the Aegean islands and the coast of Asia Minor. The Corinthian order did not develop until the fourth century BCE.

Most modern churches, synagogues, and mosques are large buildings where congregations meet to worship God. In contrast, Greek temples were relatively small because they were designed solely to house a cult statue of the god or goddess to whom the temple was dedicated. The image of the deity was placed in a walled inner sanctuary called a **cella**. Only priests and their attendants were allowed inside the temple. Most Greeks witnessed rituals held at an altar in front of the temple.

In a Doric temple, the cella, which is the central hall, is usually surrounded by a **colonnade**, or continuous row of columns, called a **peristyle**. A Doric column is strong in appearance and stands directly on a stepped platform without a decorated base (**CD Fig. 6-5**). Its fluted shaft rises to a plain capital that supports the horizontal **entablature**.

The entablature includes all the horizontal elements that rest on the columns. In the Doric order, the entablature is divided into three parts: a row of stone blocks called the **architrave**, a **frieze** made up of alternating triple-grooved triglyphs and smooth or sculpted metopes, and finally, a projection called a **cornice**. The entablature on each end of the temple supports a triangular **pediment**, which is a space in which statuary was placed.

The Ionic order (**CD Fig. 6-6**) first appeared in the sixth century BCE. It is lighter in proportion and more elegant in detail than the Doric order. Ionic columns have richly decorated bases. The Ionic capital is characterized by a scroll-like motif called a **volute**. An Ionic temple often features a continuous frieze not divided by triglyphs and metopes.

The Greeks used sculpture to decorate their temples and to make a statement about the deity to whom the building was dedicated. The sculptures were concentrated in the frieze and on the two pediments. They were usually painted with vivid colors that created a feeling of life and movement. In the model of a Doric temple (**CD Fig. 6-7**), notice how statuary is included inside the triangular pediment. The metopes of the entablature, which is below the pediment, also included relief sculpture.

The Archaic architects used numerical relationships and geometric rules to design temples that were symmetrical, proportional, and harmonious. They thus began the process of striving to achieve an ideal form that would culminate with the building of the Parthenon.

Archaic Vase Painting: Black-Figure and Red-Figure Vases

Pottery making was the first major industry to develop in Athens during the Archaic period. Because of their beauty, Athenian vases were highly prized and were exported to cities throughout the Mediterranean world. Many of the surviving vases were discovered in Etruscan tombs in Italy (see Chapter 7).

The style of decoration called **black figure** came into use around 625 BCE. In this style, the red clay of the pot itself was left untouched. Skilled artists then painted figures and details in a **slip**, which is liquefied clay. A sophisticated three-part firing process in a kiln left the figures and objects painted with the slip a black color, which is why they are called black-figure vases. Details were then incised with a sharp-pointed stylus. The most famous painters, such as Exekias, signed their works not only out of pride but also to spread the names of their workshops (**CD Fig. 6-8**).

In the sixth century BCE, Athenian artists began using a new type of ornamentation known as **red figure**. With this technique, the background, rather than the figures, was painted with a lustrous black glaze, and the unpainted areas of red clay formed the design. Additional details were brushed on, not simply scratched into the surface as with black-figure decoration. In the resulting design, the figures usually had a reddish color, hence the name red-figure vases. The red-figure technique is said to have been developed by an artist known as the Andokides Painter about 530 BCE. In less than a generation, Euphronius and other artists were creating red-figure masterpieces.

Archaic vases (**CD Fig. 6-9**) provide a vital source of information about ancient Greece. Although the Greeks were accomplished artists, virtually all their paintings have been lost. Surviving examples of ancient Greek paintings are found primarily on vases. Archaic artists abandoned the geometric use of registers to focus on one specific scene. Artists typically portrayed mythological heroes and episodes from the *Iliad* and the *Odyssey*.

Classical Art

In 480 BCE, a powerful Persian army led by King Xerxes invaded Greece. At first, the Persians forced the badly divided Greeks to retreat. Even the Athenians were compelled to evacuate their beloved city. But the Athenians had not given up. Led by Themistocles, their navy defeated the Persians at the battle of Salamis. One year later, a Greek army inflicted yet another defeat on the Persians. A dejected Xerxes was forced to abandon his dream of conquering Greece.

The Persian Wars were a watershed event in Greek history. As the only Greek city-state that challenged Persian power from the beginning, the Athenians enjoyed immense prestige. Athenian confidence soared. The pride of victory and the wealth from a new trading empire set the stage for a dazzling burst of creativity. Athens was about to enter its brief but brilliant golden age.

The period of nearly 160 years from the defeat of the Persians in 479 BCE to the death of Alexander the Great in 323 BCE is called the Classical Period of Greek Art. During this era, Greek artists, sculptors, and architects created enduring works of art that embodied the Greek concept of ideal beauty. Their achievements have had a far-reaching influence on Western art and culture. Succeeding generations of artists and patrons have used the Classical Period as a benchmark that they strove to imitate, exceed, and at times rebel against.

Classical Sculpture

The revolutionary shift from the Archaic style to the Classical style can be seen in a statue now known as the *Kritios Boy* (**CD Fig. 6-10**). In contrast to the rigidly frontal kouroi and korai, the *Kritios Boy* seems more relaxed and natural. His straight left leg bears the weight of his body, while the right leg is bent and relaxed. The *Kritios Boy's* head turns slightly to the right. Known as **contrapposto**, this relaxed, natural stance is one of the hallmarks of the Classical style.

The *Kritios Boy's* innovations were not limited to his contrapposto stance. A calm, serene expression replaces the artificial archaic smile. The statue's muscles are well defined, and his smooth flesh seems soft and natural. The *Kritios Boy* is a youthful athlete who is quietly calm and confident. No physical defects mar his perfect form.

Sculpted in about 480 BCE, the *Kritios Boy* marked the beginning of a radical change in presenting the human form. The next step in this revolutionary process can be seen in a pair of statues known as the *Riace Warriors* (**CD Figs. 6-11 and 6-12**). The statues were discovered by a scuba diver in the sea off the southern coast of Italy near Riace. An unknown master cast these rare bronze originals.

The *Riace Warriors* are remarkably lifelike. Their heads turn forcefully to the right and look at the world with alert eyes made of bone and glass paste. Silver teeth and copper eyelashes add to each statue's lifelike appearance. The realistic contrapposto stance of both statues further enhances the impression of vitality and natural motion.

The quest to sculpt the ideal male form culminated in the *Doryphoros* (*Spear Bearer*) by Polykleitos (**CD Fig. 6-13**). Long since lost, the bronze original was made between 450 and 440 BCE. Like many Greek statues, the *Doryphoros* is known through Roman copies. As discussed in Chapter 8, the Romans admired Greek sculpture and commissioned their artists to make marble copies of the bronze originals.

Figure 6-13. *Doryphoros*

Polykleitos was a renowned sculptor whose statues of young athletes and warriors embodied the Classical ideals of harmony and proportion. In a treatise he called the *Canon*, Polykleitos wrote down his theories of proportion. He then created a larger-than-life-size bronze statue, which he also called the *Canon*, to illustrate his theories.

Polykleitos created visual harmony by means of a technique called the **chiastic** pose. In this pose, the spear-bearing left arm balances the tension of the weight-bearing right leg. The relaxed but straight right arm counters the relaxed, bent left leg. The contrapposto stance of the legs—the bent, relaxed leg behind the stiff supporting leg—suggests motion, yet the figure is at rest. Action and repose are thus in perfect balance.

The *Doryphoros* is carefully and precisely proportioned. For example, the statue's head is one-seventh of the figure's height, and the distance across the *Doryphoros's* shoulders is one-fourth of the figure's height. Like other Classical artists, Polykleitos believed that following harmonious numerical ratios could create ideal human figures.

Classical Architecture

Parthenon

The Persian Wars left much of Athens in ruins. Under the leadership of Pericles, the Athenians undertook one of history's most ambitious and successful building projects. Work focused on the Acropolis (**CD Fig. 6-14**), a rocky, windswept hill that rises 260 feet above Athens. Pericles persuaded a reluctant Athenian Assembly to vote huge sums of money to pay for a small army of artisans who worked for 15 years (447–432 BCE) to build one of architecture's most influential works, the Parthenon.

The Parthenon (**CD Fig. 6-15**) was inspired by Pericles and designed by the architects Iktinos and Kallikrates. Phidias, a leading Athenian artist and friend of Pericles, supervised the sculptural decorations.

The Parthenon was primarily a temple dedicated to Athena, the patron goddess of Athens. Phidias's huge 38-foot statue of the goddess stood in the centrally located cella. Athena's flesh was composed of carved pieces of ivory, while her dress and armor were made of thin sheets of gold. One of her ivory hands rested on a huge shield; in the other, the goddess held a statue of Nike, the winged female personification of victory. Phidias's great statue faced east so that each morning the sun rising over Athens briefly lit her golden robe.

However, the Parthenon was more than just a temple to Athena; it was also a visual expression of the Greeks' long quest to build a perfectly proportioned and thus ideal temple. A colonnade of Doric columns surrounds the temple's outer perimeter. The number of columns was based on a mathematically precise formula: $x = 2y + 1$. For example, the temple's short eastern and western ends ($2y$) have 8 columns, and the long sides (x) have 17 columns ($2y + 1$). This controlling formula characterizes the entire building, thus giving the structure a harmonious design that was graceful, beautiful, and from a Classical perspective, ideal.

An extensive sculptural program enhanced the Parthenon's architectural beauty. The east pediment was more than 90 feet long and rose to a height of 11 feet. Supervised by Phidias, Athenian sculptors filled this challenging space with a series of high-relief sculptures depicting the dramatic birth of Athena. The goddess appears in the center of the pediment springing full grown from the head of her father, Zeus. Two groups of reclining goddesses witness this miraculous birth while filling the sloping spaces to the left and right. The three goddesses to the right (**CD Fig. 6-16**) are Classical masterpieces renowned for the convincing garments that cling to their bodies. A series of unfortunate events, such as warfare and removal of pieces of the structure, resulted in many of the Parthenon sculptures being scattered among various museums, but some remain at the original site.

Although the Parthenon is a Doric temple, an inner colonnade supported an entablature with a 525-foot-long low-relief Ionic frieze. The frieze features figures of more than four hundred men and women and two hundred animals. These figures represent the **Panathenaic Procession** that was held every four years to bring a sacred *peplos* to clothe an ancient wooden cult statue of Athena (**CD Fig. 6-17**). Proud young cavalry-men are shown trying to control restive horses. Four-horse chariots follow along with chariots, musicians, sacrificial animals, and a long row of young women carrying vases filled with gifts for Athena. The entire procession marches past seated gods and god-desses who have come to witness the event. Thus the frieze not only honored Athena but also celebrated the greatness of Athens.

Temple of Athena Nike and the Erectheion

The Parthenon was not the only important building constructed on the Acropolis. Significantly smaller than the Parthenon, the Temple of Athena Nike greeted visitors entering the Acropolis (**CD Fig. 6-18**). Designed by Kallikrates, the temple was the first building on the Acropolis to be built completely in the Ionic order.

The Erectheion is located on the north side of the Acropolis, opposite the Parthenon. It is a complex structure designed to hold several sacred objects, including the wooden statue of Athena that was the goal of the Panathenaic Procession. The most famous part of the building is the Porch of the Maidens (**CD Figs. 6-19 and 6-20**). The maidens are six **caryatids**—female figures that function as supporting columns. Their relaxed con-trapposto pose, graceful drapery, and serene expressions embody the classical style.

Late Classical Sculpture

The Athenian golden age was brilliant but brief. Tensions between Athens and Sparta had been building for years. Finally, in 432 BCE, the Spartans attacked Athens. Known as the Peloponnesian War, the conflict lasted 27 destructive years. In the end, Athens lost its fleet, its empire, and its political leadership.

The unceasing warfare shattered the Athenians' serene confidence. As people turned to their private lives, art began to reflect their joys and sorrows. For the first time, the faces of bronze and marble statues showed more human emotions. This trend can be seen in the work of Praxiteles and Lysippos and in a poignant grave stele of a young hunter.

Praxiteles was one of the most renowned and controversial of the new generation of fourth-century BCE sculptors. Sometime between 350 and 340 BCE, he sold a statue of the goddess Aphrodite to the city of Knidos. Although Greeks were accustomed to seeing statues of nude males, they had never seen a life-size statue of a nude female. Praxiteles's *Aphrodite of Knidos* (**CD Fig. 6-21**) created a sensation by portraying Aphrodite as she prepared to take a bath. Her discarded clothes lie in a pile on top of a nearby vase. The statue aroused so much controversy that according to one legend, Aphrodite herself visited Knidos. When she saw the realistic statue, the goddess cried out in shock, "Where did Praxiteles see me naked?"

A second great sculptor of the Late Classical period, Lysippos of Sikyon, chose typical Classical subjects but treated them in an unusual way. For example, his famous *Apoxyomenos* (*The Scraper*) (**CD Fig. 6-22**) portrays a young athlete using a scraper to remove oil and dirt from his arm. *The Scraper's* body is taller and lighter in appearance than the *Doryphoros*. While the *Doryphoros* is compact and contained, the arms of *The*

Scraper seem to break free into the surrounding space. The viewer can sense that when the athlete finishes cleaning his right arm, he will shift his weight, reverse the position of his legs, and begin scraping his left arm. While all previous Greek statues were meant to be seen exclusively from the front, *The Scraper* invites viewers' inspection from various angles.

A grave stele by an unknown sculptor also reflects the new innovations of the Late Classical period (**CD Fig. 6-23**). The stele depicts a young hunter who has died in the prime of life. A young boy buries his head between his legs and cannot control the grief he feels for his fallen brother. The hunter's aged, grief-stricken father stands to the right wondering how fate could have taken his eldest son. The hunter looks at the viewer, inviting sympathy and creating an emotional link between the spectator and the work. This emotional appeal would become one of the hallmarks of the new Hellenistic art.

Philip II and the Rise of Macedonia

While Athens and other Greek city-states were producing a cultural golden age, Macedon remained a little-known kingdom located north of Mount Olympus. The Macedonians were a tough, Greek-speaking people who lived in mountain villages rather than city-states. The Greeks looked down on the Macedonians as uncivilized because they lacked philosophers, sculptors, and writers. They did, however, have a shrewd and fearless king, Philip II.

Philip quickly proved to be a brilliant general and a ruthless politician. Realizing that the proud Macedonian nobles respected only power, Philip transformed the rugged peasants under his command into a well-trained professional army. Philip's invincible foot soldiers and fast-moving cavalry crushed a combined force of Athenians and Thebans at the battle of Chaeronea in 338 BCE. Philip's 18-year-old son, Alexander, led a successful cavalry charge that helped win the battle.

In recent years, archaeologists have made a series of dramatic discoveries that have shed new light on Philip II and life in the Macedonian court in Pella. Macedonian nobles lived in homes decorated with impressive floor mosaics. A **mosaic** is an image composed of small pieces of colored glass or stone. One of the mosaics uncovered at Pella featured two youths killing a stag. It is possible that one of the young men was Alexander.

Philip did not get a chance to realize his plan of invading Persia. In 336 BCE, he was assassinated as he strolled to see a performance in the theater at his capital city of Vergina. In 1977, Greek archaeologists excavated a tomb containing what are believed to be Philip's remains and royal treasures. One of the most impressive objects is a gold chest embossed with a 16-point star, emblem of the Macedonian dynasty. Archaeologists believe that the gold chest once held the remains of King Philip II.

Conquests of Alexander the Great

Alexander was only 20 years old when he became king in 336 BCE. Despite his youth, the new ruler proved that he had been carefully trained for leadership. Alexander especially enjoyed Homer's description of the heroic deeds performed by Achilles during the Trojan War. Since his mother claimed to be descended from Achilles, Alexander also yearned to be a great hero.

Alexander did not have to wait long to fulfill his dreams. In 334 BCE, he invaded Persia with thirty thousand infantry and five thousand cavalry. Persian messengers raced along the Royal Road to spread news of Alexander's invasion. Vowing to crush the Macedonians, the Persian king Darius III raised a huge army of at least a hundred thousand men to face Alexander at the battle of Issus.

Philoxenos of Eretria later painted a famous panel of the climactic moment of the battle of Issus. Although the painting has been lost, a mosaic discovered in Pompeii (see Chapter 8) is believed to be a faithful reproduction of the earlier masterpiece.

Known as the *Battle of Issus* (**CD Fig. 6-24**), the mosaic contains more than one million tiny colored stones called tesserae. The huge mosaic (8 feet 10 inches × 16 feet 9 inches) captures the drama and psychological intensity of the battle. Realizing that he was outnumbered, Alexander, seen at the left, fearlessly charged straight at Darius, pictured in the center with the golden helmet. The panic-stricken king fled in a chariot drawn by black stallions. One remarkable detail shows the anguished face of a young Persian about to be trampled by the wheels of Darius's chariot. Presumably in close imitation of the original painting, the mosaic successfully created the illusion of a three-dimensional world.

Alexander's victory at Issus gave him control over all of Asia Minor. Within a short time, Alexander conquered the entire Persian Empire. But Alexander did not live to build a strong and lasting empire. He suddenly caught a fever and died on June 10, 323 BCE. He was not yet 33 years old.

Hellenistic Sculpture in Pergamon

Alexander's conquests marked a pivotal moment in ancient history. As he and his army marched through the Persian Empire, thousands of Greek artists, merchants, and officials followed and settled there. They built new cities containing temples, gymnasiums, and theaters. As time passed, Greek settlers married Persian women and adopted Persian ways. A vibrant new culture called **Hellenism** emerged from the blend of Greek and Eastern customs.

Alexander's vast empire survived only a few years as his successors fought each other for power. Although the empire became fragmented, the cities of Alexandria and Pergamon emerged as thriving centers of Hellenistic culture.

Located in western Asia Minor in what is today Turkey, Pergamon played an especially important role in the development of Hellenistic art. Pergamon's rulers strove to transform their city into a new Athens. They collected Greek masterpieces and emulated Athens by erecting a number of buildings atop their city's acropolis.

The Altar of Zeus (**CD Fig. 6-25**) was soon acclaimed as a Hellenistic masterpiece. As a center of civic ceremonial activity, the monument included a colonnade of slender

Ionic columns, an elevated porch for the sanctuary, and an enormous marble frieze nearly 8 feet high and 400 feet long that ran around the base of the altar.

The lower half of the Altar of Zeus contains a frieze that portrays an epic battle, known as the gigantomachy, that pitted the Olympic gods against a race of giants. Sculpted in high relief on more than a hundred panels, the battle scenes present an unprecedented panorama of death and suffering.

The most famous scene depicts Athena attacking the giant Alkyoneus (**CD Fig. 6-26**). Crying out in terror, the giant clings desperately to Athena's arm as the goddess violently wrenches him from the protective arms of his mother, Gaia. Visibly distraught, Gaia vainly pleas with Athena to spare her son. But her anguished cry is ignored as a winged Nike flies in to crown Athena the victor. Carved in about 175 BCE, the gigantomachy frieze ushered in the new age of Hellenistic sculpture.

Hellenistic Sculpture

Hellenistic sculpture represented a new departure in Greek art. Classical sculptors portrayed gods, goddesses, and heroes with idealized bodies and serene expressions. In contrast, Hellenistic sculptors often portrayed everyday people with realistic and often aging bodies. The expressive faces of Hellenistic sculptures are intended to elicit an emotional response from the viewer. These characteristics of Hellenistic art are clearly illustrated in the *Laocoon* (**CD Fig. 6-27**) and the *Seated Boxer* (**CD Fig. 6-28**).

In 1506, Pope Julius II sent a messenger to immediately find Michelangelo. The messenger breathlessly informed the great Renaissance artist that the legendary *Laocoon* had been discovered in the ruins of the palace of emperor Titus. Michelangelo rushed to inspect the statue and supervise its recovery.

The *Laocoon* is thought to have been carved by three sculptors from the island of Rhodes sometime in the second half of the first century BCE. The statue vividly illustrates an incident from the Roman poet Virgil's account of the Trojan War. Laocoon was a priest who wisely urged the Trojans to reject the apparent Greek peace offering of a wooden horse. Furious that his clever ruse might be exposed, Poseidon sent two sea monsters to kill Laocoon and his two sons.

The sculptors focused on Laocoon's desperate struggle to free himself and his sons from the serpent's murderous grip. The merciless monsters coil around the father and his two sons, creating a unified composition. Laocoon's twisted, muscular torso and tormented face may have been influenced by the figure of Alkyoneus in the Pergamon frieze. The effect on Michelangelo of these writhing figures was enormous; their influence can be seen in his *Slaves* and in the tortured figures in his *Last Judgment* (see Chapter 17).

Cast at about the same time as the *Laocoon*, the *Seated Boxer* is a rare original bronze statue by an unknown Hellenistic master. The *Seated Boxer* is not a young athlete confidently waiting to receive an award. Instead, he is a battered veteran with broken teeth and a scarred face. While the *Laocoon* presents the image of a man struggling desperately to overcome his fate, the *Seated Boxer* presents a poignant image of an aging athlete resigned to his fate. The statue reminds us that fame and youth are both fleeting.

Figure 6-28. *Seated Boxer*, bronze, Museo Nazionale Romano, Rome

Conclusion

The ancient Greek quest to create ideal human forms and temples is fundamental to an understanding of the Western artistic tradition. Greek art evolved as artists created four distinct styles: Geometric, Archaic, Classical, and Hellenistic. This chapter has defined and illustrated each of these styles. The AP Art History committee often asks students to compare and contrast objects representing two different styles. For example, a typical question might ask you to compare and contrast an Archaic kouros and the Hellenistic *Seated Boxer*. Although all four styles are important, recent tests have asked a number of questions on the *Doryphoros*, the *Laocoon*, and the mosaic depicting the Battle of Issus.

Chapter 7

Etruscan Art

Introduction and Exam Strategy Overview

What do the movie *Mission: Impossible II* and the ancient Etruscans have in common? The answer is one word: *chimera*. In the movie, chimera was a genetically modified disease that could destroy humanity. In Etruscan art, the chimera was a famous bronze statue of a monster with a lion's head and body and a serpent's tail (**CD Fig. 7-1**). A second head, that of a goat, grew out of the lion's left side.

The Etruscans lived in central Italy from about 1000 BCE to 100 BCE. Etruscan civilization reached its peak during the fifth century BCE. During the centuries that followed, they lost their independence and were gradually absorbed into the ever-expanding Roman Empire.

Although Etruscan art is both interesting and important, it plays only a minor role on the AP Art History exam. Most exams have included only one or two multiple-choice questions on the topic. Since 1983, just one slide-based multiple-choice question and one short essay question have appeared on exams. This chapter highlights key works of Etruscan art that have been included in past AP Art History exams.

Terracotta Statues

Etruscan artists were influenced by the contemporary Archaic style being developed in Greece (see Chapter 6). The Archaic influence can be seen in the life-size terracotta *Statue of Apulu* (Apollo) (**CD Fig. 7-2**). Discovered in 1916, the statue originally decorated the roof of an Etruscan temple. Like a Greek kouros, Apulu has stylized hair and a distinctive Archaic smile.

Although influenced by Archaic Greek statues, Etruscan sculptors were not mere imitators. Unlike his Greek counterparts, the youthful Apulu is clothed. While Archaic Greek sculptors preferred to use marble, Etruscan sculptors used terracotta ("baked clay"), the same material used for making pottery. And finally, while the kouroi were stationary grave markers, the Apulu strode confidently across the roof of a temple.

Bronze Sculpture

The few surviving examples of Etruscan bronze sculpture demonstrate exceptional skill. For example, the *Capitoline Wolf* (**CD Fig. 7-3**) is a larger-than-life-size portrayal of the she-wolf that, according to Roman myth, nursed Romulus and Remus, the legendary founders of Rome. The statue vividly captures the she-wolf's protective role as she alertly confronts an unseen intruder. It is important to note that the two infants shown in most photos of the *Capitoline Wolf* are additions by the Italian Renaissance sculptor Antonio Pallaiuolo.

Underground Tombs

Like the Egyptians, the Etruscans buried their dead in elaborate underground tombs. Wealthy Etruscans stocked their tombs with prized possessions that included thousands of black-figure and red-figure vases imported from Greece. In addition, Etruscans often decorated the tomb walls with fresco paintings. Although some of the paintings depict funeral rites, most portray a zest for living by featuring banquets, sports, and dancing.

Sarcophagi

Aristocratic Etruscans had their cremated remains placed in terracotta sarcophagi. A typical sarcophagus is in the form of a sculpted husband and wife reclining on a banquet coach. The couple have long, stylized hair and gaze into eternity with contented Archaic smiles. In contrast to the Archaic kouroi and korai, the Etruscan figures stop abruptly at the waist. Also, in Greek banqueting scenes, only men are shown reclining. The Etruscan sarcophagus is distinct in its depiction of the wife reclining with her husband (**CD Fig. 7-4**). It is also interesting to notice their animated hand gestures, which create the impression of a lively conversation. To this day, Italians are renowned for "talking" with their hands.

Conclusion

The Etruscans created impressive works of art that share characteristics with Archaic Greek art. Although the Etruscans borrowed some elements from the Greeks, they also developed their own distinctive styles. Wealthy Etruscans buried their dead in elaborate tombs containing black-figure and red-figure vases imported from Greece. The terracotta *Statue of Apulu* and the sarcophagus with a reclining couple are the works of art most frequently tested on the AP Art History exam.

Chapter 8

Roman Art

Introduction and Exam Strategy Overview

What do Thomas Jefferson's home at Monticello, the New Orleans Superdome, and the California Aqueduct have in common? All three structures are modern descendants of edifices first built by the Romans. The Pantheon inspired Monticello, the Colosseum inspired the Superdome, and Roman aqueducts inspired the one in California.

The Romans conquered a vast empire that extended north to Scotland, south to the Sahara Desert, east to Mesopotamia, and west to the Atlantic Ocean. The Romans used art and architecture to help unify their empire. Temples, amphitheaters, and aqueducts were all visual expressions of the power and benefits of Roman civilization.

The rise and fall of Roman civilization is one of the most significant chapters in art history texts. Like Greece, Rome had a lasting influence on the Western tradition of art. The AP Art History exam reflects this importance by placing significant emphasis on Roman art, sculpture, and architecture. Most exams contain between four and six multiple-choice questions. In addition, a slide-based multiple-choice question or a short essay question has been included on two of every three exams since 1983. The emphasis on Roman art has been especially strong since 2001. Between 2001 and 2006, each exam included either a slide-based multiple-choice question or a short essay. And finally, Roman works of art can often be used as illustrative examples for one or both of the long essay questions.

Temple of Portunus

The Temple of Portunus (**CD Fig. 8-1**) provides a good example of an early Roman temple. Constructed around 75 BCE, the temple combines Etruscan and Greek elements to create a distinctive Roman design. Like Etruscan temples, the Temple of Portunus sits atop a high podium accessible only at the front. Much like the Temple of Athena Nike, freestanding Ionic columns support an Ionic frieze and a pediment. Roman architects also added a series of engaged Ionic half-columns on the sides and back of the cella. The engaged Ionic columns do not actually provide support because the cella is a solid wall made of concrete.

Concrete Revolution

The discovery of concrete revolutionized Roman architecture. Roman concrete was made from a mixture of lime mortar, volcanic sand, water, and small stones. Builders learned to pour this mixture into a wooden mold, where it dried and became as hard as stone. Concrete was easy to use, strong, and cheap. Unlike marble, concrete does not have to be quarried, cut, or transported.

Concrete enabled architects to build arches and to cover large spaces with barrel vaults, groin vaults, and domes. A true arch is constructed with wedge-shaped bricks or stones called **voussoirs**. A row of round arches produces a **barrel** or **tunnel vault**. A **groin vault** is formed by the intersection at right angles of two barrel vaults of equal size (**CD Fig. 8-2**).

The corbelled Treasury of Atreus at Mycenae was the largest domed space in the ancient world. Using concrete, Roman architects could build domes that surpassed the Mycenaean tombs. A **dome** is a hemispheric vault that usually rests on a cylindrical wall called a drum. Later in the chapter, you will learn how the Romans used concrete vaults and domes to construct monumental public buildings that are enduring parts of the Roman legacy.

Early Roman Portrait Sculpture

Would you prefer to be portrayed as you really look or as you would like to look? Although they were familiar with the idealized portraits of classical Greece, early Romans rejected them. Instead, during the Republic (507–27 BCE), prominent Romans preferred **veristic** or **superrealistic** portraits.

The Greeks believed that the head and body were inseparable. Romans disagreed, believing that the head was enough to constitute a true portrait. Roman sculptors often used death masks to create portraits of the head, neck, and shoulders called **busts**. The busts carefully and even proudly recorded signs of age, including wrinkles, sags, and warts (**CD Fig. 8-3**).

Veristic busts provide important insights about Roman values. As confident, experienced rulers of a rising Mediterranean power, the Romans prized a trait they called **gravitas**, or weightiness. Serious-minded Roman men and women honored strength more than beauty, power more than grace, and steadiness more than quickness of mind.

The busts served another important function. Roman aristocrats were proud of their family lineage. The portrait busts provided a visual representation of a family's genealogy. Romans kept their busts in wooden cupboards and proudly paraded them at the funerals of prominent family members and relatives.

Pompeii: Domestic Architecture

Nineteen hundred years ago, Pompeii was a thriving city of ten thousand to twenty thousand people. On August 24, 79 CE, Mount Vesuvius erupted, burying Pompeii under a layer of volcanic ash 20 feet thick.

Pompeii lay buried and forgotten until the mid-eighteenth century. Since then, excavations at Pompeii and nearby Herculaneum have uncovered a remarkable trove of information about Roman domestic architecture and art.

Aristocratic Romans wanted to be remembered as sober men of state. However, their lavish homes in Pompeii demonstrate that they also prized luxury and comfort. Private homes in Pompeii all followed a common basic plan. There were no green lawns, front porches, or picture windows. Instead, high stone walls kept strangers, noises, and odors outside.

A guest entered a typical private home through a narrow, dark foyer, which led to a large, open **atrium**, or court (**CD Fig. 8-4**). The atrium was often more than 40 feet wide, 50 feet long, and 28 feet high. Splendid paintings decorated the walls and beautiful mosaics covered the floors. Light, air, and rainwater entered the atrium through an opening in the roof called the **compluvium**. The water collected in a rectangular basin called an **impluvium**.

The atrium often connected to a beautiful **peristyle**, or open-air garden (**CD Fig. 8-5**). Peristyles were private miniparks filled with bubbling fountains, fruit trees, shrubs, and vegetable gardens. A number of small rooms surrounded the atrium and the peristyle provided places where family members slept and dined.

Pompeii: Wall Paintings

Almost all the surviving Roman wall paintings come from Pompeii and Herculaneum. The paintings are frescoes in which water-based pigments are applied directly to moist plaster. The paintings cover many subjects, including portraits, mythological scenes, landscapes, cityscapes, and **still life** compositions of inanimate objects. Hellenistic artists influenced many of these works.

During the late nineteenth century, a German art historian divided Pompeian paintings into four styles. Although this classification scheme is discussed in most textbooks, it has yet to be tested on the AP Art History exam. Instead, the committee has written several questions on what it calls "the mixture of perspective models" used by Pompeian artists.

Perspective is a system for representing three-dimensional space on a two-dimensional surface. Pompeian artists used a combination of three techniques to create the illusion of depth on a flat surface. First, objects meant to be perceived as far away from the surface plane of the wall are shown slightly smaller than those intended to appear nearby. This commonsense approach is called **intuitive perspective**. Second, Pompeian artists understood that they could create the illusion of depth by muting colors and blurring details as objects get farther away. This technique is called **atmospheric perspective**. And finally, art historians now believe that Pompeian artists employed **single-point linear perspective** (**CD Fig. 8-6**). Long thought to be a Renaissance innovation (see Chapter 16), this technique creates depth and distance by using receding lines that converge at a single point.

A skillful still life panel found in Herculaneum demonstrates the ability of Roman artists to create a realistic illusion of depth. The painting depicts green peaches and a jar half filled with water (**CD Fig. 8-7**). On first glance, the composition seems mundane. However, a close inspection reveals that the artist used touches of white paint to capture the effect of light playing on the surface of the jar. The peaches are cleverly placed on receding shelves to create the illusion of depth. Sadly, like the cities of Pompeii and Herculaneum, still life paintings would be forgotten until Dutch artists from the seventeenth and eighteenth centuries rediscovered the genre (see Chapter 21).

Age and Art of Augustus

Rome began as a collection of huts on a hill beside the Tiber River. By the middle of the first century BCE, Roman legions conquered an empire even larger than Alexander's. But the prospects for a period of peace abruptly ended when disgruntled senators assassinated Julius Caesar on the Ides of March, 44 BCE. The assassination plunged the Roman world into a bloody civil war that finally ended thirteen years later, when Caesar's grandnephew and adopted son, Octavian, defeated Mark Antony and Queen Cleopatra of Egypt at the battle of Actium.

Octavian skillfully consolidated power while claiming to be only "the first citizen." In 27 BCE, the senate granted Octavian the title Augustus or "supreme ruler." Augustus was Rome's first and ablest ruler. During his forty-one-year reign (27 BCE–14 CE) he promoted trade, commissioned public works, and inaugurated a period of peace and prosperity known as the *Pax Romana*, "Roman peace."

Figure 8-8. *Statue of Augustus from Primaporta*, marble, first century CE, Vatican Museum, Rome

As the leader of a vast and diverse empire, Augustus understood the importance of using art to create public images that projected his power and authority. The three hundred surviving portraits of Augustus were designed to create a visible image of a commanding, divinely inspired, and ageless leader. All these qualities can be seen in a famous statue now known as the *Statue of Augustus from Primaporta* (**CD Fig. 8-8**).

The statue skillfully projects several powerful images. Augustus's contrapposto pose and ideal proportions are clearly based on Polykleitos's *Doryphoros*. But unlike the *Doryphoros*, Augustus confidently raises his right arm in a gesture of command. Although more than 40 years old when the statue was carved, Augustus appears youthful and, at 6 feet 8 inches in height, larger than life. The signs of age prized on early republican busts have disappeared.

The *Statue of Augustus from Primaporta* also conveys an important message about Augustus's divine lineage. Notice the image of Venus's son Cupid next to the emperor's right leg. Because Augustus's family traced his ancestry back to Venus, Cupid proclaims his divine descent. Augustus is thus a divinely inspired leader who enjoys the approval of the gods.

The Ara Pacis (Altar of Peace) demonstrates Augustus's use of art as imperial propaganda (**CD Fig. 8-9**). Commissioned by the senate, the altar celebrates Augustus's role as a leader who brought Rome the blessings of peace and prosperity. The richly decorated altar contains a number of superb low-relief sculptures. On one side, Augustus leads a procession of priests, magistrates, and members of the imperial family. Another panel shows a figure of Mother Earth surrounded by flowering plants and peaceful animals, symbols of the fruits of the *Pax Romana* (**CD Fig. 8-10**).

Imperial Monuments

During the *Pax Romana* (27 BCE–180 CE), Romans justifiably believed that the city of Rome was unequalled in wealth, taste, and power. Augustus and his successors filled the city with columned temples, heroic statues, and imperial monuments. With so much to choose from, the AP Art History exam committee has focused special attention on the Arch of Titus, Trajan's Column, and the *Equestrian Statue of Marcus Aurelius*. All three imperial monuments illustrate how Roman rulers used art as a form of propaganda.

A second-century-CE visitor to Rome could have viewed more than thirty marble triumphal arches. These freestanding monuments commemorated notable imperial triumphs. Victorious emperors proudly paraded under a newly erected arch as trumpets blared, crowds cheered, and hapless captives groaned.

In 81 CE, Emperor Domitian erected an arch to commemorate his older brother Titus's conquest of Jerusalem (**CD Fig. 8-11**). The arch is noteworthy for two relief panels prominently located on the inside walls. One panel depicts a line of Roman soldiers carrying a sacred seven-branched candelabrum taken from the Temple in Jerusalem (**CD Fig. 8-12**). The panel on the opposite side of the arch shows Titus in a four-horse chariot. He is accompanied by statues of divinities representing the imperial virtues of victory, honor, and valor.

About forty years after Titus conquered Jerusalem, Emperor Trajan (89–117 CE) inflicted a crushing defeat on the Dacians, a warlike tribe living along the Danube River. Trajan commemorated his victory by commissioning a 125-foot-tall column (**CD Fig. 8-13**). A statue of the emperor once adorned the top of the column, and his cremated remains were placed inside a golden urn at the base.

Trajan's Column is more than just an unusual tomb; it is also a masterpiece of continuous narrative storytelling. A low-relief frieze 625 feet long winds around the column like an enormous carved scroll (**CD Fig. 8-14**). Trajan appears in one-third of the 150 episodes. He solemnly conducts sacrifices to the gods, confidently addresses his troops, and efficiently supervises the entire campaign. The Roman victory is both predictable and inevitable.

Atop the column was the *Statue of Trajan*, one of ten thousand marble and bronze statues that once adorned buildings and monuments in Rome. In 1587, Pope Sixtus V replaced the *Statue of Trajan* with the *Statue of Saint Peter* seen today. At the same time, almost all the bronze statues in ancient Rome were melted down for their metal value. But thanks to a lucky error, the bronze-gilded *Equestrian Statue of Marcus Aurelius* survived because early Christians thought it was a portrait of Constantine, considered the first Christian emperor.

The larger-than-life statue portrays Emperor Marcus Aurelius sitting calmly on a Spanish war steed. A defeated enemy may have once cowered under the horse's right foreleg while the emperor extends his right hand in a peaceful gesture suggesting clemency for the defeated adversary.

The *Equestrian Statue of Marcus Aurelius* (**CD Fig. 8-15**) has enjoyed a long and influential history. During the Italian Renaissance, it inspired sculptors who used it as a model for the first equestrian statues cast since antiquity. In 1537, Michelangelo used the statue as a centerpiece for his new design for the Capitoline Hill in Rome. The statue now stands in the Capitoline Museum, where a thorough restoration returned the famous bronze figures to their former extraordinary beauty.

Aqueducts

Romans were proud of their city's grand imperial monuments. But they boasted even more loudly about Rome's aqueducts. "Will anybody compare the idle pyramids, or those other useless though renowned works of the Greeks, with these aqueducts, these indispensable structures?" asked a practical-minded Roman engineer.

The engineer had a point. The city's eleven aqueducts used gravity to carry water from distant lakes and streams to satisfy the needs of Rome's one million thirsty citizens. The precious liquid enabled Romans to enjoy bathing in enormous baths constructed by the emperors.

As the Roman Empire expanded, its engineers built aqueducts for important provincial cities. During the reign of Augustus, engineers constructed a great aqueduct-bridge at Nimes that is known today as the Pont du Gard (**CD Fig. 8-16**). Most of the

30-mile-long aqueduct was built below ground or on a low wall. When the aqueduct reached a deep gorge cut by the Gard River, engineers built a three-story bridge that is still standing.

Figure 8-16. Pont-du-Gard aqueduct, Nimes, France

The Pont du Gard aqueduct-bridge is both an impressive engineering feat and a visible symbol of the power and greatness of Roman culture. With its three rows of true arches, one on top of the other, the imposing structure reaches a height of 150 feet. The wedge-shaped voussoirs that make up the arches weigh up to 6 tons each. The water channel runs along the top and is covered by stone slabs.

Colosseum

In 80 CE, more than fifty thousand excited spectators poured into Rome's new sports arena, the Colosseum (**CD Fig. 8-17**). The largest building of its kind in the ancient world, the Colosseum enclosed an oval-shaped arena with a floor 280 feet long and 175 feet wide. Seventy-six numbered entrances allowed spectators to efficiently enter and leave the arena.

From an architectural perspective, the Colosseum is a large amphitheater, or "double theater." The Colosseum thus resembles two Greek theaters put together. But this similarity is only superficial. Greek theaters were set into natural hillsides. The Colosseum is an artificial concrete mountain. And while Greek theaters housed refined plays, the Colosseum was the venue of bloody gladiator fights.

The AP Art History exam committee has always emphasized the importance of the architectural features of this famous building's outer walls. The Colosseum's 159-foot-high curving outer wall consists of three levels of arches culminating in a fourth-level attic or top story. The arches on each level are framed by a distinctive pair of three-quarter engaged columns. In what is known as a hierarchy of orders, the first story uses Tuscan or Doric columns, and the next two levels use Ionic and Corinthian columns. The columns did not support the wall and were purely decorative. However, this visually appealing hierarchy profoundly influenced later Renaissance architects (see Chapter 16).

Pantheon

Romans never forgot to honor the gods whose divine favor made Rome's greatness possible. Emperor Hadrian erected the Pantheon (118–125 CE) to serve as a temple literally dedicated to all (*pan*) the gods (*theoi*). The Pantheon (**CD Figs. 8-18** and **8-19**) is the best-preserved ancient Roman building and one of the world's architectural masterpieces. Its revolutionary design and awe-inspiring interior have made it one of the most influential buildings in architectural history.

Visitors to the Pantheon entered the temple through an impressive but traditional column-lined portico or porch. When they opened the temple's massive bronze doors, Romans entered an interior space unlike any that had been created in the ancient world. A 142-foot-high concrete dome covered a 142-foot-wide spherical floor. A Roman standing at the center of this perfectly proportional space could easily understand that the dome was meant to symbolize the vault of the heavens protecting the orb of the earth.

A circular opening in the center of the dome reinforced this cosmic symbolism (**CD Fig. 8-20**). With a diameter of 29 feet, the oculus allowed light (and rain) to enter the Pantheon. On a sunny day, light passing through the oculus formed a circular beam illuminating the Pantheon's marble walls and ornate statues of gods and goddesses. To the Romans, the sun's rays symbolized Jupiter's all-seeing eye.

Constructing the Pantheon's dome posed an unprecedented challenge. Roman engineers used many ingenious techniques to support the dome and lighten its enormous weight. They varied the thickness and thus the weight of the concrete. The dome is 20 feet thick along the drum but only 5 feet thick at the oculus. A series of **coffers**, or recessed panels, decorate the ceiling while also lightening the dome's weight.

The Pantheon revolutionized architectural history by combining a portico with a domed rotunda. This design influenced Renaissance architects (see Chapters 16 and 17) and the neoclassic style in Europe and America (see Chapter 23).

Diocletian and the Tetrarchy

The *Pax Romana* marked the zenith of Roman power. A long process of decline began during the third century CE. This turbulent century witnessed a series of economic disruptions, military defeats, and political upheavals that shook the empire's foundations. During one particularly chaotic fifty-year period (235–284 CE), twenty emperors seized the imperial throne only to meet violent deaths.

These dark years finally ended when Diocletian took the imperial scepter in 284 CE. A strong-willed military commander, Diocletian defended Rome's borders and revived its economy. In a bold attempt to restore political order, Diocletian created a **tetrarchy**, or rule by four. This arrangement divided power between two emperors with the title of Augustus. Each Augustus had an heir apparent with the title of Caesar.

Figure 8-21. Portraits of the tetrarchs, 305 CE, Porphyry, Saint Mark's, Venice

A revealing statue, now located in Venice, visually portrays the tetrarchs and the decline of Rome's political leadership. The statue depicts four figures: two Augusti and two Caesars (**CD Fig. 8-21**). The anonymous rulers each stand just 4 feet 3 inches tall. They embrace each other for strength and security. The four huddled figures form a stark contrast with the larger-than-life statue of Augustus raising his arm in a supremely confident gesture of command.

Legacy of Constantine the Great

Hoping that the Caesars would peacefully take his place, Diocletian voluntarily abdicated his throne in 305 CE. But the tetrarchy worked better in statues than in the reality of Roman politics. Within a few years, numerous rival leaders vied for power.

One of these rivals was a brilliant young military commander named Constantine. In 312 CE, Constantine invaded Italy only to find Rome defended by a formidable army led by Maxentius. According to tradition, on the eve of the battle, Constantine saw a fiery cross in the sky emblazoned with the words, "By this sign you shall conquer." The next morning, Constantine ordered the Christian monogram—the Greek letters *X* (chi) and *P* (rho), standing for *Christos*—inscribed on his army's shields and battle standards.

Constantine attributed his overwhelming victory over Maxentius to the power of the Christian God. He showed his gratitude by issuing the Edict of Milan. This landmark decree ended the persecution of Christians.

Although eventually hailed as the first Christian emperor, Constantine behaved more like a traditional Roman emperor. He promptly erected a huge triple arch to commemorate his great military victories. The Arch of Constantine (**CD Fig. 8-22**) includes sculptures taken from earlier monuments honoring Trajan, Hadrian, and Marcus Aurelius. In some cases, sculptors cut off the heads of his predecessors and replaced them with images of Constantine. This juxtaposition may have been intended to visually associate Constantine with the virtues of great emperors from the *Pax Romana*.

The Arch of Constantine was not the only gigantic monument commissioned by Constantine. His sculptors also carved a colossal 30-foot-tall statue of the emperor seated on a throne. Although most of the statue has been lost, Constantine's enormous 8½-foot head survives (**CD Fig. 8-23**). The head's immense size conveys an image of power and absolute authority. While early Roman leaders proudly used wrinkled faces to emphasize their gravitas, Constantine's eyes look out from an unblemished face that is eternally young.

Constantine's reign (312–337 CE) marked the end of Rome's exalted position as the capital of a great empire. In 330 CE Constantine founded a "New Rome" on the site of Byzantium. He renamed the city Constantinople, the "City of Constantine." Constantinople became the capital of the Byzantine Empire (see Chapter 10). While Constantinople flourished, Rome faltered and then fell. In 410 CE, the Vandals breached the city's once impregnable walls. By the time the Western Empire collapsed in 476 CE, the capital was a shadow of its once glorious past.

Conclusion

The artistic heritage of Rome is an essential ingredient of Western culture. Roman artistic styles varied as the empire rose and fell. Unidealized realism characterized portraiture during the republican era. In contrast, emperors such as Augustus and Constantine understood how to use art as a form of political propaganda.

The AP Art History exam committee has placed particular emphasis on Roman architectural achievements in past tests. Concrete enabled Roman architects to use barrel and groin vaults to enclose large spaces. Recent tests have included several multiple-choice and short essay questions on the characteristics and functions of aqueducts, the revolutionary design and influence of the Pantheon, and a comparison of Roman amphitheaters with Greek theaters.

Part 2
Medieval Art

Chapter 9

Early Christian Art

Introduction and Exam Strategy Overview

Could a Greek or Roman temple be converted into a Christian church? As described in Chapters 6 and 8, Greek and Roman temples were designed to contain cult statues. In contrast, a Christian church was intended to be a place where believers could gather for worship. The needs of the Christian religion thus demanded a new style of sacred architecture.

Christianity's impact on art extended well beyond building new churches. Classical art portrayed gods, emperors, mythical heroes, and victorious athletes. In contrast, Christian artists portrayed the life of Christ and the deeds of the saints.

Christianity's new, more spiritual focus required a different style of art. The first Christian artists blended Christian subjects and themes with Classical features. The term *early Christian* art refers to the preserved works with Christian subjects created during the first five centuries CE. Early Christian art is a fascinating and changing synthesis of Christian subject matter and Classical features.

Early Christian paintings, sculptures, mosaics, and buildings occupy a transitional phase between the Classical period and the art and architecture of the Middle Ages. Although early Christian art is not extensive, it has occupied an important place on past AP Art History exams. Most exams have contained between one and three multiple-choice questions. Since 1991, there have been two slide-based multiple-choice questions and three short essay questions. Each of the essay questions asked students to describe the Classical and early Christian characteristics of a specific work of art.

Life of Jesus in Art

Most art history texts devote two full pages to a chart explaining the life of Jesus as shown in art. For Christians, Jesus Christ is the Son of God, the Messiah foretold in the Old Testament of the Holy Bible. He came to Earth from Heaven to redeem humankind of its sins so that people could be united with God in Heaven. Jesus' life is usually divided into the following categories:

- *Incarnation and childhood*: The events surrounding Christ's conception, birth, infancy, and childhood.

- *Public ministry*: Key events include calling the twelve apostles, performing miracles, teaching parables, and giving sermons.

- *Passion*: The events surrounding Christ's arrest, trial, crucifixion, resurrection, and ascension.

Numerous works of art depict stories from these categories. The primary sources for these stories are the four Gospels of the New Testament attributed to the four sainted evangelists: Matthew, Mark, Luke, and John. In addition to the Gospels, Christian art draws on themes from the Old Testament, especially stories, events, and prophecies that **prefigure**, or foresee, the coming of Christ. Christian art also draws heavily on the book of Revelation, which tells about the end of Earth, the Last Judgment of humankind, and the establishment of a new heavenly kingdom to replace Earth. This chapter discusses specific Christian themes, stories, and symbols in greater depth when they are necessary for understanding a style or work of art.

Art of the Catacombs

During the first three centuries after Christ's death, Roman authorities banned Christianity and often persecuted Christians. During this long period, Christians concealed their religious practices by digging tunnels outside Rome. Known as **catacombs**, these tunnels were underground passageways and chambers where early Christians buried their dead and sometimes conducted religious ceremonies. Although originally quite modest, the catacombs gradually became extensive subterranean complexes that extended up to 90 miles. Some catacombs contained as many as five levels.

The Roman Christians sometimes decorated catacomb walls with frescoes depicting the life and teachings of Jesus. These frescoes closely resemble the style of Roman wall paintings but focused on Christian stories and themes.

The Catacomb of Priscilla contains a particularly revealing fresco that may date to the early fourth century. Christ occupies the center and is portrayed as the Good Shepherd who is concerned with the well-being of his flock (**CD Fig. 9-1**). The image refers to a passage from the Gospel of John in which Christ said, "I am the good shepherd. A good shepherd lays down his life for the sheep."

Christ's physical form is based on Greco-Roman models. He is youthful, clean shaven, and clothed in a modest classical tunic. Christ even stands in a classical contrapposto pose and physically resembles a young Apollo. Unlike Apollo, however, Christ is concerned for the welfare of his followers and willing to sacrifice himself to guarantee the salvation of those who dedicate their lives to him.

The fresco drawing of Christ and his sheep is surrounded by a circle. Four lines extend from the circle, alluding to the crucifixion. **Lunettes**, or semicircles at the end of each arm of the cross, contain scenes from the Old Testament story of Jonah, who attempted to evade God's mission by sailing away on a ship (**CD Fig. 9-2**). God pursued

Jonah by sending a violent storm that threatened to sink the ship. Realizing that God was at work and hoping to evade His calling once again, Jonah convinced the crew to throw him overboard. Soon he was swallowed by a whale and spent three days in its belly before finally repenting his disobedience to God. Then the whale spit Jonah out by the shore, and Jonah went on to fulfill God's mission.

The story of Jonah is significant. To Christians, Jonah is a **prefiguration**, or prophetic forerunner, of Christ. Just as Jonah spent three days in the belly of the whale, so Christ spent three days in the tomb. And just as Jonah was released unharmed, so Christ was resurrected from his tomb in physical wholeness. This theological analogy was later used by Michelangelo when he placed a portrait of Jonah on the ceiling over the altar in the Sistine Chapel (see Chapter 17).

Sarcophagus of Junius Bassus

Like their pagan contemporaries, wealthy Christians preferred to be buried in marble sarcophagi. The richly carved Sarcophagus of Junius Bassus (**CD Fig. 9-3**) was made for an important Roman official who converted to Christianity before his death in 359.

Two registers of five compartments, each framed by Classical columns, divide the Sarcophagus of Junius Bassus. Christ appears in the central compartment of each register. In the bottom scene, Christ appears triumphantly entering Jerusalem. The scene recalls portrayals of victorious Roman emperors entering a city. In the top register, figures of saints Peter and Paul flank an enthroned Christ. As in the Catacomb of Saints Peter and Marcellinus, Christ is youthful and unbearded. However, in this portrait, Christ resembles a Roman emperor confidently dispensing the law. As the ruler of the universe, Christ appears above a figure who personifies Coelis, the pagan god of the heavens.

The Sarcophagus of Junius Bassus is an important transitional piece that combines Christian themes with architectural and figural elements that tie the work to the Classical past. One of the compartments, for example, portrays Adam and Eve standing in the Garden of Eden. Both figures are nude and portrayed in a classical contrapposto pose. Theologically, Adam and Eve represent the Original Sin that necessitated Christ's sacrifice to redeem humankind.

Old Saint Peter's Basilica

Constantine's historic Edict of Milan legalized Christianity (see Chapter 8). Jubilant Christians were now free to leave the catacombs and build houses of worship. Because their spacious, rectangular shape could house large groups, Roman basilicas became the model for early Christian churches.

The church now known as Old Saint Peter's Basilica (**CD Fig. 9-4**) served as an important prototype for later developments in Christian architecture. Worshippers often gathered in an atrium before entering a **narthex**, or entrance hall. The narthex provided a transition from the outside to the inner sanctuary.

The Christian congregation sat in a 300-foot-long **nave**, or central area, flanked by side aisles. Old Saint Peter's also had a **transept**, a transverse aisle perpendicular to the nave. The transept and nave intersected at the crossing to form a **cruciform**, or crosslike shape. A huge marble **baldacchino**, or canopy, covered the crossing, marking the spot where Saint Peter was believed to have been buried. The basilica's architecture thus visually symbolized Christ's words when he gave Peter the keys to heaven: "Upon this rock I will build my church."

Christian rituals focused on the Mass, a body of rites that included the sacrament of Holy Communion. Priests conducted Mass at an altar located in the eastern end of the basilica. The altar usually supported a crucifix with an image of Christ facing the congregation. According to tradition, Christ was crucified facing west. A semicircular recess called an apse was located behind the altar.

Like other Early Christian basilicas, Old Saint Peter's had a timber roof. A row of windows called a **clerestory** permitted light to enter the church. The light illuminated frescoes and mosaics adorning the basilica's inner walls and apse. It is important to note that Early Christian basilicas did not have either side chapels or groin vaults.

Centrally Planned Buildings

The cruciform basilica was not the only church design. Early Christian architects also constructed centrally planned buildings. As its name implies, a centrally planned structure is circular. The main parts of the building radiate from a central point that is often reserved for the altar. A circular space called the **ambulatory** extends from the central space to the exterior walls.

Centrally planned churches (**CD Fig. 9-5**) proved to be very popular in the Byzantine Empire (see Chapter 10). In the West, the central plan was mainly used as a martyria to house sacred relics, as a mausoleum to protect the sarcophagus of an important person, or as a baptistery to provide a special place for baptisms.

Early Christian Mosaics

Like other Early Christian basilicas, Old Saint Peter's had a plain brick exterior. In contrast, precious materials, glittering mosaics, and brightly colored frescoes adorned the interior walls. According to a contemporary pope, Constantine covered the apse vault of Old Saint Peter's with gold foil and commissioned a 150-pound gold cross for the saint's tomb. The contrast between the decorated interior and the plain exterior was not accidental. It subtly reminded Christians that the beauty of the inner spirit was more important than external physical adornment. The magnificent mosaics also reminded the faithful of the splendors of the Kingdom of God.

Mosaics decorated the apse walls in the most elaborate Early Christian basilicas. A mosaic from the entrance wall of the Mausoleum of Galla Placidia in Ravenna provides a particularly important example of the development of early Christian art. Like the fresco from the Catacomb of Saints Peter and Marcellinus, the mosaic portrays Christ as the Good Shepherd (**CD Fig. 9-6**). The similarity between the two works ends there, however. In the mosaic, Christ still sits among a flock of sheep, but he wears a purple and gold robe, signifying his royal status as the future King of Heaven.

Although it was created in the fifth century CE, the mosaic depicting Christ as the Good Shepherd shows knowledge of the tradition of Roman illusionism. Christ sits in contrapposto in a spatial setting filled with three-dimensional forms. A blue sky and natural shadows also show the continuation of Greco-Roman illusionary devices.

Reminders of the Greco-Roman artistic heritage soon disappeared, however. A mosaic created in about 504 for another church in Ravenna illustrates the change. The mosaic depicts the miracle of the loaves and fishes (**CD Fig. 9-7**). A regally robed Christ stands erect directly facing the viewer. Christ and his four followers no longer look like real figures occupying real space but appear to float just above the horizon. The heavenly gold background deliberately limits the depth of the scene in favor of creating a more spiritual feeling. This mosaic thus marks the beginning of a new Byzantine style that is described in Chapter 10.

Figure 9-7. *Miracle of the Loaves and Fishes*, mosaic, 504, Sant' Apollinare Nuovo, Ravenna, Italy

Conclusion

Early Christian art marks an important transition between the Greco-Roman heritage and the emerging art and architecture of the Middle Ages. The AP Art History exam committee expects students to identify the catacombs, list characteristic features of Early Christian basilicas such as Old Saint Peter's, and be able to discuss the Classical and Early Christian styles exhibited in a work of art.

Chapter 10

Byzantine Art

Introduction and Exam Strategy Overview

Shortly after Constantine legalized Christianity in 313, he moved the capital of the Roman Empire to the Greek-speaking city of Byzantium in the East. The city of Byzantium was located on a peninsula, which was an advantage for defensive purposes. Tribes from Asia and eastern and central Europe, such as the Huns, Ostrogoths, Visigoths, and Vandals, were migrating and threatening parts of the Roman Empire. Constantine's decision to move the capital was wise because Rome was sacked soon after, whereas his new capital, which he named Constantinople, would not be conquered for several hundred years. In addition, Byzantium's location was at the crossroads of trade among Europe, North Africa, and Asia. Its location allowed it to control and tax this valuable trade.

Art produced by the eastern part of what was left of the Roman Empire is known as Byzantine art. Byzantine art has a few important characteristics. Chronologically, it succeeds early Christian art, and it has predominantly Christian themes and imagery. Byzantine art is not focused on realism and naturalism as is Classical Greco-Roman art. Early Byzantine art maintains some characteristics of Classical art, just as early Christian art does. However, these elements gradually give way to a distinctly **Byzantine aesthetic**. Once you see examples of Byzantine art and understand its basic elements, the Byzantine aesthetic becomes easy to recognize.

Past AP Art History tests have included multiple-choice questions about the Byzantine aesthetic, mosaics, ivory devotional sculptures, icons and the iconoclasm, and the Hagia Sophia (a famous Byzantine church). Other tests include a slide-based short essay that asks students to identify the classical and Byzantine elements contained in an early Byzantine work of art. Understanding the Byzantine aesthetic and its emphasis on Christianity are keys to recognizing Byzantine art.

Byzantine Art Basics: Three *F*s and a *G*

The characteristics of the Byzantine aesthetic are summarized by three *F*s and a *G*:

Flat: Although the artist includes some shading, figures appear flat, lacking the naturalistic volume that was common in Classical art.

Floating: Figures appear to hover above the ground. In Classical art, the figures have mass and rest firmly on the ground, but in the Byzantine aesthetic, the figures appear almost weightless as their feet point downward unrealistically.

Frontal: Unlike the realistic overlapping seen in most Classical art, Byzantine figures are usually oriented toward the viewer in a planar (on the same picture plane) format.

Gold backgrounds: Byzantine art shows little interest in background details or naturalism. Recall the early Christian mosaic depicting Christ as the Good Shepherd in the Mausoleum of Galla Placidia (see Chapter 9). In the background, the sky is blue and the vegetation is detailed. The background gives the mosaic a sense of spatial recession. In contrast, the gold backgrounds of Byzantine art are depthless and convey the spirituality of Christianity. Byzantine art focuses more on conveying Christian teachings and depicting important figures than on representing the details of the natural world.

Emperor Justinian

Besides Constantine the Great, Justinian is the most significant Byzantine leader to remember for the AP Art History exam. His reign, from 527 to 565, marked the early golden age of Byzantine art. His generals helped expand the Byzantine Empire through Italy, northern Africa, the Balkan Peninsula, central Europe, and part of the Middle East. While building an empire abroad, Justinian also had to deal with the Nike Riots in Constantinople and suppressed all other religions to make Orthodox Christianity the only religion of the Byzantine Empire. Justinian and the emperors after him led both the Byzantine church and state, combining the roles of pope and Caesar and creating a theocratic state.

With the same great power he used to rule the empire, Justinian promoted the golden age of Byzantine art and architecture. Like the Caesars, Justinian understood the value of impressive visual imagery. One example of art that glorifies his achievements is the *Barberini Ivory*, which shows Justinian as a world conqueror (**CD Fig. 10-1**). The ivory plaque was carved in five parts (one is missing).

The *Barberini Ivory* illustrates how early Byzantine art borrowed symbols from Classical antiquity. A figure, usually identified as Justinian, is riding victoriously on a horse similar to the *Equestrian Statue of Marcus Aurelius* (see Chapter 8). A female figure reminiscent of Tellus on the Ara Pacis is shown below the horse, and a winged-victory figure flies near Justinian. In the left panel, a figure holds an additional winged victory with a laurel crown, as if presenting it to Justinian. In the register below, conquered peoples present offerings to Justinian. These people are surrounded by a lion, an elephant, and a tiger. The exotic animals represent the diverse lands of the Byzantine Empire, such as Africa and Asia. One other Classical element to notice is the full-bodied figures of the characters. The interest in naturalism reflects the values of Classical art.

Unlike Classical artists, however, the *Barberini Ivory* artist replaced the pagan deities that supported the Roman emperors with a youthful Christ surrounded by two angels. Christ holds a cross with his left hand, and with his right, he makes a gesture of blessing, supporting the reign of Justinian. Also notice that in carving the relief of Christ, the artist sacrificed some degree of naturalism in both proportionality and three-dimensionality. This piece does not need the highly developed naturalism of antiquity to convey the importance of Christ. Thus, the *Barberini Ivory* marks an important transition from the traditions of Classical art to the spirituality of the early Byzantine period.

Hagia Sophia

Justinian commissioned the construction of Hagia Sophia, or Church of the Holy Wisdom (**CD Fig. 10-2**). It is one of the most famous holy buildings in the world today. Located in present-day Istanbul (formerly Constantinople), it first was a church and then was converted into a mosque during the reign of the Ottoman Turks. Today it is a museum. Hagia Sophia is impressive in scale: approximately 270 feet long, 240 feet wide, with a dome that is 108 feet in diameter and rises 180 feet above the ground. (The dome today is a replacement of the original, which collapsed in 558.)

Built by Anthemius of Tralles and Isidorus of Miletus, a mathematician and physicist, respectively, the church was a marvel of engineering for its time. Through the use of **pendentives**, the weight of the dome is transferred to four corner piers. In essence, Hagia Sophia has a circular dome resting on a rectangular base. This was an innovation over the Pantheon, the dome of which rests on a cylindrical drum. Anthemius and Isidorus's design created more space for other parts of Hagia Sophia, which were not possible with the restrictive form of a drum.

Figure 10-2. Hagia Sophia, 532–537, Constantinople (Istanbul), Turkey

Besides pendentives, another important aspect of Hagia Sophia is light. Its dome has forty windows around its base. The visual effect is of a dome resting on a halo of light (**CD Fig. 10-3**). Accounts of Byzantine historians describe how the entire interior of the church was bathed in light and the dome appeared to be suspended on a chain from heaven itself. Light adds to the spirituality and mysticism of Orthodox Christianity. For Byzantine Christians, it represents the presence of God. To enhance the effects of light, artists created mosaics on the interior of the dome and on the walls below. The incoming light is reflected off the tesserae (stones) and bathes the interior of Hagia Sophia.

Today Hagia Sophia has four towers surrounding its corners. These towers are minarets, which are part of the Islamic call to prayer. They were not an original part of the church but were added after the Ottoman Turks conquered Constantinople in 1453. So admired was Hagia Sophia that it was converted into a mosque for Islamic worship. Minarets are one of the hallmark features of Islamic architecture (see Chapter 11).

Ravenna and Its Mosaics

Located on the northeastern coast of Italy, Ravenna is one of the most important cities for Byzantine art and contains the largest amount of surviving Byzantine mosaics. It seems counterintuitive, because Constantinople was the capital of the Byzantine Empire. However, other than architecture, the capital city (now called Istanbul) contains a very small amount of art that has not been damaged. After the conquest of the Ottoman Turks, many of Constantinople's mosaics and icons were destroyed as a result of the religious restrictions on Islamic art. For example, the Turks plastered over the mosaics in the Hagia Sophia because a mosque cannot contain images of humans or animals. Ravenna was not a part of this conquest.

Ravenna was once a part of the Roman Empire. As the empire grew weaker, the Ostrogoths conquered the city in 493 CE. Byzantine emperors viewed themselves as the stewards of the former Roman Empire. Recall how the *Barberini Ivory*, with its depiction of Justinian as world conqueror, incorporated much Classical symbolism. Justinian's general, Belisarius, conquered Ravenna in 539, assimilating it into the Byzantine Empire. Because it gave the Byzantine Empire a foothold in Italy, Ravenna became very important and received much attention within the empire.

The most famous church in Ravenna is San Vitale (**CD Fig. 10-4**). It was named in honor of Saint Vitalis, who was martyred in the city in the second century. San Vitale is unique in Italy because it is one of the only centrally planned churches (see Chapter 9). It has an octagonal exterior and an interior octagonal arrangement of eight piers (vertical supports) with semicircular recesses between them. The walkway that separates the interior part of San Vitale from the exterior walls is an **ambulatory**, a space around which visitors may walk. The ambulatory later becomes a very important part of medieval Romanesque architecture (see Chapter 13). One unusual feature about San Vitale is the odd angle of its narthex, the vestibule in the lower part of the plan (**CD Fig. 10-5**). Its odd angle has never been fully explained.

The central space of San Vitale rises above the ambulatory and includes clerestory windows that allow light to illuminate the elaborate mosaics on its walls. Remember that light played an important part in creating the spiritual atmosphere of the Hagia Sophia. San Vitale's golden mosaics reflect light, creating a dazzling display.

San Vitale's choir and apse contain several important mosaics. In the lower apse vault, Christ is depicted as youthful and triumphant, seated on a blue globe representing his dominion over the world after the Second Coming. Two angels stand at Christ's side, presenting two important people in San Vitale's history: on the left, Saint Vitalis, to whom Christ hands the golden martyr's crown, and on the right, Bishop Ecclesius, who held office when the foundations of San Vitale were laid. Notice that Bishop Ecclesius holds a model of San Vitale in his hands (**CD Fig. 10-6**).

Justinian Mosaic

At San Vitale, Byzantine artists created a mosaic dedicated to Emperor Justinian. Justinian's central position, his purple cloak, which symbolizes royalty, and his opulent gold crown reveal his elevated status as emperor (**CD Fig. 10-7**). A halo encircles his crown as a testament to his holiness. In his hands, he holds a golden paten, a container for the Host (bread or wafers) used in the Eucharist (Holy Communion).

Figure 10-7. *Justinian, Bishop Maximianus, and His Attendants*, mosaic, San Vitale, Ravenna

Justinian possesses the symbols of leadership of both church and state; the six clergymen and six soldiers surrounding him reinforce his leadership in both arenas. One of the clergymen is Bishop Maximianus, who presided over the completion of San Vitale. He is dressed in a golden tunic, he holds a gold cross, and his name is written over his head. Other clergymen carry a jewel-encrusted Bible, representing the word of God, and a censer, which is filled with incense and used to purify the altar for religious rites. One of the soldiers holds a shield adorned with the emblem of Christ—the Greek letters *XP* (*chi* and *rho*).

Beyond contextual information, the formal qualities of the Justinian mosaic exemplify the Byzantine aesthetic. Notice that the mosaic lacks recessional space, appearing to be flat. All the characters are frontal. Their feet point downward toward the ground; rather than resting on the ground naturalistically, the figures appear to float. Lastly, a depthless golden background surrounds the figures. Therefore, the Justinian mosaic provides valuable contextual information about the position of the Byzantine emperor as well as possessing the formal elements of the Byzantine aesthetic.

Theodora Mosaic

Byzantine artists also glorified the Empress Theodora, Justinian's wife, in a mosaic on the opposing wall. Roughly the same size as the Justinian mosaic, the Theodora mosaic contains similar trappings of religious and secular authority. Theodora carries the chalice of wine for the Eucharist and has a halo indicating her holiness. Surrounded by a large entourage, Theodora proceeds as a servant opens a curtain before her. Among all the figures, Theodora with a gorgeous pearl crown and purple robe stands as the focal point. Further alluding to her status as royalty are the pictures of the kings on camels at the hem of her robe. This refers to the Magi, who bore gifts for the infant Jesus Christ. The artist reveals only two of the three Magi, leaving the viewer to consider Theodora herself as a part of this legendary trio.

Icons and Iconoclasm

An important aspect of Byzantine art, icons are images of holy figures painted on wooden panels. The holy figures include Jesus Christ, the Virgin Mary, and various saints, including Peter and Paul. Take a close look at the icon of the *Virgin and Child Between Saints Theodore and George* (**CD Fig. 10-8**). It is painted in **encaustic**, which is pigment combined with melted wax. This was a popular method of early icon painting. Later, artists painted icons with **tempera**, which is pigment mixed with egg yolks.

The Virgin Mary is painted in the center of the icon with the young Christ on her lap. She is known as the Theotokos (Christ bearer). Notice that the figures are not portrayed realistically or naturalistically. For example, the heads of the figures are disproportionately large for their bodies. The artist was not concerned with depicting realistic human proportions and focused instead on capturing the spirituality of the scene. This icon has elements of the Byzantine aesthetic as well; the figures appear flat with only moderate modeling in shadow and light, seem to float, and are arranged frontally.

Many Byzantine Christians believed that icons held special powers of healing and protection. Many Christians prayed to the icons in hopes of miracles. However, the Ten

Commandments forbid worshipping images of holy figures. It was a fine line between venerating (respecting) these icons and worshipping them. When the Byzantine Empire was challenged by the followers of the newly emerging religion of Islam, Emperor Leo III believed it was a punishment sent by God for worshipping icons. Other Christians living within the Byzantine Empire also disagreed with the use of icons. Beginning in 726, riots broke out between people who wanted to keep the icons in churches and the icon smashers, or iconoclasts.

The iconoclasts destroyed countless icons and other figural religious images. One reason the *Virgin and Child Between Saints Theodore and George* icon is such a valuable piece of art is that it survived. In addition, no images of Christ, the Virgin Mary, and saints were made during the iconoclastic struggle. Lasting more than one hundred years, the iconoclastic controversy had a profound effect upon the Byzantine Empire and its art. During that time, Byzantine artists relied on abstract religious symbols—for example, painting a throne in heaven to represent God. By 843, the production of icons resumed and the destruction of icons became heresy (that is, an act that goes against church rules). Nonetheless, for more than one hundred years, Byzantine figural art ceased to be produced and much of it was destroyed, leaving a major gap in the history of Byzantine art.

Ivory Religious Art

Before the iconoclastic struggle, Christians commissioned portable shrines made from ivory that were known as **diptychs** (two paneled) and **triptychs** (three paneled). These beautifully carved works of art were used for private devotion and prayers. Hinges on the diptychs and triptychs allowed them to fold for ease in transport during travel. Damaged by time, some of the ivory pieces are now found separately, but a close inspection would reveal small holes at the edges, indicating that hinges were once there.

After the iconoclastic struggle, artists produced more triptychs than diptychs. A fine example is the *Harbaville Triptych* (**CD Fig. 10-9**). In the upper portion of the central compartment, an enthroned Christ is flanked by the Virgin Mary and John the Baptist, Christ's cousin and the forerunner of his ministry. These religious figures are supposed to intercede in the prayers of the person praying at the triptych. In the bottom portion of the central compartment, the artist carved five of the apostles. In the wings of the triptych are four sets of figures, of which two are soldiers and two are clergy. It is not as important to correctly identify each figure in the *Harbaville Triptych* as it is to recognize the piece as Byzantine art. Among Christians who had the financial means, diptychs and triptychs were very popular for their private devotions.

Christ as Pantocrator

Another method of representing Christ in Byzantine art is as Pantocrator, which means "ruler of all" in Greek (**CD Fig. 10-10**). Mosaics of Christ as Pantocrator were popular in churches throughout the Byzantine Empire. The title refers to Christ as the final judge of humanity. To capture this persona, the artists rendered Christ with a stern expression. Placing a mosaic with Christ as Pantocrator in the dome would thus confront the congregation with the warning of final judgment by a grim and resolute deity.

Spread of Byzantine Icons

The *Vladimir Virgin* icon is another major piece of Byzantine art produced after the iconoclasm (**CD Fig. 10-11**). It has a very **stylized** appearance; that is, its visual elements adhere to the hallmark features of a specific style. The young Christ's head is too small for his body, and the folds in his robe are very linear and lack the naturalism of classical art. The icon's somewhat flat appearance and golden background reinforce the Byzantine aesthetic. Notice how Mary's nose is elongated and her face is thin yet very expressive. After the iconoclasm, in some regions of the empire, artists rendered the facial expressions and postures of religious figures to have more of an emotional impact. The *Vladimir Virgin* icon was eventually taken to Russia, and its miraculous powers were believed to have saved various Russian cities from the invasions of the Mongols, Tartars, and Poles. Another important feature of the icon is that it is painted in tempera—pigment mixed with egg yolks. This became the growing trend in icon painting both in the Byzantine Empire and the regions that its art influenced.

Saint Catherine's Monastery

A significant site of Byzantine Art beyond Eastern Europe is Saint Catherine's Monastery at the base of Mount Sinai in Egypt. Devout Christians left the main cities and towns to pursue a monastic life in the region. They chose this location believing that this was the site at which God appeared to Moses as a burning bush. The Old Testament states that God later gave Moses the Ten Commandments on top of Mount Sinai. God also appeared to the Prophet Elijah as a gentle breeze near the base of the mountain.

According to tradition, when Saint Helena, mother of Constantine, made her pilgrimage to the Holy Land, she stopped at the monastery. The monks later requested the Emperor Justinian to build a church and fortress for them as protection from incursions by nearby raiders. Another legend associated with Saint Catherine's is that the Prophet Muhammad, impressed by the piety of the monks and recognizing the importance of Moses and Elijah to Islam, ordered Muslims to protect the monastery from attackers.

Saint Catherine's Monastery is important because it is one of the greatest repositories for Byzantine icons from various periods and styles from the encaustic icons of the Early Byzantine period through the Post-Byzantine period. The collection thus includes icons that predate and survived from the eighth-century iconoclasm. Perhaps because of its remote location or because the inhabitants disagreed with the iconoclasm, Saint Catherine's retains these important works of art.

Saint Catherine's Transfiguration Mosaic

Saint Catherine's also includes a significant mosaic known as the Transfiguration. Created in the apse vault of the Katholikon (the name of Saint Catherine's main church), the Transfiguration depicts Christ's Transfiguration on top of Mount Tabor in Israel. The

Gospel of Matthew describes the event: "Jesus brought Peter, John, and James to the top of Mount Tabor. As the men watched, Jesus' appearance was transformed so that his face shone like the sun, and his clothes became as white as light. Suddenly, Moses and Elijah appeared and began talking with Jesus… the disciples were terrified and fell face down on the ground." The Transfiguration was an appropriate choice for Saint Catherine's due to Moses' and Elijah's experiences with God at Mount Sinai.

The scene contains a gold background rather than displaying a landscape setting. The figures float above the ground. The golden background and hovering bodies illustrates the spirituality of the scene, not the natural world. The figures appear rather flat, with a few traces of formulaic shading on the bodies, and seem to reside in the same picture plane. Christ's positioning as well of that of the other characters face the viewer in a frontal composition. Thus, Saint Catherine's Transfiguration mosaic is a splendid example of the Byzantine aesthetic.

Demise of the Byzantine Empire

The Byzantine Empire faced various threats to its existence over the years. It dealt with revolts in its territories and conspiracies within the empire, the iconoclasm, and threats from the outside. A major challenge to the empire was the rise of Islam, the art of which is discussed in Chapter 11. As the new religion spread throughout the Middle East, its political leaders began to challenge and win territory from the Byzantine Empire. Crusaders from Western European sacked Constantinople on their way to fight the Muslims in Jerusalem. The dogmatic differences between Western European Christians and the Orthodox Christians of the East caused an enmity that made it easier for the Crusaders to justify plundering the capital of the East. Although Byzantine control of the capital was eventually restored, the empire never regained its strength. Tribes of Turks migrating from central Asia began to threaten the Byzantine Empire, eventually winning control of all the Byzantine territory in Asia Minor and most of the Balkans. Constantinople was the last part of the empire that remained in Byzantine hands. It fell for the last time to the Ottoman Turks in 1453 and was renamed Istanbul.

Conclusion

The Byzantine Empire exerted a profound influence on the history of European art. Many Italian artists emulated the Byzantine aesthetic with its flat figures that appeared to be floating, frontal arrangements, and golden backgrounds, which lasted until the Renaissance. The Ottonian Empire of tenth-century Germany (see Chapter 12) copied the conservative Byzantine aesthetic. The Byzantine architects Anthemius and Isodorus built the first great dome since the Pantheon when they built Hagia Sophia. They even developed the support method of pendentives, which allowed a circular dome to be placed on a rectangular base. Byzantine domes became so famous that Islamic leaders summoned Byzantine architects to design some of their mosques and pilgrimage sites. What Byzantine art lacks in realism and naturalism—characteristics of ancient Greek and Roman works—it makes up for in its distinctly spiritual aesthetic, the foundation of one of the most recognizable styles in art history.

Chapter 11

Islamic Art

Introduction and Exam Strategy Overview

On the AP Art History exam, Islamic art is considered "beyond the European tradition," because Islam began in the Middle East. Historically, test writers have not consistently asked questions on Islamic art, but non-European-based art does account for 20 percent of the points on the test, and Islamic art provides more than sufficient material from which to create questions. Substantive questions have been asked about Islamic architecture, including multiple-choice and slide-based short essay questions about mosques.

This chapter introduces the basic religious guidelines to which Islamic art must adhere and how Islamic art adapted in harmony with these guidelines. Additionally, the chapter discusses the role of the mosque and analyzes its parts and their functions.

Islam and Its Rules for Art

The founder of Islam was the prophet Muhammad. He began to preach publicly about the religion in 613 CE, after he experienced a series of visions while meditating. Muhammad claimed that there was only one God (Allah) and that he was God's chosen messenger to the people. The religion Muhammad espoused, which became known as Islam, was a departure from the religion of the indigenous Arabs, most of whom were polytheists. Initially, Muhammad's teaching received limited support and was generally greeted with hostility. However, Islam gradually grew to encompass a large part of Saudi Arabia, including the holy cities of Mecca and Medina. After Muhammad's death, caliphs (his successors) continued to spread the religion throughout the Middle East, the former Persian Empire, northern Africa, and even across the Strait of Gibraltar into Spain. Through evangelism, central Asian tribes such as the Moguls and Ottoman Turks converted to Islam. The Moguls brought Islam into the Indian subcontinent, and the Ottomans continued the spread of the religion through the Anatolian Peninsula and into the Balkan Peninsula, replacing the Christian Byzantine Empire. It is difficult to overstate the impact of Islam.

Through divine inspiration, Muhammad stated the Five Pillars of Islam, which are the basic rules of the religion. The first pillar is to recognize daily that there is only one God and that his prophet is Muhammad. According to the second pillar, Muslims should pray five times a day. The third pillar is to provide for the poor. The fourth pillar dictates that Muslims must fast during the month of Ramadan. The fifth pillar requires all Muslims who are physically and financially able to make a pilgrimage to Mecca, the holiest site in Islam.

In relation to art history, the first and second pillars are the most important to comprehend because they exert an enormous influence on Islamic art and architecture. Worshipping other gods was forbidden, as was making any likenesses of gods, which is similar to Judaism and Christianity, two other monotheistic religions. Islamic art took this rule very seriously and forbade images of animals or people, which could represent gods, in sacred buildings. Therefore, the art of Islamic holy places lacks figural representations. Instead, Islamic artists created elaborate, abstract designs.

The Koran and Calligraphy

The Koran is the holy book of Islam. It is divided into 114 **suras**, or chapters, arranged from longest to shortest (**CD Fig. 11-1**). The Koran details the many visions and revelations given to Muhammad by Allah through the angel Gabriel. Reading the Koran is an important expectation of Islam because it establishes the basis for the faith. All this writing provided a major medium for artistic expression. Thus, **calligraphy** or writing as a decorative art, became a significant part of Islamic art. Skillful scribes embellished the words of the scriptures. The art of calligraphy was considered to be pure and holy and required intense training. In addition, the exteriors of Islamic buildings are often covered in calligraphic tiles. Like the illuminated manuscripts of Europe, Islamic calligraphy is both decorative and **didactic**, which means that it instructs the religion's followers.

Arabesque Designs

Although Islam prohibited zoomorphic (human or animal) images in holy places, it did not prohibit art altogether. The walls, both interior and exterior, are covered with mosaics of gardens, plants, and buildings in addition to calligraphy. Verses in the Koran describe paradise as a place of lush gardens, verdant groves of trees, and flowing streams. These mosaics help the Muslim faithful to visualize the beauty that awaits them. Artists also created intricately interlaced designs known as arabesques (**CD Fig. 11-2**). An **arabesque**, which means "Arab-like," is composed of a complex interweaving of plant motifs and geometric patterns. It can cover the entire surface of a book page, carpet, or wall. Islamic prayer rugs, which are used when Muslims prostrate themselves during prayer, contain these designs. Arabesques are one of the most distinctive features of Islamic art.

Mosque Architecture

Mosques are places of Islamic congregational worship and gathering (**CD Fig. 11-3**). They aid in fulfilling the first and second pillars of Islam. The form of the mosque follows this function. First, the **minaret**, or tower, is an important part of the mosque complex. A Muslim crier, called a muezzin, climbs to the top of the minaret to call the faithful to daily prayers. A mosque should have at least one minaret, but the number of minarets per mosque varies from culture to culture.

The Ottoman Turk architects often included four minarets (recall from Chapter 10 that their conversion of the Byzantine Hagia Sophia to a mosque added four minarets), while the Great Mosque in Mecca has seven. At the Grand Mosque in Sousse, Tunisia, the minaret appears in the left corner of the complex. Minarets can have different shapes. Some minarets are square, others are cylindrical, and the Malawiya minaret of the Great Mosque in Samarra, Iraq, is a spiraling structure.

During prayers, Muslims are expected to face Mecca, but Muslims live all over the world: How do they know the direction in which to pray? Mosque designers addressed this issue with the **qibla wall**. The qibla wall of the mosque points the faithful in the direction of Mecca and is thus very important. The qibla is part of the **prayer hall**, which is another part of the mosque. Often the prayer hall was designed as a **hypostyle**, which is a room of columns. Muslims gather in the prayer hall and pray toward the qibla. The qibla wall contains a niche, usually in its center, called the **mihrab**. The purpose of the mihrab is unclear. It can be considered decorative because it is adorned with calligraphic tiles and arabesques. The niche may also symbolically represent part of a wall in Muhammad's home, which is considered by some to be the first mosque. The photograph of the interior of the Great Mosque in Kairouan, Tunisia (**CD Fig. 11-4**), shows a view of the qibla wall inside the hypostyle prayer hall. The mihrab can be seen in the center of the wall.

A mosque usually has a dome in the roof marking the location of the mihrab (see the photograph of the exterior of a mosque). The interior of the dome is located above the mihrab and is usually very ornate. From the outside, the mihrab dome is useful in recognizing the building as a mosque. A mosque also contains a podium near the mihrab called a **minbar**. When the faithful are not praying, an imam, or religious teacher, stands at the minbar and reads verses from the Koran. Before and after worship, the faithful can gather in the forecourt, a large courtyard of the mosque complex. The forecourt encourages a spirit of fellowship and community among the Muslim faithful.

A past AP Art History test included a slide-based short essay on the parts of a mosque. The first part of the question asked students to identify that the building was a mosque. The second part of the question asked students to identify four parts of the building and explain their functions. Two slides were displayed for the question: an aerial photograph of the mosque and its floor plan. This is typical of slide-based short essay questions that refer to religious structures.

To successfully answer such a question, you will need to scan the photograph and floor plan. In the photograph, try to spot a minaret in the complex and a mihrab dome on the roof. Second, scan the floor plan for a room filled with columns, remembering that mosque prayer halls are hypostyle halls. Once you realize that the building is a mosque, remember some of the rules of Islam to help you explain the functions of the parts. Refer to the first and second pillars of Islam and other Islamic rules to provide context for your explanation. For example, a hypostyle prayer hall provides a space for Muslims to pray five times a day, which fulfills the second of the Five Pillars of Islam.

Dome of the Rock

The Dome of the Rock (**CD Fig. 11-5**) is a holy building for Muslims located in Jerusalem. It is one of the most recognizable structures in the world. The rock over which it was built was a holy platform from which Muhammad ascended, climbing a golden ladder, into heaven to meet Allah and converse with Moses. The site is also the former location of the Temple of Herod the Great, which was sacred to Jews. According to tradition, the large ridges in the rock were created when Gabriel held the rock still for Muhammad. One of the Islamic caliphs constructed the building not only to mark the site but also to show that Islam had arrived in Jerusalem, which is holy to Jews and Christians as well. The building has an octagonal structure with a large dome. The dome is 75 feet high and 60 feet wide at its base, overshadowing the design of the structure. The design of the Dome of the Rock shows the influence of Byzantine buildings such as Ravenna's San Vitale and Jerusalem's Church of the Holy Sepulcher, both of which contain domes.

Figure 11-5. Dome of the Rock, 687–692 CE, Jerusalem

The Dome of the Rock is a pilgrimage site, not a mosque. Nonetheless, it provides an excellent example of Islamic art and architecture. The interior of the dome and the walls are covered in tiles with arabesques and calligraphy. There are no images of people or animals inside this holy building. The exterior also contains brilliant blue and gold calligraphic panels of verses from the Koran (**CD Fig. 11-6**). The Dome of the Rock is one of the earliest achievements of Islamic architecture. Although Romans were the pioneers of the hemispherical dome and the Byzantine architects refined it, the legacy of the Dome of the Rock is that domes have become synonymous with Islamic architecture.

Great Mosque in Cordoba, Spain

The Muslim rulers of Spain wanted to make their capital city of Cordoba a center of culture that could rival the cities of the Middle East. In 784 CE, the ruler Abd-al-Rahman I began construction of the Great Mosque in Cordoba (**CD Fig. 11-7**). After being enlarged in the ninth and tenth centuries, the Great Mosque became the largest mosque in the western reaches of Islam. One of the most famous features of this mosque is its hypostyle prayer hall. The hall is one of the most recognizable hypostyle halls in architecture. It contains red-and-white patterned double arches that rest on 36 piers and 514 columns. The columns in the prayer hall were taken from Roman buildings in the region and were too small to provide ample interior space. To address this issue, the architects created a two-tiered arch system, with the lowest arch having a distinct horseshoe shape. Its vast number of columns and the double arches of its hypostyle prayer hall make the Great Mosque in Cordoba one of the most famous mosques in the world.

Taj Mahal

The Taj Mahal is another significant accomplishment of Islamic architecture (**CD Fig. 11-8**). Islamic leaders established a tradition of elaborate funeral monuments. The Taj Mahal continued that legacy. A famous leader of the Moguls (who conquered and ruled India, spreading Islam to the Indian subcontinent), Shah Jahan built the Taj Mahal in honor of his wife, Mumtaz Mahal. After nineteen years of marriage, his beloved wife died giving birth to their fourteenth child. The grieving monarch ordered that her tomb be built "as beautiful as she was beautiful." For twenty-two years, 20,000 workers labored on Shah Jahan's last gift to his queen.

The Taj Mahal is renowned for its symmetry and proportions. For example, its height (not including the minarets) is the same as its width, and the distance from the base of its dome is equal to the height of the facade. Surrounding the tomb are four minarets. The complex also includes lush gardens and a reflecting pool. The intended effect was for the Taj Mahal to appear weightless, a white-marble monument that could float toward the heavens. The tomb is actually elevated from the reflecting pool. A staircase ascends from the pool area to the tomb platform, but architects disguised it in the design to enhance the tomb's floating effect.

Because of its trademark dome and minarets, students often confuse the Taj Mahal for a mosque. Do not make this mistake. The Taj Mahal is a tomb, Shah Jahan's enduring gift to the wife he loved.

Conclusion

Islamic art is as diverse as the regions it covers. The AP Art History exam will test your knowledge on basic concepts that are shared throughout those regions. For example, Islamic holy buildings lack figural art, meaning they are not adorned with humans or animal shapes. Instead, artists created calligraphy and arabesques to adorn their religious structures. Regarding Islamic architecture, you should know and be able to explain the functions of several parts of a mosque. Remember that form follows function. The parts of the mosque reflect the requirements set forth in the Five Pillars of Islam, especially the first and second pillars. Two examples of Islamic holy buildings include the Dome of the Rock in Jerusalem and the Great Mosque in Cordoba, Spain.

Chapter 12

Early Medieval Art

Introduction and Exam Strategy Overview

After the collapse of the Roman Empire, Western Europe entered what is known as the Dark Ages. Power became decentralized, dispersed among various nomadic tribes. Trade among towns and outposts collapsed because the Roman legions were no longer present to maintain order. When comparing the art produced during early medieval times with the many achievements of the Roman Empire, it is obvious why historians first labeled the period the Dark Ages. However, recent discoveries and scholarship have uncovered works of art and architecture that reveal the presence of rich cultures between the years 500 and 1000 CE.

For the AP Art History exam, the early Middle Ages includes four stages: (1) Art of the Warrior Lords, (2) Hiberno-Saxon Art, (3) Carolingian Art, and (4) Ottonian Art. The 2004 exam contained a slide-based short essay comparing a picture of a purse cover from Sutton Hoo, a site during the Warrior Lord Period, to a carpet page from the *Lindisfarne Gospels*, a Hiberno-Saxon illuminated manuscript. Past tests also required students to discuss the characteristics of Carolingian illuminated manuscripts. Multiple-choice questions have tested students recognition of a famous Ottonian church and its bronze doors.

Early Medieval art is grouped with Early Christian and Byzantine Art as 5 percent to 10 percent of the points on the AP Art History exam, which is a small percentage of the total points. Nonetheless, this chapter provides you with the necessary knowledge about the early Medieval period to prepare you for possible test questions.

Art of the Warrior-Lords

In Western Europe, the power of the Roman Empire was declining. Tribes from Asia and Eastern and Central Europe immigrated into the region. The tribes continued to migrate, because even as they settled in one region, another tribe followed behind, pushing them on to another part of Europe. Warfare among these tribes was frequent. Therefore, one label used by art historians for this period from roughly 400 to 600 CE is "Art of the Warrior Lords."

Because of their migratory nature, various cultures—Visigoths, Ostrogoths, Vandals, Lombards, Franks, Anglo-Saxons, and Celts—produced art that was small and portable. Much of the art of this period has been lost, and art historians do not possess knowledge of the volume produced during this period. What art does exist consists of small possessions such as belt buckles, helmets, sword handles, fibulae (pins used to fasten a cloak, usually at the shoulder), and utilitarian objects such as plates, cups, and utensils.

These small pieces are fine art nonetheless; many are precisely shaped pieces of metal, and some are embellished with jewels or filled with brilliant enamels. Such items have been discovered in ship burials in northern Europe, buried with men who must have held a high status in their time, judging by the sheer amount of treasure that was buried with them.

Sutton Hoo Ship Burial

One such ship burial was unearthed from a hill in Sutton Hoo, England, in 1939. Although the wood of the ship itself disintegrated, the imprint of the ship and its treasures remained. Several valuable items were discovered, including golden coins; the helmet, buckle, and sword of a warrior; silver bowls and spoons; and a silver plate with the official imprint of a Byzantine emperor. One of the most significant items found in the ship burial is a remarkable purse cover made from metal, precious jewels, and enamel (**CD Fig. 12-1**). The cover was probably part of a leather change purse.

This purse cover illustrates the main characteristics of the Art of the Warrior Lords. First, it has many abstract designs based on animals. For example, along the bottom, abstract human figures are surrounded on both sides by canine figures. In the center, eagles bite on the heads of ducks. The artist gave the design a sense of unity by having the convex part of the eagle's beak blend into the concave part of the duck's beak. The artist included additional abstract animals with interlacing embellishments above the eagles in the center. Abstract animal imagery is so ingrained in the art of the warrior-lords that occasionally this type of art is referred to as the Animal Style.

Besides animal imagery, interlacing designs are a hallmark feature of the Art of the Warrior Lords. **Interlacing**, a term that refers to a ribbon that interweaves through a design repeatedly, has been used by other cultures. For example, interlace designs in Islamic Art are referred to as arabesques (see Chapter 11). A distinctive feature of the interlacing of the Art of the Warrior Lords is how it blends in with the abstract animal forms. The artists blended the design so cleverly that it takes meticulous inspection to actually locate all of the animal forms.

The artistic technique used to create the Sutton Hoo purse cover is called **cloisonné**. Cloisonné involves soldering (welding) small and thin strips of metal, which are called **cloisons** in French, to a background metal plate. After this step, the artist fills the spaces between the cloisons with colored enamels (similar to nail polish enamel) and jewels. Cloisonné was used to some extent on many of the items in the Sutton Hoo ship burial. The fact that the warrior had items produced with such a labor-intensive technique as cloisonné is a testament to this man's status.

Hiberno-Saxon Art

Hiberno-Saxon Art was produced in Britain and Ireland around the years 700 to 800. Hiberno refers to Ireland, and the Saxons settled in England. Visually, Hiberno-Saxon Art bears a striking resemblance to the Art of the Warrior Lords: it contains interlacing and incorporates abstract animal forms. However, it differs from the art of the warrior-kings in its infusion of Christian symbolism. In 432, Saint Patrick, who was a missionary from Rome, established a church in Ireland. From Ireland, missionaries began to spread Christianity throughout the British Isles. These missionaries also established monasteries on the smaller islands of Britain such as Iona and Lindisfarne.

Monasteries were seats of learning and literacy and their **scriptoria** produced beautifully illustrated and decorated Bibles, written by the hands of monks. The books they produced are called **illuminated manuscripts** because the pictures and decorations are supposed to illuminate the Christian concepts. Thus, the spread of Christianity in the British Isles affected the art of the region. Although it retains some of the characteristics of the warrior-lord period, Hiberno-Saxon Art contains imagery that conveys the concepts of the newly adopted religion.

One fine example of Hiberno-Saxon Art is the cross and carpet page from the *Lindisfarne Gospels* (**CD Fig. 12-2**). Art historians refer to it as a **carpet page** because its intricate interlacing occupying the entire page resembles oriental carpets.

The *Lindisfarne Gospels* is one of the most famous illuminated manuscripts produced during the Hiberno-Saxon Period. One of the first noticeable characteristics is the page's intricate network of interlacing blue, pink, orange, red, and green ribbons. This interlacing contains tremendous details. Several ribbons contain abstract animal forms that twist and even bite the ribbons. The monk who painted these illuminations also included a Celtic cross in the center of the page, reflecting the influence of Christianity. The cross and the border provide a geometric quality that balances against the winding interlace design, similar to the way Christianity brought order to the lives of the pagan Celts of Ireland.

Figure 12-2. Cross and carpet page, *Lindisfarne Gospels*,
ca. 698–721, British Library, London

Pages such as this carpet page resulted from meticulous planning. The artist created a grid of lines and notches onto which he drew the design square by square. The valuable pigment, some of which was imported from Afghanistan, was then carefully applied to fill in the drawing without going outside the lines. The Celtic cross was outlined and contains even more interlacing. The care that monks took in creating such illuminations reflected their zeal for the Christian scriptures.

Book of Kells

Although the *Lindisfarne Gospels* is well known, the *Book of Kells* is even more famous. The *Book of Kells* was created around 800. Records of the time praised it as the chief relic of the western world, and one priest, Giraldus Cambrensis, said it resembled the work of an angel, not a man. Within this illuminated manuscript are 680 pages, only two of which are without illuminations. One of its most famous pages is called the *chi-rho-iota* page (**CD Fig. 12-3**), based on the Greek letters for Christ, *X*, *P*, and *I*. The page contains an inscription in the lower-right corner that reads "h generatio." This page is based on the account of Christ's birth in the Gospel of Matthew. When read together with Christ's initials, it reads: "Now this is how the birth of Christ came about." Consistent with the Lindisfarne cross and carpet page, the *chi-rho-iota* page contains dense interlacing and abstract animal forms.

Unfortunately, the *Book of Kells* has had a turbulent history. First, it had to be moved in 875 from the island of Iona, where most if not all of it was produced, because of Viking raids. It was moved to Kells on the Irish mainland. In 1006, it was stolen, most likely for its golden and jewel-encrusted cover. A few months later, the *Book of Kells* was recovered from under clods of mud in a bog with its cover and several pages missing. Approximately 60 pages of the *Book of Kells*, several with detailed illuminations, are lost. Today it is restored, rebound, and displayed in Trinity College Library in Ireland.

In addition to illuminated manuscripts, stone Celtic crosses (**CD Fig. 12-4**) are another major feature of Hiberno-Saxon Art. A Celtic cross differs from other crosses in that it has a circle circumscribing the intersection of the cross arms. The *Lindisfarne Gospels* carpet page provides an example of a Celtic cross. Many of the crosses have interlacing patterns and densely packed abstract animal and human figures, which are consistent with Hiberno-Saxon Art. Occasionally, famous stories from the life of Christ adorn the cross in low relief.

Carolingian Art

In western Europe in 800, Charlemagne was crowned Holy Roman Emperor by the pope. Charlemagne was the king of the Franks, a formidable Germanic tribe, and had been solidifying the empire that was left to him by his father. By the time of Charlemagne's coronation, the Frankish Kingdom included two-thirds of Italy, all of present-day France, a small part of Spain, and all of German Saxony. It had grown larger than the Byzantine Empire. His coronation as Holy Roman Emperor made him the official protector of all Christendom (Christian Europe).

As a leader, Charlemagne wanted to revive the glory of the Roman Empire from the time of Constantine, the first Christian Roman emperor. Art provided a powerful vehicle for this revival. Much of the art and architecture are reminiscent of Roman Art during the reign of Constantine. For example, Charlemagne's Palatine Chapel in his capital of Aachen reflects the central plan of San Vitale in Ravenna (see Chapter 10). Paintings in Carolingian illuminated manuscripts have human figures with more natural body mass, which had not been evident since Roman Art. The name given to this artistic period is the Carolingian Renaissance, based on the Latin form of Charlemagne, *Carolus Magnus*.

One work of art that demonstrates a revival of Roman Art during the Carolingian period is a small bronze equestrian statue of a leader. Most art historians say that the figure represents Charlemagne, although it may represent his grandson, Charles the Bald (**CD Fig. 12-5**). Charlemagne was interested in the imagery of past leaders associated with Rome. He brought back to his capital an equestrian statue of Theodoric, the first Germanic king to rule a former Roman city, as well as a bronze statue of Justinian, neither of which survive. Of course, the main surviving precedent of equestrian portraiture is the *Equestrian Statue of Marcus Aurelius*.

In Roman antiquity, equestrian statues conveyed the power of the leader, and people of the Carolingian Period knew it. This representation would be picked up again during the Renaissance, another time in which people attempted to revive the imagery of Classical antiquity. Like the statue of Marcus Aurelius, the representation of Charlemagne is too large in relation to the horse, making him the focal point for the viewer.

Charlemagne wears the jeweled crown of the Holy Roman Emperor and holds an orb in his hand, representing world dominion. The orb as a symbol of power was used in the *Colossal Statue of Constantine* in the Basilica Nova.

On Charlemagne's agenda was a revival of learning. Thus, during the Carolingian Renaissance, illuminated manuscripts were not only an art form but a vehicle to increase literacy throughout the empire. In Charlemagne's personal copy of the Gospels called the *Coronation Gospels*, there is evidence of the revival of classical art. For example, Saint Matthew as depicted in the *Coronation Gospels* (**CD Fig. 12-6**) has the short-cropped hair and the toga of a Roman philosopher. He exudes the calm reserve of a classical figure as he contemplates his writing. The artist shows an interest in body mass because the saint's face and neck have well-developed shading and light, and the toga reveals the underlying contours of Saint Matthew's upper arm and legs. Such interest in naturalism had not been seen since Classical antiquity. The lectern and chair resemble Classical furniture. In addition, the artist shows interest in creating the illusion of a three-dimensional world, which gives this page a sense of recessional space.

Illuminated manuscripts proliferated throughout the Carolingian period and exhibit various regional styles. For example, in the *Ebbo Gospels*, named after the manuscript's patron, Archbishop Ebbo of Reims, Saint Matthew's appearance differs from the Saint Matthew of the *Coronation Gospels*. The body, the folds in the robe, and the facial expression of Saint Matthew in the *Ebbo Gospels* (**CD Fig. 12-7**) have an energized appearance, which contrasts with the classically calm Matthew of the *Coronation Gospels*. The hair on his head stands on end, and the folds in his robe vibrate with energy. His face appears anxious as he receives holy inspiration for his writing from an angel in the upper-right corner of the page. As fast as the angel pours inspiration, which is shown as ink, into the saint's inkhorn, Saint Matthew records them in his Gospel. In the pages from the *Coronation Gospels* and *Ebbo Gospels*, we have the same subject rendered differently. This reinforces that although the artists exhibited regional differences, the agenda was the same: create beautiful illuminated manuscripts.

Carolingian Architecture: The Palatine Chapel

Carolingian architecture also emulated the architecture of the Roman era. As a devout Christian, Charlemagne wanted to build a chapel for his palace in Aachen, his capital. Which model of church architecture should he use: the basilica or the central plan? His coronation as Holy Roman Emperor took place in Saint Peter's Basilica, which was built by Constantine the Great. However, Theodoric, who was the first Germanic king of a Roman city, ruled over Ravenna, in which the centrally planned San Vitale was the most important church (see Chapter 10). Charlemagne's architect, Odo of Metz, chose San Vitale as his model.

The Palatine Chapel (**CD Fig. 12-8**), as Charlemagne's palace chapel is known, has a centrally planned octagonal design similar to that of San Vitale, although the chapel's design is simplified. If you compare the two interiors, the Palatine Chapel appears sturdier, which could perhaps be a metaphor for the Frankish Empire. The interior of the chapel incorporates significant Roman architectural motifs. The lowest level is supported by thick piers (massive supports) and round arches. Upper-level galleries contain more piers, Corinthian columns, and many arches. The chapel is capped with a dome, making it the first medieval vaulted building in Western Europe. The visual elements of the Palatine Chapel revive the glory of the ancient Rome while reinforcing Charlemagne's devotion to Christianity.

Carolingian Basilicas

Although the Palatine Chapel followed a central plan, basilicas were the norm for Carolingian church designs. Carolingian architects never used the central plan to the extent that Byzantine architects did, establishing a preference for basilicas in Western Europe. The central plan was usually reserved for martyria, mausoleums, and baptisteries. No Carolingian basilicas exist in their original form, but art historians can reconstruct their appearance based on written records and architectural remains. Like early Christian basilicas, they appeared rectangular with long naves. A small number of basilicas had transepts, which shows the influence of the Early Christian Saint Peter's Basilica in Rome (see Chapter 9).

Carolingian basilicas also include a monumental western facade framed on the corners with large towers. This type of facade is called a **westwork**. The abbey church at Corvey, Germany, provides an example of a Carolingian westwork (**CD Fig. 12-9**). This design element influenced church building during the Ottonian Period (as discussed later in this chapter) and well as the later Romanesque and Gothic Periods (see Chapters 13 and 14). Carolingian architecture laid the groundwork for the subsequent evolution of Western European church architecture.

Charlemagne died in 814 and was buried in the Palatine Chapel. His son and successor, Louis the Pious, was a devoutly religious man, better suited for being a monk than the ruler of an empire. As a ruler, he was weak and ineffectual. Louis the Pious died in 840, leaving three sons: Lothair, Charles the Bald, and Louis the German. A civil war ensued as the sons fought for control of the Frankish Empire. The three men resolved their disputes by dividing the empire, so that Frankish power was never again the same. Viking raids in the west, an invasion of Magyars in the east, and a rival in the Byzantine Empire spelled the doom of the Frankish Empire.

Ottonian Art

The tenth century marked a chaotic time for Western Europe. Magyars invaded from the east, the Vikings raided the north, and the remnants of the Franks, Saxons, and Lombards vied for control of the center. Compounding this instability, the church was dealing with its own problems of disorganization and corruption. Order was restored with the rise of a line of Saxon kings collectively known as the Ottonians, after the three greatest rulers among them. Otto I ruled from 936–973 and was crowned as the protector of Christendom by the pope in 962, a role that previously had been filled by Frankish kings. Otto II succeeded his father and ruled until 983, and the reign of his son, Otto III, ended in 1002.

The Ottonians admired Charlemagne and the Franks, and each Otto dreamed of forming a new Christian Roman Empire. Charlemagne's *Coronation Gospels* became one of their treasured possessions. The three Ottos dealt effectively with the Viking and Magyar incursions, established diplomatic relations with the Byzantine Empire, and sponsored monastic reforms, all of which established a renewed period of stability and artistic creativity.

Saint Michael's of Hildesheim

The Ottonian monastery church of Saint Michael's in Hildesheim, Germany, is a good example of Ottonian architecture (**CD Fig. 12-10**). Bishop Bernward, who was a tutor to Otto III and a prominent patron of Ottonian art, commissioned the church. According to his biographer, Bishop Bernward was even skilled at sculpting and casting in bronze. Saint Michael's adheres to the basilica format established during the Carolingian Period, including a westwork facade. One notable feature is its **double transepts**. Early Christian basilicas contained only one transept, and transepts were a rare design feature in Carolingian basilicas. Towers mark each transept of Saint Michael's. Another interesting feature is that the entrances to Saint Michael's are on the sides, making the side aisles of the interior similar to narthexes, the porchlike entryways of early Christian basilicas.

One set of doors on Saint Michael's is also worthy of study (**CD Fig. 12-11**). In commissioning the doors, Bishop Bernward may have been influenced by a visit to Santa Sabina Church in Rome, a church with carved wooden doors. The doors of Saint Michael's are remarkable for their height of more than 16 feet. Each door was cast as a single piece from bronze using the lost wax casting process that the ancient Greeks used for their statues. Each door contains eight panels with figures carved in relief. The left door contains scenes from the Book of Genesis. The right door depicts scenes from the New Testament Gospels.

From top to bottom, the scenes are as follows: God's creation of Adam and Eve; God presenting Eve to Adam; Adam and Eve eating the forbidden fruit from the Tree of the Knowledge of Good and Evil; God confronting Adam and Eve for their sin; their expulsion from the Garden; the life of Adam and Eve outside the Garden, including the birth of their first son, Cain; Cain and Abel presenting offerings to God; and Cain killing Abel out of envy. The right door contains scenes from the life of Christ. From bottom to top, they include the following: the Annunciation of Christ's birth to Mary, the Nativity, the visit of the three Magi, the presentation of Christ at the temple, Christ's trial before Pilate, his crucifixion, the angel outside his empty tomb, and his appearance to Mary Magdalene after the Resurrection.

Each panel on the right door corresponds to a scene on the left door. The Old Testament scene **prefigures** a New Testament scene. For example, Christ's crucifixion panel is located across from the Original Sin panel, reflecting how Christ had to be sacrificed to redeem humankind from sin. Another example is the placement of the annunciation of Christ's birth across from Cain's murder of Abel. This juxtaposition conveys a new hope after the low of humanity's first murder. The arrangement of panels indicates a strong knowledge of biblical scripture, which suggests that Bishop Bernward may have played a more direct role in the creation of these doors than merely as patron.

Bishop Bernward also commissioned a bronze column for Saint Michael's that is reminiscent of Trajan's Column in Rome (see Chapter 8). Like Trajan's Column, the column in Saint Michael's contains a single register that winds up the column. Instead of detailing the military campaign and victories of a Roman general, Saint Michael's column illustrates stories from the life of Christ, culminating in his triumph over death with the Resurrection. This column and the bronze doors reveal the influence that Roman imagery had on Bishop Bernward.

Gero Crucifix

Another significant Ottonian work of art is a large crucifix that was commissioned by Archbishop Gero and presented to the cathedral in Cologne, Germany. The image of Christ is 6 feet tall, the size of a man. The *Gero Crucifix* (**CD Fig. 12-12**) confronts viewers with Christ's suffering. His body sags with palpable weight, giving the appearance that his arms might get torn out of their sockets. Instead of the healthy, youthful Christ of early Christian art, this Christ is an unidealized picture of agony. Blood pours down his forehead from a crown of thorns that is missing today. Christ's head hangs low, and his facial expression gives the viewer a sense of his physical pain. More blood streaks down his hands and feet. Medieval Christians who saw the *Gero Crucifix* must have been compelled to reconcile their own lives with the sacrifice of Christ.

Figure 12-12. *Gero Crucifix* (detail), painted wood, ca. 910, Rheinisches Bildarchiv, Koln, Germany

The body of Ottonian art also includes illuminated manuscripts. Church officials as well as secular leaders commissioned richly decorated books throughout the period. One manuscript of note is the *Gospel of Otto III*. Otto III was the son of Otto II and the Byzantine princess Theophanu. This intermarriage caused the importation of Byzantine culture and a great deal of luxury goods into the Ottonian Empire. Ottonian art, especially illuminated manuscripts, also exhibit elements of the Byzantine style (see Chapter 10). For example, some pages contain flat figures set against golden backgrounds, which differ from the fully modeled Saint Matthew of the *Coronation Gospels*.

In a page from the *Gospel of Otto III* (**CD Fig. 12-13**), a youthful Otto is depicted on his throne. In one hand, he holds a golden orb with a cross, symbolism that dates back to the time of Constantine. Although some figures are slightly turned, the page has a frontal organization similar to Byzantine mosaic compositions. The artist used diagonal lines to paint Otto's throne and the surrounding architecture but hardly creates a recessional space. Without convincing modeling with shadow and light, the page hardly has the illusion of a three-dimensional world. The organization and formal elements of this page resemble the Justinian mosaic (see Chapter 10).

Otto III was determined more than his grandfather and father to create a Christian Roman Empire, even moving his capital to Rome. Unfortunately, he died at the age of 21 before he could realize his dream. At his request, Otto III was buried next to Charlemagne in the Palatine Chapel.

Conclusion

Small, portable constructions; abstract animal imagery; and elaborate interlacing designs are three important features of the Art of the Warrior Lords. All these elements are revealed in the Sutton Hoo purse cover, making it a fine piece to typify this artistic period. When trying to discern whether a piece of art belongs to the Warrior Lord Period, look for the basic characteristics described in this chapter. The prows of ships resembling an animal head, carved metal pieces, and even wooden doors on buildings follow the same stylized motifs.

Hiberno-Saxon Art is from Ireland and the British Isles. Like the Art of the Warrior Lords, Hiberno-Saxon Art contains interlaced patterns and abstract animal forms. However, Hiberno-Saxon Art is distinct because it reflects the rise of Christianity. Illuminated manuscripts, such as the *Lindisfarne Gospels* and the *Book of Kells*, comprise the bulk of Hiberno-Saxon Art. Celtic crosses are also an important part of the art of this period, although they are much more monumental than the portable, illuminated manuscripts produced during the period.

The Carolingian Period marked a significant time in art history. The first revival of Roman Art and architecture in the West since the fall of the Roman Empire occurred during the Carolingian Renaissance. Charlemagne pushed for a revival in learning that resulted in the production of many beautiful illuminated manuscripts. Architecturally, the Carolingian period revived the glory of Roman architecture with the Palatine Chapel and established the basilica as the standard design for churches. The Carolingian Renaissance, though short lived, marked a trend of emulating elements of Classical art that was seen during the Ottonian Period of the tenth century, the Renaissance of the fifteenth and sixteenth centuries, and the Neoclassical period of the late eighteenth century.

Ottonian emperors viewed themselves as the successors of Charlemagne. Indeed, their reign restored a positive environment for art and architecture during the tenth century, after the instability of the Frankish decline. Ottonian monarchs, nobles, and clerics alike were responsible for this artistic revival. Similar to the Carolingian Renaissance, Ottonian Art contains Christian narratives, Roman imagery and architecture, and elements of Byzantine Art. The monastery church of Saint Michael's departed from the normal basilica with its double transepts. After the death of Otto III, the Ottonian Revival was gradually replaced by a period known as the Romanesque Period, during which nation-states began to emerge in Western Europe. In addition, the postmillennium continent burned with a religious fervor that inspired an age of pilgrimages and the Crusades to gain control of the Holy Land from the Muslims.

Chapter 13

Romanesque Art

Introduction and Exam Strategy Overview

Romanesque art and architecture encompass 3 percent to 7 percent of the points on the AP Art History exam. Multiple-choice questions often ask about the reason for the rise of church building during the Romanesque period. Questions also refer to specific features of Romanesque churches, such as the ambulatory, parts of the nave elevation, vaulting techniques, and the crossing square. Images of Romanesque church interiors have been included, and students were expected to identify the architectural style being shown. Besides the architecture of the period, Romanesque sculpture is an area from which questions have been drawn.

This chapter explains the events that precipitated the Romanesque building boom, analyzes the parts of a Romanesque church and their respective functions, and discusses Romanesque sculpture. In addition, the chapter highlights the two-dimensional forms of Romanesque art, such as manuscript illumination and embroidery.

Age of Pilgrimages: Eleventh and Twelfth Centuries

A major event failed to occur at the end of the first millennium: the Apocalypse. Many Christians believed that at or around 1000, the world would end and Christ would return to judge humanity. Do you remember the Y2K fear that gripped many people just before 2000? Well, the first millennium panic could unofficially be called the Y1K scare. When the Apocalypse did not happen, there was a surge of relief and thanksgiving among Christians.

In response, Christians became even more devout in their beliefs. Many expressed their devotion either by joining the Crusades or by making pilgrimages to holy sites. European knights, urged on by certain religious leaders, faith, and/or mercenary reasons, engaged in a quest to win control of the Holy Land from the Muslims. However, the majority of European Christians lacked the military training necessary to join the Crusades and thus turned to pilgrimages as the way to show their piety. The eleventh century is therefore referred to as the Age of Pilgrimages. Across Europe, a few major pilgrimage routes sprang up along which travelers could visit the relics (holy items) of famous holy figures and martyrs. The pilgrimage routes usually culminated at the same place: the Church at Santiago de Compostela in Spain.

Pilgrims believed that relics contained miraculous powers, similar to the way many Byzantine Christians venerated icons. Relics consisted of bones, hair, teeth, fingernails, cloth, as well as splinters and nails from the True Cross of Christ's crucifixion. Pilgrims were eager to view, pray near, and touch (if possible) these relics, which were in the possession of various churches. The churches commissioned artists to create beautiful **reliquaries** of precious metals and jewels to contain the relics and positioned them in places of honor.

During the Age of Pilgrimages, communities began to build more churches and remodel preexisting ones to accommodate the flocks of pilgrims. Influenced by the remnants of Roman architecture that were scattered throughout Europe, architects designed churches that incorporated barrel and groin vaults, round arches, columns and piers, and exterior decorative sculptures. The basilica was used as the model, continuing the legacy of Carolingian and Ottonian architects.

It was not until the nineteenth century that art historians began to refer to the architecture of the eleventh and twelfth centuries as the Romanesque (meaning "Roman-like") period because the architecture resembled Roman architecture. The visual similarities between the two periods are apparent. But do not confuse them! Roman architecture and the Romanesque period are separated by seven hundred years.

One major difference is that the Romanesque builders did not use concrete, a building material that was essential to Roman construction. Instead, Romanesque builders relied on cut stone and mortar. Another difference is the intent of the architects. Roman builders were placing the stamp of Roman authority throughout the empire, while Romanesque builders were building for the glory of God.

Saint-Sernin: A Romanesque Pilgrimage Church

Saint-Sernin was built in the city of Toulouse in southern France (**CD Fig. 13-1**). Toulouse was an important stop because of the many reliquary shrines along the road to the city. Architects built Saint-Sernin to house the reliquaries. The church was dedicated to the first bishop of Toulouse, Saint Saturninus, who was martyred in the third century. This church is a paradigm of Romanesque architecture; its design contains many hallmark features of the period.

Architects lengthened the nave of the basilica plan and doubled the aisles of Saint-Sernin to accommodate large numbers of pilgrims. The design includes a **transept**, which is an area perpendicular to the nave. The intersection of the transept and nave is called the **crossing square**. In medieval European churches, the crossing square is usually the site of a bell tower. The intersection of the transept and nave gives Saint-Sernin a **cruciform**, or cross-shaped appearance, which was intentional. The design also includes an **ambulatory** (**CD Fig. 13-2**), which is an extra walkway surrounding the apse. The ambulatory was a very important innovation of Romanesque architecture. Relics were placed in radiating **chapels**, which are semicircular niches surrounding the ambulatory. Thus, the ambulatory allowed pilgrims to visit relics in the church without disrupting the daily rituals of the priests.

Saint-Sernin's exterior also exhibits Romanesque qualities (**CD Fig. 13-3**). Notice that the windows of Saint-Sernin are small and its stone walls appear heavy. The vaulting techniques of the ancient Romans were new to Romanesque architects. Therefore, the vaulting techniques and round arches they used in Saint-Sernin did not permit much room or support for large areas of windows. Round arches encircle the windows and portals (entrances into the church), giving Saint-Sernin its Roman-like qualities. Round arches are typical of Romanesque design.

A **barrel vault** supports the nave of Saint-Sernin with transverse ribs shaped like round arches (**CD Fig. 13-4**). For the most part, architects moved away from the timber-roofed basilicas that were popular from the early Christian through the Ottonian periods. The shift toward stone vaulting is one of the marks of the Romanesque style. The nave is lined on either side by an **arcade**, which is a row of arches and piers and/or columns. The nave arcade separates the nave from the side aisles. The nave elevation, which is the height from the floor to the vaulting, consists of two levels: the nave arcade and the tribune. The **tribune** is a space above the arcade that accommodated extra visitors on special holidays. All these parts may confuse you at first and may require extra time for study.

Multiple-choice questions may target specific parts of a Romanesque church, such as the ambulatory. A slide-based short essay question might show you a Romanesque interior and ask you to identify the style and describe the visual elements that support your answer. Understanding Romanesque architecture becomes easier when contrasted with Gothic architecture (see Chapter 14).

Basis of Measurement: The Crossing Square

The architects of Saint-Sernin created a plan based on proportional relationships. In other words, the measurements of various parts of the church are interrelated. The crossing square, or the section where the nave and transept intersect, is the basis for the other measurements. Each nave bay is one-half the size of the crossing square. A **bay** is by definition a three-dimensional module. It is a section between the transverse arches in the barrel vault. A line of bays composes the length of the nave.

Additional bays in the side aisles equal one-fourth the size of the crossing square. Refer back to the plan of Saint-Sernin. Compare the size of the crossing square to the nave bays and side-aisle bays, and you will see the interrelated proportions.

Identifying the Romanesque Style Despite Regional Variations

Romanesque churches have additional distinguishing features. Stone vaulting is one of them. Early Christian and medieval basilicas built before the eleventh century had timber roofs. As you could imagine, fire was a major problem for these buildings. Yet timber roofs remained a staple in church design until the Romanesque period. A small number of Romanesque churches retained the timber roof design, but most Romanesque churches were designed with stone vaulting. Usually, the naves of Romanesque churches contain barrel vaults. Recall that in Roman architecture (see Chapter 8), a barrel vault appears like a line of round arches extending in a line through the nave. Another difference of Romanesque churches was the reemergence of exterior stone sculpture, which had not been seen since the Roman era. Early Christian, Byzantine, Carolingian, and Ottonian churches had plain exteriors with the focus on embellishing the church interiors. In contrast, Romanesque designers made sculpture an important part of a church's exterior, expressing the vision or message of each church.

Romanesque architecture varied regionally. In Normandy, France, Saint-Etienne Cathedral (**CD Fig. 13-5**) contains ribbed, sexpartite vaults (the ribs divide a square ceiling bay into six parts). The vaulting resembles that of Gothic cathedrals. But look at the overall appearance of the interior. Saint-Etienne has round arches. Its clerestory windows are not very large compared with those of Gothic churches. Saint-Etienne is a Romanesque church, and the basic features of the style remain the same.

Figure 13-5. Saint-Etienne Cathedral, ca. 1115–1120, Caen, France

Another Romanesque church that deviates slightly from the model is Durham Cathedral in England. Its nave contains ribbed groin vaults with pointed arches. This type of vault allowed for slightly larger windows in the clerestory. Durham Cathedral, like Saint-Etienne, resembles Gothic architecture. However, its windows are not as large as those in Gothic churches, and the nave arcade contains round arches. The nave arcade also contains columns, which indicate the Romanesque style. Romanesque architecture appears heavy, which is evident in Durham.

To review, most Romanesque churches have small windows because that is all the vaulting techniques would allow. Most naves of Romanesque churches have barrel vaults with round arches, but some regions may depart from this slightly. Do not let a regional idiosyncrasy confuse you. Look at the entire scope of the interior. Does it have a heavy appearance with small windows? If so, the church that you are looking at is probably in the Romanesque style.

Romanesque Cathedral Complex at Pisa

The cathedral complex at Pisa, Italy, provides another example of the regional differences among Romanesque churches (**CD Fig. 13-6**). Italian architects adhered to the tradition of Early Christian basilicas but contained Romanesque characteristics as well. The Pisa complex contains a cathedral, baptistery, and a campanile, unlike other European Romanesque churches. Another distinction is that the Pisa buildings, as well as others in Italy, have marble incrustation incorporated into the exterior design. Marble incrustation is the variously colored marble panels that decorate the building. That is why medieval Italian buildings have a colored pattern on their exteriors.

Structurally, the Pisa cathedral resembles an Early Christian basilica, but it has a longer transept, extra side aisles, and three portals, and it incorporates numerous round arches and columns. Remember, larger transepts and side aisles were added during the Romanesque period to provide room for pilgrims. The round arches and columns form arcades and reveal the influence of Roman architecture in Italy.

Pisa's baptistery is a separate building, which was an unusual feature in churches of the time. The baptistery was where infants and converts were initiated into the Christian community. Looking at the outside, you can see multiple engaged columns (columns still attached to the wall) and small windows. The building also contains Romanesque portals and an arcaded gallery on the second level.

The Pisa baptistery contains another important feature. Although its lower half has Romanesque features, it also contains Gothic-style tracery (stone ornamentation) on the exterior of the building. Notice the pinnacles, which are the pointed endings of the spires above the windows and all the frilly-looking stonework protruding from the upper half of the baptistery. The construction and modification of Romanesque buildings continued into the Gothic period. Consequently, several Romanesque buildings contain elements that indicate the transition toward Gothic architecture (another example is the bell tower of Saint-Sernin in Toulouse).

The **campanile**, or bell tower that is the world-famous "Leaning Tower of Pisa" indicates another regional difference in the Romanesque period. French Romanesque churches often incorporated bell towers as part of the main building, usually placing it over the crossing square. In the Italian style, campaniles were independent structures that were a part of the cathedral complex. The Leaning Tower of Pisa, like the cathedral and baptistery, contains multiple arcaded galleries composed of round arches and columns.

Romanesque Portals

A **portal** is an entrance to a church. It is composed of several parts, many of which contain relief sculpture. The doorway itself is outlined by vertical doorjambs and a horizontal lintel. **Doorjambs** are stone pieces on the sides of a door. Even in your home, the jambs are the sides of a doorway. The **lintel** is a beam that extends over the door. Recall that lintels were used in one of the earliest methods of architectural support: post-and-lintel construction (see Chapter 5). The doors may be separated down the middle by a **trumeau**, which is another vertical stone piece. Above the lintel is a semicircular panel called a tympanum, which serves as an ideal space for a relief sculpture of a biblical narrative. Above the tympanum are rows of round arches called **archivolts**. The archivolts were made of stones called **voissoirs**. Voissoirs are stones that make up any arches, including those in Roman aqueducts. Locate the parts of a portal in the photograph of the portal of Saint-Lazare at Autun, France (**CD Fig. 13-7**). An effective study technique is to photocopy a portal diagram, cut it into pieces to separate each part, and reassemble each part as someone calls out the name of it.

Romanesque Sculpture

Romanesque sculpture does not resemble Roman sculpture the way the architecture does. Romanesque sculpture has a closer affinity to Early Christian sculpture, which could be found on sarcophagi throughout Europe. An example of this can be seen on a frieze on the west facade of the Cathedral of Modena in Italy (**CD Fig. 13-8**). The scene depicts the creation of Adam and Eve as well as the Temptation and Original Sin. Christ is shown on the left of the frieze surrounded by a **mandorla**, an oval of light. The mandorla was shown around Christ in the sculpture of earlier periods and will be used in the next four centuries. Another characteristic of Romanesque sculpture is that its appearance is tied to the architecture of the church.

The shapes of figures conform to the architecture of which it is a part. For example, a sculpted figure on a trumeau, the vertical stone between the doors of a portal, is often elongated because of the vertical orientation of the trumeau. As a result, human figures in Romanesque art may appear thin, elongated, and angular, which means that the body joints at the head and shoulders, elbows, and hips have sharp edges. This unnatural, angular appearance gives the composition an agitated appearance.

The tympanum of Saint-Foy at Conques, France, is a fine example of Romanesque sculpture (**CD Fig. 13-9**). First impressions are important, and sculptors intended to attract the attention of the worshippers approaching the church. The tympanum contains 124 figures and is approximately 20 feet long and 10 feet high. The biblical narrative that it depicts is called the Last Judgment. The Gospel of Matthew is the main source of inspiration:

> Then He [Christ] will say to the people on His right: come you who are blessed by My Father. Come and possess the kingdom which has been prepared for you. Then He will say to those on his left: away from me, you are under God's curse, away to the eternal fire which has been prepared for the devil.

Christ is shown as the Supreme Judge in the center. He is surrounded by a mandorla. His raised right hand reminds the viewer that the souls on his right will be received into heaven. His lowered left hand directs viewers' attention to the damned souls falling and being tortured by devils. God's chosen people are walking to the right of Christ under the supervision of the Virgin Mary and Saint Peter. Note that Saint Peter holds the Keys of Heaven. The next group of people includes figures that played a role in the history of Saint-Foy and its monastery, such as Charlemagne. Abraham, who is considered the father of Israel, is shown welcoming the chosen ones. To Abraham's left are Old Testament prophets and New Testament apostles.

Figure 13-9. Tympanum of Saint-Foy, Conques, France

The door to Hell is to Christ's left on the lower level. The gaping jaws of a Leviathan (sea monster) mark the entrance, poking its head through the doorway to swallow sinners. A demon with spiked hair clubs people as they enter. Satan is enthroned in the center of Hell, surrounded by demons that torture the damned. Each of the Seven Deadly Sins is illustrated. For example, a nude man and woman stand side by side, representing lust. The tympanum of Saint-Foy provided a powerful reminder that human beings were by nature sinful and that entering the church could lead them on the path to salvation.

Scenes of the Last Judgment and the Apocalypse were very popular during the Romanesque period. Recall that the period began shortly after the millennium and that Christians were expecting the world to end. The tympanum of Saint-Pierre in Moissac, France (**CD Fig. 13-10**), is derived from the apocalyptic Book of Revelation:

And behold, a throne was set in heaven and one sat on the throne. . . . And round about the throne were . . . four and twenty elders sitting . . . and round about the throne there were four beasts . . . the first was like a lion, . . . the second was a like a calf, . . . the third beast had the face of a man, and the fourth beast was like a flying eagle.

Christ is enthroned in the center. The winged beasts that surround him symbolize the four Evangelists, or Gospel writers. The lion, calf, man, and eagle represent Mark, Luke, Matthew, and John, respectively. Collectively, these four symbols of the Evangelists are known as the Tetramorphs. The symbolism for the Tetramorphs is consistent throughout Christian art. Two attendants are on either side of Christ and hold scrolls of human deeds for judgment. Surrounding the scene, the sculptor depicts the twenty-four elders. Not only did this tympanum remind pilgrims of the impending Apocalypse but also served a didactic, or teaching purpose. Remember, that many Europeans of the eleventh and twelfth centuries were illiterate. The exterior stone sculpture of Romanesque churches instructed these Christians in the Bible.

Tympanum of Saint-Lazare and Gislebertus

The tympanum of Saint-Lazare (**CD Fig. 13-11**) is noteworthy for a special feature. Although it depicts a standard Last Judgment scene, it contains a rare signature by the artist, whose name was Gislebertus. His signature is noticeable below Christ. Art historians discuss why he signed this work, because many medieval artists worked anonymously for the glory of God. One theory is that Gislebertus hoped visitors to the church would remember to pray for him as they entered Saint-Lazare.

Devotional Sculptures and Reliquaries

In addition to stone sculpture for churches, small devotional statues and reliquaries were produced during the Romanesque period. Artists still were concerned about constructing any sculpture that would violate the Second Commandment's prohibition of idols, but as pilgrims journeyed to see relics, the popularity of small statues and reliquaries grew. Wooden statues were made of the Virgin Mary and Christ Child, such as the *Morgan Madonna* (**CD Fig. 13-12**). It shows the influence of Byzantine art by depicting the Virgin Mary as the Theotokos. She is also called the Throne of Wisdom, because her lap serves as Christ's throne in the sculpture. Notice how the bodies of the figures lack naturalism. As on Byzantine figures, the folds in the clothing are formulaic, following a pattern. However, the faces of the Romanesque Virgin Mary and Christ are more rounded that is typical of Byzantine art.

Manuscript Illumination

Illuminated manuscripts continued to be produced throughout the eleventh and twelfth centuries. They were the main form of painting and two-dimensional art during the Romanesque period. For the most part, monks and nuns created these works in remote scriptoria. However, the number of secular scribes grew in the twelfth century, as did the desire for recognition.

Most artists during the medieval period worked anonymously for the glory of God, but increasingly during the Romanesque twelfth century, artists began to sign their works. Like Gislebertus—the artist who signed a tympanum at the church of Saint-Lazare in Autun, France—other Romanesque artists desired recognition. In the frieze of Adam and Eve on Modena Cathedral, Wiligelmo not only signed his name but also carved "among sculptors, your work shines forth, Wiligelmo." Similarly, artists such as Master Hugo and Eadwine the Scribe signed the illuminated manuscripts they produced (**CD Fig. 13-13**).

Like the sculptures of the period, most figures in Romanesque illuminated manuscripts lack naturalism. Artists often conceived of the folds of the clothing and the body underneath as the same thing, rather than modeling the folds naturalistically to reflect the contours of the body underneath. Nevertheless, the religious message of a Romanesque work of art, be it sculpture or illuminated manuscript, is conveyed and represents the most important reason for art produced during this period.

Bayeux Tapestry

The *Bayeux Tapestry* (**CD Fig. 13-14**) is another example of two-dimensional art from the Romanesque period. Despite its name, the *Bayeux Tapestry* is not a tapestry but a length of linen cloth embroidered with wool thread. It recounts a famous contemporary event: the Norman conquest of the Anglo-Saxons in England. The Normans were a group of people descended from the Vikings and living in northern France. When the king of England, Edward the Confessor, died, the Norman duke, William, believed he had claim to the English throne because of his feudal ties to Edward. When Harold Godwin, a man who had pledged loyalty to William, became the new king, William decided to invade England. After defeating Harold's forces at the Battle of Hastings in 1066, William assumed kingship and became known as William the Conqueror. Bishop Odo, who was the half-brother of William and participated in the conquest, commissioned the *Bayeux Tapestry* in honor of the event. The style of the *Bayeux Tapestry* is similar to Romanesque illuminated manuscripts in that the figures are rendered in a flat manner and lack classical proportions. Another feature of the embroidered piece that resembles the illuminated manuscripts of the time is the intricate border decorated with real as well as imaginary animals.

The *Bayeux Tapestry* records the events preceding the invasion, not just the battle of Hastings. It is 20 inches high and extends across 230 feet. It is an example of **continuous narration,** which was a medieval storytelling technique. Certain characters are illustrated several times in the embroidery as the story unfolds. For example, William is shown swearing allegiance to Harold, sending representatives to Harold when he became king, and during the battle of Hastings. The politics leading up to the invasion as well as the preparations for the invasion and battle are also shown.

The purpose of this work of art, which is to tell the story of the Norman conquest of England and the reasons behind it, bears similarity to Roman works of art such as the Arch of Titus or Trajan's Column.

Conclusion

The Romanesque style flourished in Western Europe between 1000 and 1150. The design of churches during the period was a practical response to the phenomenon of pilgrimages. Because pilgrims journeyed to visit sacred relics at holy sites, churches were built to house relics and to accommodate pilgrims, as well as to provide space for worship. During what has been called the Age of Pilgrimages, the form of the church was primarily cruciform, or cross shaped, continuing the tradition established by architects of basilicas built in the Carolingian period of the ninth century. Architects incorporated ambulatories in their designs. An ambulatory is a semicircular passageway that surrounds the apse. It enabled pilgrims to walk around the apse without disturbing the daily rituals of the priests.

With the Romanesque period, stone begins to replace wood as the main material in the roofs of churches. Despite regional variations in the Romanesque style, most churches have barrel-vaulted naves with round arches. The entrance to the church, called a portal, serves as an ideal place for sculptural decoration, especially on the tympanum.

The Romanesque period marked the reemergence of exterior sculptural decoration on buildings, which had not been seen since the Roman era. The vaulting, round arches, and exterior sculpture were the reasons why nineteenth-century art historians named this the Romanesque period. However, the tenth- and eleventh-century architects used Roman building techniques in the service of Christianity rather than paganism.

Chapter 14

Gothic Art

Introduction and Exam Strategy Overview

Have you ever wondered about the meaning of *Gothic*? Chances are that you have heard of classmates who have dressed in the so-called "Goth" fashion. Or perhaps you have heard your parents discuss the Gothic or Neo-Gothic architecture of buildings you have visited. Questions concerning the Gothic period will encompass 7 percent to 10 percent of the points on the AP Art History exam. Past tests have displayed pictures of the interiors of Gothic churches and have asked two or three multiple-choice questions about parts of the churches and architectural innovations of the Gothic period. A variation of this was a slide-based short essay question that asked students to identify the style of architecture and explain its key features. This chapter addresses these questions and prepares you for some of the significant concepts and terms that you need to know.

Origin of the Term "Gothic"

Gothic was actually a derisive name coined by the famous Renaissance artist and art historian Giorgio Vasari to describe a style of architecture he found distasteful. Vasari is an important figure in art history because of his descriptions of the lives of famous Renaissance artists, and he is often referred to as the Father of Art History. Quite enamored by Classical Greco-Roman culture, Vasari likened the European structures built in the centuries preceding the Renaissance as architecture that only the Goths could have produced. The Goth tribes were blamed for the decline of classical civilization because of their incursions into the Roman Empire. Therefore, when Vasari compared the artistic and architectural creations of the thirteenth and fourteenth centuries to the work of Goths, he was deeply insulting the period.

The Gothic period began around the year 1150 and lasted through the 1200s and 1300s. Another way to say this is that the Gothic period spanned the thirteenth and fourteenth centuries.

Abbot Suger: Inventor of the Gothic Style

Abbot Suger is known as the creator of the Gothic style. The French prelate's dream was to one day become the abbot of one of France's most famous monasteries, Saint-Denis.

In his early forties, Suger did become the abbot of Saint-Denis and decided to beautify the church. In the three treatises he wrote on the topic, Abbot Suger expressed his vision for remodeling Saint-Denis in a way that differed significantly from the Romanesque-style architecture that prevailed at the time (see Chapter 13).

The church, according to Abbot Suger, should be a place of great physical beauty that inspires hope in the beauty of paradise (heaven). This was a very different approach than the fear-inspiring Last Judgment scenes of Romanesque tympanums. Throughout his treatises, Suger wrote about embellishing the church with gold and jewels. Here is Suger's description of the altar frontal of Saint-Denis:

> Into this panel, which stands in front of [Saint-Denis's] most sacred body, we have put … about forty-two marks of gold and a multifarious wealth of precious gems, hyacinths, rubies, sapphires, emeralds and topazes, and also an array of different large pearls.

In contrast, Romanesque churches were usually dark and heavy in appearance. Abbot Suger's ideas laid the foundation for Gothic architecture.

One of the first areas of Saint-Denis that Abbot Suger rebuilt was the ambulatory. You should remember this term from the Romanesque period. It is the extra walkway added around the apse so that Christian pilgrims could view a church's relics without disrupting daily masses.

Notice the intricacy of the vaulting techniques of the ambulatory of Saint-Denis (**CD Fig. 14-1**). Romanesque ambulatories usually used simpler groin vaults. During the Gothic period, architects began to use **ribbed vaults**, which were constructed by intersecting pointed arches. Look closely at the photograph to find the ribbed vaults.

Ribbed Vaults and the Quest for Height and Light

Ribbed vaults were used extensively during the Gothic period because they helped achieve the key Gothic goals alluded to by Abbot Suger, which in simple terms were height and light (**CD Figs. 14-2 and 14-3**). According to Suger, greater height provided the sensation of heaven. Suger said that the new churches should make worshippers feel like they are dwelling in a place that is above the muck of the earth but not quite heaven. Ribbed vaults provided this extra height in two ways. First, because they are composed of **pointed arches** rather than rounded arches, they literally open up more space in the church interior. Study the quadripartite rib vault in the diagram. This type of vault was often used during the Gothic period. Notice that the pointed arches give you a sense of greater verticality as well as providing more space.

Second, the steeper slope of the pointed arch more directly transfers the weight from the roof to the piers than do rounded arches. The rounded-arches scheme of a barrel vault, which was typical during the Romanesque period, caused too much outward thrust on the walls. This outward thrust limited the height of the walls of Romanesque churches. In contrast, the pointed arches of Gothic vaults enabled builders to construct walls with soaring verticality.

Pointed arches and ribbed vaulting also open up greater amounts of area for windows. Abbot Suger believed that beautiful stained-glass windows filter sunlight and provide a multicolored display of light inside the church. This light enhances the feeling of spirituality that Suger sought in church design. Abbot Suger felt that the multicolored "heavenly light" prefigures the New Jerusalem (another way of describing the Christian concept of heaven).

Flying Buttresses

Flying buttresses have become a hallmark of Gothic architecture (**CD Fig. 14-4**). A buttress is a support for a building to counteract horizontal thrust. A flying buttress has actual space or air between its vertical part and its horizontal arm, which makes contact with the side walls of the church. They are located on the outside of the church, not the inside.

Even though ribbed vaults opened up the possibility of greater nave heights, the outward thrust on most Gothic buildings was still too much for the churches to stand without collapsing. With the additional wall support provided by the exterior flying buttresses, ever-taller churches were possible.

Evolution of the Gothic Period

As more architects adopted the ideas of Abbot Suger in their church designs, the Gothic style spread, replacing the Romanesque style. The Gothic period lasted two centuries, during which it evolved. Art historians separate this evolution into subcategories based on the distinctive characteristics of each. The Early Gothic period refers to the period in the late 1100s, as French architects began to implement the ideas of Abbot Suger. Some of the designs retained Romanesque features, but specific changes in the nave elevation and vaulting techniques marked the beginning of the Gothic style. The term *High Gothic* refers to the middle of the period, the 1200s. This is when the famous Chartres Cathedral was rebuilt after a devastating fire in 1194. During the High Gothic period, architects began to decrease the surface area of the walls and incorporate more stained-glass windows. When a High Gothic church has vast amounts of windows, it is said to be built in the **Rayonnant** or radiant style. The Late Gothic period occurred during the 1300s and 1400s. In parts of France, it is called the **Flamboyant style** because the pointed arches and extensive tracery (ornamentation) on the buildings' exteriors resemble flames.

Knowing all the idiosyncrasies of each Gothic period is not essential. However, you should be able to recognize the Rayonnant style and the Flamboyant style when you see pictures of them. As Gothic architecture evolved, churches contained larger numbers of windows and less wall surface area, and the exterior ornamentation became more elaborate. In England, the High Gothic period is called the **Decorated style**, and the Late Gothic period is known as the **Perpendicular style**. It is helpful to use the adjective *English* before saying or writing these two style names because it reminds you and makes the test readers know that you understand that these styles are different from the French Gothic styles.

The Gothic style spread throughout Europe. The elements of pointed arches, ribbed vaults, and extensive stained-glass windows remained relatively consistent throughout the continent, but countries had their stylistic idiosyncrasies.

Chartres Cathedral

Chartres, officially known as the Cathedral of Notre Dame at Chartres (not to be confused with Notre Dame of Paris), was built between the Early and High Gothic periods. Many Gothic churches took several years to build, resulting in architecture that blended two or more periods. The original cathedral was begun in the Romanesque style in the early 1100s but was destroyed in the Great Fire of 1194. All that remained of the original church was its crypt and part of the western facade (**CD Fig. 14-5**). Consequently, the western facade seems to be a cross between Romanesque and Early Gothic styles, especially considering the heaviness of the stonework. The rest of Chartres, from its quadripartite ribbed vaults to its numerous stained-glass windows, is clearly Gothic.

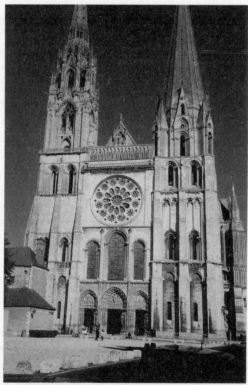

Figure 14-5. Western facade of Chartres Cathedral, begun ca. 1130, rebuilt after 1194, France

Gothic churches differ from Romanesque churches in their nave elevation—that is, the space between the floor and the vaulting. At the lowest level, a Gothic church contains a **nave arcade** like Romanesque churches. In Early Gothic churches, a **gallery** above the nave arcade provides extra seating. Gothic architects added a level above that called the **triforium**, which is a band of arcades below the highest windows. The final and highest part of the nave elevation was the **clerestory**. Churches built during the Early Gothic period thus have a four-part nave elevation: nave arcade, gallery, triforium, and clerestory. During the High Gothic period, architects did away with the gallery and increased the size of the triforium.

An important level of the Gothic church that is not a part of the nave elevation is the **crypt**. The crypt was designed to contain relics as well as the bodies of deceased monks and is usually located below the church.

The chief relic housed in Chartres was the Virgin's Veil, the head covering that the Virgin Mary wore the night Christ was born. The people of Chartres thought that when the church burned down, the Virgin's veil perished. When it was discovered that the veil survived in the crypt, the townspeople interpreted this as a miracle. Thus, reconstruction of a new cathedral in the Gothic style began soon after. Based on its appearance and the time of its completion, art historians refer to Chartres as an example of the High Gothic style.

The entrance to Chartres at the western facade is known as the Royal Portal (**CD Fig. 14-6**). The builders of Gothic churches usually oriented the structures toward the Holy Land in the East. The altar and **choir**, which is special seating for the priests on the other side of the transept, are in the **eastern** part of the church. The name Royal Portal comes from the sculptures of Old Testament kings and queens, the genealogical forerunners of Christ, that make up the doorjamb columns. These sculptures will be discussed later in the chapter.

The Royal Portal is actually three portals in one. The theme of each portal reflects the supremacy of Jesus Christ: his birth and childhood are depicted in the right portal, The Resurrection and Ascension are the focus of the left portal, and the Second Coming of Christ as the final judge of humanity at the Apocalypse is shown in the central portal. Christ's mother, Mary, also receives noteworthy attention in the tympanum of the southern portal (the portal on the right). Mary is shown reclining shortly after the birth of Christ. Remember that the greatest relic housed in Chartres was the Virgin's Veil.

When studying the Royal Portal of Chartres, it is helpful to review the parts of a portal, which were first discussed in Chapter 13. As an example, consider the central portal of the Royal Portal. The tympanum of the central portal reflects the Second Coming of Christ during the Apocalypse. Christ is seated on a throne, and encircling his body is an almond-shaped band of light called a mandorla. You will recall that the four strange creatures around Christ (winged man, lion, ox, and eagle) represent the **Tetramorphs**, also known as the Evangelists or the Gospel writers: Matthew, Mark, Luke, and John. AP Art History test writers do not expect you to know the symbolism of each Evangelist, but you should be aware that they are known collectively as the Tetramorphs or Evangelists. Fortunately for students and teachers, the iconography or symbols used to depict the events involving Christ, like the Second Coming, remain fairly consistent throughout both Romanesque and Gothic art. The lintel, the horizontal stone above the doorway, displays the twelve apostles as well as two Old Testament prophets who foretold the coming of Christ as the Messiah. The **archivolts**, or ornamental bands above the tympanum, contain the twenty-four elders described as worshipping Christ during the Apocalypse in the outer two archivolts and the apostles on the inner archivolt. Notice that the archivolts are made of pointed arches, an important Gothic feature.

Chartres Cathedral is a splendid example of the incorporation of stained-glass windows in Gothic churches. It contains 176 stained-glass windows totaling approximately 22,000 square feet. This is equivalent to half a football field of stained glass. Abbot Suger would have been proud to know that the recommendations he made for church décor about 80 years before were being implemented. The beautiful stained-glass windows of Chartres filter the natural sunlight into a multicolored display that captures the *lux nova*, or new heavenly light, that Abbot Suger sought for church interiors. The intention of including these beautiful windows was to inspire the congregation to contemplate the beauty and hope of heaven.

One famous stained-glass window that emphasizes the beauty of the art form as well as the importance of the Virgin Mary to Chartres is the *Notre Dame de la Belle Verriere* (*Our Lady of the Beautiful Window*). It depicts Mary with Christ seated on her lap. The depiction of Mary is a common one among works of Gothic art: she has a certain worldly beauty, appears youthful, and wears a gorgeous crown. The artistry of the window is enhanced as the sunlight is filtered through its multicolored glass.

Another significant window of Chartres is the rose window of its western facade (**CD Fig. 14-7**). The queen of France, Blanche of Castile, commissioned this window, and its various panels reflect the interests of its patron. For example, lancet windows below the rose windows have images of golden fleur-de-lis on blue fields, symbols of the French monarchy. The lancet windows beside those contain golden castles on red fields, representing the Kingdom of Castile in Spain, Queen Blanche's homeland. Taken together, these windows depict the unification of the two major kingdoms through marriage.

By commissioning such a beautiful and enormous rose window, Queen Blanche demonstrated her piety and love for God. Christians of the Middle Ages believed that good works such as patronage or pilgrimage would secure their position in heaven, which most likely was a concern for Queen Blanche. The window contains all the appropriate Christian iconography. Of course, Mary with the infant Christ is shown in the central panel, indicating the importance of the Virgin to Chartres. White doves and angels in circular panes of glass surround her. Square panes with the Old Testament kings who were the predecessors of Christ, his earthly royal lineage, surround those panels. The rose window also contains additional quattre-foil-shaped windows with fleur-de-lis interspersed with the other windows so that visitors do not forget who sponsored the window.

By connecting the Queen of Heaven (Mary) as well as the Old Testament kings such as David and Solomon with Queen Blanche, the window reinforces the concept of ruling by divine right. In other words, the French monarchy has the blessing of God to rule France accordingly. The concepts and goals of patronage have been the topics of long essays on past AP Art History tests. The rose window of Chartres's western facade is a fitting example to use for this topic.

Sainte-Chapelle and the Rayonnant Style

Sainte-Chapelle is a small cathedral in Paris that was commissioned by King Louis IX to hold his collection of precious relics (**CD Fig. 14-8**). These relics included the Crown of Thorns, the lance that pierced Christ's side, part of the True Cross, as well as a nail from the crucifixion. Louis IX was known for his piety and devotion to Christianity. He died while leading the Eighth Crusade, making him a martyr for Christianity. He was later canonized by the church and is considered the ideal medieval king. Because Louis built Sainte-Chapelle to hold relics, it can be considered a giant reliquary. It was also his private chapel and was connected to his royal palace. It is divided into lower and upper areas. The lower area was accessible to all visitors, such as foreign kings, dignitaries, and nobility. However, the upper area was accessible only to Louis and high-ranking clerics (priests).

Sainte-Chapelle's most distinguishing feature is that three-fourths of its surface area is stained glass (**CD Fig. 14-9**). Wall surfaces consists mostly of tracery, following the wall-covering trend of Gothic architecture. Sainte-Chapelle exemplifies the **Rayonnant** or radiant style mentioned earlier. The name is appropriate, of course, considering the beautiful, multicolored light that pours through its windows on sunny days. The stone tracery surrounding the stained-glass windows appears like thin sinews holding the massive yet beautiful windows together. Some tourists consider Sainte-Chapelle to be the most beautiful Gothic building in Europe.

Figure 14-9. Interior of upper area of Sainte-Chapelle, 1243–1248

English Gothic: Decorated and Perpendicular Styles

During its time, the Gothic style was known as *opus francigeno* or "work in the French manner." It gradually spread to other parts of Europe. Wherever it went, the Gothic style retained the basic characteristics of pointed, arched, and plentiful stained-glass windows. Yet regions adapted the style to fit their cultures. The English Gothic style can be divided into two parts: the earlier decorated style and the later perpendicular style. The hallmark of the **Decorated style** is the ornate decoration of architectural elements. For example, the English decorated style added extra ribs to the ribbed vaulting, making the ceilings of some churches look like intricate stone spiderwebs. Only some of the ribs actually have a support function; the other ribs disguised the support ribs to enhance the interior decoration, in keeping with the label of "decorated style."

The **Perpendicular style**, which succeeded the decorated style, is so named because of the more vertical emphasis of its architecture and decoration. The windows are taller, occupying more of the surface area of the wall. Gloucester Cathedral in England illustrates the perpendicular style (**CD Fig. 14-10**). Notice the large window in the choir. Its tall lancets visually unite the choir from the floor to the vaulting.

The Perpendicular style is even more ornate than the Decorated style. Remember that as the Gothic period progresses chronologically, the height, light, and decoration usually increase. The chapel has intricate **fan vaults**, a collection of ribbed vaults that meet and project downward from the ceiling like stalactites (**CD Fig. 14-11**). Largely ornamental, these fan vaults are typical of the Perpendicular style. Chronologically, you can compare the English Perpendicular style with the French Flamboyant style because they both have exaggerated decorative elements.

Comparing English Gothic and French Gothic Styles

Both of the English Gothic styles show basic Gothic features but are distinct from French Gothic. For example, compare Salisbury Cathedral in England with Amiens Cathedral in France (**CD Figs. 14-12 and 14-13**). When you examine the plans of Salisbury (**CD Fig. 14-14**) as well as the photographs of its exterior and interior, you will notice the hallmark Gothic features, such as pointed arches and a large number of windows. You should also notice that the stonework appears slightly heavier and more squat than the contemporary churches in France such as Amiens Cathedral. This shows the lingering English predilection for the Romanesque, which in England was known as the Norman style. So, Salisbury illustrates how Gothic style spread and was amalgamated with local tastes.

Salisbury has more of a horizontal emphasis in its nave than does Amiens, despite containing a nave arcade, triforium, and clerestory. The nave of Amiens Cathedral is much taller at 144 feet compared with Salisbury's nave height of about 80 feet. To accentuate this horizontality, Salisbury's nave is quite long—about 450 feet. Because Salisbury's nave walls are not as tall, the cathedral made minimal use of flying buttresses. Unlike those of Amiens, the flying buttresses of Salisbury were not necessary. Other stylistic differences between the French and English cathedrals are that Salisbury has a squared apse and a double transept, while Amiens has a round apse and a single transept.

Another difference between the churches is their locations. Salisbury Cathedral was built on the grassy Salisbury plain, separated from the town. In contrast, Amiens Cathedral was built in the heart of the city. The locations may account for the differences in height and length between the churches. Because Salisbury was built on a plain, it had more space for a longer nave. Built in the middle of the city, Amiens did not have the room to build outward, so the architects built upward. The horizontality of Salisbury and the verticality of Amiens also reflect regional tastes. Whereas the English preferred the squatness of the Romanesque period, the architect of Amiens was committed to even greater height and light than were builders of other French Gothic cathedrals.

Gothic Sculpture

The exteriors of Gothic churches were adorned with sculpture, following the trend set in the Romanesque period. Gothic sculpture evolved toward greater degrees of naturalism. The shape of early Gothic figures reflected the architecture to which it was attached. For example, the doorjamb statues of the Royal Portal are elongated and thin because they resemble the jambs. As the Gothic period advanced, sculptures became more independent of the surrounding architecture. High Gothic statues were carved in very high relief to stand out from the building. By the end of the High Gothic period, statues were almost in the round, connected to the building only by the pedestals on which they stood. As the statues became more independent, their naturalism also increased. In their representations of the human figure, sculptors began to use the Gothic *S-curve*, which is similar to, yet different from, contrapposto. The folds began to look more realistic, reflecting an understanding of how drapery flows around the body's contours.

As mentioned earlier, the Royal Portal at the western facade of Chartres contains a significant number of early Gothic sculptures (**CD Fig. 14-15**). It is called the Royal Portal because the doorjambs, which are composed of columns, contain images of Old Testament kings and queens, who were the earthly predecessors of Jesus Christ. In an interesting anachronism, they wear twelfth-century European attire. The figures stand rigidly upright following the form of the jamb columns. They are all the same height and lack naturalism. The folds flow vertically like the columns to which they are attached. The formulaic folds resemble the folds in the clothing of the Romanesque *Morgan Madonna* (see Chapter 13). Notice that the figures lack any shift in weight and express a limited amount of individuality.

High Gothic statues are still attached to the jambs, but they are far more individualized and distinctive. The southern portal of Chartres contains a trio of saintly figures that demonstrate these features (**CD Fig. 14-16**). Saint Martin, shown on the left, is a tall, intense priest with gaunt features. The central figure, Saint Jerome, is depicted as a kindly scholar holding his translation of the Bible. Saint Gregory, on the right, seems pensive, perhaps contemplating the actions of the Holy Spirit, which is symbolized by the dove on his right shoulder. Their heights, clothing, and gestures vary to reflect the personalities of these saints. In addition, notice that the statues extend farther from the building and their figures do not conform to the supports like the doorjamb statues of the Royal Portal of Chartres.

Other High Gothic churches incorporated sculptures that demonstrate a progression in naturalism. At Amiens, one of the most prominent statues is a figure of Christ as the *Beau Dieu* ("Beautiful God"), which is a part of the trumeau of the central doorway (**CD Fig. 14-17**). His facial expression, hand gesture, and drapery folds give Christ human qualities. He is almost independent of the trumeau except for the pedestal and the canopy over his head. The message being expressed about Christ is that He is a kind teacher. The art of the Gothic period, although also concerned with the Apocalypse, expresses more hope than the heavy Last Judgment scenes of the Romanesque period.

Other High Gothic statues that illustrate an increase in naturalism are the jamb statues of the central doorway of Reims Cathedral in France. The two sets of statues depict the Annunciation and the Visitation (**CD Fig. 14-18**). The Annunciation, which is shown on the left, is when the Angel Gabriel delivers the message to Mary that she is going to bear the Messiah. The Visitation, which is shown on the right, tells the story of the pregnant Virgin Mary's visit with her cousin Elizabeth, who is also with child. There is a noticeable difference between the two sets of statues. This difference indicates that they were created by different workshops. Notice that the figures of Mary and Elizabeth in the Visitation scene are almost completely independent of the columns behind them. The sculptor demonstrates knowledge of weight shift that is similar to the Classical contrapposto. In addition, these figures turn toward each other and communicate through gestures. Unlike the kings and queens of the Royal Portal, which serve as embellishments of jamb columns, the figures of Mary and Elizabeth act out a well-known biblical story.

By the Late Gothic period, the weight shift in the figures is so pronounced as to create an *S*-curve. You may recall that the Classical Greek sculptor Praxiteles created human figures that contained *S*-curves, reflecting his understanding of human anatomy and contrapposto. In contrast, the *S*-curves of the Late Gothic period seem to be forced elements—attempts to develop naturalism but obscuring the underlying forms. *The Statue of the Virgin and Child*, also called the *Virgin of Paris*, demonstrates this technique (**CD Fig. 14-19**). Her upper body shifts to the right as she supports the weight of the young Christ over her left hip. The folds in her robe are highly developed but do not reflect the natural structure of Mary's body, such as her hips and knees. Her *S*-curve, which is exaggerated and unrealistic, was nonetheless conventional for fourteenth-century statues of the Virgin Mary. It would have been sacrilegious to portray the body of the Virgin Mary in the manner of the Classical Greeks. The sculptor was balancing greater naturalism and propriety.

German Gothic Sculpture

German Gothic sculpture is known for depicting emotional scenes and human qualities and for its independence from the architecture. The sculptures are in high relief or in the round, often being connected with the surrounding architecture by only a pedestal and canopy. Demonstrating some of these characteristics is the *Death of the Virgin*, located in the tympanum of the south portal of Strasbourg Cathedral (**CD Fig. 14-20**). The sculpture depicts a mournful scene as the apostles react with grief at the passing of Mary. According to tradition, Mary merely fell asleep and was soon after transported to heaven in the Assumption. Christ, who had already ascended to heaven, is by her side in spirit, with a small representation of Mary's spirit in his hands. His presence foreshadows Mary's Assumption. The figures project significantly from the background of the tympanum. The expressions of the apostles display intense emotion, which is a hallmark of the German Gothic sculptures.

Another German Gothic sculpture that conveys intense emotion is a wooden sculpture called the *Virgin with the Dead Christ*, also known as the *Rottgen Pieta* (**CD Fig. 14-21**). *Pieta* means "pity" in Italian and refers to when Mary holds her dead son on her lap after the crucifixion. The most famous pieta is the one sculpted by Michelangelo during the High Renaissance. What the *Rottgen Pieta* lacks in naturalism it makes up for in emotion. Observe the intense grief on Mary's face. Notice also the body of Christ. The artist accentuates his suffering through his emaciated figure and grotesque wounds. The blood appears three-dimensional as it gushes from the wounds in Christ's hands and feet. This German Gothic sculpture would touch the emotions of viewers, forcing them to reconcile their sins with the sacrifices of this mother and son.

Stained Glass and Manuscript Illumination

Stained glass and manuscript illumination were the main forms of two-dimensional art produced during the Gothic period. Stained glass was not a new craft. Ancient Egyptian and Classical Greek artisans knew how to shape colored glass into works of art. Stained-glass windows had been used in a church as early as the fourth century. It was during the Gothic period, however, that craftsmen refined stained-glass windows to an intricate art form that is both decorative and narrative. The windows filtered natural sunlight into dazzling multicolored displays on the interior walls, in accordance with the ideas of Abbot Suger. Medieval theologians wrote about how the divine light created a deeper spirituality within churches. In addition, stained-glass windows often told biblical stories to the illiterate masses.

Manuscript illumination continued to thrive during the Gothic period. Production of books became secularized, moving away from remote monasteries to workshops in urban centers such as Paris. For the most part, the illustrated books were **moralizing Bibles** (which paired an Old Testament story on one page to a New Testament story on the next), **psalters** (book of Psalms), **breviaries** (selected prayers and psalms), and **books of hours** filled with prayers for different hours of the day. The human figures in these books appear flat, demonstrating the artists' lack of modeling and disinterest in the underlying anatomy, and have unrealistic proportions and body positions. Yet artists did convey the message of the Bible through their illustrations. Despite their unnatural and unrealistic depictions, the illuminated manuscripts display tremendous craftsmanship and opulence. The illustrations are carefully painted with detailed lines. The paints were often made from exotic materials that were expensive to obtain. Some of the pages include gold leaf, which are flattened sheets of gold attached to the pages.

Conclusion

The Gothic period continued the trend of church building set by the Romanesque period before it. Under the influence of Abbot Suger's treatises, Gothic architects strove to create buildings of ever-greater height and light. Pointed arches, ribbed vaults, and flying buttresses made the greater height possible. The architects included space for large and extensive stained-glass windows that filter light in a manner intended to pre-figure the New Jerusalem. The Gothic style grew in popularity during the thirteenth and fourteenth centuries, spreading from France to England and other European countries, where architects blended Gothic elements with their regional styles.

Sculpture in the Gothic period began to move toward greater naturalism and became independent of the architecture; instead of functioning solely as decoration for a church, sculpture was artwork in itself. German Gothic sculptors followed this trend and also added great emotion to the characters. Late Gothic sculptors used the S-curve to heighten naturalism, but they did not return completely to contrapposto. The return of contrapposto and the values of Classical art would reemerge in the fifteenth century during the Italian Renaissance.

Part 3
Renaissance Art

Chapter 15

Precursors of the Renaissance

Introduction and Exam Strategy Overview

Would you pay more than $40 million for a small painting of the Madonna and Child by an early fourteenth-century Sienese artist named Duccio? In 2004, the Metropolitan Museum of Art in New York did just that when it outbid the Louvre for the last known painting by Duccio still in private hands. Philippe de Montebello, the director of the Metropolitan, hailed the acquisition saying that, "the addition of the Duccio will enable visitors for the first time to follow the entire trajectory of European painting from its beginning to the present."

Few art historians would disagree with De Montebello. Between 1290 and 1310, two towering geniuses, Duccio di Buoninsegna from Siena and Giotto di Bondone from Florence, redefined Western art. Before Duccio and Giotto, medieval and Byzantine artists (see Chapters 10 and 12 through 14) painted stiff unsmiling figures who neither looked nor acted like real people. Led by Duccio and Giotto, a group of early fourteenth-century artists began to reject the Byzantine tradition. By rediscovering the human form, human emotions, and the natural world, these artists became the precursors of a new and revolutionary Renaissance style (see Chapter 16).

The fourteenth century is a pivotal transitional phase between the Byzantine tradition and the art and architecture of the Renaissance. The AP Art History committee has recognized the historical importance of Duccio, Giotto, and other fourteenth-century artists. Most exams contain between two and four multiple-choice questions on these artists. Since 1990, there have been four slide-based multiple-choice questions and four short essay questions. Six of these eight questions have focused on the work of Duccio and Giotto.

Florence

Florence is located along the banks of the Arno River in northern Italy. In 1300, a strong wall protected the city's crowded, narrow streets. Although the city was surrounded by fertile fields, banking and textiles formed the financial foundations for the city's growing prosperity. At a time when nearly everyone wore wool, Florence supplied Europe's population with highly prized fine wool cloth. The city's prosperous bankers and weavers helped finance an unprecedented burst of artistic creativity that would become the Renaissance.

The Florentines were filled with pride in their city. In 1294, they commissioned Arnolfo di Cambio to build a cathedral of such splendor and beauty "that no human power could ever conceive its equal." Begun two years later, Florence Cathedral (**CD Fig. 15-1**) required almost 150 years to complete (see Chapter 16).

Cimabue

The construction of Florence Cathedral and other new churches created a demand for altarpieces, chapel frescoes, and other works of art. During the final decades of the thirteenth century, Cimabue operated Florence's busiest artistic workshop.

Cimabue's best-known surviving work is a large altarpiece known as *The Virgin and Child Enthroned and Surrounded by Angels* (**CD Fig. 15-2**). Still steeped in the Byzantine tradition, Cimabue portrayed Mary in a frontal pose against a gold background. Golden highlights on the robes of the Virgin and Child enhanced their dignity. Although Byzantine in style, Cimabue's work showed the first signs of the new impulse toward naturalism. For example, Mary's rippling drapery prevented her from being a flat figure. The eight flanking angels also exhibited more natural poses.

Rise of Giotto

Giotto di Bondone (1267–1337) grew up in a small village about 14 miles from Florence. According to one of art history's best-loved stories, the young Giotto spent his days sitting in a field tending a flock of sheep and goats. Instead of daydreaming, Giotto drew a picture of a sheep on a large flat stone. As fate would have it, Cimabue passed by and was amazed by Giotto's natural skill. The master at once asked permission to take Giotto to Florence to serve as his apprentice.

Whether or not this charming story is true, Giotto did become Cimabue's apprentice. During his formative years, Giotto learned about the pioneering work of the Roman painter Pietro Cavallini and the Pisan sculptor Nicola Pisano. Both artists created works that showed an interest in a more natural representation of figures based on classical models.

Giotto's naturalistic approach can be seen in a large altarpiece of the *Madonna Enthroned*, which he painted for the Church of All Saints (Ognissanti) in Florence (**CD Fig. 15-3**). Like Cimabue, Giotto portrayed the Madonna sitting on a throne holding the Christ Child. The gold background and the lack of proportion between the Virgin and the other figures are lingering vestiges of the Byzantine tradition. However, unlike his predecessors, Giotto placed the Virgin on a realistic three-dimensional throne. Her body has both volume and form. The angels surrounding Mary also appear more natural and realistic. Indeed, two of the angels offer Mary vases containing lilies and roses drawn from nature.

Giotto and the Arena Chapel

Giotto's great fame rests on a series of fresco paintings he completed inside the Arena Chapel in Padua (**CD Fig. 15-4**). Built by Enrico Scrovegni in 1302, the Arena Chapel received its name because it stood near the ruins of a Roman theater. Enrico's enormous wealth had been inherited from his father, Reginaldo, a notorious money-lender whose exorbitant interest rates were castigated by Dante in his *Divine Comedy*. It was later said that Enrico defended his family name against a verse by Dante with a church painted by Giotto.

The Arena Chapel contains forty major fresco paintings. Giotto begins his narrative with the lives of Joachim and Anna, the Virgin's parents. He then depicts key events from Mary's life and the Ministry and Passion of Christ. The narrative cycle concludes with a dramatic painting of the Last Judgment placed over the entrance wall.

Figure 15-4. Interior of the Arena Chapel (Scrovegni Chapel), 1305–1306, Padua, Italy

Giotto's paintings demonstrate his extraordinary ability to convey a range of human emotions. For example, in *The Lamentation*, Mary is torn with sorrow as she holds her son's lifeless body and stares into his unseeing eyes (**CD Fig. 15-5**). A grief-stricken Mary Magdalene looks hopelessly at the wounds in Christ's feet while Saint John the Evangelist flings his arms back in a gesture of complete despair. Meanwhile, a group of inconsolable angels, unable to contain their anguish, hover above the mourners.

Giotto's revolutionary management of light and shade enhanced his expressive powers. Unlike the flat Byzantine figures, the people in Giotto's paintings appear to have weight and bulk. Giotto created this illusion of volume by allowing light to illuminate parts of each figure while leaving the rest in shade. This marks the first step toward the development of **chiaroscuro**, the use of dramatic contrasts of light and dark to produce modeling.

The Arena Chapel frescoes ushered in a new era in painting. Giotto abandoned the stiff forms of Byzantine art and restored the naturalistic approach developed by Greek and Roman artists. Giotto thus began a style in Western art that would endure for seven centuries.

Giotto spent his final years supervising the construction of the campanile, or bell tower, that stands beside Florence Cathedral. In an unprecedented honor for an artist, the Florentines buried Giotto's remains inside Florence Cathedral. An epitaph engraved on his tomb proudly proclaimed Giotto's role as the Father of Western Art: " I am the man who brought painting to life . . . whatever is found in nature may be found in my art."

Siena

Siena is located just 30 miles south of Florence. During the thirteenth and fourteenth centuries, the two cities competed for political power, commercial wealth, and artistic prestige.

The Sienese sought to visually express their growing prosperity through grand building projects. As evidence of their confidence and stable government, they built a Gothic city hall, the Palazzo Pubblico (**CD Fig. 15-6**). The building also included a 330-foot campanile. Each day, sharp-eyed lookouts climbed the tower's steep winding stairs to survey the surrounding countryside for approaching visitors and enemies.

While the Palazzo Pubblico served as a focus of civic pride, the city's great Gothic cathedral served as a focus of religious devotion. During one of the Sienese's many wars with the Florentines, the entire population of Siena retreated to the cathedral to pray to the Virgin Mary. Believing that Mary had listened to their fervent prayers, the Sienese army rushed out of the cathedral and routed the Florentine invaders. From then on, the Sienese looked to Mary as their special protector.

Duccio's *Maestà*

Siena proudly called itself "the Virgin's ancient city." In 1308, the directors of Siena's cathedral commissioned Duccio di Buoninsegna (ca. 1255–1318) to paint a huge altarpiece for the church's high altar. The completed two-sided work contained more than fifty panels, all painted using the technique of tempera on wood. Because the central and largest panel depicts the Virgin and Child in majesty, the entire altarpiece is called the *Maestà* (**CD Fig. 15-7**).

Figure 15-7. Duccio, Virgin and Child Enthroned with Saints, from the *Maestà* altarpiece, tempera on wood, 1308–1311, Museo dell'Opera del Duomo, Siena

The *Maestà*'s central panel reveals a strong Byzantine influence. Mary is shown enthroned as the Queen of Heaven. Dressed in a rich blue robe, she towers above the surrounding saints, angels, and apostles. A traditional gold background reminds viewers that the splendid scene takes place in heaven. The precious materials thus reinforce the work's timeless spiritual message.

Although indebted to the Byzantine tradition, the *Maestà* also reveals the new naturalism. The smaller panels on the front and back vividly demonstrate this influence. For example, the *Betrayal of Christ* panel portrays the dramatic sequence of events triggered by Judas's treacherous kiss (**CD Fig. 15-8**). Like Giotto, Duccio painted figures who show a range of emotions. The terrified apostles flee while a furious Peter cuts off the ear of the high priest's servant. Only Jesus, dressed in a purple robe reserved for royalty, remains calm amidst the chaotic scene.

The robes of each figure also display the new naturalistic impulse. Unlike the flat and rigidly erect Byzantine forms, the convincing figures that Duccio created seem animated by three-dimensional life. He achieved this illusion by carefully depicting the fall of light and shade across each figure.

The completed altarpiece was a triumph for both Duccio and Siena. A contemporary chronicler wrote that shops closed, bells rang, and townspeople flocked to see the *Maestà* installed inside Siena Cathedral. Duccio expressed his justifiable pride by writing the following prayer alongside his signature at the base of Mary's throne: "Holy Mother of God, be the cause of peace to Siena, and of life to Duccio because he painted you thus."

Simone Martini

Duccio's influence surpassed the *Maestà*. His use of luxurious colors and love of ornamental details guided a new generation of Sienese artists led by Simone Martini.

Art historians believe that Martini may have been one of Duccio's assistants on the *Maestà*.

In 1333, Martini received a commission from the directors of Siena Cathedral to paint an Annunciation altarpiece (**CD Fig. 15-9**) that would complement Duccio's *Maestà*. Martini portrayed the moment when the angel Gabriel approached Mary and pronounced the words, "Hail, Mary, full of grace, the Lord is with you." Gabriel seems almost weightless as he kneels before Mary wearing a magnificent golden gown and a richly decorated cloak. His iridescent wings point toward heaven as he presents Mary with a sumptuous vase of lilies that symbolize her purity. Startled by her heavenly visitor, Mary closes her Bible and seems stunned as she receives Gabriel's momentous news.

Martini spared no expense to create a regal setting. Both Gabriel and Mary are silhouetted against a gold background generously decorated with gold leaf. Gabriel's words are revealed in raised golden letters that form an arc connecting him to Mary. Martini's use of brilliant colors, lavish costumes, and exquisite ornamental details contributed to the development of the International Gothic style at the beginning of the fifteenth century (see Chapter 19).

Ambrogio Lorenzetti

Just five years after Simone Martini completed the *Annunciation* altarpiece, another Sienese artist, Ambrogio Lorenzetti, received a very different commission. Siena's ruling Council of Nine asked Lorenzetti to decorate the walls of their meeting hall in the Palazzo Pubblico with a vast painting contrasting the effects of good and bad government. The painting represented the first secular commission since the fall of the Roman Empire.

Lorenzetti's *Effects of Good Government in the City and in the Country* is remarkably well preserved (**CD Figs. 15-10 and 15-11**). More than 13 feet high and 27 feet long, the painting provides a realistic picture of what Siena must have looked like in the first half of the fourteenth century. The benefits of peace can be seen everywhere: prosperous merchants sell goods in well-stocked stores, attentive students listen to knowledgeable teachers, and joyous maidens clad in fashionable silks dance to the beat of a tambourine.

The blessings of peace also extend to the countryside just beyond Siena's walls. The *Peaceful Country* portion of Lorenzetti's fresco provides a sweeping view and is one of the first landscapes painted since antiquity. Groups of contented peasants work in terraced vineyards and bountiful fields that stretch to distant hills. In the upper-left corner, an allegorical figure representing Security holds a scroll with an inscription promising safety to all who live under the rule of law.

Art and Death

Lorenzetti completed the *Effects of Good Government in the City and in the Country* in 1339. At that time, both Siena and Florence appeared to be flourishing cities capable of supporting an emerging golden age of art and culture. No one could have predicted that just ten years later an outbreak of bubonic plague would devastate the population of both cities. By 1348, more than half the people of Florence and two-thirds of the citizens of Siena were dead.

Known as the Black Death, the plague spread inexorably across Europe, killing as much as one-third of the population. Anguished survivors believed that this unprecedented disaster was God's punishment for humanity's earthly sins. Art reflected this sense of mourning, misery, and self-reproach. It would take fifty years for Italy to recover and for a new generation of artists to remember the pioneering achievements of Giotto and Duccio.

Conclusion

Giotto and Duccio are the principal founders of Western European painting. The naturalistic impulse, which inspired both artists, created a style that supplanted Byzantine art and endured until Modern artists led by Picasso and Matisse changed the rules.

During the last ten years, the AP Art History committee has placed particular emphasis on the pioneering works of both Giotto and Duccio. Students should give special attention to *The Lamentation* as they review Giotto's paintings in the Arena Chapel. Do not neglect Siena's artistic contributions. Duccio's *Maestà* and Lorenzetti's *Effects of Good Government in the City and in the Country* are both landmark works. And finally, closely examine a picture of the Palazzo Pubblico. Recent tests have expected students to know that it is a Gothic structure located in Siena.

Chapter 16

The Early Renaissance

Introduction and Exam Strategy Overview

What do fifth-century Athens, Republican Rome, and fifteenth-century Florence have in common? Florence's proud citizens had a ready answer to this question. They believed Florence was the new Athens and the heir of the ancient Roman Republic.

The Florentines had a strong argument. By the beginning of the fifteenth century, Florence had become one of the most prosperous cities in Europe. It was also the most historically self-conscious. Led by intellectuals known as **humanists**, the Florentines devalued their medieval past and looked instead to the ancient Greeks and Romans for inspiration and knowledge.

During the fifteenth century, or *Quattrocento*, Florence became the acknowledged center of the **Renaissance**—the rebirth of classical learning, literature, and art. Humanists revived the ancient Greek ideal that "man is the measure of all things." They believed that contact with the classical past would enrich their own culture by promoting civic responsibility, encouraging artistic creativity, and rewarding individual excellence.

Art historians have traditionally divided the Italian Renaissance into two distinct phases. The first phase, the Early Renaissance, began in Florence and lasted most of the fifteenth century. The second phase, the High Renaissance, began in Rome in the early 1500s and later spread to Venice. This chapter will focus on the early Renaissance, and Chapter 17 will describe the High Renaissance.

The Early Renaissance is a particularly important topic on the AP Art History exam. As you learned in Chapter 1, the exam devotes approximately 25 percent of its questions to architecture, 25 percent to sculpture, and 50 percent to painting. Because the Early Renaissance made pivotal contributions in all three areas, it has generated a large number of exam questions. Most AP Art History exams have four to six multiple-choice questions on the Early Renaissance. In addition, since 1984, there have been twelve slide-based multiple-choice questions and twelve short essay questions. Early Renaissance works of art can also be used as illustrative examples in your long essays. The Early Renaissance is clearly an essential building block in constructing a coalition of points for your "drive for a 5."

The Baptistery Competition

In 1401, the Guild of Cloth Merchants decided to sponsor a competition to determine who would win a commission to cast a new set of doors for the octagonal-shaped Baptistery. Located in front of Florence Cathedral, the Baptistery was a venerated building where every child in Florence was baptized.

The competition rules called for each contestant to submit a trial panel based on the story of Abraham's sacrifice of Isaac. As described in Genesis 22:2–13, God ordered Abraham to sacrifice his only son, Isaac. Obedient to God's will, Abraham prepared to use a long, sharp knife to slash Isaac's throat. At the last moment, an angel intervened, and Abraham sacrificed a ram instead.

The competitors spent a year translating this biblical story into a bronze panel. After much debate, the judges and the people of Florence were divided between the merits of panels submitted by two young goldsmiths: Filippo Brunelleschi and Lorenzo Ghiberti (**CD Figs. 16-1 and 16-2**). In Brunelleschi's panel, Abraham lunges forward and violently seizes Isaac's throat. An angel swoops in from the left to grasp Abraham's arm and thereby saves Isaac.

Brunelleschi's panel conveys power and dramatic action. In contrast, the figures in Ghiberti's panel are more graceful and elegant. Ghiberti cast Abraham in a traditional Gothic *S* curve. Isaac, however, is a beautifully idealized nude, clearly inspired by classical models. Ghiberti's successful blend of Gothic and classical styles won the judge's approval. The victorious Ghiberti gloated, "I had surpassed everyone."

Brunelleschi and the Dome of the Florence Cathedral

The Baptistery competition marked a turning point for the careers of both Ghiberti and Brunelleschi. Ghiberti spent the next twenty years casting twenty-eight door panels depicting scenes from the New Testament. As discussed later in the chapter, pleased church officials then offered him an even more prestigious commission that won Ghiberti lasting fame and glory.

While the triumphant Ghiberti worked on his first set of doors, Brunelleschi angrily left Florence and traveled to Rome. Fascinated by the ancient ruins, he measured Roman monuments to rediscover the exact measurements of the Doric, Ionic, and Corinthian orders. Brunelleschi devoted special attention to studying the Pantheon and its dome.

Brunelleschi's meticulous study of Roman architectural principles fired his imagination and prepared him for a historic achievement. In 1417, Florentine officials announced a competition to design and construct a dome for the Florence Cathedral. Although begun in 1296, the cathedral still lacked a dome to cap its 138-foot-wide crossing. Many baffled architects considered the task impossible.

Undaunted, Brunelleschi submitted a winning plan and began work in 1420. He combined his knowledge of Roman engineering principles with innovative building techniques to construct a 100-foot-high dome that seemed to reach heavenward without any visible means of support (**CD Fig. 16-3**). In fact, the dome's weight is borne by eight white marble ribs that span the dome from its base to the marble lantern at the peak. These eight ribs are in turn supplemented by sixteen concealed ribs radiating from the center.

The completed dome became a visible symbol of Florence's piety, power, and ingenuity. Today, visitors who climb the 463 steps to reach the lantern are rewarded with a magnificent panoramic view of Florence and its surrounding countryside.

Brunelleschi and the Renaissance Style of Architecture

Brunelleschi's work on the dome did not prevent him from accepting other commissions. In 1419, the Silk Merchants Guild hired him to design a hospital for abandoned children. The Ospedale degli Innocenti (Hospital of the Innocents) enabled Brunelleschi to apply the principles of balance, harmony, and proportion he discovered during his study of ancient Roman buildings (**CD Fig. 16-4**).

A continuous **loggia**, or covered walkway, dominates the hospital's facade. The loggia illustrates Brunelleschi's conviction that good architecture lay in choosing harmonious proportions. The loggia is divided into square bays with sides equal to the height of the columns. The beautifully proportioned columns support classical round arches that give the facade a rhythmic harmony.

The loggia's precise mathematical ratios and graceful rhythm embody the new Renaissance style of architecture. Brunelleschi applied these principles to the interior of the Church of Santo Spirito (**CD Fig. 16-5**). He rejected the soaring vertical emphasis that was the hallmark of Gothic cathedrals. Instead, Santo Spirito's nave arcade is composed of a series of arches supported by Corinthian columns. The row of columns guides the worshipper's eye toward the altar.

Brunelleschi divided Santo Spirito's side aisles into square bays that govern the church's interior design. The nave is twice as wide as the side aisle, and the crossing square is four times as large as the side aisle. The arcade and the clerestory are each as high as the nave is wide. Santo Spirito thus fully expresses the new Renaissance commitment to graceful symmetrical buildings that reflect the classical quest for harmonious and perfect proportions.

Brunelleschi and Linear Perspective

In addition to establishing the principles of Renaissance architecture, Brunelleschi is credited with the invention of **linear perspective** (**CD Fig. 16-6**). Linear or one-point perspective is a geometric method of creating the illusion of depth on a flat two-dimensional space. It is one of the most significant discoveries in the history of Western art.

As conceived by Brunelleschi, linear perspective theory is based on two ways the eye perceives an object. First, parallel lines receding from us seem to converge at one point on the horizon. These receding parallel lines running at right angles to the front edge of a painting are called **orthogonals**. The point where they converge is called the **vanishing point**. Second, figures or objects that are farther away from the eye appear smaller than those that are closer. This effect is called **diminution**. Brunelleschi proved that the diminution in the size of objects is in direct proportion to their distance from us and that space is, therefore, measurable.

Brunelleschi demonstrated his theory of linear perspective in two paintings that are now lost. Fortunately, Leon Battista Alberti described Brunelleschi's theory in his *De Pictura* (*On Painting*), written in 1435. Alberti compared the picture surface to "an open window through which the subject painted is to be seen."

Renaissance artists quickly incorporated linear perspective into their work. The idea of a painting being a window through which the viewer sees a scene dominated Western art for the next five hundred years.

Ghiberti and the Gates of Paradise

As mentioned earlier, Ghiberti won the competition to create a set of doors for the Baptistery. As a result of his successful completion of this project, he received a commission to create a second set of doors devoted to ten episodes from the Old Testament. Ghiberti began work in 1425 and twenty-seven years later completed the doors known as the Gates of Paradise (**CD Fig. 16-7**).

Ghiberti used two techniques to create the illusion of depth. Most importantly, he applied the principles of linear perspective discovered by his great rival, Brunelleschi. He also skillfully varied the relief of his figures by placing high-relief objects in the foreground and low-relief objects in the background.

The *Jacob and Esau* panel clearly illustrates how Ghiberti used these two techniques to create a convincing illusion of depth (**CD Fig. 16-8**). The squares marked out in the pavement establish orthogonals that recede to a central vanishing point under the main arch. At the same time, the foreground figures are all cast in high relief, and the figures and classical buildings in the background are cast in ever-diminishing low relief.

Ghiberti's work combined classical figures and architecture with a firm understanding of the newly discovered rules of perspective to create a work of matchless grace and beauty. When Michelangelo saw the doors, he proclaimed them worthy to serve as the "Gates of Paradise."

Masaccio and the "Hole in the Wall"

In 1425, startled visitors gathered inside the church of Santa Maria Novella in Florence to view a revolutionary painting by a young and previously unknown artist nicknamed Masaccio ("Careless Tom"). Named the *Holy Trinity*, the fresco created the illusion of depth so successfully that viewers gasped in awe at what they called "the hole in the wall" (**CD Fig. 16-9**).

The *Holy Trinity* presents a deceptively simple group of figures. God the Father stands in the center holding a cross and presenting his crucified son to us. Mary and John the Evangelist stand at the foot of the cross. The kneeling figures standing outside the sacred space are the two donors who commissioned the painting. The bottom portion of the painting contains a skeleton resting on a ledge. Above the skeleton, a somber inscription warns, "I was once what you are; what I am, you will be."

The four holy figures occupy a chapel that closely resembles contemporary works by Brunelleschi. Two graceful classical columns support a painted round arch. The chapel's barrel-vaulted ceiling appears to recede into the distance. Masaccio created this illusion of depth by making the ceiling's receding lines orthogonals that converge at a vanishing point at the base of the cross.

Holy Trinity also provides a particularly vivid example of a **pyramid or triangular composition**. Rather than placing his figures along a horizontal line, Masaccio linked them in a series of interlocking pyramids. For example, the heads of Mary and John the Evangelist are the base of a triangle with apexes at the heads of both Christ and God the Father. A similar set of triangles is formed with the heads of God the Father, Christ, and the two donors. First used by Masaccio, the pyramid configuration became one of the hallmarks of Renaissance art.

Masaccio and the Brancacci Chapel

The remarkable success of the *Holy Trinity* contributed to Masaccio's growing fame and led to a prestigious commission to paint a series of frescoes for the Brancacci Chapel of the Church of the Santa Maria del Carmine in Florence. The frescoes depict scenes from the life of Saint Peter. Masaccio painted about half of the twelve frescoes.

The *Tribute Money* provides a highly praised example of Masaccio's bold innovations (**CD Fig. 16-10**). The painting is a **continuous narration** in which the same figure appears more than once in the same space at different stages of the story. In the center, a Roman tax collector demands that Christ and his apostles pay a tax. The apostles are worried and fearful because they do not have enough money. But Christ, with a majestic sweep of his arm, tells Peter to go to the nearby Sea of Galilee where he will find a gold coin in the mouth of a fish. Although incredulous, Peter obeys Christ, finds the coin, and pays the tax collector.

Figure 16-10. Masaccio, *Tribute Money*, fresco, ca. 1427, Brancacci Chapel of the Church of the Santa Maria del Carmine, Florence

Masaccio's figures represent a revolutionary step in Western art. The tax collector, apostles, and Christ are solid three-dimensional figures, all standing in balanced contrapposto. A constant light source creates a realistic blend of light and shade. This chiaroscuro gives each figure the illusion of volume. Masaccio thus completed Giotto's pioneering innovations by depicting real people who occupy real space.

Like Giotto, Masaccio created figures whose faces and gestures express powerful emotions. In Masaccio's most dramatic painting, Adam and Eve are expelled from the Garden of Eden because they yielded to temptation (**CD Fig. 16-11**). Overwhelmed with guilt, Eve throws her head back and helplessly cries out in anguished pain. She covers herself with her hands to hide her nakedness. Standing helplessly beside Eve, Adam stoops with shame as he hides his face.

Masaccio's brilliant career was tragically cut short when he was 27 years old and suddenly died in Rome under mysterious and still unexplained circumstances. Some historians theorize that jealous rivals poisoned him. Despite his premature death, Masaccio's influence continued. As part of their training, Michelangelo and other aspiring artists carefully studied Masaccio's paintings in the Brancacci Chapel. And to this day, visitors still stand in awe as they look at Masaccio's famed "hole in the wall."

Nanni di Banco and Donatello at Or San Michele

During the fifteenth century, Florentine artists worked in an environment that encouraged creativity and rewarded excellence. As we have seen, city officials often used competitions to attract talent and heighten interest in a project. In 1406, the city assigned each niche on the exterior wall of Or San Michele to a specific guild. The guild was then responsible for decorating the niche with a statue of its patron saint. The guilds competed to hire the best sculptors, who in turn competed to create the most impressive statues.

The Guild of Wood and Stone Carvers hired Nanni di Banco to fill their niche with four life-sized marble statues of their martyred patron saints. During the late third century, these four Christian sculptors refused Diocletian's order to carve a statue of a pagan deity. Diocletian, who was well known for persecuting Christians, promptly executed the four Christian sculptors.

Nanni chose to portray the crucial moment when the four sculptors debate whether to compromise their religious beliefs by carving the idol or submit to death. The four figures stand in a tight semicircle. The figure on the right speaks while two of his colleagues listen intently and a third gazes into the distance, weighing their grim choices.

Known as the *Four Crowned Saints*, the sculptural group closely resembles Roman portrait statues (**CD Fig. 16-12**). All four wear full Roman togas that partially cover their feet. Their grave, determined faces command the viewer's attention and respect.

The Linen Weaver's Guild, perhaps eager to surpass Nanni's successful sculpture, turned to Donatello to fill their niche with a statue of Saint Mark. Donatello had unusual credentials. Although still only in his mid-twenties, he had worked for Ghiberti and traveled to Rome with Brunelleschi.

The commission gave Donatello an opportunity to demonstrate what he learned from studying ancient works of sculpture. Saint Mark's powerful hands grip a copy of his gospels, while his alert eyes seem to survey the street (**CD Fig. 16-13**). Unlike medieval statues that were rigidly attached to a wall, Saint Mark seems ready to step out of his niche at any moment.

Saint Mark's pose closely resembles ancient Greek and Roman figures. Like the *Doryphoros* (see Chapter 6), Saint Mark's straight right leg supports his weight while his relaxed left leg is bent at the knee. Saint Mark's flowing robe reveals his contrapposto pose while cleverly reminding viewers of the linen weavers' products.

Figure 16-13. Donatello, *Saint Mark*, 1411–1413, Or San Michele

Saint Mark helped launch Donatello's long and amazingly versatile career. Both his contemporaries and modern art historians consider Donatello the most important Renaissance sculptor before Michelangelo.

The Medici

Florentine artists depended on churches, guilds, and wealthy families for commissions. The Medici family dominated Florence's economic, political, and artistic life for much of the fifteenth century. The Medici earned their wealth as bankers and spent much of it as humanists. Led by Cosimo (1389–1464), Piero (1416–1464), and Lorenzo the Magnificent (1449–1492), the Medici financed libraries, built churches, sponsored the Platonic Academy of Philosophy, and commissioned hundreds of artworks. Like Pericles and Augustus, the Medici understood how the power of imagery could be used to extend their fame and influence.

The Medici and Donatello

The Medici recognized Donatello's great talent. Sometime between the late 1420s and the late 1450s, they awarded Donatello a commission to cast a bronze statue of the biblical hero David. In the Bible, David, armed only with a sling and a rock, places his faith in God and slays the Philistine giant Goliath. The Florentines identified with David. As David had conquered Goliath, so had Florence overcome the boastful Duke of Milan when he attempted to conquer their city in 1402.

Donatello's bronze *David* marked a milestone in Early Renaissance art (**CD Fig. 16-14**). Possibly inspired by Greek and Roman statues in the Medici collection, Donatello chose to portray David as a nude youth. The statue thus became the first freestanding, life-size nude statue cast since antiquity. Holding Goliath's sword in one hand and a rock in the other, David triumphantly stands over the Philistine's severed head in a relaxed contrapposto pose.

The Medici installed *David* in the courtyard of their Florence palace. David's courage and faith may have been a daily reminder of the qualities needed to administer the Medici banks while guiding the Florentine Republic.

The Medici and Pollaiuolo

Given the Medici's desire to associate their family with Florence's symbolic heroes, it is not surprising that they commissioned Antonio Pollaiuolo to cast a bronze statue of Hercules. The Florentines identified with the Greek hero and even placed his image on their state seal.

Pollaiuolo created a small but remarkable statue (**CD Fig. 16-15**). Standing only 18 inches high, the statue depicts Hercules locked in a ferocious struggle with Antaeus, the son of the earth goddess. Since Antaeus gains renewed strength from contact with the earth, Hercules must lift him off the ground and then crush his waist. Pollaiuolo depicted the intertwined figures locked in a mortal struggle. Antaeus gasps for air as he desperately attempts to break free from Hercules's grip. Most statues were designed to be viewed from the front, but Pollaiuolo intended *Hercules and Antaeus* to be viewed from all sides.

Hercules and Antaeus gave Pollaiuolo an opportunity to display his skill in depicting the human figure in action. He continued to explore this subject in an engraving titled *Battle of the Ten Nudes* (**CD Fig. 16-16**). Although the classical origin of this print is unknown, its purpose is clear. Pollaiuolo portrays naked men fighting each other in a variety of poses. Their lean and muscular figures enabled Pollaiuolo to demonstrate his detailed knowledge of human anatomy.

The Medici and Botticelli

The Early Renaissance reached its peak during the lifetime of Lorenzo the Magnificent. Lorenzo established the Platonic Academy of Philosophy, consisting of scholars, poets, and artists who discussed ancient philosophy at a Medici country villa. This intimate circle of friends included an artist affectionately nicknamed Botticelli ("Little Barrel").

Sandro Botticelli had served as an apprentice under Antonio Pollaiuolo. But where Pollaiuolo's lines emphasize action, Botticelli's are renowned for their grace and rhythm. Recognizing Botticelli's talent, the Medici commissioned a number of paintings, including the *Birth of Venus*, to adorn private rooms in their country villa.

The *Birth of Venus* is one of the most famous and beautiful paintings created during the Early Renaissance (**CD Fig. 16-17**). The painting illustrates the birth of Venus, goddess of love. Blown by Zephyr and the nymph Chloris, Venus floats ashore on a scallop shell. Flora welcomes Venus to her earthly home and prepares to clothe the naked goddess in a garment embroidered with delicate flowers.

Botticelli borrowed ancient forms while updating ancient philosophy. A Roman statue owned by the Medici and known as the *Medici Venus* served as the model for Botticelli's Venus. Her beautiful but sad expression may be a portrait of Simonetta Vespucci, a renowned beauty who unexpectedly died at the age of just 22. Venus may also be a Neoplatonic symbol of the rebirth of beauty and divine love.

Palla Strozzi and Gentile da Fabriano

The Medici family was not the only powerful Florentine family committed to supporting the arts. Palla Strozzi's wealth and learning made him a formidable rival. In 1422, Strozzi commissioned Gentile da Fabriano to paint an altarpiece for his family chapel in the church of Santa Trinita.

Completed in 1423, Gentile's *Adoration of the Magi* is a particularly ornate example of the International Gothic style (**CD Fig. 16-18**). A magnificent triple-arched gilt frame encloses the altarpiece. In the central scene, the Three Kings lead a splendid procession of lavishly dressed aristocrats who have come to venerate the Christ child. The procession includes a portrait of Palla Strozzi that proclaims his piety and displays his aristocratic rank.

Although the altarpiece clearly embodies the International Gothic style, Gentile did demonstrate knowledge of Early Renaissance innovations. The **predella**, or base of the altarpiece, contains scenes depicting the Nativity, the Flight into Egypt, and the Presentation in the Temple. The Presentation scene takes place in a Renaissance architectural setting inspired by Brunelleschi's work. In the central panel, Gentile abandoned the conventional gold background and created an atmospheric landscape with a real blue sky. And finally, the Nativity scene includes modeled figures that demonstrate an awareness of chiaroscuro.

The Rucellai Family and Alberti

Giovanni Rucellai was a wealthy merchant who made a fortune manufacturing highly prized red dye. Rucellai used his wealth to build a palace for his family and a new façade for his church. He hired Leon Battista Alberti to perform both tasks.

Although others might have been daunted by these commissions, Alberti welcomed the challenge. Personifying the spirit of the Renaissance, he confidently proclaimed, "Man can do anything if he will." This was not an idle boast. As previously noted, Alberti had written a treatise, *On Painting*, that described Brunelleschi's system of linear perspective. In addition, Alberti studied Vitruvius's ancient texts and then wrote his own work, *On Architecture*. The Rucellai commissions thus provided an opportunity for Alberti to apply his principles of harmonious proportions to actual buildings.

Alberti began by using classical elements to embellish the Palazzo Rucellai's façade (**CD Fig. 16-19**). He employed horizontal entablatures to divide the palazzo's flat surface into three equal stories. Inspired by the Roman Colosseum (see Chapter 8), Alberti chose Tuscan pilasters for the ground floor, Ionic for the second floor, and Corinthian for the third floor. Round arches frame the second- and third-story windows, thus enhancing the classical effect. And finally, a projecting cornice crowns the third floor and completes Alberti's harmonious classical design.

Pleased by Alberti's work, the Rucellai family hired him to design a facade for the thirteenth-century Gothic church of Santa Maria Novella (**CD Fig. 16-20**). Alberti used the commission to once again create a mathematically proportional and thus harmonious design.

Alberti divided the church façade into a system of three squares. The two lower squares flank a classical portal formed by two Ionic pilasters and a round arch. The second story includes a third square that supports a triangular pediment. A pair of graceful scrolls frame the upper scroll and hide the clerestory. The height of Santa Maria Novella equals its width, so the entire facade can be inscribed in a square.

Princely Courts Outside Florence

Florentine artists created a revolutionary new style of art based on linear perspective, chiaroscuro, and a pyramid or triangular configuration. These hallmark traits soon spread to princely courts across Italy. Wealthy rulers hired Florentine artists to design buildings and create works of art intended to underscore their power and enhance their fame.

Alberti in Mantua

The marquisate of Mantua was located in northern Italy between Venice and Milan. Its ruler, Marquis Ludovico Gonzaga (1412–1478), dreamed of transforming Mantua into a center of Renaissance art and culture. In 1470, he enticed Alberti to work in Mantua by offering him a highly prized commission to redesign the church of Sant' Andrea.

Alberti's ambitious design called for a facade that combined a classical temple portico with a Roman triumphal arch (**CD Fig. 16-21**). Visitors approaching the church must have been surprised by the absence of statues and other Gothic features. Instead, they saw a majestic arch framed by colossal pilasters that ran uninterrupted through three stories. The pilasters supported a classically inspired pediment.

Alberti's innovative design did not end with the facade. In his voluminous writings, Alberti had long criticized the use of columns in the nave arcade. He argued that a colonnade prevented many members of the congregation from fully seeing holy ceremonies taking place at the altar. Therefore, Alberti replaced the columned arcade with a barrel-vaulted nave.

Figure 16-21. Leon Battista Alberti, west facade of Sant' Andrea, ca. 1470, Mantua

Sant' Andrea marked a decisive break with Christian building traditions. By achieving the Renaissance ideal of combining ancient forms with Christian uses, Alberti created a "Christian temple" that strongly influenced the design of future Renaissance and Baroque churches.

Mantegna in Mantua

While Alberti worked at Sant' Andrea, another renowned artist, Andrea Mantegna (1431–1506), painted for the Gonzaga family at their Ducal Palace in Mantua. Mantegna served as court painter to the Gonzagas for almost fifty years. Although he painted many masterpieces, Mantegna created his most famous work in a chamber of the Ducal Palace called the Camera Picta ("Painted Room").

The Camera Picta celebrates both the Gonzaga's brilliant court and Mantegna's extraordinary skill (**CD Fig. 16-22**). Mantegna covered the walls with detailed portraits of the Gonzaga family, their courtiers, and even their pet dog. The scenes provide historians with a wealth of information about courtly manners and dress.

As impressive as the Camera Picta's walls were to visiting dignitaries, its ceilings often left them speechless with wonder. In a triumphant demonstration of his command of perspective, Mantegna painted an illusionist oculus that appears to be an opening to a cloud-filled sky. Young women seem to look over a marble balustrade while several **putti**, or nude children, play along its edges. Many startled visitors called for help, afraid that the "children" would fall and hurt themselves.

Perugino in Rome

Florence and other northern Italian cities dominated the Early Renaissance. However, as the fifteenth century drew to a close, a new generation of popes led by Sixtus IV began to assert Rome's religious and cultural leadership. In 1481, Sixtus commissioned a cycle of paintings for the newly built Sistine Chapel.

Pietro Vannucci, better known as Perugino, was one of the artists summoned to Rome. In just two years, Perugino completed a large fresco titled *Christ Delivering the Keys of the Kingdom to Saint Peter* (**CD Fig. 16-23**). Christ and Saint Peter dominate the center of the painting. Christ calmly and deliberately hands the keys to the Kingdom of Heaven to the apostle Peter. This symbolic transfer of authority provided the biblical support for the papacy's claim to infallible and total authority over the Roman Catholic Church.

Perugino used all the major Early Renaissance innovations to create a convincing pictorial space for this vital theological message. Christ and Saint Peter stand amid an imaginary gathering of the Twelve Apostles and a number of Renaissance contemporaries. Perugino used chiaroscuro to carefully model each figure.

The apostles and Renaissance contemporaries all stand in the foreground of a large piazza. The vertical lines perpendicular to the picture plane are orthogonals that converge at a vanishing point located in the door of the church positioned at the center of the horizon line. Two triumphant arches modeled after the Arch of Constantine flank the church. The arches form the base of a triangle whose apex consists of the all-important keys Christ is handing to Saint Peter!

The Decline of Florence

Perugino's painting accurately symbolized the papacy's rising power. While Rome began to assert its leadership, Florence experienced a series of setbacks. In 1492, the last of the great Medici leaders, Lorenzo the Magnificent, unexpectedly died. A Dominican monk named Girolamo Savonarola quickly moved to fill the power vacuum.

Savonarola called on the people of Florence to repent their sins. He denounced the Medici as irresponsible rulers and condemned humanism as heretical nonsense. Savonarola told the Florentines to burn their "vanities"—their jewels, their fancy dresses, their foolish classical books, and even their paintings. Fervent converts, including Botticelli, hurled their treasures into a great bonfire.

Savonarola's power proved to be short lived. Supported by the pope, the Florentines turned against Savonarola. In 1498, the Florentines executed him in the same square where only a year before they had eagerly made a bonfire of their vanities.

Historians still debate the impact of Savonarola's rise and fall. Art historians, however, have a far more definitive viewpoint. The fall of the Medici and Savonarola's fiery tirades denouncing humanism ended Florence's golden age. As the sixteenth century began, Rome became the center of a new and momentous period of art known as the High Renaissance.

Conclusion

The Early Renaissance marked a watershed in the history of Western art. Led by Masaccio, artists learned to use chiaroscuro and one-point perspective to create the illusion of three-dimensional space. Sculptors, led by Donatello, revived contrapposto and gave their statues human emotions. Architects, following the lead of Brunelleschi and Alberti, combined classical forms with Christian traditions to create a new style of church architecture. The AP Art History committee has always devoted a number of questions to these figures and the masterpieces they created.

Chapter 17

Giants of the High Renaissance

Introduction and Exam Strategy Overview

Who would you rank as the most famous artist in world history? The chances are very good that you named either Leonardo da Vinci or Michelangelo. Both are renowned for creating some of the most celebrated works in the history of art.

Da Vinci and Michelangelo worked during a period of art history known as the High Renaissance. The High Renaissance began in the late fifteenth century and extended to the middle of the sixteenth century. Although Florence and Venice were important artistic centers, Rome dominated the period. Artists from all across Italy came to Rome to decorate palaces, paint altarpieces, and build the new St. Peter's Cathedral.

Although many artists worked during the High Renaissance, the accomplishments of Leonardo da Vinci, Michelangelo, Raphael, Bramante, and Titian profoundly influenced both their contemporaries and succeeding generations of artists. These artists all mastered the laws of perspective and understood how to depict the human form. Patrons and critics measured their greatness by their inventiveness, imagination, and ability to create works of ideal beauty. Taken together, the five giants of the High Renaissance dramatically elevated the prestige of artists. No longer mere artisans, artists came to be regarded as almost divine creative geniuses.

The AP Art History exam reflects the importance of the High Renaissance. Most exams have three to four multiple-choice questions on the period. In addition, since 1983, eight slide-based multiple-choice questions and eleven short essay questions have appeared in exams. It is important to note that four of the slide-based multiple-choice questions and five of the short essay questions have focused on the works of Michelangelo. It is also important to remember that High Renaissance works of art can frequently be used as illustrative examples in long essays.

Leonardo da Vinci and the *Last Supper*

Leonardo da Vinci (1452–1519) personifies the Renaissance spirit of curiosity and exploration. Blessed with unique and varied gifts, he produced paintings of unequalled beauty. But his notebooks reveal that painting was just one of the many activities that interested him. Da Vinci was also skilled in anatomy, botany, geology, architecture, music, military science, and much more.

Da Vinci was born in Vinci, a little village lying between Florence and Pisa. His father recognized his son's precocious talents and sent him to the studio of Andrea Verrochio. A highly regarded sculptor and artist, Verrochio trained the young artist for ten years.

Da Vinci left Florence in 1482 to work for Ludovico Sforza, the duke of Milan. As one of Italy's richest and largest cities, Milan seemed like an ideal location for an aspiring artist. Da Vinci thus joined the ranks of great artists and humanists who spent their lives drifting from court to court in pursuit of commissions.

In 1495, Duke Ludovico commissioned Da Vinci to decorate the refectory of the Dominican monastery of Santa Maria delle Grazie. Because the refectory is the room where monks meet to eat their meals, artists traditionally used the space to portray the theme of the Last Supper. For example, a half century earlier, Andrea del Castagno painted his *Last Supper* for a Benedictine convent in Florence. Following tradition, Castagno separated Judas by placing him alone on the opposite side of the table from Christ and the other disciples (**CD Fig. 17-1**).

Da Vinci's *Last Supper* portrait represented a dramatic break with this tradition. Christ and his twelve disciples are seated behind a long table placed parallel to the picture plane and to the monks seated below. Christ seems to offer the bread and wine from the picture to the real diners outside the painting (**CD Fig. 17-2**).

While Castagno had not fully mastered linear perspective, Da Vinci created a fictive room that appears to be a continuation of the real refectory. Da Vinci achieved this depth by placing the central vanishing point behind Jesus' head in the exact middle of the painting. The three windows behind Jesus symbolize the Trinity while also giving the work greater depth. Equally symbolic, the light behind Jesus' head forms a halo, reminding viewers of Christ's role as the "light of the world."

Da Vinci's innovations extended beyond his placement of the disciples and his mastery of linear perspective. In one of his notebooks, Da Vinci wrote, "A good painter has two chief objectives to paint—man and the intensity of his soul. The former is easy, the latter hard, for it must be expressed by gestures and movement of limbs."

Da Vinci attempted to portray the intensity of man's soul by depicting the dramatic moment when Christ announced the fateful words, "One of you shall betray me." Symmetrically arranged in four groups, the apostles react with varying degrees of shock, incredulity, and horror. Judas, his face cloaked in shadows, recoils from Christ, knowing that he is a traitor.

Preferring to work slowly, Da Vinci scorned the customary technique of painting swiftly on wet plaster. Instead, he used oil, varnish, and pigments mixed in his own proportions. His experiment proved to be a tragic error. An irreversible process of deterioration set in during Da Vinci's own lifetime. Numerous attempts to repair the damage have failed to fully restore the painting.

Leonardo da Vinci and the *Mona Lisa*

In 1499, the French invasion of Milan prompted Da Vinci to return to Florence. Within a short time, he began work on a portrait of Lisa di Antonio Maria Gherardini, the 24-year-old wife of a prominent Florentine merchant. The *Mona Lisa* has become the world's most famous painting. Because it is surprisingly small (2 feet 6 inches by 1 foot 9 inches) and does not tell a story, the *Mona Lisa* often disappoints visitors who try to glimpse it through the crowds that always surround it at the Louvre (**CD Fig. 17-3**).

Figure 17-3. Leonardo da Vinci, *Mona Lisa*, ca. 1503–1505

Despite these limitations, the *Mona Lisa* is a revolutionary painting. Before the *Mona Lisa*, most female portraits showed profile views that emphasized the woman's expensive clothing and jewelry. In contrast, Da Vinci used a three-quarter pose. The *Mona Lisa* wears no jewelry and seems to directly face the viewer. Her enigmatic smile and the mysterious mountain landscape behind her give the painting its timeless appeal.

The *Mona Lisa* also demonstrates Da Vinci's mastery of aerial perspective and a technique he invented called **sfumato**. As a result of his use of aerial perspective, the landscape seems to fade away into the muted blues and greens of the horizon. At the same time, Da Vinci's use of sfumato, or misty haziness, softens his forms so that one color area subtly blends into the next.

The *Mona Lisa* is one of just twenty paintings completed by Da Vinci. However, Da Vinci's fame does not rest entirely on his paintings. He filled his notebooks with more than 5,500 pages of drawings that illustrate his astounding range of interests. Precise drawings such as *Embryo in the Womb* corrected longstanding errors and began the scientific study of human anatomy (**CD Fig. 17-4**).

Bramante and the Tempietto

Da Vinci was not the only famous artist who left Milan in 1499. After the city fell to the French, the renowned architect Donato Bramante traveled to Rome. Like Brunelleschi and Alberti, Bramante carefully studied the ancient Roman ruins.

Within a short time, Bramante received a commission from King Ferdinand and Queen Isabella of Spain to build a small shrine to mark the site of St. Peter's crucifixion. Bramante chose to design a circular temple. Centrally planned churches often served as a mausoleum for early Christian martyrs. In addition, Bramante and other Renaissance thinkers believed that the circle represented an ideal geometric form. Lacking a beginning or end, the circle symbolizes the perfection of God and the harmony of the world (**CD Fig. 17-5**).

Known as the Tempietto, or "Little Temple," the completed building exemplifies High Renaissance architectural ideals. The Tempietto is constructed in concentric circles. Its circular peristyle of sixteen Doric columns surrounds a cylindrical cella and supports an elegant balustrade. The distance between the columns is four times their diameter, demonstrating the Renaissance use of simple mathematical ratios to create harmonious proportions. A tall drum, or circular wall, supports a hemispheric dome. The Tempietto's small dome inspired domes from St. Peter's Basilica to the Capitol in Washington, D.C.

Julius II, Bramante, and the New St. Peter's

The Tempietto established Bramante as Rome's leading architect and brought him to the attention of Pope Julius II. A leader of vast energy and sweeping vision, Julius II strove to revitalize Rome and reassert papal authority. Like the Roman emperors, he understood the ability of artists to create visible symbols of power.

In 1506, Julius II entrusted Bramante with the task of rebuilding St. Peter's Basilica. Although Old Saint Peter's was one of the most revered churches in Christendom, it had fallen into disrepair. Julius II boldly demanded a magnificent new church that would simultaneously mark the burial spot of the first pope and overshadow all the monuments of imperial Rome.

Bramante promptly proposed to replace the Early Christian basilica with a centrally planned church. His design called for a huge round dome that would crown the crossing of the barrel-vaulted arms of a Greek cross. While the cruciform shape of Old Saint Peter's symbolized salvation, the central plan would express the Renaissance ideals of harmony and order **(CD Fig. 17-6)**.

Rebuilding St. Peter's proved to be an enormous undertaking that required vast sums of money. Although Julius II laid the cornerstone in 1506, the cathedral was not completed until 1626. As we will see, succeeding architects substantially altered Bramante's design.

Michelangelo's Early Sculptures

Like Leonardo da Vinci, Michelangelo (1475–1564) is representative of the artistic achievements of the High Renaissance. To his awed contemporaries, Michelangelo was a supremely gifted genius who could not be limited by normal artistic rules. For Michelangelo, art was a compulsive inner calling rather than a profession. His towering achievements and dominating personality forever changed the status of artists.

Michelangelo's artistic style was formed in Florence. He learned fresco techniques in the workshop of Ghirlandaio. Michelangelo often visited the Brancacci Chapel where he carefully copied Masaccio's masterpieces. Lorenzo de' Medici recognized Michelangelo's immense gifts and invited him to live in the Medici Palace where he would be surrounded by artists, poets, and scholars. Inspired by the Medici's collection of ancient statues, Michelangelo studied sculpture and was soon recognized as one of Florence's foremost sculptors **(CD Fig. 17-7)**.

In 1497, Michelangelo received a commission to sculpt a marble pieta for a French cardinal living in Rome. The contract stipulated that the completed sculpture would be "the most beautiful work of marble in Rome." Michelangelo more than met this stipulation. Michelangelo's *Pieta* is the first great sculpture of the High Renaissance. The eloquently simple figures of Mary and Christ convey a range of poignant emotions. Still a tender young mother, the Virgin cradles the limp body of her crucified son. She extends her left hand, presenting Christ's sacrifice to the viewer. Every fold of Mary's drapery is finely sculpted and polished. The *Pieta's* exquisite finish and technical brilliance enhanced Michelangelo's reputation. When Michelangelo returned to Florence in 1501, city officials awarded him a major commission—the famous *David* **(CD Fig. 17-8)**.

Figure 17-8. Michelangelo Buonarroti, *David*, 1501–1504

Sculpting a statue of David presented Michelangelo with a formidable challenge. As we have seen, Donatello had already sculpted an innovative *David* statue (see Chapter 16). In addition, Michelangelo received an enormous but partly mutilated block of marble that had been lying abandoned for almost forty years.

Undeterred by these obstacles, Michelangelo carved a 13-foot statue of the Old Testament hero. Michelangelo chose to portray *David* just before his battle with Goliath. *David's* contrapposto pose recalls works of art from Greece and Rome. However, unlike the serene classical statues, *David* defiantly faces his adversary. His muscular body is tense with gathering power as God's champion prepares for the battle ahead.

A special committee that included Leonardo da Vinci and Boticelli promptly installed *David* at the entrance to the Palazzo della Signoria, the center of Florence's civic government. To the proud Florentines, *David's* alert vigilance and heroic courage symbolized their own willingness to defend their republic against unwanted tyrants.

Florentine officials rewarded Michelangelo with a prestigious commission to carve statues of the Twelve Apostles for Florence Cathedral. Before he could begin the project, Julius II summoned Michelangelo to Rome to design his tomb. As envisioned by the Pope and Michelangelo, the tomb would be a colossal monument that would contain as many as forty life-size figures. Julius intended to place the grandiose monument inside the new St. Peter's Cathedral.

The immense scale of the project fired Michelangelo's imagination. But as Julius diverted ever-greater funds to building the new St. Peter's, the Pope's interest in the project waned. Although bitterly disappointed, Michelangelo later completed a magnificent statue of Moses for the much-reduced project.

Sistine Chapel Ceiling

In 1508, two years after suspending the tomb project, Julius II offered Michelangelo a commission to paint the ceiling of the Sistine Chapel (**CD Fig. 17-9**). The Pope wanted Michelangelo to replace the old, star-spangled blue ceiling with portraits of the Twelve Apostles. Declaring that this would be "a poor thing," Michelangelo conceived of a far more complex and ambitious plan.

The 5,800 square-foot ceiling presented Michelangelo with a number of formidable challenges. Painting a curved vaulted ceiling was much more difficult than painting a flat wall. In addition, the fresco technique demanded both speed and precision.

Michelangelo overcame these obstacles and finished the ceiling after four years of intense work. In his *Lives of the Artists*, Giorgio Vasari wrote that "the whole world came running to see what Michelangelo had done . . . and certainly it was such as to make everyone speechless with astonishment."

Visitors had good reason to be astonished. A narrative sequence of nine history paintings taken from the Book of Genesis begins over the altar and ends near the chapel entrance. Alternating in size, the nine panels tell the story of the Creation, Fall, and Redemption of humanity. Hebrew prophets and pagan sibyls who foretold the coming of Christ face each other across the ceiling. As seekers of the truth, the prophets and sibyls steadily build up in the degree of their contemplation and enlightenment, finally reaching a climax in the figure of Jonah over the altar. Because of his miraculous salvation, Jonah prefigures the coming of Christ, humanity's final Redeemer.

Renaissance artists strove to combine Ancient Classical form with Christian subject matter. The three hundred figures in the Sistine Chapel ceiling represent a stunning fulfillment of this goal. For example, the *Creation of Adam* history panel marks the culmination of a century of Renaissance research into the nature and possibilities of human anatomy. While Adam's body has the beauty of a Greek god, his face burns with an inner intensity inspired by his closeness to God (**CD Fig. 17-10**).

Raphael

Julius II's lavish patronage transformed the Vatican into the creative nerve center of the High Renaissance. On a typical day in 1508, Bramante oversaw the construction of the great piers at the new St. Peter's, while Michelangelo painted part of a scene from the Book of Genesis. Undaunted by the expense, Julius II turned his attention to a group of four rooms, or *stanze*, located on the third floor of the papal apartments just 200 feet from the Sistine ceiling.

Julius II overlooked a number of established artists and awarded the commission to decorate the rooms to a 25-year-old artist known as Raphael. Raphael's charm and talent more than compensated for his relative youth. After apprenticing under Perugino, Raphael lived in Florence, where he painted a number of highly praised portraits of the Madonna and Child (**CD Fig. 17-11**). Raphael's Madonnas were renowned for their sweetness of expression and their graceful, fluid forms.

Julius II's commission inspired Raphael to create works of enduring genius. His four frescoes in the Stanza della Segnatura ("Room of the Signature") illustrate the disciplines of philosophy, theology, poetry, and law. Studied together, each of these disciplines leads to a revelation of higher truths and ultimately to knowledge of the Divine.

The *School of Athens* (**CD Fig. 17-12**) is the most famous of the four frescoes in the Stanza della Segnatura. The painting depicts a gathering of ancient philosophers from various eras. The sages seem to move freely in a carefully designed space that resembles the appearance of the new St. Peter's in 1509.

Figure 17-12. Raphael, *School of Athens*, 1509–1511

The toga-clad figures of Plato and Aristotle dominate the center of the painting. Plato points upward to the abstract world of ideas, and Aristotle gestures toward the earth, where he can observe and study nature. The painting's vanishing point is located between these two giants of Western philosophy.

Raphael underscored the rising status of Renaissance artists by including portraits of his contemporaries among the ancient philosophers. For example, Plato is a portrait of Leonardo da Vinci, and the brooding figure of Heraclitus seated on the front step is a portrait of Michelangelo. Raphael also included a portrait of himself on the far right, looking out at the viewer.

The *School of Athens* brilliantly illustrates the High Renaissance ideals of order, unity, and symmetry. Young, handsome, and supremely talented, Raphael quickly became a favorite of the papal court and wealthy Roman families. Patrons showered him with commissions for portraits, Madonnas, and even a mythological portrait of *Galatea* (**CD Fig. 17-13**). All of Rome mourned when Raphael unexpectedly died of a sudden violent fever on his thirty-seventh birthday. At the artist's request, the Romans buried Raphael inside the Pantheon.

Michelangelo and the *Last Judgment*

Pope Julius II died in 1513, less than four months after Michelangelo completed the ceiling of the Sistine Chapel. The next twenty years witnessed a far-reaching upheaval that shook the Catholic Church. Led by Martin Luther and John Calvin, Protestant reformers challenged the authority of the pope, questioned church doctrines, and demanded the end of nepotism and other corrupt practices. As Protestantism spread across northern Europe, the Catholic Church launched a Counter-Reformation to revive the faithful and reform the church.

Elected pope in 1534, Paul III understood the importance of using imagery to instruct worshippers and restore the church's prestige. Shortly after becoming pope, Paul III commissioned Michelangelo to paint a monumental *Last Judgment* that would be located behind the altar of the Sistine Chapel (**CD Fig. 17-14**). Michelangelo spent the next six years (1534–1541) painting more than four hundred figures. He completed the 1,940-square-foot painting on October 31, 1541—twenty-nine years to the day after the Sistine ceiling was unveiled. When he first saw the painting, Pope Paul III fell to his knees in prayer asking for forgiveness.

The pope's stunned reaction was more than justified. Deeply disturbed by the Protestant Reformation and perhaps haunted by his own fear of death, Michelangelo created one of the most pessimistic Last Judgment depictions in the history of European art. He portrayed Christ as a stern and threatening Judge. Surrounded by Mary, numerous saints, and apostles, Christ raises his powerful arm in a gesture of condemnation. Terrified, the damned plummet into the mouth of Hell, where demons gleefully torture them. Even the ascent of the saved souls is a hazardous struggle for survival that requires mutual cooperation. Michelangelo thus refuted Luther's teaching that salvation can be achieved by faith alone. Consistent with Catholic doctrine, in the *Last Judgment*, salvation must be earned by faith and good works.

The Campidoglio and St. Peter's

The *Last Judgment* marked Michelangelo's culminating achievement as an artist. He devoted most of his remaining years to architecture.

In 1537, Michelangelo began work on a plan to reshape the Campidoglio, the top of Rome's Capitoline Hill, into a new civic center (**CD Fig. 17-15**). Because an important temple to Zeus had once stood on this site, the project offered an opportunity to showcase the church's authority over Rome. Michelangelo boldly accomplished this goal by symbolically turning the piazza's entrance away from the old Roman forum and toward the new St. Peter's. Subsequent architects followed Michelangelo's design, and the Campidoglio became an impressive civic center that influenced city planners throughout Europe.

After completing his design for the Campidoglio, Michelangelo turned his attention to the new St. Peter's. In the forty years since Julius II had laid the foundation stone, the project had experienced sporadic progress as leadership passed through the hands of many popes and architects. Although he was 71 years old, Michelangelo infused the project with new energy and purpose. He devoted particular attention to designing the dome. Completed by Giacomo della Porta, Michelangelo's dome served as a model for generations of architects to come.

Michelangelo's Final Sculptures

Michelangelo never completely abandoned sculpture. During his final years, he began but did not complete three pietas. These pietas reveal much about Michelangelo's changing style. As his physical capacity declined, Michelangelo became more introspective and spiritual. For example, the *Rondanini Pieta* portrays Mary and Christ in a standing position (**CD Fig. 17-16**). Their figures seem to merge into one. Michelangelo's identification with Christ's suffering imbues the statue with a poignant and powerful spirituality.

Michelangelo worked on the *Rondanini Pieta* until six days before his death in 1564. Friends took his body to Florence, where a great assembly of painters, sculptors, and architects carried his coffin to a final resting place inside Santa Croce Church. According to Vasari, "All desired the glory of having borne to Earth the remains of the greatest man ever known to the arts."

Venice and the Primacy of Color

Venice stood proudly apart from the other Italian cities. Known as the "Queen of the Adriatic" because of its location on a group of islands, Venice became a wealthy commercial center. The city's prosperous merchants supported a thriving community of artists.

The Venetians had a different attitude toward life and art than the other Renaissance cities. Florence is typically dry and clear. In contrast, Venice is bathed in mists from the sea. The lagoon's shining water and the sky's constantly changing light had a profound effect on Venetian artists. While Florentine artists were interested in form and line, the Venetians delighted in color and sensuality. Because of their interest in color, Venetian painters were the first Italian artists to adopt the new oil paints that had been developed in Flanders.

Giovanni Bellini

Giovanni Bellini (1430–1516) is often called the Father of Venetian Painting because of his pivotal role in creating the Venetian style. Bellini abandoned fresco and tempera after learning how to use oil paints. The new medium enabled Bellini to develop a more sensuous style that employed a wide range of lustrous colors. During his later years, Bellini had a thriving workshop that included two artists destined for even greater fame than their teacher. They were Giorgione and Titian.

Giorgione

Details about Giorgione's life are scarce. He apprenticed under Bellini, worked with Titian, and produced works for sophisticated private patrons. He died at the age of 32, struck down by the plague.

Though few in number, Giorgione's paintings are both original and influential. For example, the *Dresden Venus* (**CD Fig. 17-17**) portrays a naked goddess lying asleep under a rock. The soft shading of Venus's body and the rich colors of the cloth she is lying on demonstrate Giorgione's mastery of the new technique of oil painting. As you will see, the **recumbent** or reclining nude became one of the most popular images in European art.

Giorgione's paintings are also known for their poetic qualities and ambiguous meanings. In the *Pastoral Symphony* (**CD Fig. 17-18**), Giorgione created a beautiful natural setting in which two clothed musicians are seated on a hill overlooking a beautiful valley filled with floating clouds and lacy trees. The men seem to ignore two naked women standing nearby. One of the women dips water from a fountain, while the other is about to play a flute. The painting does not tell a story but instead seems intended to evoke a romantic idyllic mood.

Titian

The unexpected deaths of Giorgione (1510) and Raphael (1520) left a vacuum in Italian art. Without any serious rivals, Titian soon became a dominant figure in Venetian and Italian art. During his long and prolific career, Titian painted religious altarpieces, voluptuous pagan goddesses, and a series of exceptional portraits that form a gallery of many of the most important leaders of the sixteenth century.

The Church of Santa Maria dei Frari in Venice offered Titian his first important commission. Known as the *Assumption of the Virgin*, Titian's completed altarpiece caused a sensation (**CD Fig. 17-19**). The Madonna ascends to heaven in a golden halo of light, watched by astonished apostles gathered beneath her. Titian used a color triangle formed by the vermilion robes of the two apostles at the base and the Virgin's crimson robe at the apex to unite the composition.

Impressed by Titian's work, Bishop Jacopo Pesaro asked the artist to paint a second altarpiece for the church of the Frari. Pesaro commissioned the altarpiece to express his gratitude for leading a successful naval expedition against the Turks.

The *Madonna of the Pesaro Family* (**CD Fig. 17-20**) enabled Titian to once again demonstrate his talent for using vibrant colors to realistically portray figures in an innovative composition. Following the example set by Da Vinci and Raphael, previous artists had arranged their figures in a pyramid composition with the apex at the center of the painting. Titian boldly placed his figures along the arms of a right triangle that culminated with a portrait of Mary holding the Christ Child. This innovative composition allowed Titian to place members of the Pesaro family along the base of the triangle just below portraits of Saint Peter and Saint Francis. In a particularly dramatic example of a **sacra conversazione**, or holy conversation, the two saints introduce the members of the Pesaro family to Mary and the Christ Child.

Titian's triumphant altarpieces established him as Venice's foremost artist. He further enhanced his reputation by painting highly praised portraits of Emperor Charles V and the Renaissance's most prominent female patron, Isabella d'Este.

Venetian Architect: Palladio

Palladio was the most prominent Venetian architect during the Renaissance period. His work espoused the classical elements that the Renaissance so admired. To become more informed on classical architecture, Palladio spent a significant amount of time in Rome. He studied a Renaissance era copy of Vitrivius' landmark *De Architectura* and even illustrated it. In addition, Palladio wrote his own treatise called *The Four Books of Architecture* that would influence architecture in the American colonies. Thomas Jefferson owned all four volumes.

Because of increased competition both in glass making and trade with the East as well as wars, Venice lost its position of economic dominance. Responding to this challenge, Venetian businessmen diversified their possessions by developing agriculture on the mainland. Demand for villas (country homes) thus increased. As first architect of the Venetian Republic, Palladio received many commissions and made his reputation designing villas. Palladio's most significant design is the Villa Rotonda on the Venetian mainland (**CD Fig. 17-21**).

Figure 17-21. Palladio, Villa Rotonda, 1566–1570

The Villa Rotonda demonstrates the influence of both Roman architecture and the work of earlier Renaissance architects such as Alberti and Bramante. It contains a central rotunda from which four porticoes project. Each portico resembles the front of a Roman temple with Ionic columns, an entablature, and pediment. Palladio must have looked to the Roman Pantheon as one of his inspirations. Like Etruscan and Roman temples, the Villa Rotonda contains statues on its roof.

The porticoes are of identical length and are perpendicular to the central rotunda. Such symmetry satisfied the Renaissance aesthetic of balance and harmony. Also, the owner (a retired priest from the Vatican) and his guests would have access to four different vistas of the surrounding countryside. The Villa Rotonda follows a central plan, which Bramante advocated during his lifetime as the most balanced form (recall Bramante's Tempietto and his design for the New Saint Peter's) (**CD Fig. 17-22**).

The Villa Rotonda set the benchmark for villas. One estimate states that one thousand versions of the Villa Rotonda have been created since it was made in the sixteenth century. Famous examples include Chiswick House in England and Thomas Jefferson's design for his home, Monticello.

Conclusion

The giants of the High Renaissance created masterpieces that awe students and inspire AP test questions. The AP Art History committee expects students to be able to analyze Da Vinci's *Last Supper*, explain the significance of Bramante's Tempietto, evaluate the artistic contributions of Michelangelo, describe how Raphael's *School of Athens* embodied the High Renaissance style and describe the characteristics of Venetian art. Students should also know the following:

- Da Vinci's notebooks include anatomical drawings.

- Michelangelo's *Moses* was intended to be part of Julius II's tomb.

- Raphael's *Galatea* is a mythological painting.

- Isabella d'Este was a prominent female patron of Renaissance art.

Chapter 18

Mannerism

Introduction and Exam Strategy Overview

After the High Renaissance, what was left for artists to accomplish? Brunelleschi and Alberti rediscovered the concept of linear perspective and shared it with artists. This solved the problem of creating the illusion of three dimensions in art. Leonardo da Vinci was able to demonstrate unparalleled understanding of the human anatomy in his paintings and drawings. Michelangelo carved tour de force sculptures and converted his sculpturesque figures into magnificent paintings in the Sistine Chapel. Raphael assimilated the qualities of Leonardo and Michelangelo to create paintings of unparalleled detail, balance, and grace. In Venice, Titian and his fellow artists painted with the rich colors that would profoundly affect the future of painting. With the great artistic advancements of the Renaissance, would artists be doomed to simply repeat what had already been done?

The answer is no. Some artists began to change the appearance of their paintings slightly after the Renaissance. They still used chiaroscuro for modeling and developed generally naturalistic human figures. Yet features of their paintings and sculptures departed from some of the values of the Renaissance. These artists came to be known as the Mannerists.

Despite being an interesting topic, **Mannerism** has received little coverage on past AP Art History exams, usually one or two multiple-choice questions. A past test did display an image of a famous Mannerist painting in conjunction with a short essay, which asked students to identify the style and its characteristics. This chapter will prepare you for these questions.

How Mannerism Fits into Art History

Mannerism is the name given to the style of European art in the mid-sixteenth century, or the mid-1500s. The name reflects the idea that artists of the period adopted certain elements in their painting that became the acceptable style or manner. The Italians referred to this style as *il maniera*. Mannerism appeared during the High Renaissance and lasted throughout the sixteenth century. It has certain qualities that reflect the artistic interests of the Renaissance. However, its key characteristics differ significantly from the Renaissance.

Key Characteristics of Mannerism

Mannerism can be divided into a few important characteristics that make it easy to recognize on the AP Art History exam. First, the human figures have **elongated features**. The figures can look somewhat realistic (the influence of the Renaissance), but their necks, torsos, limbs, hands, and feet appear unnaturally long.

A second noticeable trait is that Mannerist compositions are often **asymmetrical**, or unbalanced. In other words, you may have a large group of figures on one side of a painting, and no figures on the other. Similarly, Mannerist paintings usually lack a focal point. This aspect differs from the focused, symmetrical, and balanced pyramidal compositions of the Renaissance. Unlike Renaissance order and rationality, the arrangements of Mannerists work are sophisticated and complex.

Mannerist paintings also have **unusual light sources**. During the Early Renaissance, Masaccio perfected the use of one uniform light source in his compositions, which would influence artists throughout the Renaissance. In contrast, finding a single light source in Mannerist paintings is difficult. Light and shadows dance about in Mannerist works.

A final point that helps identify Mannerist paintings and sculptures is the use of *figura serpentinata*. The term *figura serpentinata* refers to the twisting of human bodies, reminiscent of the movement of a serpent or snake. Often in Mannerist paintings, bodies contort into unnatural positions and figures intertwine with each other.

The elongated features, unusual lighting and compositions, and the twisting poses of human figures gave Mannerist paintings grace and elegance. Mannerism became the accepted style of cultured and refined patrons. It was difficult to receive commissions if one did not paint in *il maniera*.

Pontormo

Pontormo's paintings contain the hallmarks of Mannerism. He took traditional religious scenes, such as Christ's descent from the cross, and turned them into Mannerist masterpieces. In the *Descent from the Cross,* various figures crowd around the dead Christ, including his grief-stricken mother, Mary, and the apostle John (**CD Fig. 18-1**). Christ's body is elongated and twisted. A young man, who helps to support the lower half of Christ's body, hunches and squats under Christ's dead weight while rising on his toes. His body positioning is unnatural. Would you be able to squat that way with a man's weight on your shoulders? Yet the young man's positioning looks elegant and graceful.

The *Descent from the Cross* lacks a central focus. Christ is being carried just below and to the left of the center. Mary stands just right of the center. Instead, the hands of several figures, including Christ's, move about in the central space. Mannerists believed that a person's qualities could best be expressed through their hands. Departing from the centrally organized pyramid composition that characterized Renaissance art, Pontormo's *Descent from the Cross* leaves space in the center for expression through the hands of the characters.

Parmigianino

Parmigianino, another well known sixteenth-century painter, created the *Madonna of the Long Neck*, which contains several characteristics of *il maniera* (**CD Fig. 18-2**). Using a traditional theme, the Madonna and Child surrounded by angels, he displayed several pictorial elements that typified the tastes of the time. The Madonna has a small oval head, a long neck, an elongated body, and long elegant feet. Her facial expression, the pose of her long-fingered right hand, and the expressions of the angels on the right convey the delicacy and refinement sought for in sixteenth-century Italian painting. In addition to these features, the Madonna's body as well as that of the infant Christ display *figura serpentinata*.

The composition is crowded with angels on the left side but is mysteriously empty on the right, containing only some tall white columns and a man reading a scroll. Notice the similarity between the tall white columns and the Madonna's long neck. Fitting with courtly sophistication of the time, Parmigianino probably created this painting as an illustration of medieval hymns that compared the Madonna's neck to a white tower. The asymmetrical composition adds complexity to the painting, a desirable trait in the courts of nobles.

Figure 18-2. Parmigianino, *Madonna with the Long Neck*, ca. 1535

Bronzino

Bronzino was an esteemed painter of the sixteenth century. His paintings often contain *figura serpentinata* and unusual lighting effects. Bronzino was famous for portraiture. Even in his portraits, he elongated the necks of his sitters, captured a slight twist in their bodies, and accentuated their hands. Mannerists believed that the extremities of the body revealed a person's grace. Careful depiction of these features indicated artistic ability. Bronzino's mannered style made him popular with sixteenth-century aristocrats. His skill and popularity helped him rise to court painter for Cosimo I, the first grand duke of Tuscany.

One painting by Bronzino that exemplifies aristocratic tastes is *Venus, Cupid, Folly, and Time* (**CD Fig. 18-3**). The painting contains obvious Mannerist devices, such as elongated hands and feet, *figura serpentinata,* and delicate features. It contains yet another Mannerist element: eroticism. Educated patrons enjoyed intricate allegories with erotic undertones. Cupid is fondling and kissing his mother, Venus, in an exaggerated, *figura serpentinata* pose. A figure on the right, possibly representing the concept of folly, playfully prepares to toss rose petals at the incestuous couple as masks lie on the floor by his feet. A severe, old man stands above the scene, balancing an hourglass on his back while pulling back the curtain on this forbidden love affair. Meanwhile, a seemingly innocent female figure in the background on the right holds a sweet honeycomb in one hand, while concealing a scorpion's tail in her other. Her own lower half contains a serpent's tail with dragon's claws.

Interpretations of this allegory vary. One idea is that couples may be seduced by the pleasures of forbidden love, but time eventually exposes the true results of this deceit, such as envy and wrath, represented by the figures on the left. Nonetheless, *Venus, Cupid, Folly, and Time* illustrates the Mannerist tastes for complex paintings containing mild eroticism.

Tintoretto, a Venetian Mannerist

Tintoretto, whose real name was Jacopo Robusti, claimed to be a student of Titian. He is considered a great Venetian Mannerist. His paintings demonstrate the complexities that define the style. One of his most famous paintings is his rendition of the *Last Supper* (**CD Fig. 18-4**). Unlike Leonardo's, Tintoretto's is set on a steep diagonal with the table receding into space. Jesus is still shown in the middle of the long table but stands and turns sideward as he passes the bread. In contrast to Leonardo's orderly arrangement of apostles, Tintoretto's overlap each other and also recede in size based on where they sit at the table. Servants move to and fro bringing food and carrying plates.

The composition lacks the balance of Leonardo's *Last Supper,* with the greatest weight of figures being on the left of the painting on one side of the table. On the other side of the table, there is an open floor with a few servants moving about. Tintoretto creates multiple light sources. A lamp in the left corner, above the table, emits a powerful light. Glowing, translucent angels fly about near the ceiling, escaping the notice of all earthly figures. Their presence at the significant occasion contributes another light source. Each of the apostles minus Judas, who sits on the other side of the table, has a halo, which adds light to the scene. And of course, the most brilliant light source of all comes from Jesus' halo. The overall effect of these elements is a very spiritual scene, which reflects Tintoretto's religious nature later in life.

Cellini

Benvenuto Cellini was a famous and controversial Mannerist sculptor with international notoriety. Although his personal exploits (detailed in his autobiography) may have been controversial for the time, kings and nobles throughout Italy and France commissioned his work. His greatest patron was Francis I, King of France. One of Cellini's most famous works for Francis was the *Genius of Fontainebleau.* The female Genius, or spirit, represents both Diana, the Roman goddess of the hunt, and the concept of spring. The Genius extends one arm around a stag, which was sacred to Diana, while reclining on a pitcher, which spews forth water.

The visual elements of the *Genius of Fontainebleau,* which is cast in bronze, demonstrate Mannerism in a sculptural form (**CD Fig. 18-5**). Notice her elongated legs and torso. The Genius twists in an unnatural position, illustrating *figura serpentinata.* Her disproportionately small head combined with a long neck is similar to Parmigianino's *Madonna of the Long Neck.* The crowded but decorated background, filled with animals, and elegantly elongated features of the Genius reflect the courtly tastes of the time.

Giovanni da Bologna's *Rape of the Sabine Women*

Giovanni da Bologna was really a Netherlandish sculptor named Jean de Boulogne. Probably drawn to opportunity for commissions in Italy, he migrated to Italy. His famous sculpture, *Rape of the Sabine Women*, exhibits important qualities of Mannerist sculpture. First, notice the erotic quality of the work: a nude woman is being lifted by a nude man while a nude older man kneels raising his hand below them. This may depict the story of how early Roman men stole the women of the neighboring Sabines to take them as their wives and populate Rome.

The *Rape of the Sabine Women* has a vertical, spiraling composition that displays *figura serpentinata* (**CD Fig. 18-6**). To appreciate this work, a viewer must walk around the sculpture and see it from multiple angles. This differs from Renaissance sculptures, which were often viewed from one angle. Another significant innovation of this work is the incorporation of open spaces into the composition, as seen in the space between the woman's upraised arm and body.

Do the poses of the older man and women remind you of an ancient work? Giovanni da Bologna most likely used the *Laocoon* group (see Chapter 6) as the model for the upraised arms and expressive qualities of the women and older man.

Conclusion

Mannerism is a highly recognizable style of European art that was popular during the sixteenth century. Catering to the manners and tastes of wealthy patrons, the paintings and sculptures exuded gracefulness through facial expressions and the elongation of the human form and *figura serpentinata*. Reflecting the sophistication of these patrons, Mannerist works contain complex compositions that are often asymmetrical, lack a central focus, and contain multiple light sources. Mannerist sculptures extended these qualities into three dimensions, with spiraling compositions intended for viewing from all sides. The amalgamation of these unusual features invited the contemplation of a sophisticated audience.

Although Mannerism lasted into the early seventeenth century, it was soon eclipsed by the need for a new, dramatic art style. A religious crisis in Christendom called for a bolder art style that superseded the refined tastes of the aristocracy. Reflecting the short-lived nature of this movement, AP Art History tests contain few questions on Mannerism.

Chapter 19

The Northern Renaissance

Introduction and Exam Strategy Overview

So far, Italy appears to have been the only location of remarkable artistic advancement during the fifteenth and sixteenth centuries, but appearances are deceiving. Northern European artists began to create works that emerged from the constraints of earlier medieval art. Artists from Flanders (present-day Belgium and the Netherlands) traveled to Italy throughout the period, absorbing Italian artistic concepts and sharing their own. Art historians refer to the developments in Flanders, the Netherlands, and Germany during the fifteenth and sixteenth centuries as the Northern Renaissance.

The AP Art History test writers include the Northern Renaissance as part of the art of the fourteenth through sixteenth centuries, which accounts for 12 to 17 percent of the total exam points. Typically, a test contains two to four multiple-choice questions that refer to the hallmark features of Northern Renaissance painting or include a slide-based short essay question asking students to compare and contrast Northern Renaissance art to another style, most often the Italian Renaissance.

This chapter describes the basic features of Northern Renaissance art and chronicles its development from its early roots in the International Gothic style through the blending of the Northern and Italian Renaissance in the work of Albrecht Dürer.

Jan van Eyck and the Arnolfini Marriage Portrait

A good introduction to Northern Renaissance art is the painting by Jan van Eyck titled *Giovanni Arnolfini and His Bride* (**CD Fig. 19-1**).

The subject is an Italian merchant with his new bride, Giovanna Cenami, inside their wedding chamber. Giovanni Arnolfini was a representative of the Medici family (see Chapter 16) in the Flemish city of Bruges, one of the foremost commercial centers of northern Europe. As an agent of the powerful Italian family, Arnolfini was a wealthy man, and the wedding portrait contains many of the trappings associated with the rising status of the bourgeoisie. Notice Giovanni's expensive beaver fur coat and Giovanna's beautiful green gown. Their wedding chamber contains oriental carpeting, an extravagant possession for a person of fifteenth-century Europe.

This exquisite Flemish masterpiece contains many hallmarks of Northern Renaissance painting, the first of which is **hidden symbols.** Van Eyck depicts several objects in the room with the couple, such as a dog at the couple's feet, wooden clogs cast to their side, oranges on a windowsill, and a solitary lit candle in a chandelier. Although these objects seem odd for a wedding portrait, they contain hidden meanings. The dog represents fidelity. Wooden clogs were a common wedding gift in Flemish culture, and depicting both Giovanni and his bride with their shoes off (notice a second red pair in the center background) symbolizes the sanctity of marriage. Oranges on the windowsill may refer to the couple's Italian heritage (oranges did not grow in Flanders) and allude to casting aside the temptation of marital infidelity. The solitary lit candle represents the presence of God in the sacrament of holy matrimony and was part of the Flemish wedding custom. Even the green of Giovanna's gown is symbolic, representing fertility and alluding to her future childbearing.

Van Eyck painted this wedding portrait in **tremendous detail.** Notice the finely articulated hairs of the dog and the highly developed textures of each object in the painting, from the wooden clogs to the wooden floor panels, the metal chandelier, and Giovanni's beaver skin overcoat. A convex mirror in the background contains carefully carved medallions depicting the Passion of Christ (**CD Fig. 19-2**). The mirror also reflects Giovanni, his bride, and two witnesses (one of whom is most likely the artist), in keeping with Flemish law concerning matrimony.

Jan van Eyck painted the wedding portrait in **oil.** This medium had two advantages for artists of the period: its lengthy drying time enabled artists to work slowly applying the level of detail they wanted, and oil gave paintings the desired **lustrous** appearance. Historians give credit to Van Eyck and his brother Hubert as two of the earliest artists to use the medium (another Flemish artist named Melchior Broederlam began using oils in the 1390s). Flemish artists then shared oil painting with Venetian artists during their excursions to Italy. The Venetians became famous for popularizing the medium in Italy. Thus, northern European artists preceded the Italians in using oil painting, which would become the staple of artists for the next five hundred years.

In one final touch, Van Eyck claims credit for this masterpiece by signing the wall above the mirror *Johannes de Eyck fuit hic* ("Johannes of Eyck made this"). In so doing, he exhibited the same desire for status as the Italian Renaissance artists.

Jan van Eyck created this famous painting at roughly the same time as Masaccio painted the *Holy Trinity* and Donatello created *David* (see Chapter 16). Therefore, Italy was not the only site of an artistic renaissance. *Giovanni Arnolfini and His Bride* illustrates the main characteristics of Northern Renaissance painting. Northern Renaissance paintings are famous for their hidden symbols (often with a religious connotation), exquisite detail, and the use of oil as a medium to create paintings with a lustrous appearance.

International Gothic Style

The developments of fourteenth century European painting presaged the coming of the Northern Renaissance, just as the works of Giotto and Duccio served as precursors to the Italian Renaissance (see Chapter 15). As artists traveled throughout Europe in search of commissions, an International Style of painting began to emerge, exhibiting the common tastes of fourteenth-century patrons. These works contained exquisitely painted details, elegant and colorful costumes, and splendid processions of people. All these characteristics typify the international Gothic style, the elegant and courtly style that was quite popular in Europe in the fourteenth and fifteenth centuries.

Recall that the style emerged with Simone Martini's Annunciation altarpiece in the fourteenth century (see Chapter 15) and remained popular during the *Quattrocento* in Italy, as seen in the work of Gentile da Fabriano (Chapter 16).

Limbourg Brothers and the Duc de Berry

Qualities of the International Gothic style are evident in *Les Tres Riches Heures du Duc de Berry,* or *The Very Sumptuous Book of Hours of the Duke of Berry. Tres Riches Heures* is a Book of Hours—a book of prayers to be recited at various hours of the day, including the Office of the Blessed Virgin. A famous component of any book of hours was its calendar pages illustrating the labors that were to be performed in each month of the year.

Jean, the duke of Berry, was the brother of the king of France. Jean had eclectic tastes that included collecting chateaux (castles), jewels, and wild animals, as well as books. Jean owned an impressive library, and religious books comprised a major part of this collection. Among them were fourteen Bibles, sixteen psalters, eighteen breviaries, six missals, and fifteen books of hours, including, of course, *Les Tres Riches Heures*. Most of these books were medieval illuminated manuscripts (see Chapter 12). Art historians consider Jean, the duke of Berry, to be one of the greatest connoisseurs of the visual arts in fifteenth-century Europe.

Jean commissioned three brothers—Paul, Hennequin, and Herman Limbourg—to paint his very sumptuous book of hours. The Limbourg brothers included elements of the International Gothic style as well as the illusion of three-dimensional space in their paintings for the book.

The page for January shows a feast hosted by the duke of Berry, who is seated at the right (**CD Fig. 19-3**). Jean and all his guests wear brilliant costumes. Notice Jean's extravagant blue robe. The Limbourg brothers included amazing details in the painting, such as the decorations on each of the costumes, various dishes of food on the table, interesting facial expressions, and the individual hairs on the duke's pet dogs. The background contains an elaborate tapestry with scenes that may be a reference to the Trojan War. All the guests appear to form a procession to greet the duke, whose attendant welcomes them with the words "Approach, approach," which are painted in gold lettering. The guests follow a pattern based on the splendid processions of the international Gothic style. The styles of their clothing and headdress also adhere to the pattern of the period. The Limbourg brothers painted the duke as a gracious host. A fire screen behind his head resembles a halo.

Northern European artists shared ideas with artists of Italy, who were beginning to rediscover works of classical civilization. As such, like the Italian artists, Northern European artists became acquainted with the artistic techniques of the classical world, such as creating the illusion of three-dimensional space in painting. The Limbourg brothers figures overlap and recede in size in the background. The grand table and the columns in the background contain diagonal lines to create the illusion of recessional space. Although the Limbourg brothers did not depict one-point linear perspective accurately, their efforts indicate the growing interest of painters to render the real world in their art.

The calendar pages in *Les Tres Riches Heures* alternate between scenes of the nobility and scenes of the peasants who worked for the duke. Illuminations on the book's pages show splendid processions of nobles during the month of May and dutiful and content peasants working the land in October (**CD Fig. 19-4**). At the top of each calendar page is the appropriate sign of the zodiac as well as a chariot pulling the sun, showing the seasonal progression through the year. The Limbourg brothers included illusionary devices throughout the pages, such as trees receding into distant forests and peasants casting shadows on the land, indicating the direction of the sun.

The Limbourg brothers conveyed the patterns common in the International Gothic style while exhibiting their interest in the new naturalism, which was also occurring in Italy. Figures and objects cast shadows, revealing the artists' interest in a uniform light source. Figures, both human and animal, contain naturalistic details and proportion, and the background appears as a three-dimensional space. Painting since the fall of the Roman Empire neglected these elements, focusing instead on more spiritual and didactic (teaching) elements.

Tragically, the Limbourg brothers and Jean, the duke of Berry, died in 1416 probably from an epidemic. An unknown court illustrator completed *Les Tres Riches Heures* about 70 years later. Nevertheless, this work is one of the most famous illuminated manuscripts in art history, ranking in prominence with the *Book of Kells* (see Chapter 12).

Jan van Eyck and the *Ghent Altarpiece*

Jan van Eyck painted the *Ghent Altarpiece* before he received the commission for the Arnolfini marriage portrait. As court painter to Philip the Good, Van Eyck was well known for his talents. Jodocus Vyd and his wife, Isabel Borluut, commissioned Van Eyck to create this **polyptych** (a work that contains multiple panels). Polyptych altarpieces were popular in fifteenth-century churches because they conveyed didactic narratives to the congregation, many of whom were illiterate. Altarpieces also inspired devotion during services, giving the congregation a visual representation of Christian doctrines. Polyptychs contained hinges and could be viewed closed or opened.

When closed, the *Ghent Altarpiece* illustrates key stylistic features of the Northern Renaissance (**CD Fig. 19-5**). Notice the Annunciation depicted through the middle panels. The costuming of Gabriel and the Virgin Mary is very detailed, as is the cityscape that can be seen through the window. The Annunciation scene contains hidden symbols. Gabriel holds a stem of white lilies representing Mary's purity. A shining washbasin hanging in a niche in the back wall is a reference to her holy womb. The dove over Mary's head symbolizes the Holy Spirit. A single candle behind Mary refers to the presence of God the Father at the incarnation of Christ (the conception of Christ).

The lower panels also contain important elements. Jan van Eyck renders the piety of Jodocus and Isabel, the donors of the *Ghent Altarpiece*, as they kneel in the corner panels. Painted in the lower-center panels are Saints John the Baptist and John the Evangelist, the patron saints of Ghent. They are painted in grisaille (graying tones used to simulate sculpture). The upper lunettes contain prophets and sibyls, whose writings foretold the coming of Christ.

The opened *Ghent Altarpiece* contains images of God the Father flanked by the Virgin Mary and John the Baptist (**CD Fig. 19-6**). Notice the intricate patterning and detail in the crowns of God and the Virgin Mary. As in the Arnolfini Marriage Portrait, Van Eyck mastered textures, as seen in the jewels and metal of the crowns, the robes of the saints, and the hairy garment of John the Baptist. Scenes contain symbolism as well. For example, Mary's crown contains twelve jewels, representing the twelve tribes of Israel. On the sidelines, choirs of angels worship with singing to the accompaniment of a pipe organ. Van Eyck painted Adam and Eve on the outer panels of the wings. In the lower-central panel, the community of Christians approaches a bleeding lamb from the four corners of the earth. The scene of a lamb, which symbolizes Christ, bleeding into a chalice represents the shedding of His blood for the remission of sins. The rite of the Eucharist (Holy Communion) commemorates this event. The crowds comprise apostles, martyrs, and clergy. In addition, groups symbolizing various Christian virtues approach. For example, the group of knights represents the cardinal virtue of fortitude.

Van Eyck's Adam and Eve present a remarkable contrast to Masaccio's *Adam and Eve* from the Brancacci Chapel (see Chapter 16). Van Eyck renders the bodies naturalistically, even down to the hairs on Adam's legs. Yet the proportions of Adam and Eve adhere to medieval standards, including Eve's pronounced abdomen. In contrast, Masaccio gave his Adam and Eve idealized body types, exhibiting the influence of the newly discovered classical sculptures in Renaissance Italy. Northern European artists did not include these references until the work of Albrecht Dürer.

The Ghent Altarpiece contains the exquisite details, naturalism, and symbolism of the Northern Renaissance. It also reveals the lack of classical references in Northern European paintings of the fifteenth century.

Merode Altarpiece

The wealthy commercial centers of Northern Europe commissioned art for public use, just like their Italian counterparts. Also like their Italian counterparts, wealthy patrons commissioned works for private enjoyment and devotion. The *Merode Altarpiece* is an example of one such work (**CD Fig. 19-7**).

The *Merode Altarpiece* is a small (about 2 feet high by 4½ feet across) triptych, indicating its purpose for private rather than public devotion. When the altarpiece is opened, we can see a miraculous event—the Annunciation—transpiring in a middle-class Flemish home. On the left panel, the donors, Peter Ingelbrecht and his wife, appear at the doorway of the home, witnessing the sacred event.

Figure 19-7. Robert Campin (Master of Flémalle), Merode Altarpiece (open), 1425–1428

Following the northern tradition, the triptych contains hidden symbols. Lilies, a washbasin, and candles in the central panel represent Mary's purity and the incarnation of Christ. Above Gabriel's head, a tiny white figure carrying a cross flies in through a window at the left toward the Virgin Mary. It is none other than Jesus. The candle on the table is thus extinguished with the presence of God the Son (Jesus) in the world. In the right panel, Joseph, the earthly father of Christ, works in his carpentry shop. A mousetrap on the table symbolizes how Christ will be used as the bait to trap the devil. Strawberries and violets in the garden on the left panel symbolize Mary's other virtues, such as humility.

The details of the *Merode Altarpiece* are masterful, credited to an artist known as the Master of Flémalle. Art historians recognize an artist named Robert Campin as the Master of Flémalle. His rendering of the subject includes knots in the wood, feathery wings on Gabriel, the textures of fabric, metal, pages, and flowers. Outside the garden in which the Ingelbrechts kneel, people move about on the street surrounded by intricately painted buildings.

Rogier van der Weyden: Flemish Master

Rogier van der Weyden, a contemporary of Jan van Eyck, created paintings that not only contained the stylistic elements of the Northern Renaissance but also expressed tremendous emotion. The *Deposition* depicts Christ being brought down from the cross by his followers. Mary, Christ's mother, has fainted (**CD Fig. 19-8**). The positioning of her body echoes that of Christ—a pose that is commonly used in paintings of this scene. The apostle John, whom Christ charged with caring for His mother, attends to Mary. Nicodemus, a wealthy merchant who became a secret follower of Jesus, holds

Christ's legs as Mary Magdalene, one of Christ's close female followers, stands to the right weeping. Every character expresses sorrow at the event.

The *Deposition* contains symbolism. The skull on the ground below John is a reference to Adam and the original sin. The skull is often included in Crucifixion and Deposition scenes to demonstrate the necessity of Christ's sacrifice. Christian sources refer to Christ as the Second Adam. The decorative crossbow tracery in the corners of this panel represents the donors, the Archer's Guild of Louvain. A man holds a jar of ointment, a symbol of when Mary Magdalene poured perfume and ointment on the feet of Christ.

Van der Weyden demonstrates great control of the medium of oil. The colors are deep and lustrous. The oil also provided time for Van der Weyden's exacting use of line and detail. On close inspection, a viewer can see details such as the reddish eyes and tear-streaked cheeks of the mourners. It is with good reason that art historians consider Rogier van der Weyden a great Flemish master.

Bosch and the Surrealists

Have you ever seen work by the twentieth-century Surrealists such as Salvador Dali or René Magritte? The works of the Surrealists (see Chapter 29) create fantastic worlds with odd juxtapositions of objects that defy rational explanation. Did you know that a Northern Renaissance artist set the precedent in the early 1500s for the works of modern Surrealist artists?

The artist's name is Hieronymous Bosch, and his most discussed work of art is a large triptych called the *Garden of Earthly Delights* (**CD Fig. 19-9**). The left panel contains an image of a clothed male figure between a male and female figure. Exotic animals surround the figures and are scattered throughout the land. A strange fountain shaped like a sinister, grinning face sits in the middle of the painting. A small window in the fountain reveals an owl peering out at the viewer.

In the central panel, groups of nude people are involved in unusual activities. Women bathe in a pond in the center as men ride horses around them. Men and women kiss and embrace in glass spheres, clamshells, and fruit skins. Some people bite fruit while others carry fish. The people interact in a dreamlike landscape surrounded by strange structures.

The right panel is much darker. People are being tortured. One man is crucified on a giant harp. Demons poke, bite, and grope other human figures. Another man is being devoured by a birdlike creature with a pot on its head. The creature appears to be seated on a toilet, for below you can see excrement traveling into a hole in the ground. Meanwhile, fires burn within a dark city in the distance.

What does all this mean? One interpretation of the *Garden of Earthly Delights* is that it is a complex allegory about the fall of humankind into depravity and the consequences of sin. The right panel represents the Garden of Eden, where God introduces Eve to Adam. But trouble lurks in this paradise. Some animals begin to devour each other, and a sinister fountain with an owl (the medieval symbol for witchcraft) foreshadows the original sin. A spiky tree near Adam and Eve signifies the Tree of Knowledge with its forbidden fruit. The middle panel represents what would be sexual depravity by using medieval iconography. The consequence for such behavior is punishment in hell. Using more medieval symbolism, sinners are punished by methods that reflect their sins, such as lust, adultery, pride, and gluttony.

Art historians cannot agree on the precise meaning of Bosch's triptych. Nor can they reach a consensus on the purpose of this work. However, they do agree that its unusual imagery was revolutionary. Looking at the *Garden of Earthly Delights,* it is evident that Bosch was the sixteenth-century forerunner to the Surrealist movement of the twentieth century.

Protestant Reformation

A watershed event in history occurred in 1517. A German friar by the name of Martin Luther posted ninety-five criticisms of the church in Rome as points of discussion for his students. He nailed them to the church door in Wittenberg, Germany. Luther directed much of his criticism toward the teachings of the church and the corrupt practices of the clergy, such as the sale of indulgences (pardons from penance). He did not anticipate the full ramifications of his act. A citizen copied Luther's "Ninety-Five Theses" and brought them to a printer. People then dispersed these copies throughout Europe. Because the printing press evolved during this period, copies reached a wider audience than Luther ever intended.

At that time, Luther's ideas were controversial, even heretical (*heresy* is an action or belief that violates church doctrine, for which the penalty can be excommunication or even execution). One of Luther's heretical ideas was that the Holy Bible, not the church hierarchy, was the true source of the Word of God. According to Luther, the pope was the Antichrist and the church was the "whore of Babylon." He thought that the church needed to be cleansed of its impurities to return to the true doctrines of Jesus Christ. Luther also believed that people should read the Holy Bible themselves to ascertain God's will. This contradicted the church's recognition of the pope as the supreme authority on the Word of God.

The spread of the "Ninety-Five Theses" produced several effects. First, Pope Leo X sent a bull (a papal order) to Martin Luther, warning him to recant his heretical writings or face excommunication. Luther responded to the papal bull by tossing it into a public bonfire.

Next, the Holy Roman Emperor Charles V, who was the ruler of Germany and an ally of the pope, compelled Luther to stand trial at the Diet of Worms in 1521 and recant his teachings. Martin Luther refused and consequently was proclaimed an outlaw; no one was to provide him with shelter or food. However, Luther's ideas struck a chord with many Germans, who resented the authority of the Roman pope and the corruption of the church. After the Diet of Worms, Luther lived comfortably in Germany for 25 more years, during which he continued writing, including a German translation of the New Testament.

In his lifetime, Luther even began to see his teachings put into practice. The clergy in Wittenberg gave up their colorful robes for more modest attire, and they began to conduct masses in German rather than Latin. Luther's translation of the Bible into German meant that more people could read God's Word. The clergy also began to marry, which was allowed by scripture, according to Luther. Over time, the people who disagreed with the church in Rome became known as Protestants. Martin Luther's actions were the beginning of the Protestant Reformation.

The Protestant Reformation exerted a profound effect on art as well as religion. Previously, western Europeans followed only one church. After the Reformation, Christians were split into the categories of Protestant and Catholic, which was the newly adopted name of the church in Rome. Several other denominations developed within Protestantism. King Henry VIII of England split from the Roman Catholic Church and created the Church of England, also known as the Anglican Church. John Calvin, a religious leader in Switzerland, created a new denomination of devout Protestants who became known as the Calvinists. Calvinists shunned displays of worldly ostentation, such as colorful clothing and jewelry. Also forbidden was figural art, whether painting or sculpture, in church interiors. Even Jan van Eyck's *Ghent Altarpiece* was a target of the zealous Calvinists. People hid it to save it from being burned.

The Protestant Reformation influenced the art of the later Northern Renaissance. Artists conveyed the teachings of Martin Luther in their works. Calvinists shunned figural religious art and whitewashed the interior walls of churches. The effects of the Reformation continued to be felt into the seventeenth century, as the Catholic Church launched its own reformation and the Protestant Reformation expressed itself in the Netherlands (see Chapters 20 and 21).

Allegory of Law and Grace

A small **woodcut** by Lucas Cranach the Elder, an artist from Wittenberg who befriended Martin Luther, expresses a difference between Catholic and Protestant teachings (**CD Fig. 19-10**). A woodcut is a print made by carving a picture into wood, inking it, and pressing paper onto the design. The woodcut by Cranach is split in two by the image of a tree. The scene on the left depicts the Last Judgment, a scene common in Romanesque artworks (see Chapter 13). Christ is enthroned in the clouds as a skeleton drives a sinner into the fires of hell. Adam and Eve appear in the distance committing the original sin, while Moses stands on the right, holding a copy of the Ten Commandments. According to Luther, the Catholic Church stressed that Christians could attain salvation by good works and obedience to God's law, but by those standards, all humans would fail. Cranach's scene illustrates Luther's message that no matter how hard humans try to follow the Ten Commandments, they are doomed to fail because of their sinful nature.

In the scene on the right, Cranach depicts a sinner bathing in the sanctifying blood of Jesus Christ. Because he has faith in Christ as the Redeemer of humankind, he will be saved. Just as Moses lifted a serpent on a pole to alleviate a deadly plague that affected the ancient Hebrews (which can be seen in the background), so too does the elevation of Christ on the cross save sinners. Cranach also includes Christ's emergence from the tomb to reinforce the concept of salvation.

Cranach's message is that Christians could not attain salvation by trying to lead a holy life alone, because people ultimately succumb to sin. Instead, Christians should follow the Lutheran interpretation of the New Testament, which held that Christ's sacrifice provided the grace necessary for salvation. No good works could earn this salvation; it was God's gift to humanity.

Woodcut prints such as the *Allegory of Law and Grace* circulated widely in northern Europe. Printers could make multiple copies of the woodcut. Woodcut prints were more affordable than paintings. The modest woodcuts were an efficient way to convey the new teachings of Luther and served as private devotional items. Because of these advantages, the printing of woodcuts and engravings (incised designs on metal plates) spread throughout northern Europe during the sixteenth century.

Grünewald's *Isenheim Altarpiece*

In contrast to Lucas Cranach the Elder's woodcut, the *Isenheim Altarpiece* displays prominent Catholic iconography (**CD Fig. 19-11**). The artist, Matthias Grünewald, painted the scenes on the *Isenheim Altarpiece* some time between 1510 and 1515, prior to the spread of Luther's ideas.

The monks of the hospital order of Saint Anthony in Isenheim, Germany, commissioned the work. At the time, a plague was spreading throughout Germany. The symptoms of the plague included convulsions, oozing boils, and gangrene, which often resulted in amputation.

The monks placed the *Isenheim Altarpiece* in the choir of a church adjacent to the hospital. It inspired increased piety among the monks and plague victims as well as the hope of miraculous healing.

When closed, the polyptych contains panels that convey suffering. A Crucifixion scene in the center panels displays the torturous death of Christ and the agony of his closest followers. Christ's skin contains the same oozing boils associated with the plague, an image that expresses the message that Christ can empathize with suffering. The center panels also contain a lamb, whose blood trickles into a chalice, which is traditional Catholic symbolism. The predella panels contain a Lamentation scene. It is interesting to note, that when one of the lower panels is opened, Christ's legs appear amputated. Likewise, if only one of the upper panels is opened, Christ's right arm appears amputated.

Grünewald depicts Sebastian and Anthony, Catholic saints associated with suffering and healing, in the side panels. Just as Saint Anthony stands in the panel on the right, a demon breaks through the window in the upper corner, spewing plague vapors into the room.

What a contrast when the polyptych is opened. It contains sculptures of enthroned saints created by Nikolaus Hagenauer and additional paintings by Grünewald. When fully opened (the Isenheim Altarpiece contains two sets of doors), Christ appears at the Resurrection, fully healed and in all His glory. Likewise, Saint Anthony is no longer being afflicted by demons but converses with Saint Paul in heaven. These images inspired plague victims living at the Hospital of Saint Anthony. According to accounts from that time, some victims even experienced healing.

The *Isenheim Altarpiece*, like many other famous religious works of art, is no longer in its original location. Today you can see the Isenheim Altarpiece at the Musee d' Unterlinden, in Colmar, Germany. Removed from its original context, it may seem as nothing more than a spooky or gory Crucifixion scene when closed. Without contextual knowledge, present-day visitors have no idea of how this work inspired ill and dying people with the hope of healing and salvation.

Albrecht Dürer: Leonardo of the North

Albrecht Dürer is the most acclaimed artist of the Northern Renaissance for several reasons. A master goldsmith, he also mastered oil and watercolor painting, as well as the print mediums of woodcut and engraving; it is the latter for which he is most famous. He was also one of the most widely traveled artists of his day, spending time in many of Europe's major cities. He took two significant trips to Italy, which made a lasting impact on his art. Dürer was also a businessman. He marketed his prints, which were affordable for people of modest means, and had his wife and mother sell them for him at market. When an Italian artist attempted to steal one of his prints, Dürer sued him. This may be the first noted case of copyright infringement.

Art historians draw parallels between the life of Albrecht Dürer and Leonardo da Vinci. Like Leonardo, Dürer was a man of many talents. Also like Leonardo, Dürer kept a notebook and diary of his work and life. Dürer learned to observe nature, as did Leonardo, who considered nature to be his greatest teacher. Dürer produced a number of intricately detailed watercolors of plants and animals. Botanists can actually identify each of the plants in his *The Great Piece of Turf*. In contrast to Leonardo, Dürer completed and published his works and his diary, which is an articulate and readable story of his life.

Dürer elevated the status of artists in Northern Europe. The Northern European conception of the artist was as a craftsman, no higher than a blacksmith or carpenter. Traveling to Italy allowed Dürer to witness how Italians elevated the status of their artists. Artists such as Leonardo, Michelangelo, and Raphael were acquaintances of dukes, kings, and even popes. Albrecht Dürer's response to this inequity in status was to produce self-portraits. In creating these detailed paintings, Dürer displayed his talents for line and color while portraying himself as a sophisticated and fashionable gentleman. The artist used these works not only to chronicle his life and development as an artist but also to elevate the status of the artist in Northern Europe.

Dürer's The Fall of Man

Although skilled in various mediums, Dürer is most famous for his **engravings**. An engraving is produced when an artist uses a metal tool known as a burin to incise a design into a metal plate. This metal plate can then be inked and used to create multiple copies. The advantages of engravings are obvious: multiple copies of the original that are affordable to a broad audience.

The Fall of Man engraving by Dürer is an important work to study (**CD Fig. 19-12**). It depicts the original sin, which would necessitate the coming of Christ. You can see Eve receiving the forbidden fruit from the devil, represented as a snake. Meanwhile, Adam stands by her side. Dürer created this engraving after his first trip to Italy. Unlike other Northern European artists, who traveled to Italy mainly for commissions, Dürer was the first who seemed genuinely interested in understanding Italian art and its classical influences. Unlike Jan van Eyck's *Adam and Eve*, Dürer's figures possess the idealized body types of a classical god and goddess. Most likely, Dürer was responding to copies of classical statues from Italy.

Figure 19-12. Albrecht Dürer, *The Fall of Man*, engraving, 1504

Dürer also pays significant attention to naturalism. Using cross-hatching (incising lines over other lines in a perpendicular fashion to create modeling), Dürer develops shadows and textures. We can see the fur of animals, the smooth flesh of people, the rough texture of tree bark, and jagged mountains in the distance. These qualities provide evidence of Dürer's interest in representing the natural world. In addition, his highly developed naturalism is consistent with the Northern Renaissance style.

The animals are not merely creatures of the Garden of Eden but also function as hidden symbols. The cat, rabbit, moose, and ox represent *humors*—body fluids that medieval physiologists believed dictated human personality. Each humor had specific attributes, and the ratios among the various humors determined the qualities of the person. Notice the intense gaze of the cat at the mouse in the foreground. This may symbolize the tension building up to the original sin. It may also symbolize the relationship between Eve, who sinned first, and Adam, who consumed the forbidden fruit at her suggestion. Another interpretation is that the cat represents the devil as he is about to pounce on humanity. A goat stands on distant cliff to the far right. Goats represent lustfulness. As the goat is about to leap from the precipice, humanity is about to leap into sinfulness.

The Fall of Man is important because it demonstrates key characteristics that typify the work of Albrecht Dürer. It is an engraving, the medium for which Dürer is most famous. It contains the detailed naturalism, controlled use of line, and hidden symbols of Northern Renaissance art. Most significantly, *The Fall of Man* represents Dürer's synthesis of the Northern Renaissance style with the classical body types of the Italian Renaissance.

Dürer and the Protestant Reformation

The teachings of Martin Luther influenced Albrecht Dürer. One work that demonstrates this influence is *The Four Apostles* (**CD Fig. 19-13**). No one commissioned Dürer to create this oil painting. Instead, Dürer created the diptych and donated it to the Nuremberg City Hall. This act demonstrates his feelings regarding the reforms proposed by Martin Luther.

Dürer depicts four biblical figures associated with Christianity: John and Peter in the left panel and Paul and Mark in the right panel. Paul and Mark were not actually apostles. Paul was an important Christian missionary, who wrote several epistles (letters) admonishing the early Christian churches. Paul authored the majority of the New Testament. Mark is one of the evangelists.

The organization of the left panel does a great deal to explain Dürer's religious viewpoint. Rather than giving Peter pride of place in the front of the painting, Dürer places him in the background. Recall that Peter symbolized the popes. Instead, the apostle John stands in the foreground holding his gospel of Christ's life. A verse from John 1:1 is visible on closer inspection. In German, it states: "In the beginning was the Word, and the Word was with God, and the Word was God." Choosing this passage represents how Protestants looked to the Holy Bible as the Word of God rather than to the pope.

A second work that exemplifies Dürer's religious leanings is the engraving of *Knight, Death, and the Devil* (**CD Fig. 19-14**). The image visually represents a passage from Paul's Epistle to the Ephesians. Paul made an analogy between the armor of a warrior (in this case, a medieval knight) and the spiritual armor of Christians. Christians are supposed to wear the helmet of salvation and the breastplate of righteousness, and hold the shield of faith and the sword of the Spirit, which is the Word of God.

A hideous image of death stands by the warrior's side. His rotten corpse holds an hourglass, attempting to shake the faith of the warrior by reminding him of his mortality. The devil, depicted as a goatlike creature with crooked horns, appears menacingly behind the warrior. Nonetheless, the Christian warrior is dauntless, striding forward on his steed with his trusted canine companion accompanying below.

Knight, Death, and the Devil contains elements of art from both the Middle Ages and the Renaissance. The costuming represents a medieval warrior, which was not the intention when Paul wrote the passage (although it is applicable). The hourglass and a skull below the horse's front hoof symbolize mortality. Art historians refer to skeletons in paintings of this nature as *memento mori* ("reminders of death"). The castle in the background and the layout of the figures resembles medieval illuminated manuscripts. Artists of the Middle Ages often included dogs with images of knights as symbols of fidelity, which was integral to medieval chivalry.

Yet, Dürer's work surpasses medieval art. He has absorbed the Italian Renaissance conventions of figural proportion. Dürer copied Leonardo's drawings of horses and was familiar with the equestrian portraits produced by Donatello and Verrocchio during the Renaissance. In *Knight, Death, and the Devil*, Dürer's representation of the knight and his steed resembles those Italian statues. The level of naturalism in this work supersedes any medieval take on the subject. Dürer mastered modeling with light and shadow with cross-hatching. His control of line conveys various textures. This scene contains the illusion of a three-dimensional world in a two-dimensional space, one of the major interests of the Renaissance.

Hans Holbein the Younger

Hans Holbein the Younger was a Northern Renaissance artist famous for his portraiture. Originally from Germany, Holbein moved to England and averted the disasters that befell his homeland as Protestants and Catholics faced off in religious wars. The famous Renaissance thinker Erasmus recommended Holbein to Sir Thomas More, who was the chancellor of England and an associate of King Henry VIII.

His portrait titled *The French Ambassadors* represents his tremendous skill (**CD Fig. 19-15**). The two men are Jean de Dinteville and Georges de Selve, the French ambassadors to England. Notice the monumental forms of the subjects, which reveal the influence of Italian Renaissance art. Holbein depicts the subjects in all their finery. Jean de Dinteville wears an elegant, fur-lined overcoat over a black tunic with a fancy red shirt. He wears golden jewelry and has an additional gold medallion on his saucy hat. This costuming is befitting of a noble landowner. Georges de Selve is more modestly attired but no less dignified. His sober ensemble is appropriate for a bishop.

Holbein's double portrait holds many symbols in fitting with the stylistic tendencies of the Northern Renaissance. A table between the two men contains various status symbols. Globes, compasses, astronomical devices, opened books, an oriental rug, and a lyre indicate that these are cultivated men of arts and letters. One book on the table is a hymnal, which is opened to a hymn translated by Martin Luther into German. The Ten Commandments are visible in the other book. The lyre behind the books has a broken string. Behind a richly brocaded curtain in the background, a crucifix emerges (see the left corner). Then there is the strange gray shape that cuts across the foreground. What do these objects symbolize?

The book pages may be a commentary on the religious tensions occurring on the Continent. The broken lyre string represents discord. Even the different statuses of the ambassadors (an aristocrat and a cleric) hold the potential seeds for discord (secular versus religious authority). The crucifix refers to the death of Christ, and the shape on the floor is a skull. Using a special device or standing at the appropriate acute angle to the right allows the viewer to spot the skull. This may serve to remind the viewer that even such powerful men must deal with the prospect of mortality.

Holbein's portraits do more than record people's physical features. His paintings elevate the status of the subjects and provide insight into their personalities. He deftly straddles the line between realism and flattery. He absorbed the sculptured human proportions of the Italian Renaissance through the work of Dürer and maintained the Northern attention to detailed line, naturalism, and symbolism. Secondary objects are detailed enough to be treated as independent still-lifes. The talent of Holbein gained him the recognition he needed to become court painter to the King of England. Holbein is very famous for his paintings of King Henry VIII and the royal family.

Pieter Bruegel the Elder

One last Northern Renaissance artist of note for the AP Art History exam is Pieter Bruegel the Elder. Although he traveled to Italy, he did not incorporate the classical elements of the Italian Renaissance. Instead, signs of his travels can be seen in the distant Alpine peaks he often includes in his landscapes. There is no way that those mountains in Bruegel landscapes can be part of the Low Countries (Flanders and the Netherlands).

Returning to the Netherland tradition of depicting various seasons (recall the work of the Limbourg brothers), Pieter Bruegel created a series of paintings representing the seasons of the year. Today, only five survive, making them very rare and valuable. Bruegel's landscapes were unusual for the sixteenth century because they focus on naturalism and the lives of peasants independent of a religious context. Artists usually used landscape as a backdrop to religious allegory. In contrast, Bruegel's landscapes stand alone.

In *The Harvesters*, Bruegel painted a group of peasants enjoying a respite from the work of harvesting grain (**CD Fig. 19-16**). A group in the foreground comprises a man taking a nap (maybe intoxicated) and peasants eating their lunch. A few men are still working in the field while other harvesters, both male and female, trod along a path in the grain that recedes into the distance. The background contains the mountains with which Bruegel became familiar during his trips to Italy. Additional peasants engage in leisure activities in the distance. Behind some trees to the right, Bruegel also painted a church. It is interesting that the peasants occupy the foreground while the church is obscured behind trees.

Bruegel's painting is Northern Renaissance in style. The priority he gives to his peasant subjects signifies the new humanism of the Renaissance. Some historians nicknamed him "Peasant" Bruegel to distinguish his work from the works of his sons and grandsons. Art historians refer to paintings that depict the lives of ordinary people as **genre paintings.** Bruegel is thus one of the first genre painters since the fresco painters of Pompeii. His paintings were precursors to the genre paintings of the Dutch baroque artists of the seventeenth century as well as the nineteenth-century realists in France.

Another Renaissance feature evident in *The Harvesters* is naturalism. Despite caricaturizing some of the human figures, their proportions to the landscape, including how they recede in the distance, are realistic. Bruegel remains true to the Northern Renaissance attention to detail in the landscape and the figures. We can see the facial expressions of workers, details in their clothing, the bowls of porridge they consume, and the games they play in the distance.

Bruegel also displays knowledge of linear perspective and Italian landscape composition. He does not use obvious elements such as orthogonal lines. Yet he subtly creates a three-dimensional world through the use of atmospheric perspective and the creation of a recessional space. Bruegel presents a realistic view of a day in the life of these peasants during harvesting.

Conclusion

Although each Northern Renaissance artist possessed personal idiosyncrasies, the Northern Renaissance contains basic stylistic tendencies, such as detailed naturalism and hidden symbolism. Most Northern Renaissance paintings were painted in oil, making these artists pioneers in this medium. Also, Northern Renaissance artists did not follow classical body types in their depictions of human figures. Albrecht Dürer, the "Leonardo of the North," was the first northern European artist to fully grasp the innovations of the Italian Renaissance.

AP Art History test writers are fond of questioning students about the stylistic tendencies of the Northern Renaissance, especially in comparison with the Italian Renaissance. Consider the contrasting depictions of Adam and Eve by Jan van Eyck and Masaccio.

Past tests have included multiple-choice questions about all the artists discussed in this chapter. Slide-based short essays tend to favor the works of Jan van Eyck, Albrecht Dürer, and Hans Holbein the Younger. Questions usually ask students to discuss the medieval elements of these works as well as their Renaissance innovations. To do this, consider just how far painting of fifteenth- and sixteenth-century northern Europe had progressed from the flat and unnatural depictions of Romanesque and Gothic illuminated manuscripts.

Part 4
Baroque Art

Chapter 20

Baroque Art

Introduction and Exam Strategy Overview

What thoughts come to your mind when you think of Baroque art? If you are like most students, Baroque art may have meant very little to you before you began studying AP Art History. For well-informed students, however, Baroque art calls to mind the sculptures of Bernini, the churches of Borromini, and the paintings of Caravaggio.

The Baroque style began in Rome in the late 1500s and spread to the rest of Western Europe during the seventeenth century. This chapter focuses on Baroque art in Italy, Spain, and Flanders. Chapter 21 will discuss the golden age of Baroque art in Holland. Finally, Chapter 22 will describe both Baroque and Rococo art in France.

Baroque art has been one of the most heavily tested artistic styles on AP Art History exams. Since 1983, there have been twelve slide-based multiple-choice questions and ten short-essay questions on the Baroque period in Italy, Spain, and Flanders. Seven of these questions have been devoted to Bernini and three to Caravaggio. The concentration of questions on Bernini is second only to the collection of questions on Michelangelo. In addition, most tests have three multiple-choice questions on the Italian, Spanish, and Flemish phase of the Baroque era. Therefore, Baroque art must be viewed as an essential building block in your drive for a 5.

Characteristics of Baroque Art

The Protestant Reformation represented the greatest challenge to the Catholic Church since the Roman persecutions during the third century. Led by a series of reforming popes, the Church launched the Counter-Reformation to halt the spread of Protestantism and reenergize the faithful. The Counter-Reformation began in the 1530s and extended into the middle of the seventeenth century.

The Catholic Church commissioned works of art designed to communicate the spirit of the Counter-Reformation. Known as Baroque, the new artistic style was eventually called "a style of persuasion." Painters, sculptors, and architects tried to speak to the faithful by creating dramatic works of art that involved worshippers by appealing to their emotions.

Baroque art has also been described as "the style of absolutism." Absolute rulers led the Catholic Church and the nation-states of Western Europe. Both the popes and the kings supported the Baroque style, acting as patrons to artists and using art and architecture to overwhelm their subjects with a sense of awe. Thus, the characteristic features of the Baroque style were dramatic theatricality, grandiose scale, and ornate decoration.

Bernini's Sculpture

In 1609, Pope Paul V demanded to meet an 11-year-old boy named Gianlorenzo Bernini. The pope wanted to see a demonstration of the boy's artistic talent. Already hailed as an artistic prodigy, Bernini did not disappoint the pope. Paul V turned to Cardinal Maffeo Barberini and said prophetically, "We hope that this youth will become the Michelangelo of his century."

Within a few years, Bernini demonstrated his awesome skills in a series of statues carved for Cardinal Borghese. In his sculpture *David* (**CD Fig. 20-1**), Bernini displayed the power of the new Baroque style. The work depicts the dramatic moment when David was about to sling the stone that would kill Goliath. David's tense muscular body, knitted brows, and focused eyes express his unwavering resolve.

Bernini's *David* is often called the first Baroque statue because it focuses on a dramatic moment and involves the spectator in the work. When Bernini's *David* was first unveiled, many viewers ducked. They reacted this way because Bernini successfully expanded David's space by implying Goliath's presence somewhere behind the viewer. In contrast, the statues of David created by Donatello and Michelangelo were self-sufficient works that did not demand additional space.

David helped establish Bernini as Italy's foremost Baroque sculptor. In 1647, Cardinal Federigo Cornaro commissioned Bernini to create a memorial chapel for his illustrious Venetian family. Bernini responded by designing a stunning multimedia work that successfully combined sculpture, painting, and architecture.

The chapel's focal point is a vision experienced by Saint Teresa of Avila (**CD Fig. 20-2**). In her autobiography, Saint Teresa describes how an angel plunged into her breast a golden spear symbolizing Divine Love. As depicted by Bernini, figures of the angel and Saint Teresa are perched on a floating cloud. Natural daylight from a small window in the vault of the chapel illuminates the figures and highlights Teresa. To complete the illusion, Bernini created balconies resembling theater boxes. Standing in the boxes are marble figures depicting members of the Cornaro family discussing the vision taking place in the chapel below them.

Completion of Saint Peter's Basilica

While Bernini was carving *David*, he was also serving as an assistant to Carlo Maderno. A talented architect, Maderno had been given the task of completing Saint Peter's Basilica. The commission proved to be a formidable challenge. As we have seen, Bramante envisioned a centrally planned church (see Chapter 17). Pope Clement

VIII, however, ordered Maderno to add a nave and a narthex to the west end, thereby converting the church into a basilica plan. The pope ordered the extra space so that Saint Peter's Basilica could accommodate the large crowds of worshippers drawn to Rome by the Counter-Reformation.

Figure 20-3. Carlo Maderno, facade of Saint Peter's, 1606–1612

Maderno finally completed Saint Peter's Basilica in 1626, culminating 120 years of work (**CD Fig. 20-3**). The new church was a masterpiece of both Renaissance and Baroque styles. Michelangelo's dome, for example, embodies Renaissance principles of balance and proportion. In contrast, Maderno's facade utilizes enormous columns and pilasters that embody the Baroque taste for grandiose scale. Unfortunately, lengthening the nave pushed the dome further back, causing it to gradually become hidden by the facade as visitors approach the church.

Bernini and Saint Peter's Basilica

Carlo Maderno died in 1629, just three years after completing the façade of Saint Peter's. Pope Urban VIII promptly named Bernini "Architect of Saint Peter's." Bernini spent the next fifty-one years designing and executing large-scale projects in and around the church.

Saint Peter's enormous 600-foot-long nave confronted Bernini with a challenging problem. Bernini persuasively argued that the nave's vast open space required a dramatic focal point. He therefore proposed to build a **baldachino**, or canopy, which would cover the holy altar where only the pope could say mass (**CD Fig. 20-4**). Located directly under Michelangelo's dome and over the tomb of Saint Peter, the papal high altar marks Rome's most sacred site.

Bernini's baldachino boldly fused architecture and sculpture to create a dazzling Baroque monument. Its four bronze spiral columns soar 95 feet upward to the dome. Supported by Pope Urban VIII, Bernini stripped 90 tons of bronze from the Pantheon. The dark bronze stands out against the cool white of the surrounding marble walls. This contrast of light and dark is one of the hallmarks of the Baroque style. The spiral columns support four colossal angels who stand guard at the corners of the canopy. A globe and cross symbolizing Christ's universal triumph mark the apex of the baldachino.

Visitors to Saint Peter's Basilica are often surprised to discover that the baldachino is literally covered with decorative bees. The bees are symbols of Pope Urban VIII's Barberini family. Like any powerful seventeenth-century patron, Pope Urban VIII wanted his family emblem on whatever he commissioned. Needless to say, Bernini was only too happy to oblige his powerful benefactor.

Bernini's creative energies were not limited to the inside of Saint Peter's. He also designed a magnificent oval piazza, or plaza, for the front of the church. Bernini's bold plan called for a colonnade comprising 284 freestanding columns and crowned by ninety larger-than-life statues of saints. The colonnade marks the boundaries of a large open piazza where thousands of people gather to receive the pope's blessing from either Saint Peter's Basilica or the adjacent Vatican Palace. Bernini proudly described the curved colonnade as a pair of "arms" spread out to embrace visitors to Saint Peter's Basilica (**CD Fig. 20-5**).

Borromini's Undulating Walls

Bernini's growing fame aroused the jealousy of his greatest professional rival, Francesco Borromini. In 1634, the Trinitarian monks awarded Borromini a commission to design their new church, San Carlo alle Quattro Fontane (Saint Charles at the Four Fountains). Borromini responded by creating a daring Baroque design.

During the Renaissance, architects such as Brunelleschi and Alberti built flat, symmetrical facades. Borromini abandoned this approach by creating an undulating facade that seemed to be in motion. He achieved this unprecedented effect by designing alternating concave and convex bays on the ground level. The bays on the facade's upper level are all concave. Borromini's undulating walls thus resemble the twisted columns of the baldachino. Both works create an illusion of movement and a play of light and dark, which are hallmarks of the Baroque style (**CD Fig. 20-6**).

Borromini's innovative plans did not stop at San Carlo's facade. He replaced the Renaissance system of modular units with an elongated centrally planned church whose undulating walls created a sense of movement. A highly innovative oval dome contains a mix of coffers in the shape of hexagons, octagons, and crosses. These coffers decrease in size as they approach the apex, creating an illusion of upward motion (**CD Fig. 20-7**).

Baroque Ceiling Paintings

As we have seen, Renaissance artists such as Mantegna, Correggio, and Michelangelo created illusionist ceiling paintings (see Chapters 16 and 17). Whether executed for palaces, private homes, or churches, a painted ceiling conveyed the patron's lofty status and power. During the Baroque period, Italian artists created elaborate ceiling paintings that vividly communicated the exuberance and theatricality of the Baroque style.

In 1597, Cardinal Odoardo Farnese commissioned Annibale Carracci to paint a ceiling fresco to celebrate his brother's wedding. Influenced by Michelangelo's nude youths and painted architecture, Carracci produced the first great Baroque ceiling painting. Carracci ingeniously painted a number of panels to resemble framed easel pictures. This type of simulation of easel paintings for ceiling design is called **quadro riporato** (**CD Fig. 20-8**).

Impressed by the Farnese ceiling, Pope Urban VIII commissioned Pietro da Cortona to paint a decorative ceiling fresco for the great hall of the Barberini Palace in Rome. The enormous painting glorifies Urban's triumphant reign. Appearing in a halo of radiant light, an allegorical female figure representing Divine Providence directs Immortality to bestow eternal life on the Barberini family. Meanwhile, allegorical figures representing Rome and religion carry the papal tiara and the keys of Saint Peter, symbols of Urban VIII's papacy (**CD Fig. 20-9**).

Baroque ceilings reached their ultimate expression in the paintings created for Counter-Reformation churches. In 1679, Giovanni Battista Gaulli completed his awe-inspiring *Triumph of the Name of Jesus* (**CD Fig. 20-10**) for the vault of the Church of Il Gesu in Rome. As the mother church of the Jesuit order, Il Gesu played a particularly prominent role in the Counter-Reformation. Gaulli's composition focuses on the illuminated letters *IHS*, the monogram of Jesus and the insignia of the Jesuits. Figures of the elect joyfully rise to the great golden aura surrounding Christ's monogram. In contrast, figures of the damned seem to plummet through the ceiling toward the nave floor. Gaulli successfully combined architecture, painting, and sculpture to create a dramatic work that celebrates the glory of Christ and His Church.

Caravaggio

While Carracci painted the Farnese ceiling (1597–1601), his leading rival, Caravaggio, completed a major commission for the Contraelli Chapel inside San Luigi dei Francesi in Rome. Caravaggio's painting, The *Calling of Saint Matthew* (**CD Fig. 20-11**), contained a combination of three distinctive features that had a far-reaching impact on Western art.

The tax-gatherer Levi (Saint Matthew's name before he became an apostle) and four assistants form a horizontal block on the left side of the painting. Seated around a table, Levi and his agents are counting the day's proceeds. The five men are clearly not idealized High Renaissance figures. Instead, Caravaggio portrays them as contemporary men who not only lack perfect features but also wear ostentatious costumes that include plumed hats and velvet doublets. Caravaggio's deliberate naturalism both shocked and fascinated contemporary artists, patrons, and critics. The figures of Christ and Saint Peter suddenly interrupt Levi and his agents. As Christ enters, a beam of light shines into the room highlighting Levi's face while creating deep pockets of shadow in the rest of the painting. This sharp contrast between light and dark is called **tenebrism.**

Figure 20-11. Caravaggio, *Calling of Saint Matthew*, 1597–1601

Christ's unexpected appearance focuses a dramatic spotlight on the astonished Levi. In a gesture borrowed from the portrayal of God giving life to Adam that dominated the Sistine Chapel ceiling, Caravaggio shows Christ extending His arm towards Levi. Stunned by what is happening, Levi draws back and gestures towards himself with his left hand as if to say, "Who, me?" Christ's commanding gesture leaves Levi with only one option. We know that in another second, Levi will stand up and follow Christ.

The *Calling of Saint Matthew* illustrates the power of Caravaggio's style. Although his artistic career proved to be tragically short, Caravaggio's use of naturalistic figures, vivid tenebrism, and dramatic portrayals of decisive moments had a profound effect on Baroque art.

Artemisia Gentileschi

Caravaggio's vigorous realism and revolutionary tenebrism influenced a number of followers known as the Caravaggista. Following Caravaggio's death in 1610, Artemisia Gentileschi established herself as Italy's most prominent Caravaggista. Born in Rome, Artemisia first worked under her father, Orazio Gentileschi. However, her life irrevocably changed when, at the age of 19, she was raped in her home by her teacher, Agostino Tassai.

The rape and subsequent trial left indelible marks on Artemisia's life and work. Possibly to escape the notoriety generated by this scandal, Artemisia left Rome and moved to Florence. The Medici family recognized her talent, and with their support, Artemisia became the first female member of the prestigious Florentine Academy of Design. She later left Florence and eventually settled in Naples.

Artemisia's paintings reflect Caravaggio's influence as well as her own life story. For example, she executed at least five portraits depicting a scene from the Book of Judith, an apocryphal work of the Old Testament. According to the biblical account, Judith saved her besieged town from the Assyrian army by seducing its general, Holofernes, getting him drunk, and then cutting off his head with his own sword.

Although the story of Judith had been painted by other Italian artists, none captured its intense drama with the extreme realism employed by Artemisia. In *Judith Slaying Holofernes* (**CD Fig. 20-12**), Artemisia depicts Judith as a determined woman who has the physical and emotional strength necessary to sever Holofernes's head. As Judith plunges the sword into the general's neck, blood spurts into the air and even drips down the sheets. Like Caravaggio, Artemisia uses a beam of light to spotlight the decisive moment when Holofernes realizes that Judith will kill him.

Baroque Art in Spain

Although the Counter-Reformation began in Rome, it drew much of its leadership from Spain. For example, both Saint Ignatius Loyola and Saint Teresa of Avila were born in Spain. In addition, the Spanish monarchs championed the Catholic Church by spreading Catholicism to the New World and using the Inquisition to suppress heresy.

Given their loyalty to the Catholic Church and unwavering support for the Counter-Reformation, the Spanish kings embraced the Baroque style. Like their counterparts in Italy, Spanish Baroque artists sought to emotionally involve worshippers and encourage greater religious devotion. As a result, Spanish artists often produced powerful paintings depicting martyred saints. For example, José de Ribera portrayed the *Martyrdom of Saint Bartholomew* (**CD Fig. 20-13***)* and Francisco de Zurbarán portrayed the *Martyrdom of Saint Serapion*. Influenced by Caravaggio, both artists used bright light to call attention to the sacrifices of their heroic martyrs.

Diego Velazquez

Diego Velazquez (1599–1660) was Spain's greatest and most influential Baroque artist. Many art historians as well as renowned artists such as Manet and Picasso rank Velazquez as the greatest painter of all time.

When he was just 20 years old, Velazquez demonstrated his enormous talent in a painting called *The Water Carrier of Seville* (**CD Fig. 20-14**). This intensely detailed and realistic work portrays an old water seller offering a youth a glass of water sweetened by a fresh fig. The heat of the day and the coolness of the water are revealed in the delicate beads of water running down the earthenware jug. Caravaggio's influence can be seen in the dark background, strong light, and dignified portrayal of the proud Spaniards of humble means.

Velazquez hoped his masterpiece would attract the attention of King Philip IV and his royal court. He was not disappointed. Impressed by the young artist's talent, Philip invited Velazquez to Madrid, where the artist quickly became a royal favorite. Velazquez spent the remainder of his career painting portraits that proclaim the greatness of Philip IV and the royal family.

Las Meninas (*The Maids of Honor*) is indisputably Velazquez's greatest master-piece and one of the most acclaimed paintings in all of Western art (**CD Fig. 20-15**). On first glance, the painting appears to be a portrait of the 5-year-old Infanta (Princess) Margarita, her two maids-in-waiting, and her favorite dwarfs. However, closer inspec-tion reveals a mirror on the back wall with the images of King Philip IV and Queen Mariana. Some scholars argue that the royal couple have entered the studio and are the real subjects of the painting.

While no consensus exists on the meaning of *Las Meninas,* it is clear that the paint-ing is more than a portrait of the infanta and her royal parents. It is also a self-portrait of Velazquez proudly standing at his easel. Throughout his career, Velazquez sought respect for himself and for the act of painting. Deep in concentration and at the same time supremely self-assured, Velazquez seems to proclaim the importance of painting and his own status as a respected royal courtier.

Flanders

As we have seen, the Netherlands produced an impressive flowering of artistic talent during the Northern Renaissance (see Chapter 19). The religious and political upheav-als caused by the Protestant Reformation ended that period of artistic creativity. Led by the House of Orange, the northern Netherlands won their independence from Spain and became a Protestant nation with their own distinctive artistic style (see Chapter 21). Meanwhile, the southern Netherlands, or Flanders, remained under Spanish control. As a result, Flemish artists retained close artistic connections to the Baroque art of Spain and especially Italy.

Peter Paul Rubens

Handsome, cultured, and talented, Peter Paul Rubens (1577–1640) dominated Flemish art and became the most renowned artist in early seventeenth-century Europe. After train-ing in Antwerp, Rubens spent eight years studying in Rome. His contact with the paintings of Michelangelo and Caravaggio dramatically transformed his artistic style.

On retuning to Antwerp in 1608, Rubens painted a monumental triptych known as *The Raising of the Cross* (**CD Fig. 20-16**). In the central panel, muscular figures, show-ing the influence of Michelangelo on Rubens, strain to raise the cross containing Christ's crucified body to an upright position. Lit by a beam of bright light, the body of Christ forms a powerful diagonal that cuts across the picture. Christ's classical figure clearly shows the influence of the ancient statues Rubens studied in Rome.

Rubens demonstrated his talent for portraiture and monumental historical works in a cycle of twenty-one paintings glorifying the life of Marie de' Medici, the widow of King Henry IV of France (**CD Fig. 20-17**). Completed in just four years, the cycle established Rubens as Europe's most popular and prolific Baroque artist. Rubens' paintings successfully bridged the gap between northern and southern Europe.

Figure 20-17. Peter Paul Rubens, *Arrival of Marie de' Medici at Marseilles*, 1622–1625

Conclusion

Baroque art is one of the most heavily tested artistic styles on the AP Art History exam. The exam committee expects students to be able to recognize and discuss the characteristics of the Baroque style. Particular attention should be devoted to the works of Bernini, Borromini, and Caravaggio. Students should know that Bernini created works such as the baldachino that glorified papal power, that Borromini's churches have undulating walls, and that Caravaggio's use of tenebrism and naturalism influenced followers called Caravaggista. Artemisia Gentileschi was the most notable Caravaggista. In addition, students should know that the ceiling of the Sistine Chapel influenced Carracci's ceiling paintings, that Velazquez worked primarily for the Spanish court, and that Rubens received important commissions from Marie de' Medici.

Chapter 21

The Golden Age of Dutch Art

Introduction and Exam Strategy Overview

Why were Catholic officials and royal monarchs not important patrons of Dutch artists during the seventeenth century? At that time, the Dutch Republic was a Protestant nation without an absolute ruler. This made the republic very different from the centers of Baroque art in Rome and Madrid. As we have seen, Baroque artists working in those cities created works of art designed to glorify the Catholic Church and inspire awe toward the ruling monarchs (see Chapter 20).

Lacking commissions from the Catholic Church and from royal officials, Dutch artists turned to their nation's prosperous merchants. The cities of Amsterdam, Leiden, Haarlem, and Delft were proud, free, and wealthy. Successful merchants liked paintings and could afford to buy them. As self-made entrepreneurs and patriots, they wanted to purchase portraits of themselves, their families, their possessions, and their land. As a result, Dutch Baroque artists focused on painting portraits, still lifes, landscapes, and genre scenes of everyday life.

During the 1600s, the Dutch Republic supported an astonishing number of great artists. Led by Frans Hals, Rembrandt van Rijn, and Jan Vermeer, the Dutch enjoyed a golden age of artistic achievement. The AP Art History exam has always included a significant number of questions on seventeenth-century Dutch art. Each exam typically has two or three multiple-choice questions on this period. In addition, since 1983, there have been five slide-based multiple-choice questions and nine short essay questions. Because three of every five exams have either a slide-based multiple-choice question or a short essay on seventeenth-century Dutch art, this topic merits close study.

Frans Hals

Frans Hals was the first great master of the golden age of Dutch painting. Almost all his surviving paintings are portraits. Hals chose his subjects from everyday life. His goal was not to idealize his sitters but to capture each person's most characteristic expression. Few artists have depicted smiles and laughter so convincingly. Hals's works form a portrait gallery of the men and women whose exuberant spirit turned the Dutch Republic into the most prosperous country in Europe.

Hals particularly excelled at painting portraits of local civic groups. Originating in the sixteenth century, the group portrait was a Dutch innovation that responded to demands from officers of guilds, militia companies, and charitable organizations for paintings to decorate the walls of their meeting houses. A portrait might include as many as twenty people, each of whom contributed to the painter's fee. As a result, artists traditionally arranged the sitters in rows or crescents. Hals broke this convention by skillfully creating arrangements that portrayed his subjects from various angles (**CD Fig. 21-1**).

Judith Leyster

Judith Leyster also developed a successful career as a portraitist. While still in her early twenties, Leyster became the only female member of the Guild of St. Luke in Haarlem. Her *Self-Portrait* was probably a presentation piece designed to display her skills as a painter of both portraits and genre scenes (**CD Fig. 21-2**). Leyster depicted herself as a confident artist seated in front of an easel that contained a painting of a fiddler.

Rembrandt's Portraits

Hals, Leyster, and other artists from Haarlem originally dominated Dutch portrait painting. However, they were soon superseded by Rembrandt van Rijn, a young artist working in Amsterdam. During the 1600s, Amsterdam became Europe's financial commercial center. Its prosperous middle-class merchants played an active role in their city and wanted to be portrayed as hard-working, worthy citizens or as contributing members of important civic organizations.

Born and trained in Leiden, Rembrandt moved to Amsterdam in 1631 and quickly established himself as the city's foremost portrait artist. Working with enormous energy, Rembrandt painted more than sixty-five portraits during the 1630s.

His most famous painting from this time, *The Anatomy Lesson of Dr. Tulp*, demonstrated how far Rembrandt had advanced beyond his rivals (**CD Fig. 21-3**). Rembrandt brilliantly placed the members of the surgeon's guild to the left side of the painting. They watch intently as Dr. Tulp, a celebrated surgeon, dissects a corpse spread diagonally across the picture plane. Rembrandt used an interplay of glances and gestures to connect Dr. Tulp and the members of the group.

The acclaim received by *The Anatomy Lesson of Dr. Tulp* helped Rembrandt become Amsterdam's most sought-after portrait painter. In 1642, he received a prestigious commission to portray the musketeers of the Amsterdam Civic Guard. Now known as *The Night Watch* (**CD Fig. 21-4**), the painting shows the group assembling for Marie de' Medici's state visit to Amsterdam (recall Rubens's famous series for this monarch in Chapter 20). Captain Banning Cocq proudly gestures to his lieutenant, indicating that it is time for the company to assemble. While the officers stride forward, the rest of the men load their muskets and prepare to march. A golden natural light illuminates the lieutenant's lemon-yellow costume and the red sash across Captain Cocq's chest.

Rembrandt's Etchings

Rembrandt stood apart from all other seventeenth-century Dutch artists. While other artists specialized in a certain type of painting, Rembrandt exhibited a range of interests that extended to etching. An **etching** is a kind of engraving in which the design is incised in a layer of wax or varnish on a copper plate. The parts of the plate left exposed are then etched or slightly eaten away by the acid in which the plate is immersed. The medium's softness enabled artists to create tonal gradations that were far more subtle than those created by sixteenth-century woodcutters and engravers.

Rembrandt proved to be a supreme master of the etching technique. One of his most dramatic etchings, *Christ with the Sick around Him, Receiving the Children,* shows Christ surrounded by followers who have come to hear Him teach the Gospel and heal the sick (**CD Fig. 21-5**). It became known as *The Hundred-Gilder Print,* in reference to the high price paid for the work during Rembrandt's lifetime.

Rembrandt's Late Work

The direction of Rembrandt's life and career abruptly changed in the 1640s. The sudden deaths of his mother and his beloved wife, Saskia, left emotional voids from which Rembrandt never fully recovered. Possibly as a response to those losses, Rembrandt began to paint a series of introspective self-portraits (**CD Fig. 21-6**). Rembrandt portrayed himself with unflinching honesty as an aging human being who nonetheless looks at us with a steady gaze informed with a lifetime of experiences.

Figure 21-6. Rembrandt van Rijn, Self-Portrait, ca. 1659–1660

The Return of the Prodigal Son illustrates Rembrandt's late work while also demonstrating his mastery of light and shade to portray powerful human dramas. Painted less than a year before he died, *The Return of the Prodigal Son* illustrates the final scene in one of Christ's best-known parables (**CD Fig. 21-7**). Impoverished and filled with remorse, the prodigal son drops to his knees to beg his father's forgiveness. As others watch from the shadows, the father embraces his son in a memorable gesture that combines forgiveness and tenderness.

Landscape Painting: Jacob van Ruisdael

The Dutch reclaimed their land from the sea and then won a long struggle to liberate it from the Spanish. As a result of their deep attachment to their homeland, the Dutch loved landscapes. Although many landscape artists filled this demand, Jacob van Ruisdael's extraordinary skill established him as the Dutch Republic's foremost landscape artist. His *View of Haarlem from the Dunes at Overveen* portrays flat, carefully cultivated fields and a vast sky filled with soft billowy clouds (**CD Fig. 21-8**). It is interesting to note that Ruisdael would be buried in the distant church he so carefully included.

Still Lifes

Prosperous Dutch families accumulated prized possessions that symbolized their success. It is not surprising that they purchased still lifes that portrayed dishes and glasses created by local craftsmen and exotic objects imported by the Dutch East Indies Company. Willem Claesz Heda and Harmen Steenwyck emerged as the most popular and skilled still life artists.

On first glance, the typical Dutch still life seems to be a straightforward display of material possessions. A closer inspection, however, reveals a deeper level of meaning. As devout Calvinists, the Dutch believed that pride in material possessions should be tempered by humility and a realization that possessions and life itself are both fleeting. Dutch artists skillfully underscored the transience of life by including clocks, broken glasses, and extinguished lamps in their still lifes. These works are often called **vanitas** paintings because of their references to life's brevity and the inevitability of death (**CD Fig. 21-9**).

Flower Painting: Rachel Ruysch

Like landscapes, paintings of flowers expressed the Dutch love for their homeland's natural beauty. Because flower painting was the most highly paid form of still life, it attracted many noted artists. Rachel Ruysch earned a reputation as the most distinguished of these painters (**CD Fig. 21-10**). Her keen interest in flowers may have been sparked by her father, who was a professor of botany and anatomy. Ruysch's paintings are renowned for their vivid colors and almost photographic depictions of blossoms, insects, and even snails.

Genre Painting: Jan Steen

The Dutch particularly enjoyed genre paintings that depicted aspects of daily life. Jan Steen captured the raucous and sometimes comical home life of many Dutch families. In his famous *The Feast of St. Nicholas*, Steen portrays what happened after Saint Nicholas's visit (**CD Fig. 21-11**). Needless to say, the children are in an uproar as they open their presents. A little girl in the center is smugly content as she clutches a doll and secures a bucket filled with sweets she has no intention of sharing. Meanwhile, her older brother cannot hold back his tears because he only received a birch rod. Steen slyly lets us know that the boy's tears will soon turn to joy. In the background, his grandmother opens a curtain to indicate where a special present is hidden. Even today, chaotic Dutch households are referred to as "a Jan Steen family."

Figure 21-11. Jan Steen, *The Feast of Saint Nicholas*, ca. 1660–1665

Jan Vermeer

While Steen's paintings revel in the uproarious home life of many Dutch families, Jan Vermeer presents us with an entirely different view of Dutch domesticity. Vermeer is now regarded as one of the greatest Dutch masters. Unfortunately, very little is known about his life. He probably spent all his life in Delft, where he worked as an art dealer and ran a tavern to support his family of eleven children.

Although Vermeer only painted about thirty-five works, he perfected a unique style (**CD Fig. 21-12**). His best-known paintings are set in a room filled with light entering from a window on the left side of the painting. One or two figures quietly read, write, play a musical instrument, or perform a domestic task. The figures are usually women. Many of Vermeer's paintings employ a distinctive harmony of blue and yellow. Vermeer's colors often sparkle with reflected light. The total image creates a mood of calm serenity.

Art historians believe that Vermeer may have created these perfectly balanced paintings with the help of a *camera obscura*. First used during the seventeenth century, this device created an image by means of a hole for light on the inside of a dark box. The hole acted as a primitive lens and a scene from outside the box can be seen, inverted inside it. However, Vermeer did not merely copy the image. The *camera obscura* was simply a tool that helped Vermeer compose his paintings.

Conclusion

During the seventeenth century, the Dutch Republic supported a brilliant golden age of art. Having just won their independence from Spain, the Dutch enjoyed a unique status as a Protestant country with no absolute ruler. Prosperous Dutch merchants purchased portraits, landscapes, genre scenes, and still lifes. Among the most prominent artists, Hals painted group portraits, Rembrandt created etchings, Vermeer focused on domestic interiors, Judith Leyster produced popular portraits, and Rachel Ruysch specialized in exquisite paintings of flowers.

Chapter 22

French Art, 1661–1789

Introduction and Exam Strategy Overview

When and why did France replace Italy as the center of Western art? As we have seen, Italy's dominant role in Western art began in the early 1300s with the pioneering work of Giotto and Duccio. This leadership continued during the Early Renaissance, the High Renaissance, and the Baroque periods. In 1661, however, Louis XIV took the reins of royal power into his own hands and became the king of France. As the ruler of Europe's most populous and powerful nation, Louis also became the era's preeminent patron of the arts. During his fifty-four-year reign, France became the center of European art.

This chapter reviews French art from the reign of Louis XIV (1661–1715) to the outbreak of the French Revolution in 1789. It begins with a look at Louis XIV and the construction of the palace at Versailles and then describes how Rococo became the artistic style favored by the French aristocracy. During the period, Louis XIV and his successors dominated, dazzled, and in the end, almost destroyed France with their dreams of grandeur and empire.

Although this era of French dominance played a pivotal role in European history, it occupies a relatively modest place in AP Art History exams. Most exams have two to four multiple-choice questions on French art from 1661 to 1789. Since 1983, there have been five slide-based multiple-choice questions and three short essay questions. It is interesting to note that the most frequently tested figures are Louis XIV and his architects and the artists Élisabeth Vigée-Lebrun and Adélaïde Labille-Guiard.

Louis XIV and the Pursuit of Glory

Like Augustus and Charlemagne, Louis XIV understood the power of art as propaganda and the value of visual imagery for cultivating a public image. In a revealing entry in his diary, Louis wrote, "The peoples over whom we reign, being unable to apprehend the basic reality of things, usually derive their opinions from what they can see with their eyes."

The king was very insightful. In France, "the basic reality of things" was that Louis XIV ruled as an absolute monarch by divine right. Louis formulated foreign

policy, commanded the army, and supported the arts. Louis's self-proclaimed description of himself as the "Sun King" was accurate. In France, all aspects of life and culture
revolved around Louis XIV.

Louis determined to use his enormous wealth and power to pursue his dominant
passion—"a love of glory." This all-consuming love expressed itself in the construction
of a royal palace that would serve as a proper setting for Louis and his court.

Versailles Palace

The tiny village of Versailles was located about 11 miles southwest of Paris. Before
Louis XIV's reign, its only tie to royalty was the presence of a modest hunting lodge built
by Louis XIII. The quiet village was to change forever, however, when Louis XIV decided
to transform his father's lodge into a palace of matchless grandeur (**CD Fig. 22-1**).

Beginning in 1668, Louis regularly rode out to Versailles to oversee the construction of his new palace and gardens. Supervised by the architects Louis Le Vau and
Jules Hardouin-Mansart, 36,000 workmen translated the Sun King's dream into reality.
Although work continued until 1710, the impatient king officially moved into Versailles
on May 6, 1682.

The palace and gardens created by Louis XIV were unprecedented in European
history. Unlike all previous royal residences, Versailles was completely unfortified.
Instead of being surrounded by unsightly walls and a moat, it overlooked a magnificent
garden.

Everything about the palace of Versailles was immense. It faced a huge royal court
dominated by a statue of Louis XIV. The palace itself stretched for a distance of about
700 yards. It was so long that food from the kitchens was often cold by the time servants
reached Louis's chambers.

While the nobles lived in relatively small rooms, Louis and his Spanish queen,
Marie Therese, enjoyed spacious royal suites. Located in the exact center of the palace,
Louis's royal bedroom faced east toward the rising sun.

Although the King's bedchamber was impressive, the palace's most famous room
was the Hall of Mirrors (**CD Fig. 22-2**). This remarkable room was 246 feet long and
33 feet wide. Seventeen towering windows gave guests a splendid view of palace gardens. Light from these windows flooded into the room and reflected off seventeen huge
gold-framed mirrors on the opposite wall. During the evening, the mirrors reflected the
glimmer of four thousand wax candles set in silver chandeliers.

Located outside the Hall of Mirrors, the palace's formal gardens covered almost
250 acres. Designed by Andre Le Notre, the park of Versailles contained 150,000
plants, one hundred statues of classical heroes, and fourteen hundred fountains. In
one fountain, a sculptural group depicts Apollo, the triumphant god of the sun and
symbol of Louis XIV, being pulled from the sea in a magnificent four-horse chariot.

As the royal residence and center of French government, the palace of Versailles dominated French political and cultural life. Yet Versailles was also something more. Its gardens, royal suites, and elaborate daily rituals provided a visual display of Louis XIV's absolute power. Like all the great monuments we have studied thus far, Versailles both expressed and symbolized the culture of its times. As the cathedral of Chartres was built to glorify God, so the palace of Versailles was built to glorify Louis XIV.

Two Images of Royal Power

Befitting Europe's most powerful ruler, Louis XIV commissioned numerous portraits of himself. The most famous and enduring of these images were a bust carved by Bernini and a portrait painted by Hyacinthe Rigaud.

In 1665, Louis and his ministers persuaded Pope Alexander VII to permit the 66-year-old Bernini to travel to Paris to submit designs for the east facade of the Louvre. Although the king's ministers rejected Bernini's plans, the great sculptor did carve a magnificent portrait bust of the young Sun King.

Bernini's *Bust of Louis XIV* is often described as the pinnacle of Baroque portraiture (**CD Fig. 22-3**). Carved in 1665 when Louis was just 27 years old, the life-size bust captures the king's features while creating a dynamic image of royal power and energy. Louis's luxurious hair forms a profusion of curls and swirls framing the smooth surface of his face, and the young king's head is turned to his right as if to give a command. At the same time, his drapery flows to his left, creating a Baroque sense of motion and energy.

Thirty-six years later, Hyacinthe Rigaud portrayed the 63-year-old monarch in his coronation robes (**CD Fig. 22-4**). The life-size painting depicts Louis as the very embodiment of absolute power. Symbols of royal power enhance Louis's image of omnipotence. He holds a royal scepter in his right hand while wearing a sword thought to have belonged to Charlemagne. An enormous wig covers Louis's balding head. But the vain monarch insisted that Rigaud portray his shapely silk-covered legs!

Rococo Style

The death of Louis XIV in 1715 left a void in French high society. With the passing of the Sun King, aristocrats reasserted their traditional social and economic privileges. Many nobles left Versailles and moved to fashionable hotels or townhouses in Paris. These hotels soon became centers of a new artistic style called Rococo.

The Rococo style emphasizes elegant designs that feature pastel colors. The nobles enjoyed life and commissioned works of art that reflected their lighthearted and sometimes frivolous mood. Although Louis XIV had pursued glory and grandeur, the French nobles were far more interested in love, ladies, and seduction.

Figure 22-4. Hyacinthe Rigaud, *Louis XIV*, 1701

Antoine Watteau

Antoine Watteau's paintings capture the Rococo style and spirit. He is best known for inventing the *fête galante* paintings—depictions of festive gatherings in which elegant nobles converse, dance, and enjoy music in pastoral settings. Watteau's *fête galante* paintings portray carefree nobles enjoying a fantasy world that was far removed from reality.

Watteau's most acclaimed work, *Return from Cythera,* depicts a group of romantic couples preparing to depart from Cythera, the island sacred to Venus, the goddess of love (**CD Fig. 22-5**). As elegantly costumed couples reluctantly prepare to leave the idyllic island, they momentarily pause to gaze one last time at a statue of Venus draped with flowers. While powder-pink cupids frolic in the sky, the lovers slowly board a golden barge that will return them to reality.

Watteau completed *Return to Cythera* in 1719. Ill with tuberculosis, he died two years later at the age of 37.

François Boucher

Following Watteau's death, François Boucher became France's foremost Rococo artist. As the favorite painter of Louis XV's mistress, Madame de Pompadour, Boucher received numerous commissions that brought him honors and a lucrative career. Boucher delighted in painting voluptuous goddesses. *Cupid a Captive*, for example, portrays a nude Venus teasing her naughty son, Cupid (**CD Fig. 22-6**). Lively and lighthearted, Boucher's paintings reflect the fantasy life of the decadent French aristocracy in the mid-1700s.

Jean-Honoré Fragonard

Jean-Honoré Fragonard's art constituted a final flowering of the French Rococo style. Once one of Boucher's students, Fragonard's skill at times surpassed his master's. Fragonard's delicate pastel paintings are often witty commentaries on the frivolous fantasies of his patrons. *The Swing*, for example, portrays a beautiful young mistress perched on a swing, flying through the air with the lightness and beauty of a butterfly (**CD Fig. 22-7**). Her lover, a young baron, reclines in a bower of flowers and foliage strategically positioned to catch a glimpse of his mistress's legs. The young woman exuberantly kicks off her shoe at a statue of Cupid, who slyly holds his finger to his lips.

Élisabeth Vigée-Lebrun

During the Rococo era, women often distinguished themselves as leading portraitists. The most famous was Élisabeth Vigée-Lebrun (**CD Fig. 22-8**). At the age of just 24, Vigée-Lebrun painted the first of what was to be a series of more than thirty portraits of Queen Marie Antoinette (**CD Fig. 22-9**). With the queen's support, the Royal Academy accepted Vigée-Lebrun. However, royal patronage made it much too dangerous for Vigée-Lebrun to remain in France once the revolution began. Fleeing the revolution, Vigée-Lebrun traveled the continent painting portraits of the European, particularly Russian, aristocracy. Vigée-Lebrun returned to Paris in 1802 and wrote a memoir describing her eventful life.

Adélaïde Labille-Guiard

Vigée-Lebrun's contemporary and sometimes rival, Adélaïde Labille-Guiard also established a reputation as a skilled portraitist. The French Academy admitted both women on the same day in May 1783. Although Labille-Guiard painted many portraits of members of the royal court, her best-known painting is a self-portrait showing her training two female students (**CD Fig. 22-10**). The painting demonstrated Labille-Guiard's talent, underscored her role as a teacher, and called for an improvement in the status of women artists.

Clodion

Rococo sculpture is best seen in the work of Claude Michel, called Clodion. Like other Rococo sculptors, Clodion is known for small terra-cotta statuettes designed to decorate tabletops. For example, his *Nymph and Satyr* illustrates the amorous frivolity of the Rococo style by showing an eager nymph pouring wine into the mouth of a laughing satyr (**CD Fig. 22-11**).

Figure 22-11. Clodion, *Nymph and Satyr*, ca. 1775

Chardin and the Reaction Against Rococo

The Rococo style mirrored the self-indulgent lifestyle of the French aristocracy during the 1700s. While Boucher, Fragonard, and Clodion captured the period's superficial fun, Jean-Baptiste-Siméon Chardin strove to depict a new morality rooted in the simple goodness of ordinary people. His portraits of industrious middle-class youth and domestic scenes featuring mothers instructing their young children marked the beginning of a reaction against Rococo that would lead to the Neoclassical movement we will review in Chapter 23 (**CD Fig. 22-12**).

Conclusion

During the reign of Louis XIV, France eclipsed Italy as the center of European art. Louis XIV was the preeminent patron of the arts, and the palace of Versailles was the era's most important architectural project. After Louis XIV's death, many nobles moved to Paris, where they supported a style of art known as Rococo. The Rococo style used pastel colors to depict lighthearted scenes of aristocrats pursuing pleasure.

The AP Art History committee expects students to know that Watteau, Boucher, and Fragonard were the leading Rococo artists and that Élisabeth Vigée-Lebrun and Adélaïde Labille-Guiard were accomplished portraitists. In addition, you should know that Bernini sculpted a famous Baroque bust of Louis XIV, that Clodion's small terracotta statuettes embody the Rococo style, and that Chardin's portraits and scenes of middle-class life signaled a reaction against Rococo.

Part 5
Nineteenth-Century Art

Chapter 23

Neoclassical Art

Introduction and Exam Strategy Overview

What do the Grand Tour, the excavations at Herculaneum and Pompeii, and the publication of *The History of Ancient Art* by Johann Joachim Winckelmann have in common? Each event fueled an interest in Greek and Roman history and art. This revived interest in classical antiquity fired the imagination of artists, sculptors, and architects who created a new style of art known as Neoclassical.

During the eighteenth century no gentleman's (and increasingly, gentlewoman's) education was complete without extensive travel throughout Europe—a grand tour, as it was called—which included a prolonged visit to the major cultural sites of Italy. While in Italy, these young connoisseurs visited the just-discovered remains of Herculaneum and Pompeii. Fascinated by what they saw, the future social and political leaders returned to northern Europe and America with a taste for classical art.

The writings of the German scholar J. J. Winckelmann also played a pivotal role in the rise of Neoclassicism. In his book *The History of Ancient Art*, Winckelmann extolled Greek art for its beauty and high moral qualities. Unlike the frivolous and overly ornate Rococo art, the Greek masterpieces embodied what Winckelmann called a "noble simplicity and calm grandeur." Neoclassical artists strove to create works that expressed these aesthetic goals.

The Neoclassical style played a major role in European art from the 1760s to about 1820. The AP Art History committee has always recognized the importance of this style and its leading artists. Most exams contain two or three multiple choice questions devoted to Neoclassical art. In addition, since 1983, there have been seven slide-based multiple-choice questions and nine short essay questions on this style. It is important to note that four of these sixteen questions focused on the sculptures of Jean-Antione Houdon, three asked about the paintings of Jacques-Louis David, and two required students to discuss the architectural contributions of Thomas Jefferson.

Angelica Kauffmann

Born in Switzerland and trained in Italy, Angelica Kauffmann earned unprecedented acclaim and financial success while painting in England during the 1770s.

Contemporary accounts described Kauffmann as an attractive woman who spoke several languages and played a number of musical instruments. She first encountered the new classicism in Rome and painted a portrait of J. J. Winckelmann. While contemporary female artists such as Vigée-Lebrun specialized in portraiture, Kauffmann excelled at history painting, considered at that time the most prestigious artistic category.

Like other Neoclassical artists, Kauffmann drew her themes and stories from Roman history. In *Cornelia, Mother of the Gracchi* (**CD Fig. 23-1**), she illustrated a famous second century BCE story about Cornelia, the mother of the future political leaders Gaius and Tiberius Gracchus. Cornelia reveals her character when a guest proudly shows off her fine jewelry and then haughtily requests that Cornelia display hers. If this were a Rococo painting, Cornelia would no doubt have produced a dazzling array of jewels. Instead, Cornelia responds by proudly introducing her two sons and saying, "These are my most precious jewels."

Kauffmann's painting embodies the striving for a new morality that energized Neoclassical art. In *Cornelia, Mother of the Gracchi*, Neoclassical virtue replaced Rococo vice. Kauffmann underscored this point by creating a triangular composition culminating in Cornelia. It is interesting to note that Cornelia's features resemble Kauffmann's.

Figure 23-1. Angelica Kauffmann, *Cornelia, Mother of the Gracchi* (or *Cornelia Presenting Her Children as Her Treasures*), 1785

Benjamin West

Angelica Kauffmann was not the only artist devoted to Neoclassical history painting. Her American-born friend Benjamin West had also traveled to Rome, met Winckelmann, and established a reputation for painting uplifting scenes from Roman history.

West shocked Kauffmann and other Neoclassical artists when he completed a contemporary history painting, *The Death of General Wolfe* (**CD Fig. 23-2**), that represented the figures in contemporary costume. At the time, traditional academic rules demanded that heroic figures should be dressed in antique clothing so as to elevate a subject to its universal significance. Although West had followed this precept in his previous paintings, he argued that *The Death of General Wolfe* had to be different. General Wolfe died a heroic death while leading his troops to a decisive victory that enabled the British to defeat the French and gain control over Quebec City. West defended his decision to use contemporary uniforms saying that he had to accurately represent "the facts of the event."

West's decision proved to be successful. The painting enjoyed an enthusiastic reception from both the British public and previously skeptical critics. Although West avoided classical dress, he used a traditional composition borrowed from Van der Weyden's *Deposition* (see Chapter 19). Like Christ, General Wolfe is a fallen martyr surrounded by grieving followers who frame the painting. An Iroquois brave contemplates the scene and helps emphasize that the event took place in Canada.

Jean-Antoine Houdon

Jean-Antoine Houdon is recognized as the greatest European portrait sculptor of the last half of the eighteenth century. Houdon established his reputation by carving portrait busts of leading philosophers, inventors, and political figures of the Enlightenment. Houdon's portrait busts combine a remarkable degree of physical accuracy with extraordinary psychological insight. These traits can be seen in Houdon's portraits of Voltaire and George Washington.

Houdon executed a statue of Voltaire shortly before the great philosopher died. The statue shows the aging but still alert writer seated on an antique-style chair. Although Voltaire was bald, Houdon gave him enough hair to hold a classical headband. The sculptor further classicized Voltaire by dressing him in a Roman toga.

A comparison of Houdon's *Voltaire Seated* with Bernini's *Bust of Louis XIV* illustrates important differences between the Neoclassical and Baroque styles (**CD Figs. 23-3 and 23-4**). Houdon classicized Voltaire by dressing him in a toga. In contrast, Bernini used Louis XIV's royal robes to create a Baroque sense of motion. Both Houdon and Bernini captured the looks and personalities of their sitters. Known for his sharp wit, Houdon's Voltaire turns his head and smiles as if amused by one of the human foibles he so cleverly satirized. In contrast, Bernini's Louis XIV imperiously turns his head as he prepares to issue a royal command.

Houdon also carved busts of Benjamin Franklin, Thomas Jefferson, and other American leaders. Impressed by his work, the Virginia legislature commissioned Houdon to carve a statue of George Washington. Eager to create a realistic work, Houdon modeled Washington while staying at the general's home at Mount Vernon.

Houdon's life-size statue captures Washington's likeness while using both American and classical features to symbolize the general's historic accomplishments (**CD Fig. 23-5**). Houdon presented Washington as a retired general dressed in uniform. He stands in a relaxed contrapposto pose and looks confidently toward a future he helped create. In his left hand, Washington holds a bundle of 13 fasces, or rods. Once symbols of Roman authority, the fasces in the general's grasp symbolize each of the thirteen original states. Houdon's statue also includes a sword and a plow to indicate Washington's return from military duty to a life dedicated to peaceful pursuits.

Neoclassical Architecture

The appeal of classical antiquity extended beyond painting and sculpture to architecture. Republican leaders in America rejected both the grandiose splendors of Baroque architecture and the intricate ornamentation of Rococo decoration as inappropriate for a young democratic nation. Led by Thomas Jefferson, America turned to Greece and Rome for models of dignified private and public buildings.

Monticello

Jefferson's design for Monticello, his country home in Virginia, reflects his classical education. Although Jefferson had not seen the Pantheon, he was aware of its distinctive use of a front portico and a rotunda consisting of a drum supporting a dome. As the owner of the first copy in America of Palladio's *Four Books on Architecture*, Jefferson carefully studied the Villa Rotonda's classically inspired design. The Villa Rotonda in turn served as a model for Lord Burlington's home, Chiswick House (**CD Fig. 23-6**).

Begun in 1790 and finally completed in 1806, Monticello is a synthesis of Jefferson's ongoing study of Classical and Neoclassical designs. The final version of Monticello is reminiscent of both the Villa Rotonda and Chiswick House. Monticello featured a classical front portico with Doric columns, an octagonal-shaped dome, and symmetrical wings that reach out toward the surrounding landscape.

Virginia State Capitol

As we have seen, Baroque churches and palaces inspired awe in worshippers and subjects. In contrast, Jefferson believed that in a republic, public buildings should be dignified expressions of civic virtue. While serving as U.S. minister to France, Jefferson carefully studied a well-preserved temple at Nimes that was very similar to the Temple of Portunus in Rome (see Chapter 8). Jefferson wrote that he gazed at the temple for hours, "like a lover at his mistress."

Jefferson used the temple at Nimes as a model for the new Virginia State Capitol (**CD Fig. 23-7**). Much larger than its predecessor, the State Capitol features an Ionic portico, pediment, and classical proportions that confer a solemn, dignified appearance. Known in America as the **federal style**, this Neoclassical look soon became widely used in government buildings in the new republic.

David and *The Oath of the Horatii*

Like Jefferson, the French philosophers and Neoclassical theorists looked to Republican Rome for models of order, justice, and civic virtue. Denis Diderot and other leading philosophers called for art to embody grand ideas that would educate and uplift the public. This goal fired the imagination of Jacques-Louis David, an artist whose work personifies Neoclassicism and French revolutionary fervor.

David burst into public consciousness with the triumphant showing in 1785 of his landmark painting, *The Oath of the Horatii* (**CD Fig. 23-8**). The painting depicts a story by the Roman historian Livy. According to Livy, the warring cities of Rome and Alba agreed to settle their conflict by a mortal combat between three Roman brothers (the Horatii) and three Alban brothers (the Curatii). Complicating the story, one of the Horatii brothers is married to one of the sisters of the Curatii, and a Horatii sister is betrothed to one of the Curatii brothers.

Figure 23-8. Jacques-Louis David, *The Oath of the Horatii,* 1785

David chose to portray the dramatic moment when the three Horatii brothers swear an oath to their father that they will fight to the death. Standing together as one, the brothers resolutely raise their hands to receive the gleaming swords held by their father. The brothers and their father ignore the distraught women, who huddle together knowing the tragic losses that await them.

David's composition is a model of Neoclassical style. The setting is a room defined by three Doric arches. Each group or individual—the brothers, the father, and the women—is framed by one of these arches. The carefully modeled figures are all parallel to the picture frame. David's meticulous brushwork is precise and imperceptible.

The Oath of the Horatii vividly illustrates the theme of the conflict between patriotic duty and family love. Faced with this dilemma, the brothers and their father do not waver. They unhesitatingly choose loyalty to Rome. Although the story is taken from the classical past, David's theme of civic duty and self-sacrifice offered a guide for moral behavior in the troubled times facing France.

David and *The Death of Marat*

As a result of the success of *The Oath of the Horatii*, David became the most influential painter in France. His themes of duty, patriotism, and sacrifice underscore his growing opposition to the privileged French Old Regime. When the French Revolution began in 1789, David became a powerful figure in the new Republic. As a member of the National Convention, he supported the Reign of Terror, voted to execute Louis XVI, and used his art to serve the Revolution.

In 1793, members of the National Convention called on David to create a painting that would commemorate the death of Jean-Paul Marat (**CD Fig. 23-9**). An outspoken writer and friend of David, Marat had been stabbed to death as he lay in his bath by the royalist Charlotte Corday. David had visited Marat the day before the assassination. As a result, the image of the journalist hard at work in his bath was fresh in David's mind.

David faced a difficult challenge. Marat was an unattractive man who was disfigured by a painful skin disease. David ignored Marat's gruesome appearance and placed the dying man in a heroic pose. Like the dead Christ in Michelangelo's Saint Peter's *Pieta*, Marat's head is gracefully inclined, and his arm hangs limply by his side. He still holds a quill pen he was using to write a letter offering money to support a soldier's widow. David thus portrayed Marat as a martyr who died while serving the state.

David and Napoleon

Despite the assassination of Marat, the Revolution seemed to fulfill David's political and artistic goals. However, the bloody Reign of Terror and the fall of Robespierre ended David's dream of serving the Revolution. In August 1794, authorities arrested David for supporting Robespierre and imprisoned the artist for five months. Shattered and confused, David retreated from politics and devoted himself to painting portraits and classical events.

But David's retreat from the political arena proved to be brief. Napoleon's swift rise to power rekindled David's ambition to be part of the historic events unfolding before him. Realizing that David's talent could be used to glamorize his public image, Napoleon offered him the position of First Painter of the Empire. David enthusiastically accepted the opportunity of serving Napoleon. Dazzled by Napoleon's power and charismatic personality, David portrayed Bonaparte as an invincible hero. For example, in the painting *Napoleon at the Pass of St. Bernard*, David depicted Napoleon as a modern Charlemagne astride a white charger fearlessly pointing the way across the Alps (**CD Fig. 23-10**).

After being crowned emperor in 1804, Napoleon commissioned David to create a painting to commemorate the event. David's *The Coronation of Napoleon* is a monumental painting that successfully captured the drama and pageantry of the historic event (**CD Fig. 23-11**). He faithfully recorded the lavish scene inside Notre Dame Cathedral, focusing on the moment Napoleon crowned his wife, Josephine, while Pope Pius VII gave his blessing. Interestingly, David also included a portrait of himself witnessing the momentous ceremony.

Napoleon and the Arts

Like other rulers before him, Napoleon understood how to use art as a form of propaganda. During his brief reign, Napoleon commissioned artists, sculptors, and architects to create monumental works designed to glorify his public image.

David was not the only well-known artist to portray Napoleon. The emperor awarded important commissions to Antoine-Jean Gros and to Jean-Auguste-Dominique Ingres. Both artists created portraits depicting Napoleon as a commanding and almost divine ruler. As a result of these commissions, Napoleon became the most portrayed ruler during the Neoclassical period.

While Napoleon lavished patronage on leading artists, he did not completely neglect sculptors. The emperor's favorite sculptor was Antonio Canova. During the early 1800s, Canova was the most famous Neoclassical sculptor in the world. Although Canova created statues of Napoleon, he is best known for a marble portrait of Napoleon's sister, *Pauline Borghese as Venus* (**CD Fig. 23-12**).

Figure 23-12. Antonio Canova, *Pauline Borghese as Venus*, 1808

Napoleon's grandiose ambition extended beyond commissioning portraits of himself and statues of his family. He also ordered the construction of monuments designed to recreate the grandeur of Imperial Rome. Inspired by Trajan's Column in Rome, Napoleon commissioned a huge freestanding Doric column decorated with spiral reliefs depicting events from his victorious campaigns in 1805. A year later, he commissioned a huge Arc de Triomphe (Arch of Triumph) based on the Arch of Titus in Rome. The arch was not completed until 1836, twenty-one years after Napoleon lost the battle at Waterloo. Napoleon's final defeat marked a watershed in European history that inaugurated a new political order and ushered in a new Romantic style of art.

Conclusion

The Neoclassical style provides a particularly vivid example of how artists are affected by historic and social events. Given the AP Art History committee's current emphasis on contextual art, it should come as no surprise that recent tests have featured a number of questions on Neoclassical art. Students preparing for the exam should carefully review the portrait busts of Jean-Antoine Houdon, the Federal style buildings designed by Thomas Jefferson, and the paintings of Jacque-Louis David. In addition, students should know that the Villa Rotonda and Chiswick House influenced the design of Monticello, that Canova was the foremost Neoclassical sculptor in the early nineteenth century, and that Napoleon was the most portrayed ruler during the Neoclassical period.

Chapter 24

Romanticism

Introduction and Exam Strategy Overview

What do paintings of a harem in Algiers, a slave ship captain throwing his human cargo overboard, and a gentleman standing on a craggy mountain peak contemplating a magnificent vista have in common? These paintings reveal the range of subjects explored by Romantic artists. Although the paintings and artists are not linked by a common style or subject, the Romanticists are united by an overriding desire to express their personal emotions. Their intense feelings were often inspired by exotic locations, atrocities, and the awesome beauty of nature.

Romanticism is a complex artistic movement. It began in the late 1700s as a reaction to the constraints imposed by Neoclassical rules of beauty and morality. Romantic artists, sculptors, and architects all shared a desire to freely express their feelings and emotions. Whereas Neoclassicism emphasized reason and deliberate thought, Romanticism focused on emotion and spontaneous feeling.

Although art historians disagree on exactly when the Romantic movement began, most agree that it reached its peak in 1830 and began to decline after 1848. During that period, the romantic movement influenced artists throughout Western Europe and the United States. This chapter focuses on key artists working in France, Spain, Germany, England, and America.

Approximately 10 percent to 15 percent of the questions on the AP Art History exam are devoted to the nineteenth century. Because Romanticism dominated the first half of the twentieth century, it has enjoyed a prominent place on the exam. Each exam typically contained two to four multiple-choice questions on Romanticism. Since 1983, there have been nine slide-based multiple-choice questions and six short essay questions. It is important to point out that eight of those fifteen questions focused on works by French artists and sculptors.

Henry Fuseli and *The Nightmare*

While Neoclassical artists strove for an orderly presentation of objective reality, Romantic artists were more interested in the mysteries of human psychology. The pioneering work of Henry Fuseli (1741–1825) illustrates this aspect of Romantic art.

Swiss by birth, Fuseli settled in England, where he specialized in unconventional subjects that often portrayed his dark fantasies. His painting *The Nightmare*, for example, depicts a beautiful woman lying across a bed (**CD Fig. 24-1**). As she sleeps, a demonic-looking incubus, an evil spirit believed in medieval times to prey on sleeping women, squats menacingly on her stomach. At the same time, a horse with glowing phosphorescent eyes bursts into the room. Although the meaning of this disturbing work remains a puzzle, its emphasis on the human mind as a site of unexplained mysteries marks the beginning of Romantic art.

Figure 24-1. Henry Fuseli, *The Nightmare*, 1781

Theodore Gericault and *Raft of the Medusa*

The Romantic movement in France began with Theodore Gericault's impassioned reaction to a contemporary disaster at sea. In 1816, a French frigate, the *Medusa*, ran aground on a reef off the west coast of Africa while transporting four hundred soldiers and settlers to the colony of Senegal. The incompetent captain was a nobleman who had been appointed by the government of Louis XVIII as a reward for his loyalty to the royal family.

The captain commandeered all six lifeboats for government officials and senior officers. His callous action left 150 people he saw as his social inferiors to fend for themselves. The desperate castoffs built a makeshift raft from the planks of the disintegrating ship. Drifting helplessly for thirteen days, the abandoned people gradually succumbed to disease and starvation. Only fifteen emaciated survivors were saved when a rescue ship finally spotted the raft.

Despite the government's attempt to cover up the tragedy, an account by one survivor exposed the full extent of the scandal. Because wealthy patrons still purchased most works of art, there seemed little likelihood that anyone would create a critical painting of the disaster. Gericault, however, represented a new type of outspoken artist. Unlike most young painters, Gericault was independently wealthy and thus free to express his personal feelings. Outraged by the travesty, Gericault worked feverishly for eight months to create a painting that not only dramatized the plight of the victims but also castigated the government. His painting *Raft of the Medusa* (**CD Fig. 24-2**) is the result.

Influenced by the Baroque artists he had studied while touring Italy, Gericault chose to depict the dramatic moment when the survivors first sighted the rescue ship. He placed the raft at the edge of the picture plane, compelling viewers to become witnesses to what is taking place. Most of the figures are arranged along two crossing diagonals. The diagonal that begins on the lower left rises from the depth of despair to the men frantically waving clothes that they hope the rescue ship will spot. The diagonal that begins with the dead man on the lower right directs our attention to a huge wave representing the implacable force of nature.

Although Gericault's composition is Baroque, his mood is clearly Romantic. He condemned the injustice that created the tragedy and at the same time invited viewers to respond to the compelling themes of hope against despair and humanity against nature.

The *Raft of the Medusa* established Gericault as France's foremost Romantic artist. During the next few years he created a remarkable series of portraits of inmates at hospitals and institutions for the insane. Unfortunately, Gericault died in 1824, at the age of 32. His death gave his friend and colleague Eugene Delacroix an opportunity to become France's preeminent Romantic artist.

Eugene Delacroix

Delacroix was young, independent, and largely self-taught. He moved comfortably in fashionable circles where people found him elegant and witty. At the same time, an intensely passionate nature smoldered beneath his outward charm. The poet and critic Charles Baudelaire described him as "a volcanic crater artistically concealed beneath bouquets of flowers."

Like Gericault, Delacroix rebelled against the careful drawing and morally uplifting subjects from ancient history favored by the Neoclassicists. Instead, contemporary events taking place in Greece riveted his attention. In 1822, the Turks massacred 20,000 defenseless Greeks on the small island of Chios. Sensing a chance to distinguish himself, Delacroix decided to paint a picture of the atrocity.

The completed painting, *Scenes from the Massacre at Chios*, exemplifies the new Romantic style (**CD Fig. 24-3**). Set on an exotic island, the painting depicts remorseless Ottoman soldiers guarding a group of exhausted Greeks waiting to be either executed or enslaved. Delacroix replaced the precise edges and smooth surfaces of Neoclassical painting with thick brushstrokes and vivid colors.

Delacroix applied his understanding of the expressive power of color to yet another exotic subject, the death of the last Assyrian king, Sardanapalus. Inspired by Lord Byron's play *Sardanapalus*, Delacroix portrayed the besieged despot reclining on his ceremonial bed about to die (**CD Fig. 24-4**). Resigned to his fate, Sardanapalus indifferently watches as his servants slaughter his favorite horse and the women of his harem. Only the rich red cover on his bed unites the chaotic scene. Delacroix offered no redeeming moral, just violence and terror.

Moments of supreme emotion fascinated Delacroix. In 1830, the people of Paris spontaneously revolted against the arbitrary rule of Charles X. Although Delacroix did not fight for his country, he vowed to paint for it. Working with his usual passion, he produced the monumental *Liberty Leading the People* in just three months (**CD Fig. 24-5**).

Delacroix focused the viewer's attention on an allegorical figure who personifies Liberty. Liberty holds a rifle in her left hand as her right hand defiantly raises the republic's tricolor flag. She urges the street fighters to move forward over the rubble. The rebels wear various hats, indicating that all social classes supported the revolt. Liberty wears a scarlet Phrygian cap, the symbol of a freed slave in antiquity.

Buoyed by the acclaim awarded to *Liberty Leading the People*, Delacroix next visited North Africa. The sun-drenched landscape and the people's colorful robes made a lasting impression on the artist. He tried to capture the exotic culture and its vibrant colors in a series of paintings that depicted tiger hunts and the secluded world of a harem. Delacroix recorded his observations about color and brushwork in a journal that later influenced the Impressionists.

Francois Rude and La Marseillaise

Romanticism championed the ability of the human imagination to capture moments of supreme emotion. The soaring emotional surge of the Romantic spirit can be seen in the enormous high-relief sculpture by Francois Rude that decorates one of the piers of the Arc de Triomphe (**CD Fig. 24-6**). A resolute figure representing both France and Liberty soars above a group of soldiers urging them to defend France from an Austrian-Prussian invasion in 1792. Rude depicted the soldiers in classical nudity or wearing ancient armor to express the universal theme of humanity's fight for liberty.

Although Rude's soldiers are dressed like classical heroes, a Romantic spirit clearly energizes them. An intense nationalistic zeal carries the densely packed soldiers forward into battle. When unveiled in 1836, the sculpture so stirred the patriotism of French viewers that it quickly became known as *La Marseillaise*, the name of the French national anthem written in 1792.

The AP Art History committee has frequently asked students to compare *La Marseillaise* with Athena Battling Alkyoneos from the Altar of Zeus. (see Chapter 6). Both sculptures are incorporated into structures—the Arc de Triomphe and the Altar of Zeus—that served as focal points of civic ceremonial activities. In addition, both works feature dynamic and highly developed Realistic qualities.

Antoine-Louis Barye

The raw beauty of the animal world fascinated Antoine-Louis Barye. His sculptures often portrayed exotic animals locked in a fierce fight to the death. For example, in *Tiger Devouring a Gavial Crocodile of the Ganges* (**CD Fig. 24-7**), Barye provides a graphic depiction of a tiger attacking a crocodile. Barye's bronze statuettes appealed to the Romantic passion for strong emotion and chaotic struggle in an untamed natural setting.

Figure 24-7. Antoine-Louis Barye, *Tiger Devouring a Gavial Crocodile of the Ganges*, 1831

Francisco de Goya y Lucientes

Goya and *Los Caprichos*

Although French artists and sculptors played a dominant role in the Romantic movement, the Spanish artist Francisco de Goya y Lucientes (1746–1828) emerged as one of the greatest artists of the Romantic period. Goya first earned his reputation by painting cartoons for Rococo tapestries. A **cartoon** is a full-scale drawing used to transfer the outline of a design onto a surface to be painted. A series of outstanding portraits of leading Spanish aristocrats earned Goya further acclaim.

The outbreak of the French Revolution in 1789 had a dramatic effect on Goya's art. At first he welcomed the Revolution's promise of political enlightenment and individual freedom. But Goya soon became disillusioned when the hoped-for reforms proved to be short lived.

The apparent failure of the French Revolution prompted Goya to create a folio of eighty etchings called *Los Caprichos* (*The Caprices*). The best-known print, *The Sleep of Reason Produces Monsters* (**CD Fig. 24-8**), shows a personification of Reason sound asleep, slumped over a writing table. As Reason sleeps, an ominous flock of owls (representing folly) and bats (representing ignorance) suddenly appear to symbolize what happens when humanity abandons logic and reason. Other prints from *Los Caprichos* satirize a broad range of superstitions and follies of Spanish life.

Goya and the Royal Commissions

Although *Los Caprichos* did not sell well, Goya's career nonetheless continued to advance. In 1799, Charles IV appointed Goya as First Painter to the King. The following year, Goya painted a group portrait of the royal family.

The Family of Charles IV (**CD Fig. 24-9**) provides a revealing comparison with Velazquez's *Las Meninas* (see Chapter 20). Standing in the center, Queen Maria Luisa strikes the same pose as the Infanta Margarita in *Las Meninas*. Although resplendent with their lavish costumes and gleaming medals, Charles IV and his family appear to be dull, stiff, and inept. Whereas Velazquez portrayed himself proudly standing with the royal family, Goya painted himself standing in the shadows, as if to express his ambivalence about the king and queen.

Events justified Goya's doubts about the royal family. In 1807, mass protests forced the corrupt Charles IV to abdicate in favor of his son, Ferdinand VII. Within a year, Napoleon put his brother, Joseph Bonaparte, in Ferdinand's place. The French occupation provoked bloody rioting in Madrid on May 2, 1808. Determined to suppress the revolt, French troops retaliated by executing almost a thousand Spanish rebels.

Six years later, Goya commemorated the atrocity in a painting that, like Gericault's *Raft of the Medusa* and Delacroix's *Scenes from the Massacre at Chios*, confronts viewers with a horrible act of inhumanity. In *The Third of May 1808* (**CD Fig. 24-10**), Goya portrayed the French firing squad as a row of ruthless and faceless executioners who are indifferent to their victims' pleas for mercy. Faced with death, the condemned men react with emotions ranging from terror to despair. Goya focused our attention on an unforgettable central figure dressed in yellow and white, the colors of the papacy. He defiantly raises his arms in a Christlike gesture of martyrdom.

Goya's Black Paintings

As Goya aged, he became increasingly disillusioned and pessimistic. Among his later works is a series known as the Black Paintings. Drawn on the walls of his farmhouse just outside Madrid and created solely for himself, these works reveal a terrifying and even disturbing vision. In *Saturn Devouring One of His Children* (**CD Fig. 24-11**), for example, Goya depicted a wild-eyed Saturn eating one of his sons to thwart a prophecy that his children would overthrow him. Still haunted by the fears expressed in *The Sleep of Reason Produces Monsters*, Goya may have used the myth to express his feeling about the irrationality of old age.

Romantic Landscape Painting

Romantic artists shared an overriding desire to express powerful personal emotions. Like atrocities and exotic experiences, nature could elicit deep feelings. During the

Romantic era, landscape painting took on a new significance. For artists in Germany, England, and the United States, landscapes became a means of celebrating the natural world and the divine power that created it.

Caspar David Friedrich

Germany's greatest Romantic artist, Caspar David Friedrich, devoted his career to landscape painting. Many of his landscapes feature figures seen from behind the back, contemplating a compelling and often mysterious natural setting. In *Wanderer Above a Sea of Mist* (**CD Fig. 24-12**), a solitary figure stands on a rocky cliff looking out over a landscape shrouded in thick mists. Absorbed in thought, the wanderer looks to nature for spiritual guidance.

John Constable

John Constable, perhaps the best known of the English landscape artists, is renowned for his views of the Stour Valley in Suffolk, north of London. Constable's most famous painting, *The Haywain* (**CD Fig. 24-13**), depicts a tranquil summer day at Flatford Mill. Only the dog looks up as an empty hay wagon crosses the Stour River. In the distant meadow, a group of farmhands load hay onto a second wagon. Billowy clouds float across the sky, throwing patches of shadow across the green fields.

The Haywain provides no hint of the Industrial Revolution then transforming rural England. No pollution mars Constable's sky or fouls the Stour's pristine waters. No displaced workers drift across the verdant fields. "Painting," Constable asserted, "is but another word for feeling." In *The Haywain*, Constable ignored the effects of the Industrial Revolution to portray his nostalgic feeling of oneness with nature.

J. M. W. Turner

Constable's calm landscapes exemplify the Romantic yearning for a personal connection with nature. In contrast, the paintings of his contemporary Joseph Mallord William Turner strive to portray the uncontrollable and frightening power of nature.

Turner's quest to capture the awesome power of nature can be seen in his historical landscape titled *Snowstorm: Hannibal and His Army Crossing the Alps* (**CD Fig. 24-14**). Turner shows the army of the great Carthaginian leader Hannibal, who, like Napoleon, invaded Italy by marching through the Alps. But Turner does not glorify Hannibal. Instead, he focuses the viewer's attention on a swirling snowstorm that threatens to overwhelm Hannibal and his battered army. Whereas the Neoclassical painter David portrayed Napoleon as an invincible leader who commanded both his troops and nature (see Chapter 23), the Romanticist Turner reduced Hannibal to a tiny speck on the horizon.

Turner's theme of humanity's insignificance faced with the awesome and terrifying forces of nature can also be seen in *The Slave Ship* (**CD Fig. 24-15**). The painting is based on the true story of a ship's captain who callously threw his cargo of 132 sick and dying slaves overboard so he could collect insurance that paid for humans lost at sea but not for death from illness. Although the limbs and chains of the victims are discernible in the foreground, Turner focuses on the slave ship heading into the fury of a typhoon. Like the captain, nature is indifferent and implacable.

Turner used sweeping brushstrokes and vivid colors to intentionally blur forms. His swirling colors overwhelm both Hannibal's army and the fleeing slave ship. Turner's innovative use of freely applied colors had a significant impact on the development of modern art. Because of his willingness to reduce shape and blur form, Turner is often thought of as the first "modern" artist.

Hudson River School

Landscape paintings were popular in both Europe and the United States. One group of American artists known as the Hudson River School formed the country's first art movement. Led by Thomas Cole, Hudson River artists painted the unspoiled woods and valleys of the Hudson River and Catskill Mountains in upstate New York. During the 1860s, Albert Bierstadt traveled west and produced many paintings depicting the sublime majesty of the Rocky Mountains and the Yosemite Valley. Taken together, these paintings capture the immense scale and many moods of America's landscape.

Hudson River School artists painted their landscapes with a realist's attention to detail and a Romantic's choice of imagery. Let us examine Albert Bierstadt's *Rocky Mountains, Lander's Peak* (**CD Fig. 24-16**). Bierstadt painted minute details of the location he observed firsthand during an expedition to the Rocky Mountains with the U.S. Army. When he exhibited this painting, he made magnifying glasses available to enable viewers to inspect tree leaves, flower petals, and mountains crags, as well as the Native American tribe engaged in daily activities.

Bierstadt painted a glorious light emanating from the clouds and illuminating the mountain waterfall at the center of the painting. This beautiful sight inspired many Americans to move westward. This is a salient point because America was dealing with the issue of westward expansion. Many Americans believed in Manifest Destiny, which meant that it was Americans' God-given right to expand westward. Bierstadt focused on the pristine and uncontaminated beauty of the American West. The lighting in the center almost looks like a divine light sanctioning Manifest Destiny. Thus, Bierstadt also romanticized the American West, a technique that drew many spectators to view exhibits of his paintings.

Romantic Architecture and the Gothic Revival

As we have seen, classical buildings inspired Neoclassical architects (see Chapter 23). In contrast, Romantic architects looked to their nation's Gothic past for inspiration. The Gothic revival began in England during the 1750s, when Horace Walpole "Gothicized" his country villa outside London. When completed, Strawberry Hill (**CD Fig. 24-17**) featured exterior turrets, buttresses, and tracery along with interior fan vaulting.

The Gothic revival in England received additional impetus when the old Houses of Parliament burned down in 1834. After much debate, Sir Charles Barry won a commission to rebuild the Houses of Parliament in the Gothic style (**CD Fig. 24-18**).

The Gothic revival spread to America, where it played an important role in church architecture. Richard Upjohn, the leading proponent of the Gothic style, built more than forty Gothic revival churches. He is best known for Trinity Church in New York City (**CD Fig. 24-19**).

Whereas the Gothic revival looked to the past, the invention of cast-iron skeletons and prefabricated parts ushered in a new era in architectural design and construction (see Chapter 28). At the same time, photography posed an unprecedented challenge to artists. As discussed in Chapter 25, a new group of artists, called the Realists, chose to emphasize the experiences and sights of contemporary life.

Conclusion

Romantic artists emphasized feeling, imagination, and personal intuition. They found inspiration in exotic cultures, human atrocities, and the sublime beauty of nature. French artists and sculptors played a dominant role in the Romantic movement. You should carefully review the work of Gericault, Delacroix, Rude, and Barye. It is important to know that Baroque art influenced the *Raft of the Medusa*, that the Romantic approach to color and brushwork influenced Impressionism, that Barye specialized in statuettes of animals, and that Turner's innovations with color made a significant impact on the development of modern art. In addition, review Fuseli's *The Nightmare*, noting that it is an early Romantic painting that explores human psychology.

Chapter 25

Realism and the Birth of Photography

Introduction and Exam Strategy Overview

Times were changing for Western civilization during the nineteenth century. Europe experienced major revolutions in science, industry, technology, and social systems. All these revolutions significantly affected a simultaneous artistic revolution. Realist artists sought to visibly manifest in their works the changes that were occurring in their world. The technological revolution produced another method of visually recording the world other than painting or sketching—photography.

Because of the artistic changes that occurred during the Realist era (1850s), it has been and will remain a popular topic on the AP Art History exam. Tests typically have two to four questions on artists and events of the Realist era. Test writers have developed slide-based multiple-choice questions about a Realist painting juxtaposed with a photograph of a similar theme. A slide-based short essay has asked students to compare and contrast a portrait by Ingres with a photograph by Nadar.

This chapter provides context for Realism and introduces you to the major Realist artists as well as key events. It also familiarizes you with terms related to photography while comparing and contrasting Realism and photography.

Nineteenth-Century Revolutions

The nineteenth century built on the spirit of the Enlightenment and the Scientific Revolution. The late eighteenth century and early nineteenth century were times in which scientists began to use the scientific method rather than accept explanations for the universe with faith. This Age of Reason inspired industrial and technological revolutions in which science was used to improve the efficiency of everyday tools. The Industrial Revolution began in central England during the late 1700s and primarily affected the textile industry. The second half of the nineteenth century witnessed another wave of the Industrial Revolution that included technological advances and a rash of new inventions, such as the train and—most important for art history—photography. Industrialization caused urbanization. Cities grew as peasants from the countryside moved in search of factory work. Many workers lived in cramped and filthy apartment buildings near the factories and earned low wages for long hours of work.

A revolution occurred among the social classes of Europe, which was written about by Karl Marx in *The Communist Manifesto*. Industrialization, the growth of capitalism, and urbanization expanded class differences with the creation of a new, urban working class, which Marx called the proletariat. Another element of the social revolution was the expanding class of the newly rich, which Marx referred to as the bourgeoisie. Comprising mostly business and factory owners, the bourgeoisie controlled capital and the government. Tension escalated between the proletariat and the bourgeoisie and eventually erupted into violent revolutions in France in 1830, 1848, and 1870. Several other European countries also experienced revolutions in 1848.

What Is Realism?

Art historians still disagree about the meaning of *Realism*. For the purposes of the AP Art History exam, it represents a movement in mid-nineteenth-century art to depict what can actually be seen in the world. Since the Enlightenment, people had begun to embrace the philosophy of **empiricism**, which held that people should search for knowledge based only on observation and direct experience. How does this translate into the world of art? Gustave Courbet may have said it best: "Show me an angel, and I'll paint one."

Social Revolution and the Realists

Gustave Courbet, whom you will learn about shortly, applauded the 1870 revolution that overthrew France's Second Empire and Napoleon III. The Socialist Commune even made Courbet director of artistic affairs. Another Realist, Jean-Francois Millet, looked to peasants in the countryside for inspiration. The artist Honoré Daumier created lithographs that captured important social events and rallied against France's repressive regimes. A female realist, Rosa Bonheur, looked beyond human affairs to make animals her subjects. Not long after its birth in France, Realism spread to the United States, Great Britain, and Germany.

Realism: The Artistic Revolution

Realist artists departed from the subjects of previous styles. If asked to recall the glories of Rome, Neoclassicists would have enthusiastically taken on the task. Realists, on the other hand, would have responded, "Who cares? Ancient history is just that—ancient. It has no relevance to the new Industrial Age." Romanticists were concerned with nature and with imagining great things. That was nice, but Realists believed imagination was for dreamers. People of the nineteenth century did not actually see angels or the figures from the Bible, so religious figures were also out. And paintings of grand historical events and figures did not strike a chord with the Realists because they did not experience the events and had never met the people.

The new style of art focused on subjects that were grounded in the modern world and part of the artists' personal experience. Peasants, the working class, the struggles of life, and satires on the bourgeoisie were popular topics among the Realists.

"Precursors" to Realism

Although Realism was born of the nineteenth century, some artists from the sixteenth to eighteenth centuries were interested in the lives of peasants. Realists particularly admired three earlier artists who had depicted peasant and middle-class life: Bruegel, Le Nain, and Chardin.

Pieter Bruegel (1528–1569)

Recall that Pieter Bruegel the Elder was a sixteenth-century Netherlandish painter who depicted the activities of peasants during various seasons of the year (see Chapter 19). Remember *The Harvesters*? At a time when artists from other European countries were depicting dramatic religious frescoes or learned religious allegories, Bruegel closely examined peasants while they worked, hunted, ate, drank, and played. Remember, paintings of the activities of commoners are called **genre painting**.

Louis Le Nain (1593–1648)

Louis Le Nain painted pictures of peasants during the Thirty Years' War of the seventeenth century. Foreign armies invaded the countryside and harassed the peasantry, stealing, raping, and burning villages. Frustrated by their condition, peasants in the French countryside revolted against wealthy nobles. The nobles, with support from the monarchy, brutally suppressed the peasant revolts. During that time, Le Nain painted *Family of Country People* to portray the plight of the peasants (**CD Fig. 25-1**). The mother on the left has a worn face, the father in the background looks tired, and their children look too serious for people their age. You can see that the family is poor (the children have no shoes, the father has holes in his jacket, and the oldest daughter wears a filthy dress) and tied closely to the land. Yet, Le Nain presented the peasants with dignity. They have stoic faces, seeming to accepting their station in life with patience and dignity.

During the seventeenth century, when the Baroque style of Poussin and others reigned supreme, wealthy patrons preferred classicism. How might they have reacted to a genre painting like *Family of Country People*? Most probably responded well to Le Nain's depiction of the peasants as peaceful and orderly.

Jean-Baptiste-Simeon Chardin (1699–1779)

Chardin painted during the Rococo period of the eighteenth century (see Chapter 22). Chardin dismissed the frivolities of the Rococo and instead depicted quiet, middle-class scenes praising the simple goodness of ordinary people. *Grace at Table* (**CD Fig. 25-2**) displays a mother setting a table and looking down approvingly on her younger daughter, who folds her hands in prayer. The older daughter is seated at the table and also looks in the direction of her sister. The room's sparse decor, the plain tablecloth, and the ordinary place settings convey the humility of this family. Notice that Chardin used muted colors (browns and grays) to portray the simplicity of these folk. He focused on their morality, as embodied in the youngest daughter learning the important lesson of thankfulness. At a time in which Rococo artists expressed the decadence of the French aristocracy, Chardin's *Grace at Table* extolled the virtue of the lower class.

Gustave Courbet

Courbet is the father of Realism, although he did not like such stylistic labels. Realism as a label derives from his independent exhibit, which he called the Pavilion of Realism. He was the son of a well-to-do farmer, born in the remote town of Ornans in eastern France. He moved to Paris at age 20 and struggled for years to gain recognition as an artist. Courbet's chance came after the 1848 revolution. (That year, revolutions broke out in Austria, German, Italy, and France. It was also the year that Marx published *The Communist Manifesto*.) He was hailed as the leader of the new Realist school. Courbet's letterhead read, "Gustave Courbet, master painter, without ideal and without religion."

Courbet created the *Realist Manifesto* to explain the aims of his work. He was committed to contemporary social issues of the working class. In his art, he focused on the common people and subjects that surrounded him. He wanted to translate the customs, ideas, and appearances of his time as he saw them. Therefore, his subjects had to be visible and tangible, things that were real and existing. Courbet went on to say that abstract objects and things nonexistent or invisible (Romantic art) did not belong in the domain of painting and concluded with his famous "show me" saying.

The Stone Breakers

To our eyes, there is nothing offensive about Courbet's *The Stone Breakers*. The painting depicts a youth assisting an older man in breaking stones for a roadbed. But the painting shocked and angered critics and the French public alike. Stone breaking was a job usually performed by the lowest in French society. Courbet did not romanticize their labor. He used muted colors such as brown and gray to convey the monotony of the work. We feel compassion for the younger fellow, because one day he will be that older worker hunched on the ground, having performed backbreaking labor for the greater part of his life. Released shortly after the 1848 revolutions, *The Stone Breakers* provoked criticism for its socialist undertone (**CD Fig. 25-3**). Many art historians now view *The Stone Breakers* as the first socialist painting. Critics also attacked the two-dimensional quality of his painting technique. Courbet used loose brushwork and did not fully model the volume and mass of the figures with chiaroscuro.

Burial at Ornans

Courbet's *Burial at Ornans* is a huge painting measuring 10 feet high by 22 feet wide (**CD Fig. 25-4**). It contains nearly sixty life-sized figures. Courbet depicts the townspeople of Ornans gathered together, possibly for the funeral of his grandfather,

Oudut. (Men in the foreground wear clothing contemporary with the French Revolution, in which his grandfather had participated.) This is death at its simplest and most ordinary. Courbet referred to his creation as "the death of Romanticism." We can see the clergy and the male and female mourners separated, in accordance with Catholic custom.

Figure 25-4. Gustave Courbet, *Burial at Ornans*, 1850

Critics hated the painting for several reasons. On seeing it, Emperor Napoleon III cried, "Great God! How ugly!" The painting depicted the life of common people without romanticizing their existence. Courbet created the painting on a monumental scale that had been reserved for paintings with religious or historical themes or for portraits of monarchs. He thus elevated the common people to the level of God and the monarchy. Instead of a traditional pyramidal composition, Courbet lined the figures in rows across the picture plane, an arrangement that he considered more democratic. Critics once again complained about Courbet's painting technique, which they viewed as crude and unrefined. Occasionally, he used a painter's knife to apply big patches of paint. This was improper by academic standards. Courbet set the stage for the reexamination of the qualities of paint, which would influence the loose brushwork of the impressionists. What was the purpose of painting: to create the illusion of a three-dimensional world or to call attention to the issues of the nineteenth century? Courbet would have subscribed to the latter.

The Salon and the Pavilion of Realism

The Salon, a state-run art exhibition held every two years in Paris, convened a jury of noteworthy artists and critics to accept or reject artists' work for display. At the time, being accepted for the Salon was extremely important because it was the artist's only real contact with critics, the public, and collectors. One young painter, on learning that the jury refused his paintings, committed suicide.

Courbet submitted his work to the 1855 Salon, a part of Exposition Universelle. The jury rejected his work because his subjects and content were too coarsely depicted and smacked of socialism. In fact, the Salon rejected at least twenty of his paintings that year. The jury's rejection may have been one of the most fateful decisions in art history.

Undaunted, Courbet rented space near the Exposition and created his own exhibition called the Pavilion of Realism. He displayed forty of his paintings. The public ignored the show and the critics derided it, but its effect on other artists was profound. Courbet showed that it was possible to challenge the Salon.

Courbet and other Realists continued to submit works to the Salon, eventually gaining more public acceptance. In fact, by 1870, Napoleon III offered Courbet the Legion of Honor, the highest award an artist could win. Staying true to form, Courbet rejected it. The Salon remained an important venue for recognition into the late 1800s. Yet Courbet's boldness foreshadowed the Impressionist exhibitions and the future importance of private galleries.

Jean-Francois Millet

Jean-Francois Millet was the son of a farm laborer. He moved to Paris to study art and began his career by painting portraits and pastoral scenes in the eighteenth-century style. Then, in 1848, he chose to submit *The Winnowers* to the Salon. Because the painting depicted peasants working, critics accused him of allowing socialist sympathies to creep into his work. He responded that he wanted to capture the human side of life. In 1849, he joined a group of artists who worked in Barbizon, a small village outside of Paris. These artists specialized in landscapes and truthfully depicted the countryside and the people who worked the land. Millet would spend the rest of his life in Barbizon. Art historians call Millet and his fellow artists the **Barbizon School**. Millet and the other members of the Barbizon School influenced later painters such as Monet, Pisarro, Seurat, and Van Gogh.

One of Millet's most famous paintings is *The Gleaners* (**CD Fig. 25-5**). It depicts three peasant women performing the grueling task of gleaning the last scraps of wheat. The owners of the land usually permitted the most impoverished women to pick up the remainders left in the field after the harvest. Millet's *The Gleaners* is similar to Courbet's *The Stone Breakers* in that it frankly reveals the difficulties of peasant life. Notice the realism that Millet employed. He did not idealize the beauty of these women or exaggerate their actions. Their bodies possess a certain monumentality of form that brings dignity to their labor. Critics called Millet the "Michelangelo of the peasants." He used muted colors for the clothing that these peasant women wore and created a recessional space that allows us to survey the land around them.

Another famous painting by Millet is *The Angelus* (**CD Fig. 25-6**). A peasant couple has stopped their toil to say the early morning prayer called the Angelus. Notice the realism that Millet employs and the muted colors characteristic of the Realist style. He portrays the couple as hardworking (you can see all the land that they have tilled) and pious.

Rosa Bonheur

Rosa Bonheur was the daughter of an artist. She specialized in painting pictures of animals, including sheep, tigers, horses, cows, and wolves. In her home in Paris, Bonheur had peacocks, chickens, and goats to use as models. To increase her understanding of animal anatomy, she would study the carcasses at a slaughterhouse. Bonheur became the most successful female artist of her time. In 1865, Napoleon III awarded her the Legion of Honor, making her the first woman to win the award. One of her most famous paintings hangs in the Metropolitan Museum of Art. Called *The Horse Fair*, it displays her tremendous talent for realistically rendering animal anatomy (**CD Fig. 25-7**). She sketched at the Paris horse fair for a year and a half disguised as a man in preparation for the 8-by-16-foot masterpiece. We see horses trotting and rearing up. She captures the muscles, tendons, and veins of their well-defined bodies, articulated by the effects of light. A recessional space in the distance enables the viewer to see people through the trees. The horses are the focal point; the men who parade them for sale are mere accessories.

Honoré Daumier

Honoré Daumier was a bold political satirist. He created cartoons and **lithographs** for the popular press in a newspaper called *La Caricature*. A lithograph is a print made by pressing a page over a specially prepared stone using a complex technique, which transfers the design or picture onto the page. One of Daumier's key works depicted Louis Philippe, the king of France, as *Gargantua*, a fictional figure in literature known for his insatiable appetite (**CD Fig. 25-8**). Louis Philippe's authoritarian policies and sumptuous life style made him a target of the popular press. Daumier depicts a never-satisfied king exploiting his subjects and growing fat at their expense. In response, the government charged Daumier and his publisher with inciting contempt and hatred of the French government and for insulting the person of the king. The artist was sentenced to six months in jail.

Undeterred, Daumier created another work for the popular press, a lithograph called the *Rue Transnonain* (**CD Fig. 25-9**). In April 1834, workers in Paris rioted to demonstrate against harsh working conditions and the recent passage of an anti-unionization law. On the night of April 14, a sniper in Paris killed a police officer. In retaliation, police killed a number of innocent residents of the sniper's building, including the father and son depicted in Daumier's lithograph. Daumier's printer wrote, "This is not a caricature . . . it is a blood-stained page in the history of our days, traced by a vigorous hand and inspired by noble indignation. . . . He has created a picture which will never lose its worth or duration."

Daumier also created Realist paintings, such as *The Third-Class Carriage* (**CD Fig. 25-10**). It gives us a glimpse into a cramped and grimy railway carriage of the 1860s. Railway owners crammed third-class passengers together on hard wooden benches. Although several people are in the painting, only one looks in our direction. Every person seems to be in his or her own world. Daumier thus expressed the alienation of the third-class passengers.

Edouard Manet

Art historians consider Edouard Manet to be one of the most influential painters of the nineteenth century. Chapter 26 investigates his influence on the impressionists and modern art. Here we explore his work as a Realist.

Manet came from a respectable bourgeois family. His father was a high-ranking official from the Ministry of Justice, and his mother came from a long line of diplomats. His family wanted him to study law, but he failed the entrance exam. Then his father insisted that he join the navy. Manet spent time traveling on a vessel known as the *Havre et Guadeloupe*. Life at sea did not agree with him, and he was incapable of tying nautical knots. However, the captain did employ Manet's artistic skills to paint spoiled food to make it look more palatable.

Despite his family's wishes, Manet announced his plans to become an artist. Manet would become one of the most revolutionary artists in history, ranking with Giotto and Caravaggio. Demonstrating a commitment to realist principles, Manet's painting technique would inspire modernism. Let us examine the paintings that made him famous (or notorious, according to the nineteenth-century critics).

In *Le Dejeuner sur l'Herbe* (*Luncheon on the Grass*), the foreground figures are portraits of contemporary people (**CD Fig. 25-11**). The seated nude is Victorine Meurend, who modeled for other Manet paintings. The gentleman to the right is Manet's brother, Eugene, and the man on the left is the sculptor Ferdinand Leehof. In the background, Manet included a woman wading in a stream with a two-dimensional-looking forest behind her. In the left foreground, we see a still life with a basket of fruit and rolls. Manet submitted this painting to the Salon of 1863, and it was rejected.

Salon des Refuses and *Le Dejeuner sur l'Herbe*

Of the 5,000 submissions to the Salon of 1863, the jury rejected 2,800. Responding to the complaints of artists and their supporters, Emperor Napoleon III ordered a separate exhibition for the rejected works of art. The government called this exhibition of rejected works the **Salon des Refuses**. "People entered it as they would a horror chamber at Madame Tussaud's Wax Museum in London," recalled one artist whose works were displayed. "They laughed as soon as they passed through the door."

The Salon des Refuses marks a watershed event in art history because critics subsequently divided artists into academics (those whose work was worthy of the official salon) and the independents (those who were too modern for official tastes). The exhibition was the first step toward avant-garde art (see Chapter 26).

The organizers of the exhibit displayed *Le Dejeuner sur l'Herbe* in the farthest room of the Salon des Refuses. Critics reacted negatively to it, using expressions such as "indecent" and "shocking." One critic wrote, "This is a young man's practical joke, a shameful open sore not worthy of exhibiting." Most critics accused Manet of wanting to shock people.

Why did they react this way? First, it was scandalous to display a nude woman of contemporary times looking shamelessly at the viewer. Critics considered this vulgar. Critics also thought the painting was amateurish. Manet did not fully model the skin of Victorine with chiaroscuro. Her skin appears very pale and flat compared with the rest of the scene. Critics thought the painting possessed too many incongruous features and had an absurd composition: a poorly modeled nude lolling about between two fully dressed men, a realistically rendered still life in the left foreground, an enigmatic woman in the background who is disproportionately large for the painting, and a flat-appearing background that did not contain the illusionary devices of the Old Masters.

In reality, Manet possessed academic training and spent many hours in the Louvre studying and sketching works by the Old Masters. He was particularly fond of Velazquez (see Chapter 20). When he created *Le Dejeuner sur l'Herbe*, he was imitating pastoral (rural) landscapes by Giorgione (see Chapter 17) and a famous engraving of a Raphael painting called the *Judgment of Paris* (the story of the Trojan prince Paris judging a beauty contest among three goddesses). The original Raphael painting had been lost, but Manet knew of the engraving.

What set Manet's painting apart was its expression of his desire for new art. It is doubtful that he painted *Le Dejeuner* with flatness, because he lacked the skill to render illusionary space. More likely, he was imitating the flat qualities of Japanese woodblock prints (see Chapter 26) and the loose brushwork of Velazquez and Delacroix, both of whom he admired. Therefore, Manet's painting synthesized classical sources with unconventional painting technique to create a novel and enormously influential style. One vanguard critic stated that *Le Dejeuner sur l'Herbe* dazzled and inspired; it had piquancy and was the astonishment of the exhibition.

Olympia

Aware of the tradition of the recumbent nude (Giorgione, Titian, Velazquez, Goya), Manet created his own version titled *Olympia* (**CD Fig. 25-12**). The model is Victorine Meurend. She is wearing a black ribbon about her neck, a red orchid in her hair, silk slippers, and a gold bracelet. A black cat is at her feet. Her maid is holding a bouquet, presumably sent by an admirer. Based on the subject's nudity and accessories, critics interpreted *Olympia* as a portrait of a prostitute. One critic described Olympia as "a courtesan with dirty hands and wrinkled feet . . . her body has the livid tint of a cadaver displayed in the morgue; her outlines are drawn in charcoal and her greenish bloodshot eyes appear to be provoking the public, protected all the while by a hideous Negress."

The 1865 Salon accepted *Olympia*. Anticipating the negative reaction of the public and critics, the organizers of the Salon "skied" the painting (moved it to an inconspicuous place high on the wall). Nevertheless, huge crowds gathered to see the controversial portrait. Two guards stood below the painting to protect it from the outraged citizens who wanted to attack it.

Why did the public and critics react so vehemently? Olympia's nudity was not a problem. Many of the 2,242 paintings displayed at the Salon of 1865 were nudes. For instance, Alexander Cabanel exhibited his *Birth of Venus* (**CD Fig. 25-13**). However, his nude was popular with the public for several reasons: Cabanel used a classical theme as the context for the nudity, he idealized the female form so that Venus's body had classical beauty, and Venus does not look out at the viewer but allows the viewer to observe her. In addition, Cabanel's painting developed chiaroscuro and naturalism, as can be seen in the human forms and the ocean waves.

Manet's *Olympia* was a modern woman with frank, realistic, features that Manet painted in his new style. Although the mainstream did not accept it, a new generation of artists greatly admired Manet's work.

Pre-Raphaelite Brotherhood

A group of English Realists banded together to form a group of Realistic painters called the Pre-Raphaelite Brotherhood in 1848. Their paintings possess enormous detail and convincing illusionism. The Pre-Raphaelites desired to depart from the tired classical themes being propagated in the academies since the time of Raphael. But unlike their contemporaries, the French Realists, the Pre-Raphaelites disdained industrialization and the world it created. Instead, the Pre-Raphaelites escaped from the present reality into the world of medieval stories and spirituality. Writers such as John Ruskin and William Shakespeare influenced these English artists.

Ophelia by the Pre-Raphaelite John Everett Millais has an almost photographic quality (**CD Fig. 25-14**). He exhibited the painting in the 1855 Salon Universelle in Paris (the event next to which Courbet set up his Pavilion of Realism). Millais studied nature and the human form very closely to create this painting. He had the wife of one of his friends lay in a warm bath for hours as he tried to capture the scene from Shakespeare's *Hamlet* in which Ophelia, whose love for Hamlet is unrequited, drowns herself. In one verse, Shakespeare wrote how Ophelia's clothes spread wide and mermaid-like, appearing to make her float. Millais captured this effect as well as the illusion of a Shakespearian world so well that the famous modern writer Baudelaire described Millais as the master of meticulous detail. The medieval theme, the realism, and the detail are hallmarks of the Pre-Raphaelite Brotherhood.

Birth of Photography

Photography exerted an enormous influence on nineteenth-century artists. The advantage of photographs was obvious. A photo could record an object exactly as it was at a particular moment, including the lighting, proper proportions, and spatial relationships. Some artists reacted against the medium, fearing it would render certain types of art obsolete. Other artists, such as Delacroix, Ingres, Courbet, and Degas, used the new technology to enhance their paintings as well as a means in itself. You will recall that the Dutch painter Vermeer was famous for his use of the *camera obscura* (see Chapter 21), an early predecessor to nineteenth-century cameras.

The first surviving photograph dates to 1826, when a French chemist named Nicephore Niepce made an image of the courtyard outside his home; he exposed the pewter plate for eight hours to capture the image. In 1839, Louis Daguerre inadvertently took the first known photograph of a human being, a man having his shoes shined. Soon people began to visit studios to have their image captured in a **daguerreotype**, an early type of photograph that Daguerre invented. The disadvantage of daguerreotypes was that they required a lengthy exposure time and thus demanded extreme patience from the sitters, many of whom used props to hold up their bodies.

Another inventor came up with a process called the **calotype**, which developed the first photo negatives. Light could then be shined through the negative onto photo-sensitive paper to produce a positive image. In 1851, the invention of a new process called **wet plate** reduced exposure time to seconds and produced prints almost as precise as Daguerre's. By the 1880s, inventors created portable handheld cameras and roll film.

Types of Popular Photography

Louis Daguerre created the first popular type of photography with his still lifes. He arranged his photos like seventeenth-century Dutch vanitas paintings. Other photographers took daguerreotypes of events, such as the first operations in which patients were anesthetized with ether. Josiah Johnson Hawes, a painter, and Albert Sands Southworth, a pharmacist and teacher, recorded an early operation from the vantage point of the gallery, making the viewer feel like a medical student (**CD Fig. 25-15**).

People wanted their likenesses captured by the accurate medium of photography, beginning the tradition of portrait photography. Photographers and painters occasionally cooperated to blend the desirable elements of the two mediums. Photography could portray a precise likeness, and painting created a mood and captured the sitter's personality. Early portrait photographers posed their subjects with special lighting and draped cloth over their bodies to create the mood of painted portraits.

Nadar was one of the most famous portrait photographers. Born Gaspard-Félix Tournachon, Nadar was also a caricaturist, novelist, and journalist who rode in a hot air balloon called the Giant to take the first aerial photographs. He said that in his work, he sought an instant understanding that would help convey the personalities of his models. In 1855, he took a famous photographic negative of the Romantic painter Eugene Delacroix (**CD Fig. 25-16**). At that point, Delacroix was a well-known celebrity. Nadar captured in Delacroix's pose the dignity and spirit of one of France's greatest painters.

Julia Margaret Cameron was another famous portrait photographer. However, she often posed her female sitters not as themselves but as characters from literary works, as in *Ophelia, Study no. 2* (**CD Fig. 25-17**). Recall that Millais, the Pre-Raphaelite painter, painted a picture of Ophelia. Cameron's photographs possess a hazy quality because she used a short lens that allowed only a small area of the picture to be sharply focused. The hazy quality gives her portraits a mystical, dreamy quality, which is compatible with the characters her sitters imitated.

War photography became popular as well. Early photographers captured the first war scenes in the Crimean War of the 1850s. However, the medium expanded greatly during the American Civil War. Photographers such as Timothy O'Sullivan and Matthew Brady exposed the grim realities of the Battle of Gettysburg by capturing images of dead bodies strewn across the battlefields. Brady took more than 7,000 photographic negatives of Civil War scenes.

Eadweard Muybridge and Sequential Motion Photography

Eadweard Muybridge was a British photographer who immigrated to the United States and made a reputation for himself by taking landscape photographs of the American West. Muybridge was eventually hired by the U.S. government to take photographs of survey and military expeditions.

An interesting opportunity catapulted Muybridge to greater notoriety. A politician and racetrack owner named Leland Stanford (who eventually became governor of California) involved himself in a debate about whether all four of a horse's hooves are airborne during a gallop. He took the position that a horse is fully airborne during parts of a gallop. Stanford hired Muybridge to resolve this debate. Muybridge captured a photographic still that revealed that all four horse's hooves are indeed airborne during a gallop (**CD Fig. 25-18**). To demonstrate this further, Muybridge positioned 50 cameras at the racetrack to capture Stanford's horse *Occident* in motion. Muybridge connected a tripwire to each camera which, when triggered by the passing horse's hooves, would snap a picture. Once again, photos revealed that Stanford was on the right side of the debate. Thus, Muybridge developed the technique of **sequential motion photography**.

Muybridge continued his sequential motion photographic studies, which influenced the development of motion pictures. Of particular interest was the movement of wild animals of the West and humans engaged in athletic activities.

Ingres versus Nadar

The 2001 AP Art History exam showed a slide of Ingres's painting *The Comtesse d'Haussonville* and Nadar's photograph *Sarah Bernhardt* (**CD Figs. 25-19 and 25-20**). The question asked students to discuss specific ways in which Ingres's painting both reflects and ignores the newer medium of photography, as represented by Nadar's photograph. To earn a 4 on this response, you had to discuss at least three issues related to these works together, at least one way Ingres's painting displays elements of traditional painting techniques and at least one way Ingres's painting reflects an awareness of photography.

The last time we examined Ingres was in Chapter 23 as a Neoclassical artist. Ingres went on to have a long, illustrious career, winning the Legion of Honor and being the most esteemed academic painter in all France. When examining *The Comtesse d'Haussonville*, realize that this is one of the last great Realist portraits.

Let us consider how Ingres's painting and Nadar's photograph are similar. Ingres captures every realistic detail in the comtesse, just as Nadar captures every detail of Sarah Bernhardt, who was a famous nineteenth-century actress. In Ingres's portrait, we can detect various textures: her satin dress and soft skin, the smoothness of her hair, the textiles of the chair in the foreground, and the delicate flower petals in the background. Ingres poses the comtesse in a manner that conveys her personality, just as Nadar poses Sarah Bernhardt to capture her personality, one of the key goals of Nadar's style. Ingres is able to render more detail than in traditional painting—for example, the way the light hits the corner of the wall in the background and the amazing reflection of the comtesse's back. In addition to using nude models (Ingres wanted to render the comtesse's anatomy as realistically as possible) and the comtesse herself, Ingres used photography to enhance his realism.

Yet there is something that paintings could capture that nineteenth-century photography could not. Can you guess what it is? Ingres was able to capture specific colors and their richness in the painting in ways that black-and-white photography could not. We can see the luster of the oil paint, which captures the extraordinary highlights of the satin dress, the highlights in her hair, the shine of the mirror, the material on the chair, and the glimmer of her jewelry. Like the photograph, Ingres presents tremendously accurate detail. However, he uses colors to show that painting still retains certain advantages for capturing a person's likeness.

Conclusion

Realism was a major artistic period of the mid-nineteenth century. It challenged the academy by departing from traditional subjects, taking instead the working class, peasants, and Realistic landscapes as themes. The Realists responded to the various revolutions around them and demonstrated an interest in social issues. Realists looked to earlier painters such as Bruegel, Le Nain, and Chardin as influences.

Courbet was the first artist to hold his own one-man art show challenging the institution of the Salon. His work elevated the status of ordinary people and workers. Meanwhile, Millet and the other Barbizon School artists glorified the landscape and peasant life. Manet's revolutionary blend of classical training and his unique style influenced future painters. The Salon des Refuses of 1863 diminished the authority of the academy and increased the power of independent artists, which would revolutionize art later in the nineteenth century.

Daguerreotypes and calotypes were the earliest photographic methods. You should be prepared to see a question that juxtaposes a Realist painting with a photograph and asks you to explain the advantages and disadvantages of each medium. Realize that although some Realist painters felt threatened by photography, others used it to their advantage.

Chapter 26

Impressionism and Post-Impressionism

Introduction and Exam Strategy Overview

Impressionism and Post-Impressionism were two important artistic periods that comprised the last thirty years of the nineteenth century. Both movements continued the revolutionary changes in art set in motion by the Romantics, who explored feelings and emotions in their art, and the Realists, who chose subjects that challenged the standards of the academies. Impressionists deviated from the academics in both their subject matter and their methods. Post-Impressionists deviated even further by exploring abstract depictions of color and shape as well as the inner mind of the artist.

Remember that art of the nineteenth century makes up 10 percent to 15 percent of the points on the AP Art History test. Because Impressionism and Post-Impressionism comprise thirty years of the nineteenth century, they are an important focus of study. The test assesses your knowledge of these periods in various ways. Typically, an exam includes two to four multiple-choice questions on the topics. On past tests, slide-based multiple-choice questions have examined both an Impressionist work and a Post-Impressionist work side by side. Additional slide-based short essays have asked students to recognize a work that may be associated with either movement and discuss its basic stylistic tendencies. Another popular question asks students to describe the influence of Japanese woodblock prints on Impressionist and Post-Impressionist paintings.

A recent testing trend is to include a written primary source pertaining to nineteenth-century art in the short essay part of the test. In 2005, a short writing by Eugene Delacroix accompanied his painting *The Barque of Dante*. In 2006, a quote by Charles Baudelaire, a famous modernist writer and art critic, discussed the shift in subject matter in nineteenth-century art. Test writers asked students to explain the primary source and cite examples of nineteenth-century art as support.

This chapter provides essential information about both Impressionism and Post-Impressionism. It also discusses the developments of the nineteenth century that provide context for the two periods.

What Is Impressionism?

It would be inaccurate to describe Impressionism as a cohesive movement similar to Neoclassicism. The term *impressionism* was actually used as a derisive description of a work by Claude Monet called *Impression: Sunrise.* Eventually, Monet and his fellow painters referred to themselves as Impressionists. Although the Impressionists share some qualities, the main link among them was that they exhibited together at eight impressionist shows between 1874 and 1886. However, they did not all consistently exhibit at every show and had serious disagreements about art and society at the time. Their art also displayed differences in subject and method.

Nonetheless, Impressionist works do share some common elements. First, Impressionist artists created works that captured an impression, a **momentary slice of life.** Consequently, the brush strokes in their paintings often appear short and choppy. Second, they sought to capture the **effect of light on color** at a certain moment in time. Third, most Impressionist painters **limited the use of black paint**, which they did not view as a color. To create shadows, Impressionists used dark green, blue, purple, and brown. Impressionists **juxtaposed complementary colors** (for example, orange and blue) to create vibrant contrasts between light and shadow. Fourth, Impressionists created compositions that have **cropped edges** and unusual angles. The asymmetrical composition helps to convey the feeling of a moment in time.

A fifth characteristic of Impressionist art is that modern Parisian life provided inspiration to the painters. Although Monet focused primarily on the outdoors, the **Parisian middle class**, or bourgeoisie, is a recurring theme in many Impressionists' works. Paris was becoming a bustling metropolis with a population of more than one million people. Modernity reached the streets of Paris. Emperor Napoleon III ordered that the streets be widened to accommodate large crowds and that more lights be added on the boulevards. Trains increased the urbanization of Paris and enabled the urban bourgeoisie to make short excursions to the French countryside. Parisians were on the move, and the Impressionists attempted to capture that.

An Important Concept: The Avant-Garde

The actions of the Impressionists gave rise to an important term in art history: **avant-garde**. Before its use in art criticism, the French military used the word to describe the units that advanced farther than the rest of the army. In art, *avant-garde* refers to artists who led the way with bold concepts and works. Generally misunderstood by the public who frequented the salons (state-run art exhibitions), the artistic concerns and techniques of the Impressionists were largely appreciated only by other artists. These artists were thus ahead of the mainstream, much like the avant-garde in the French military. When a style becomes mainstream (as did Impressionism by the 1890s), it is no longer avant-garde.

Another result of the expansion of the avant-garde was that the venue for viewing new art shifted from the salon to the private gallery. Salons usually rejected the avant-garde work in the nineteenth century. Because it did not keep up with the times, salons declined and private exhibitions grew.

Importance of Japanese Woodblock Prints

Japan had remained closed to Western trade and influence until the mid-nineteenth century. In the 1850s, the U.S. fleet compelled Japan to open itself to trade with the West. Soon European countries formed trade agreements with Japan as well. The "opening of Japan" affected the Western art world dramatically.

Similar to Rome's favorable response to Greek art and culture, Japanese culture captivated Europeans, especially the Parisian bourgeoisie. Among various other goods, they imported Japanese tea sets, folding screens, fans, and kimonos. The French even created a word to express the influx of Japanese culture: *Japonisme*.

For art history, the most important Japanese imports were **woodblock prints**. It is difficult to overstate the importance of Japanese woodblock prints to the Impressionists and Post-Impressionists. Japanese artists, such as Suzuki Harunobu (**CD Fig. 26-1**) and Katsushika Hokusai, created designs and carved them into blocks of wood used to create colored prints. Although many of the print artists were unknown, their creations were immensely popular with nineteenth-century Europeans. This graphic art form was inexpensive, and several Impressionist and postimpressionist artists collected them. At a large exhibit of Japanese woodblock prints in 1890, the American Impressionist Mary Cassatt wrote in a letter: "You must not miss it. . . . You couldn't dream of anything more beautiful. I dream of it and don't think of anything else." She even created her own series of prints called *The Ten*, which reflects the influence of the Japanese prints.

The Japanese aesthetic, which was called the *Ukiyo-e*, or "floating world," emphasized fleeting moments, snapshots of Japanese culture. Favorite subjects included theater, dance, and intimate moments of daily life. The world-famous Mount Fuji was another popular subject, as seen in the series by Katsushika Hokusai titled *Thirty-six Views of Mount Fuji* (**CD Fig. 26-2**).

Figure 26-2. Katsushika Hokusai, *The Great Wave off Kanagawa*, from *Thirty-six Views of Mount Fuji* series, ca. 1826–1833

Recalling the definition of the movement presented in the earlier section titled "What Is Impressionism?," you can understand that the qualities of Japanese woodcuts appealed to the Impressionists. An efficient way to remember these qualities is the acronym C-FID. *C* stands for "cropping": the Japanese artists created designs with cropped edges. *F* stands for "flatness": the woodblock prints do not convey volume with gradations of light and shadow; instead, the artists use steep angles and diagonals to give the illusion of another world. *I* stands for "intimate moments": the subjects of many woodcuts were small groups of people eating, drinking, or interacting in private. *D* stands for "decorative patterns": these are evident in the kimonos of the figures in the prints.

As we investigate Impressionism and Post-Impressionism, you should make mental comparisons between these styles and Japanese woodblock prints. If a test question asks you to describe the influence of Japanese woodblock prints, remember C-FID: cropped, flatness, intimate moments, and decorative patterns.

Major Artists of the Impressionist Style

We have established the important stylistic elements of Impressionism. Past AP tests do not usually require you to differentiate among the various artists associated with the Impressionist exhibitions. However, test writers do want to see if students can identify the names of artists associated with various styles, whether it is Venetian Renaissance, Realists, or Impressionists. The following sections introduce you to the major Impressionist artists and briefly describe their works.

Edouard Manet

Edouard Manet was one of the most influential figures to the Impressionists (see Chapter 25). Much of his work lacks Impressionist elements, but his revolutionary paintings established him as an iconoclast (rebel) to academicians. Manet received classical academic training as an artist, but he aspired to do more than merely copy the works of classical artists and the Old Masters such as Raphael. When his instructor was running late one day, Manet ordered the male model, who was supposed to pose nude, to put on his street clothes and pose for him and his classmates. When asked to paint a cast of a Roman portrait bust, he copied it upside-down saying it looked more interesting that way.

Manet's style is difficult to categorize. Chronologically, he was a contemporary of the Realists Courbet and Daumier, as well as the Impressionists. Stylistically, his flat, barely modeled figures with their pale skin juxtaposed with darker, muted colors also resemble the Realist works. However, his subjects reflect the bourgeoisie, which is more akin to the Impressionists than the Realists, who preferred the working class and peasants. Manet began to associate with the Impressionists, accompanying Monet and Renoir on painting trips along the Seine River. But Manet never exhibited in the Impressionist shows, so he was not officially part of the group.

Nevertheless, Manet's impact on the Impressionists is clear. Just as Manet had tired of his academic training, the young Impressionists abandoned their formal, indoor training for painting **plein air** (outdoors). Renoir best expressed the role of Manet when he said, "Manet was a whole new era of painting."

Claude Monet

Claude Monet was one of the first Impressionists, and his painting *Impression: Sunrise* became the group's namesake (**CD Fig. 26-3**). Monet displayed the revolutionary painting at the First Impressionist Exhibit of 1874. It contains stylistic elements of this group of artists. First, Monet captured a moment as people move about in boats on the water early in the morning. The human figures lack detail and modeling but we can nonetheless see them and their shadows on the water. The reddish orange sun turns everything around it into a hazy purplish blue. Surrounding the sun are blue clouds. Monet painted the orange reflection of sunlight with glints of yellow on the blue water. The colors are complementary and create vibrancy in the center of the picture. Imagine how different the colors of this painting would look by midday, or even in thirty minutes.

Conveying the moment in time, Monet used choppy brushstrokes for the small waves in the water. He used the same technique for the clouds. The vertical lines on the horizon appear to be the masts of docked ships. This picture lacks the controlled line used by academic artists, and the academic critics of the nineteenth century considered the painting unfinished.

Monet's main subject matter consisted of landscapes and seascapes. He painted series of certain topics chronicling how the objects looked at different times of day and different seasons of the year. For example, he created a series of paintings of Rouen Cathedral at different times of the day (**CD Fig. 26-4**). At a certain hour, the building has a creamy yellow color, while at another hour, it appears lavender. Monet also created well-known series based on grain stacks in the countryside, poplar trees, and water lilies.

Pierre-Auguste Renoir

Pierre-Auguste Renoir was Monet's friend, and the two of them would often take painting excursions along the Seine. Renoir is famous for his genre paintings of the Parisian bourgeoisie. One of his most famous paintings is *Luncheon of the Boating Party* (**CD Fig. 26-5**). It depicts a collection of middle-class Parisians enjoying a weekend afternoon on the Seine River. Food and bottles of wine decorate the tables of the café. People laugh, converse, and flirt. It looks like a beautiful, sunny day as boats sail in the distance.

Figure 26-5. Pierre-Auguste Renoir, *Luncheon of the Boating Party*, 1881

Notice the sketchy brushstrokes that Renoir used to capture this moment in time. Flecks of lighter-colored paint indicate spots of sunlight that hit the members of the boating party. Lavender and blue tones indicate the shadows on the skin of the revelers cast by the roof of the café. The colors have greater vibrancy because they are complementary; Renoir juxtaposed creamy yellow skin highlights with lavender shadows, and reddish orange beards are juxtaposed with blue shadows and water in the distance. The colors pop out at the viewer.

Renoir placed the figures in a natural and informal composition. Some sit, others stand, some have their backs to us, the owner of the café leans on a railing. The painting lacks a classical, pyramidal composition. Instead, we see the figures moving about in a moment of time. Renoir gave us a slice of the bourgeois life by cutting off the figures on the right side of the painting. He also cropped the table in the foreground. By doing so, he created the transitory feeling of this moment, which will soon be lost. However, before it could be lost, Renoir caught it using his short, choppy, brushstrokes.

Gustave Caillebotte Creates a Variation of Impressionism

Gustave Caillebotte was a wealthy engineer and boat builder who befriended the Impressionists. He helped finance exhibits and collected more than sixty Impressionist paintings, which he left to the French people. The paintings form the core of the great Impressionist collection at the Musée d'Orsay. Renoir even included him in his *Luncheon of the Boating Party*.

Caillebotte was also a fine artist. Let us examine his painting *Paris: A Rainy Day* (**CD Fig. 26-6**). Should we consider this a Realist or Impressionist painting? When Caillebotte painted this, a man named Baron Georges Haussmann, appointed by Emperor Napoleon III, instituted modernization projects in Paris that included erecting more streetlights and widening the Parisian streets to create roomy boulevards. Additionally, as industrialization expanded, so did locomotive use and urbanization. Caillebotte and other impressionists, like Camille Pissarro in *La Place du Théâtre Francais* and Monet in *Saint-Lazare Train Station* (**CD Fig. 26-7**), captured this evolution.

Paris: A Rainy Day lacks the loose brushwork and color of *Impression: Sunrise*, although it does have a slightly unfinished appearance. Yet the subject of Caillebotte's painting is bourgeois life. The Parisian middle-class walks about the streets fashionably dressed and equipped with umbrellas. Notice the asymmetrical composition of the painting and how Caillebotte cropped the figure at the far right. A streetlamp bisects the painting, and the weight of the painting favors the right, where a gentleman and lady stroll on the sidewalk sharing an umbrella. Caillebotte most likely planned this composition to give the viewer an impression of Paris undergoing its changes. Therefore, despite its more finished appearance, the subject matter, composition, and overall effect make Caillebotte's *Paris: A Rainy Day* an Impressionist painting.

Edgar Degas

Degas focused on interior scenes more than Monet. He was reluctant to be described as a member of the Impressionists as well because he felt that his goals differed from those of Monet and Renoir. Degas had no interest in plein air painting and believed that paintings should have carefully planned compositions. These opinions would seem to exclude him from the group.

However, a survey of his work displays several Impressionist features. His most famous series illuminates the lives of dancers, not just during performances but also backstage performing limbering exercises, and during practices and rehearsals (**CD Fig. 26-8**).

Degas provided a "snapshot" of their experiences. His arrangements are asymmetrical, have cropped edges, and include unusual viewpoints such as steep diagonals. (Photography, which was evolving in the nineteenth century, influenced Degas's compositions. In fact, Degas snapped photographs as studies for his paintings.) Degas also utilized loose brushwork or strokes with pastels. These qualities enhance the transitory feeling of Degas's works.

Degas is also famous for his series of women bathing and grooming themselves. He captured the private moments of these women performing their daily routines. Notice the cropped edges of *The Tub* (**CD Fig. 26-9**). To the right, a pitcher on a shelf is cut off at the side. The unusual viewpoint is reminiscent of the *Ukiyo-e* woodblock prints. The visible strokes of the pastels, the cropped edges, and the theme provide the slice of life that interested Impressionists.

Berthe Morisot and Mary Cassatt

Berthe Morisot was married to Eduoard Manet's brother, Eugene. Although she associated and exhibited with the Impressionists, social propriety limited a bourgeois woman's access to certain areas the artists frequented (cafés, for example) during the nineteenth century. Therefore, Morisot focused on the outdoor leisure of the Parisian middle class, who often escaped Paris on weekends for resorts by the sea or along the Seine. Morisot's paintings often contain a main female figure with either a male companion or a child relaxing in the outdoors. Like Monet, her paintings are often plein air. The paintings contain loose brushwork, express an interest in natural light and how it affects color, and an informal arrangement of the figures that enhances the feeling of the moment.

Mary Cassatt was born into a wealthy, American family from Pennsylvania. As a child, she and her family took trips to Europe. When she reached early adulthood, she left the United States to live in Europe and study art. She too became acquainted with the Impressionists, exhibited with them regularly, and befriended Degas, who became her mentor. Like Morisot, Cassatt was forced by the social restrictions placed on upper-class women to limit the subject matter of her work.

Most of her paintings focus on mothers alone with their children (**CD Fig. 26-10**). Although she usually places the figures in the center of the painting, Cassatt used sharp diagonal viewpoints, similar to the works of Degas and Japanese woodblock prints. The cropped edges and unusual angle of her paintings makes the viewer feel like a witness to the intimate and tender interaction as a mother cares for her child.

What Is Post-Impressionism?

The works of the Impressionists affected the next group of artists, the Post-Impressionists. Yet the works of the Impressionists dissatisfied the Post-Impressionists. First, Impressionists focused only on reproducing the natural world. In their rush to capture a moment in time, the Impressionists lost the traditional elements of picture making—namely, line, shape, and color. Lines dissolved and shapes lacked solidity in Impressionist paintings because of the loose brushwork. Color merely reflected the lighting of a given moment. Artists of the Post-Impressionist period sought to restore some of these elements to painting.

Post-Impressionism was not a specific art movement like Neoclassicism or Realism. Post-Impressionism refers to a group of French artists painting in the 1880s and 1890s. Nonetheless, these painters did share some common ground. Some wanted to restore **color** and **shape** to art, which were formal elements that they felt the Impressionists compromised. Others wanted to restore the **subjectivity** of the artist in creating a picture rather than merely copying nature. Paul Gauguin, for example, encouraged Vincent van Gogh, to stop looking at nature during his painting in exchange for painting from memory.

Since the Renaissance, art was a means to express the natural world, a mere means to an end. Artists sought to obscure all evidence of brushstrokes and, using chiaroscuro and accurate perspective (both linear and atmospheric), attempted to re-create their view of the real world. The more polished the painting and the more an artist controlled line and the gradations of shadow and light, the more society recognized the artist's ability. Post-Impressionists deviated from this expectation. Instead, they created abstract versions of the natural world to reinforce that art is indeed different from nature.

Henri de Toulouse-Lautrec

Henri de Toulouse-Lautrec frequented the cafés, bars, and brothels of the Montmartre district in Paris, which had a reputation for its nightlife. He created paintings and prints that contain a great deal of subjectivity and deviate from the natural world. Perhaps expressing the more depressing elements of the nightlife, his paintings exaggerate human features. In *At the Moulin Rouge*, women have green, masklike faces, and other people's faces seem like caricatures (**CD Fig. 26-11**). On the surface, the painting is an intimate glimpse at a group of people drinking and talking together. But the masklike faces of its subjects give the painting a sinister and unpleasant quality that suggests a decadent society so rich and pleasurable that it is on the verge of decay.

There are other reasons for these qualities. Toulouse-Lautrec also designed posters and prints in which caricature was popular. Gaslight became popular to illuminate these night destinations, and it projected a strange greenish glow on these interiors.

Some critics have dubbed Toulouse-Lautrec a "mini-Degas" because his work has much in common with Degas. The similarity lies in the influence that Japanese woodblock prints had on both artists. (Remember the C-FID mnemonic from earlier in the chapter.) Notice how the face of the woman in the right foreground is cropped, as is the shelf in the left foreground. Toulouse-Lautrec did not fully model the figures, so they appear flat. The painting also contains decorative elements, such as multicolored streaks of paint in the background as well as the red lipstick and orange hair of the green-faced woman in the foreground.

Toulouse-Lautrec's use of Japanese influences in his printed works is evident in *Le Jockey*, a picture of two jockeys racing (also influenced by a work by Degas). Its flatness resembles Japanese woodblock prints (**CD Fig. 26-12**). Other elements of Japanese influence can be seen in how Toulouse-Lautrec cropped the edges and placed the jockeys to the far left, suggesting informality. This work is a combination of crayon and splash lithograph, and contains six colors. A print like this is part of the graphic arts (etchings, lithograph, etc.). Toulouse-Lautrec was a major figure in elevating the status of the graphic arts, which in the late nineteenth century was not yet considered part of fine art.

Georges Seurat

Georges Seurat is famous for his use of **divisionism**, also known as **pointillism**. Divisionism (the more academic description) involves using small dabs of unmixed colored paint on a canvas. Using this technique, Seurat applied scientific principles to the use of color. His paintings reflect nineteenth-century **color theory**, which was proposed by the French chemist Michel-Eugene Chevreul. The theory explained that when a person focuses on a color for a significant amount of time and then removes that color from sight, the person will momentarily perceive that color's complementary color. For example, if you focus on the color red for at least 20 seconds and then the red is removed, you will temporarily see a splotch of green color in your line of vision.

Following color theory, Seurat juxtaposed dabs of complementary colors directly on the canvas instead of mixing them on his palette. Because of the way the eye works, Seurat reasoned that complementary colors set side by side on the canvas would mix in the viewer's eye with greater luminosity than if mixed on the palette. Thus, divisionism is an accurate description; the colors are divided and applied to the canvas in their pure form and optically mixed by the viewer.

Let us examine Seurat's use of divisionism in *A Sunday on La Grande Jatte* (**CD Fig. 26-13**). First, notice all the dots. Seurat meticulously placed them side by side, following the theory of complementary colors. For the subject, Seurat chose the leisure of the Parisian middle-class, as the Impressionists did. He painted men and women reclining and strolling on the Grande Jatte, an island in the Seine River. Seurat placed a mother and child as a still point around which the other figures move. Notice the couple in the right foreground: a man is accompanied by a woman who is fashionably dressed, with a tightly corseted waist and bustle, and holds a monkey on a leash. Other women in the painting are fishing on the banks of the Seine.

An unusual feature of the painting is its painted frame. To produce exactly the right optical effect in the eye of the spectator, Seurat dispensed with the conventional golden frame and painted his own border around the picture. He designed the frame so that, in any one section, it contains the complementary colors of the adjacent part of the painting. For example, the part of the frame by the sky contains more orange, blue's complementary color.

Seurat applied meticulous methods in creating this painting. Going beyond merely giving the viewer an impression of the middle class, Seurat presented a theory of color and a new painting technique called **divisionism**. Later, other artists, such as Henri Matisse (see Chapter 29) would experiment with divisionism before developing their own styles.

Seurat methodically dedicated himself to divisionism. In his work *The Models* (**CD Fig. 26-14**), notice the same elements as in his earlier work, *A Sunday on La Grande Jatte. The Models* was much more challenging for Seurat. Divisionism worked effectively in plein air to capture the effects of light on the water, grass, and foliage. But to take a common theme—nude models (or one model in three poses)—and complete it on a large scale using divisionism was unprecedented. Although he wrote of his difficulties with the painting, Seurat maintained his consistent small dabs of pure paint that mix in the eye. In the background, you can even notice Seurat's earlier masterwork leaning against a wall.

Paul Gauguin

Paul Gauguin also developed his own unique artistic style. He began painting privately during his twenties. When he became a stockbroker at the age of 23, Gauguin seemed to have settled for a conventional middle-class life. He was prosperous, married, and eventually had five children. Gauguin seemed content, but adventure was in his blood. At the age of 35, he abandoned his business career to devote himself to painting and his desire for personal and artistic freedom. He left his wife and family and spent the rest of his life painting and traveling. He lived in Paris, Brittany (northwestern France), and Arles (with Vincent van Gogh), as well as the exotic locales of Tahiti and the Marquesas Islands, where he died and is buried.

Gauguin's bold colors and shapes expressed his own **inner vision** rather than external reality. When he died, Gauguin was virtually forgotten. But an exhibition in Paris in 1906 revealed his genius, and since then he has been one of the greatest influences on twentieth-century art.

Gauguin's painting *The Vision after the Sermon* (also known as *Jacob Wrestling with the Angel*) illustrates several qualities of his work (**CD Fig. 26-15**). The scene is a churchyard in rural Brittany. We see a group of Breton women on the left, a brown tree bisecting the picture diagonally, and a man wrestling an angel on the right. The women are deep in prayer and experiencing a vision.

The real world is on the left, with the simple Breton women and a straying cow that paws the red earth. On the right is the visionary world, where an angel and Jacob wrestle (Jacob wrestling the angel is a well-known Old Testament story). This spiritual battle takes place on a blood-red field. The red ground symbolizes the theme of struggle. In choosing it, Gauguin freed himself from the traditional use of color to describe nature. Here Gauguin used color in an abstract, expressive way.

Note that Gauguin used **flat planes of color**, not dabs or dots like Seurat. Gauguin drew inspiration from stained-glass windows, cloisonné designs (see Chapter 12), as well as Japanese woodblock prints. These types of art are known for their two-dimensional qualities. Flat planes and the expressive use of color are key elements of the work of Gauguin.

Gauguin traveled to the South Pacific in search of a civilization that was uncontaminated by the mores and values of Western culture. During his stay, Gauguin captured the lives of Tahitian women and local myths in his paintings and sculpture. One example is *Where Do We Come From? What Are We? Where Are We Going?* (**CD Fig. 26-16**). Gauguin painted this shortly after he received news that his favorite daughter died. He was determined to create a *magnus opus*, a culminating work. This painting represents the cycle of life from childhood through old age. The sleeping baby represents the first stage of life. Two figures dressed in purple discuss their destiny. A crouching figure raises her arms in astonishment. A figure in the center is picking fruit, which symbolizes the pleasures of life. The idol with upraised arms reminds us of the inevitability of death. The old woman seems to accept and be resigned to her own fate.

Where Do We Come From? What Are We? Where Are We Going? contains flat planes. Gauguin did not model the figures with chiaroscuro, which reveals the influence of two-dimensional art forms such as stained glass and Japanese woodblock prints. In the painting, he expressed his spirituality and inner vision of the cycle of life; Gauguin did not represent a literal reality. In addition, he used folk tales and exotic imagery to depict this theme.

After completing the work, Gauguin went into the mountains and ingested poison. However, he survived and recovered. Thanks to the patronage of a European gallery owner, Gauguin began to sell some of his work on the Continent, which improved his livelihood in the South Pacific. But after bouts of sickness and a serious injury to his foot, an exhausted Gauguin succumbed to death, leaving the world a legacy of expressive paintings that continued art history's path through modernism.

Vincent van Gogh

Vincent van Gogh was born in Holland, the son of a Protestant minister. He trained to be an art dealer and then left to become a missionary in his early twenties. At the age of 27, he dedicated himself fully to his art. Largely self-taught, Van Gogh first painted pictures of the peasants in Holland. Later he moved to Paris and was supported financially by his brother, Theo, who was a successful art dealer. Van Gogh met many of the Impressionist and Post-Impressionist artists in Paris.

Although Van Gogh has been the subject of many monographs, documentaries, and movies, typically his life is not a concern of AP test writers. The same can be said for most of the artists discussed in this book. Test writers focus on discerning whether students understand Van Gogh's style.

Van Gogh painted with vibrant colors and swirling brushstrokes. Like Gauguin, he did not want to copy the natural world but presented his vision of the world, which was infused with his religious upbringing and his inner feeling. Adding to the expression of the brushstrokes, Van Gogh applied the paint in thick globs known as *impasto*.

The Night Café expresses several key elements of Van Gogh's style (**CD Fig. 26-17**). In a letter, Van Gogh described the night café as a place for tramps, drunkards, and prostitutes. Van Gogh explained that he used the most alien reds and greens to create a clash and convey the feeling of intense human alienation. As we look at the painting, we have an uneasy feeling. People are hunched over tables with their bottles in front of them as a man ominously stares at the viewer. There is a sense that these people are all alone. Van Gogh, also influenced by Japanese woodblock prints, created a steep diagonal with the billiard table and floorboards, reminiscent of the *Ukiyo-e* style. This intense angle heightens the tension in the painting.

Van Gogh's series *Sunflowers* is considered among his happier paintings. They also contain the important elements of his technique. Why did he paint this painting the way he did? To clarify this, it is interesting to contrast his depiction of *Sunflowers* with Da Vinci's drawing of the *Star of Bethlehem*, which was among the art and writing in his notebooks (**CD Figs. 26-18** and **26-19**). Both artists demonstrate evidence of their observations of nature, yet their depictions are significantly different.

We know that Da Vinci was a Renaissance artist who was interested in science, anatomical drawing, and studying nature. His drawing is a precise record of his observation of nature. He once wrote, "The most praiseworthy form of painting is the one that most resembles what it imitates." The contours of the plant and its anatomy illustrate Da Vinci's fascination with the natural world, which he referred to as his greatest teacher. Just as he spent hours dissecting human cadavers, precisely recording his observations and demonstrating a knowledge of human anatomy that of European doctors of his time, Da Vinci spent hours studying horses, birds, tidal flows, and flowers. His *Star of Bethlehem* drawing records his artistic objectives of great realism and naturalism.

Although Van Gogh also observed sunflowers, he presents a unique vision of the subject. He used the color yellow to express his happiness. In letters, Van Gogh compared yellow to music, explaining that at the time of the painting, he felt like he was on a high yellow note. He also wrote that yellow represented the sun, another source of happiness for him. The swirling brushstrokes on the petals of the flower display some naturalism but also express Van Gogh's feelings. The sunflowers are at various stages of life; some are in bloom while others are dying. Van Gogh may have been expressing the brevity of life. The use of *impasto* heightens the expressiveness of his brushwork.

Van Gogh painted *Sunflowers* while in Arles, as a decoration for the room his friend Paul Gauguin was to stay in. Did you notice that Van Gogh used flat planes of color for the vase, table, and background? Like his contemporaries, Van Gogh expressed his interest in the pictorial devices of Japanese woodblock prints. His goal was not to express the fleeting effects of light, as did the Impressionists, but to present his feelings through color and his unique vision of nature in *Sunflowers*.

Paul Cézanne

Paul Cézanne was the illegitimate son of a wealthy, domineering father. At first, Cézanne studied law and worked in the family bank, but eventually he broke away and moved to Paris to paint. Through contact with the impressionists, he began to paint nature and gradually developed a completely new pictorial language, which was to help establish him as the Father of Modern Art. Cézanne exhibited with the Impressionists, but since the formulation of his style occurred more in the 1880s and early 1890s, Cézanne is a Post-Impressionist.

Spending most of his mature years working alone in remote Provence, Cézanne dedicated his life to art. Fame came late to him. In 1895, a one-man show revealed his genius to an unsuspecting public. He died at the age of 67, of an illness he contracted after being caught in a storm while painting.

Impressionism turned Cézanne into an outdoor painter and he became famous for **landscapes**. However, Impressionism dissatisfied Cézanne. He had a stronger sense of pictorial construction than his contemporaries, whose choppy brushwork dissolved objects into the play of dazzling light. Cézanne sought to retain the brightness and freshness of Impressionism but make of it "something solid and durable."

Cézanne created a series of paintings of *Mont Sainte-Victoire* near his home in Aix-en-Provence (**CD Fig. 26-20**). He used a few important techniques in representing this mountain and the surrounding land. First was the technique of **color patches**. Cézanne believed that by using color patches, he could capture the true colors that existed beneath the transitory effects of light. In other words, unlike Monet, he was not looking to give the viewer an impression of the moment but a view of Mont Sainte-Victoire that was more permanent. He would constantly look from his canvas to the vista to be sure to catch the underlying colors.

Figure 26-20. Paul Cézanne, *Mont Sainte-Victoire*, 1902–1904, Philadelphia Museum of Art

Second, Cézanne **varied the colors** in the landscape. He painted with warmer colors—such as orange, gold, and green—in the middle ground, closer to the viewer, while cooler colors like blues and purples convey air and distance. Although using bluish tints to convey depth is part of atmospheric perspective, Cézanne did not use traditional linear perspective and chiaroscuro to convey the illusion of depth. The sky does not appear to exist behind Mont Sainte-Victoire but instead exists on the same plane. Cézanne conveyed distance and the flatness of paint simultaneously.

A third important element of Cézanne's painting is that, as you look at objects in the painting, you have the feeling of **multiple viewpoints**, or different perspectives. Instead of creating the painting as a camera would capture the scene, with a single viewpoint, Cézanne's vision of *Mont Sainte-Victoire* varies, as our vision of the location would vary if we were actually there. No person actually keeps their eyes perfectly set on one viewpoint in real life. Thus, Cézanne's multiple viewpoints may be more reflective of "real" human vision than is a traditional landscape with a fixed vanishing point and linear perspective.

A final key point for Cézanne's painting style is his attention to the **underlying shapes** of objects. In an abstract way, *Mont Sainte-Victoire* is an assemblage of small rectangles, triangles, and trapezoids. Cézanne once wrote to an aspiring artist, "Treat nature by the cylinder, the sphere, the cone." Of course, rudimentary drawing begins when students find the underlying geometric shapes of objects. However, Western art tradition since the Renaissance sought to hide the underlying shapes with chiaroscuro, overlapping, perspective, and other illusionary devices. In contrast, Cézanne retained the importance of these shapes in this landscape.

Cézanne's **still lifes** reinforce the key characteristics of his painting. Still-life arrangements allowed Cézanne to work with a limited set of variables to refine his style. He used flat color patches to reinforce the solidity of the fruit and table (**CD Fig. 26-21**). He explored the underlying shapes of the objects. He captured the still life through multiple viewpoints that reinforce the solidity and underlying shapes of the objects. The table, dishes, and fruit are not optically realistic. Their slightly askew shapes display the multiple viewpoints that Cézanne wanted to capture. Cézanne's paintings, although misunderstood by many of his contemporaries, became an inspiration to later artists, such as the Cubists.

Conclusion

Impressionism and Post-Impressionism are difficult to categorize as coherent artistic movements because the artists within the movements had varied objectives. The movements are described by their chronological placement as well as basic similarities shared by the artists in each period. Impressionism occurred in the 1870s and 1880s and Post-Impressionism in the late 1880s and 1890s. Impressionist artists were interested in capturing a moment in time, the fleeting qualities of light at the moment, and how the momentary light affected color. Cropped edges, informal arrangements of characters, and unusual viewpoints enhance the transitory feel of their paintings.

Post-Impressionists such as Seurat, Gauguin, Van Gogh, and Cézanne were dissatisfied with the limitations of Impressionism. Seurat and Cézanne explored the science of color and shape, while Gauguin, and to a lesser extent Van Gogh, transcended faithfulness to nature in exchange for their inner, unique visions of the world.

Both Impressionism and Post-Impressionism illustrate the influence of Japanese woodblock prints, with their flat qualities, cropped edges, and depictions of a moment in time.

Chapter 27

Other Late Nineteenth-Century Art Styles

Introduction and Exam Strategy Overview

Major developments occurred in the history of art and architecture during the late nineteenth century. Artists continued the path of Modernism that the Realists and Impressionists established. Artists continued to probe the inner mind in their art, influenced by the work of their Post-Impressionist contemporary Paul Gauguin. These artists formed a completely new pictorial language known as Symbolism. Sculptors also began to depart from faithfully copying the real world. Rodin's sculpture blended Realism with abstraction to capture the inner essence of forms. In addition, wealthy patrons commissioned decorative objects for interior design. The *fin de siècle* ("end of the century") culture was extravagant and desired opulent, decorative objects.

Past AP Art History tests contained few multiple-choice questions on topics from some of the styles you will read about in this chapter. Slide-based multiple-choice questions have examined Horta's Tassel House and Gaudi's Casa Mila, the influence of arts and crafts on art nouveau, and the chronology of the *fin de siècle* (1890s–1910s) relative to other periods. Certain topics such as the sculpture of Rodin lend themselves well to a slide-based short essay. So many major developments transpired during nineteenth century art history (Romanticism, photography, Realism, Impressionism, and Post-Impressionism) that they can eclipse the *fin de siècle* period. Nonetheless, this period is the transition from the nineteenth century stirrings of Modernism to its full employment during the twentieth century.

The Symbolists

Symbolism was a reaction against the nineteenth-century belief in the advance of science and technology. The artists discarded the visible world of surface appearances. Instead, they wanted to give visual form to **states of mind.** The following topics are commonly treated in the works of the Symbolists:

* The inner world of fantasy, in which imagination takes precedence over nature

- A state of mind, emotion, or idea

- Images that portray irrational aspects of the human mind; these irrational images can be disturbing

The major Symbolists include Odilon Redon, Gustave Moreau, Henri Rousseau, and Edvard Munch. Their influences were Goya's etchings and black paintings and Gericault's depictions of the insane (see Chapter 24), as well as Gauguin's paintings of the inner vision (see Chapter 26). Gauguin's followers even called themselves the Nabis taken from the Hebrew word meaning "prophet." A notable amount of Symbolist literature accompanied this artistic movement.

Pierre Puvis de Chavannes

The work of Pierre Puvis de Chavannes was among the first to abandon the world of reality and turn to a remote other world. Puvis's painting *The Sacred Grove*, completed in 1884, preceded even the work of Gauguin (**CD Fig. 27-1**). Art historians consider Puvis a precursor to the Symbolists. While Impressionists recorded the fleeting effects of light on the natural world, Puvis created a whole other dimension.

The Sacred Grove has groups of figures with classical body types. Puvis barely modeled his subjects with chiaroscuro, giving them a shallow quality similar to the figures in classical frieze. Consistent with the modern art of his time, he emphasized the two-dimensional aspect of painting. He placed the figures in a classical paradise in which they recline, contemplate, converse, and gather flowers. Puvis rendered the figures in various states of suspended animation, heightening the painting's dreamlike effect. In a modern sense, it is as if Puvis hit the pause button on a DVD player. How strange it looks.

The world depicted in *The Sacred Grove* is nothing like the world examined by the Realists or Impressionists. Yet both the academicians and the avant-garde accepted it. It is important for us to understand why. Puvis includes classical references, including the body types, the architecture, and the landscape, all of which appealed to the academicians. Its similarity to a classical frieze and finely articulated details also met the expectations of the academy. However, the painting's mystical feel appealed to the avant-garde's sense that art should transcend the natural world and capture the artist's unique vision.

Odilon Redon

Odilon Redon is now regarded as one of the greatest French Symbolist artists. He remained an obscure provincial painter until his late forties. During his early years, he pursued a solitary course in opposition to the prevailing naturalism, producing prints and charcoal drawings of macabre and fantastic subjects. It was only in the late 1880s, when the reaction to Impressionism became widespread, that Redon received recognition. As his work became better known, young artists responded to his novel technique and visionary images and came to regard him as a leader.

Let us examine Redon's painting titled *Closed Eyes* from 1890 (**CD Fig. 27-2**). He modeled the female figure on his wife. This is not a Realist or even Impressionist rendition. Instead, Redon treated the subject of the inner vision. The closed eyes and the tranquil expression all suggest a spiritual state of mind. The imagery of Redon resembles that used by science fiction television shows like *The X-Files* and *The Outer Limits*.

Another Symbolist painting by Redon is *The Cyclops* (**CD Fig. 27-3**). Redon chose a subject from Greek mythology, Polyphemus the Cyclops. According to the myth, Polyphemus desired to have a beautiful mortal woman named Galatea as his wife (Raphael created a famous fresco of this story). He killed her husband and pursued her. Redon projects a figment of the imagination as if it were real. Polyphemus, with his huge loving eye rises, above the sleeping Galatea. Notice the depiction of the fantasy world around them, rendered through a spectrum of various colors and loose brushwork.

Gustave Moreau

Gustave Moreau was a reclusive Symbolist painter who gained a reputation late in life. Because he was older, his fellow Symbolists viewed him as a source of wisdom and inspiration. Let us examine his painting *The Apparition*, also known as *Dance of Salome* (**CD Fig. 27-4**). Salome was the niece of Herod the Great, king of Judea. According to the biblical account, Salome performed a dance for all the guests at Herod's party, and it so pleased him that he swore to give her anything she wanted. After consulting her mother, she asked for the head of Saint John the Baptist, whom Herod had imprisoned. Herod honored his oath and gave Salome John's head on a platter, which she presented to her mother.

Renaissance versions of this story depict John's head on the platter being carried by Salome, but Moreau illustrates the story with Symbolist devices. The painting is **macabre**, with blood dripping from a levitating head surrounded by a golden halo. There is an intense gaze between John and Salome that conveys an underlying psychological tension. A variation of the story says that Salome wanted John the Baptist as a lover, but he spurned her. Moreau expresses the tension between them through that gaze. The whole scene seems otherworldly.

Symbolist Interest in Mythology

Both Moreau and Redon are known for alluding to mythology, which demonstrates their departure from the mundane topics of the real world. Recall that Redon's *The Cyclops* referred to a mythological monster. Moreau referenced Roman mythology with his rendition of *Jupiter and Semele*. Semele was a mortal love of Jupiter (**CD Fig. 27-5**). She asked him to reveal himself to her in all his majesty. But on seeing his glory, Semele died. Moreau drew inspiration for the opulent decorations from Byzantine mosaics, Indian miniature paintings, medieval cloisonné, and exotic decorations. With its elaborate designs, fantasy arrangement of strange figures, and mythological otherworldliness, Moreau's *Jupiter and Semele* is an interesting Symbolist piece.

Henri Rousseau

Henri Rousseau was a retired customs collector who started to paint in middle age without any academic training. Because he was an untrained amateur, art historians refer to Rousseau as a **naive** painter. This did not exclude him from the Symbolist group, who actually enjoyed his naive style.

The Sleeping Gypsy depicts Rousseau's fantasy of a gypsy occupying a silent and secret desert world and dreaming under a perfectly round moon (**CD Fig. 27-6**). A lion sniffs at the gypsy. A critical encounter occurs between the sleeping gypsy and lion. The viewer feels uneasiness at seeing the encounter because of the gypsy's vulnerability. It reminds us of our own vulnerability when we sleep.

Notice how the bodies of the lion and gypsy do not look realistic. This is not for lack of effort. On the contrary, Rousseau put a great deal of effort into depicting the animal and person with great naturalism. However, because he was a naive painter, the world lacks the optical realism that a trained artist could create. Unwittingly, Rousseau created a painting that would be praised by his avant-garde contemporaries for its abstraction, which accentuated its fantasy atmosphere.

Edvard Munch

Edvard Munch is Norway's most famous painter. He was a major proponent of Symbolism and a forerunner of the Expressionists (see Chapter 29). The tragic loss of his mother and sister in early childhood brought a morbid tone to much of his work. Munch wrote, "Illness, madness, and death were the black angels that kept watch over my cradle and accompanied me all my life."

Trips to Paris put Munch in touch with the Symbolists. He produced unprecedented images of the innermost feelings and mental anguish of modern man. His painting *The Scream* (also known as *The Cry*) exemplifies his achievement (**CD Fig. 27-7**). He created the painting after he moved to Berlin in 1893. About the painting, he wrote, "I sensed a scream passing through Nature; it seemed to me that I heard the scream. I painted this picture, painted the clouds as actual blood. The color shrieked." The famous volcanic eruption on the island of Krakatoa in 1883 may have inspired Munch as well. It produced the most powerful sound ever heard by humans, and its ashes spread around the atmosphere, affecting European sunsets for six months afterward. Munch was very religious and may have viewed the event as apocalyptic.

The skull-like head of the figure in the foreground displays an anguished expression. We feel the figure's psychological terror. The intense colors, swirling brushwork, and steep diagonal of the painting escalate the tension. *The Scream* invades our space and confronts us with the figure's madness. The painting's formal devices are reminiscent of Van Gogh's *Night Café*. The works of Van Gogh and Gauguin influenced Munch during his stay in Paris. Nevertheless, Munch was a Symbolist.

Late Nineteenth-Century Sculpture

Because of its three-dimensional nature, nineteenth-century sculpture could not display the many transitory effects that the Impressionists captured in painting. Sculpture of the second half of the nineteenth century inherited the features of Neoclassical and Romantic art. As painting shifted toward Modernism, sculpture was being used for little more than monuments, and academic propriety held sway. Sculpture lacked the avant-garde spirit.

We will examine two late nineteenth-century sculptors and their work: Jean Baptiste Carpeaux, whose style is relatively traditional and academic, and Auguste Rodin, whose work exhibited the move toward Modernism. The work of the former was revered by his contemporaries, while the work of the latter was reviled. Yet today, the work of the former is more obscure, while whole museums are dedicated to the work of the latter.

Carpeaux's *Count Ugolino and His Sons*

Jean-Baptiste Carpeaux modeled this statue in 1861. It depicts the story of Count Ugolino, who in 1288 was convicted of treason and sentenced by Pisa to die of starvation locked in a tower with his sons. In the *Inferno*, Dante describes his encounter with Count Ugolino in hell. Count Ugolino told Dante how he bit his own hands because of his intense grief. His sons, seeing their father do this, interpreted it as hunger and offered him their own flesh.

Count Ugolino and His Sons was carved in marble under Carpeaux's supervision and displayed at the Universal Exposition in Paris in 1867 (**CD Fig. 27-8**). In this work, Carpeaux pays homage to his favorite sculptor, Michelangelo, with the twisted figures and exaggerated musculature. Michelangelo included Count Ugolino as one of the anguished figures being pulled toward hell in his *Last Judgment* fresco (see Chapter 17). Carpeaux also credited the Hellenistic *Laocoon* group as one of his influences (see Chapter 6).

Carpeaux finished the original model while studying at the French Academy in Rome. It was very popular and brought Carpeaux many commissions. At the direction of the French Ministry of Fine Arts, it was cast in bronze and displayed at the Salon of 1863, which was the Salon that rejected some 2,800 of the 5,000 submissions. The bronze was then placed in the Tuileries Palace, where it was displayed with a bronze rendition of the *Laocoon*.

Why was this work so popular? This is an important question to answer. Carpeaux depicted a scene from a popular Renaissance story, which was acceptable to the academicians. He used the work of Michelangelo, a venerated Old Master, and a work from classical antiquity as his sources of inspiration, which was also recommended by the academies. Finally, *Count Ugolino and His Sons* has a highly finished appearance (it is smooth and polished) and displays great knowledge of human anatomy. The group is optically realistic and, in fact, idealizes the bodies of its characters in keeping with the standards of the academicians.

Auguste Rodin

According to the twentieth-century sculptor Constantin Brancusi, "In the nineteenth century, the situation of sculpture was desperate. Rodin arrived and transformed everything." In fact, sculpture had declined into little more than decorative public monuments.

Auguste Rodin single-handedly revived sculpture as a medium worthy of an original artist. His work serves as an interesting counterpoint to that of Carpeaux.

His major work was called the *Gates of Hell* (**CD Fig. 27-9**). He won the prestigious commission in 1880 to design the doors to a new decorative arts museum. The project had multiple sources, including Dante's *Inferno*, the nineteenth-century poet Baudelaire's *Flowers of Evil*, and Ghiberti's "Gates of Paradise" (see Chapter 16). We see a continuous sequence of rising and falling figures condemned to hell, including Adam and Eve after the original sin. Despite Rodin's dedication to the project, it was not cast during his lifetime. Today a plaster cast of the finished project is displayed at the Musee d'Orsay in Paris.

Rodin did turn individual figures from the *Gates of Hell* project into independent masterpieces. *The Thinker* is one example (**CD Fig. 27-10**). The figure, which occupies the center of the lintel in the plaster cast, represented Dante contemplating his journey through the Inferno. Rodin modeled a separate 27.5-foot sculpture based on Dante, which artisans then cast in bronze. Notice his physical resemblance to the *Slave* figures created by Michelangelo, one of Rodin's biggest influences.

Rodin used the real world as his inspiration, but his works capture the steps of his creative process. Rodin worked with pliable materials such as plaster or terra cotta. He did *not* use the subtractive method (when material is removed) with hard materials such as marble or wood. Pliable materials provided Rodin the opportunity to create a textured appearance in his work. We can see indentations, smooth edges, and round edges that reflected the actions of his hands. His final products lack the highly finished and smooth exterior of the Neoclassical and academic sculptors of the nineteenth century.

In *Walking Man*, Rodin omitted the head and arms of the figure (**CD Fig. 27-11**). He did this because the head and arms would distract the viewer from the essence of walking, which he was trying to express. He intended the design to depict John the Baptist in the act of preaching. This sculpture's appearance became emblematic of Rodin's work. Rodin combined a deep understanding of human anatomy and movement with his own individual expression. Notice how the rough edges and textured appearance capture light. Aware of the Impressionist interest in the effects of light, Rodin provided a sculptural equivalent. Also, like the Symbolists, Rodin avoided the limitation of objectively copying every part of the body in exchange for the **essence**, which reveals itself on the surface. Rodin once wrote, "The sculptor must learn to reproduce the surface, which means all that vibrates on the surface, soul, love, passion, life."

Rodin received a commission from the city of Calais to create a monument known as the *Burghers of Calais* (**CD Fig. 27-12**). The monument would commemorate an event from the Hundred Years' War. In 1347, six male citizens of Calais surrendered themselves to the English king, Edward III, in exchange for lifting his siege of their city and sparing its inhabitants. When the city fathers commissioned Rodin to do the project, they probably envisioned something like Michelangelo's *David*, which was the symbol of Florence. *Burghers of Calais* would be their *David*. The city fathers probably expected six colossal-sized, muscular men whose expressions would show defiance towards death and the English king. The city fathers probably wanted the work to have a smooth and highly finished appearance like earlier heroic monuments. In addition, they probably expected the work to be placed on a tall platform. However, Rodin's work displeased the city fathers. Let us examine why.

Rodin evoked the emotions that these men must have felt. He worked for two years on models of faces and bodies. Rodin's rendition contains ordinary men who are dealing with the various emotions one would experience while walking toward imminent death: tension, anguish, fear, resignation. The arrangement allows the viewers to see the burghers from all sides. Rodin did not use the traditional high base that would elevate a heroic monument. This contrasts with preceding nationalist monuments such as the Romantic era *La Marseillaise* group from the Arc de Triomphe. By placing the burghers at eye level, Rodin hoped that the citizens of Calais could connect with them. Rodin's humanizing of the Calais heroes did not strike a chord with the city fathers. Besides hiding the *Burghers of Calais*, they had it placed on a taller base.

Arts and Crafts Movement

By the late nineteenth century, most people accepted the changes being caused by industrialization and urbanization. Some writers and artists living in Great Britain, the most industrialized country of Europe, rejected what they saw as runaway industrialism. Suspicious of machines and capitalism, they advocated handcrafting objects that were useful and aesthetically beautiful. Their influence gave rise to the Arts and Crafts movement.

The Arts and Crafts movement relied on hand production of everyday household items. Artists beautified the objects to bring pleasure to both the person using the object as well as the maker. The movement rejected artificial patterns, turning instead to natural floral patterns, which in turn influenced the next movement, Art Nouveau. Artisanship was integral to their creations, and the leaders of the movement reinforced this by forming guilds and workshops. The process was just as important as the end result, a theme that we will see again in artists such as Jackson Pollock during the twentieth century. William Morris and another advocate of the movement, Charles Rennie Mackintosh, created arts and crafts theme rooms in which all elements, from tea sets to tables to wallpaper to stained-glass windows, were harmonized. Creations such as theirs could not result from industrialism but from the thoughtfulness and craftsmanship of an individual.

Art Nouveau

Art Nouveau was a short-lived art movement in the late nineteenth century that focused on the decorative arts and architecture. It took its name from a decorative arts store in Paris, L'Art Nouveau, which translates to "New Art." Influenced by the arts and crafts movement, Art Nouveau became popular in France, Belgium, Holland, Great Britain, and America. Art Nouveau also became popular in Germany, where artists called it *Jugendstil*, and in Austria, where artists referred to it as the Austrian Secession. Art Nouveau works contain **organic designs**. The term *organic* refers to artwork that has qualities of organic life, such as plants. The designs often contain leafy tendrils, meandering vines, and elaborate floral patterns.

Victor Horta and Art Nouveau Architecture

Examine the interior of the Tassel House in Brussels, Belgium. The Belgian architect Victor Horta designed this paragon of Art Nouveau style. The banisters of the stairs contain metal bar tracery with plantlike forms (**CD Fig. 27-13**). Along the walls are the outlines of flowers, leaves, and tendrils, which extend to mosaics in the floors. Malleable wrought-iron columns were shaped into leafy designs that resemble slender Corinthian columns.

The organic motif also unites Horta's design in the Van Eetvelde House (**CD Fig. 27-14**). The skylight contains metal bar tracery resembling vines and leaves. Once again, he used wrought iron to create plantlike tendrils in the banister for the stairs. The organic designs on the walls and floor blend to give the effect of an exotic forest, which transforms the normal boxy feel of an enclosed space.

Gaudi's Casa Mila

Antonio Gaudi was a Spanish architect who adopted Art Nouveau style. In his Casa Mila apartment house (**CD Fig. 27-15**), the facade has pronounced undulations (curving surfaces). It lacks the rigid edges often associated with architecture; instead, its features are organic. For example, metal railings on the balconies have the shape of seaweed. The undulating facade of the building itself and its colored stone imitates the seaside cliffs of Spain's Mediterranean coast. Gaudi built the Casa Mila in Barcelona, which had a significant economic and geographical relationship to the sea. Even the various curvy shapes of the chimneys resemble sand castles. Gaudi also considered Moorish architecture in Spain and the Baroque period as influences, which is evident with the color of the stone and the undulating surface. Nevertheless, Gaudi's use of organic forms, although geographically specific to southern Spain, makes the Casa Mila distinctly part of Art Nouveau design.

Tiffany Stained Glass

Louis Comfort Tiffany created Art Nouveau designs for stained-glass windows and interior décor out of his high-end store in New York City. The materials, time, and craftsmanship he allocated to his creations made them expensive. For example, a lotus lamp that his workshop produced in 1906 cost $750 (**CD Fig. 27-16**). Demonstrating the influence of the Arts and Crafts movement, Tiffany's store only produced one lamp at a time, because the craftsmanship in his creations was time consuming. Tiffany's stained-glass creations reflect Art Nouveau because they contain organic elements. For example, the table lamp shown here is shaped like lotus petals, leaves, and stems. Its metallic stand represents the lotus's main stem, which branches out into a base with rootlike metallic braces. Even the bulbs of the lamp resemble flower petals.

Aubrey Beardsley: Art Nouveau Illustrations

Aubrey Beardsley was an English artist who incorporated Art Nouveau elements into his illustrations. His most famous series of illustrations were for the writer Oscar Wilde's *Salome* (**CD Fig. 27-17**). His drawings contain organic motifs. For example, in one of his pictures, an evil-looking Salome kisses the head of John the Baptist as it rests on a platter. The blood dripping from John's severed head swirls into plantlike shapes as it pools on the ground below. Out of the pool, a flower grows. Beardsley avoided color in his illustrations, working instead in black ink on white paper. In addition, he reinforces the two-dimensionality of objects and figures by not modeling them with shadow. Beardsley often includes intricate decorations in the patterns of clothing while leaving other parts of the pictures bare. Beardsley's use of flatness, line, and decorative pattern reveal the influence of Japanese prints.

Gustave Klimt

The works of Gustave Klimt combine elements of Symbolism, Arts and Crafts, and Art Nouveau. He created a series of paintings of the kiss, which reflected his love life. In *The Kiss*, we see two lovers embracing so tightly that they almost blend into one figure except for their faces (**CD Fig. 27-18**). Klimt's painting represents a fantasy world, demonstrating a Symbolist quality. The couple kneels on a precipice of tiny flowers with a depthless gold background. The man is so enthralled he is about to fall off the cliff. The painting shimmers with gold and smaller color patterns reminiscent of Byzantine mosaics, which Klimt studied firsthand in Ravenna. The flowers and the organic lines of the couple's robes and bodies reflect Art Nouveau. Lastly, the painting captures the tension between two- and three-dimensional worlds, which captivated other late nineteenth-century artists. Klimt was part of a movement known as the **Austrian Secession**, the Austrian equivalent of Art Nouveau.

Conclusion

The years of the 1890s through the early twentieth century were busy for art and architecture. During the late nineteenth century, artistic movements such as Post-Impressionism, Symbolism, Arts and Crafts, and Art Nouveau grew simultaneously. The artists of each movement separated themselves from creating the illusion of a three-dimensional world in their work. Instead, their work expressed greater individual subjectivity and reinforced "art for art's sake." (In other words, art did not have to serve solely as a means of imitating the real world, which had been the trend since the Renaissance.) In addition to various artistic movements, sculpture also entered the Modern era, as seen in the work of Rodin.

Questions on past AP Art History tests pertaining to the late nineteenth century have assessed students' ability to:

• Recognize that various art movements were contemporary with each other.

- Observe and comprehend complementary formal terms, such as flat versus modeling, decorative versus simple, and organic versus artificial.

- Apply knowledge of contextual events to interpret formal elements. For example, the Art and Crafts movement and Art Nouveau reacted against industrialism.

Chapter 28

Nineteenth-Century Architecture

Introduction and Exam Strategy Overview

Architects of the modern era (after the French Revolution) revived the ideas of past styles in their designs through the eighteenth and nineteenth centuries. Whatever style was in vogue at the time, architects followed with designs that reflected that style. Around the middle of the nineteenth century, architectural design began to change. The incorporation of new building materials such as cast iron (in the late eighteenth century) and steel and glass (in the nineteenth century) created new opportunities. At first, architects responded with ambivalence; they were willing to use these materials but obscured them below decorative embellishments. Then, around the mid-nineteenth century, architects began to fully embrace and glorify the materials that expanded the creative possibilities of architecture.

The guidelines for the AP Art History test state that questions related to architecture are worth 25 percent of the points. Major developments occurred in architecture from the eighteenth to the early twentieth century, and test writers reflect this in their questions. For example, the 2006 exam contained a slide-based short essay question about how Louis Sullivan's Carson, Pirie, Scott Building (1899–1904) inspired the modern skyscraper.

This chapter explains the architectural trends that occurred during the modern era. As they do with nineteenth-century painters and sculptors, art historians label architects "modern" when the influences of past styles decrease and architecture becomes functional and expresses a new aesthetic.

Revivalist and Thematic Architecture

The running order of nineteenth-century architecture was revivalism. In other words, the architects borrowed from previous architectural styles. Also, as European countries like Britain practiced imperialism abroad, they amalgamated their revivalist styles with the exotic architectures of their colonies.

In the eighteenth century, architects used classical and Renaissance architecture as an inspiration to develop the Neoclassical style (see Chapter 23). Neoclassical buildings contained the architectural vocabulary of the Roman Pantheon (118–125 CE) and

Palladio's Villa Rotonda (1566–1570) in that they contained porticoes, classical orders, and rotundas. We see examples of the Neoclassical style in Chiswick House (1729) in England. During the early nineteenth century, Thomas Jefferson adopted Classical and Renaissance influences to create a fitting architecture for the new United States. This American take on neoclassical architecture became known as the Federal Style. Monticello (1790–1806) and the Capitol in Washington, D.C. (1803–1807) represent the Federal Style.

As Romanticism became popular in the early nineteenth century (see Chapter 24), so did reviving Gothic-style architecture. The Gothic period preceded the resurgence of classical humanism and reason seen during the Renaissance. Because of its intense interest on spirituality and otherworldliness, Gothic architecture was simpatico with Romantics' interest in the sublime and disdain for the rationality of the Neoclassical period. Romantics enjoyed the style of Gothic castles, which reminded them of medieval times and things that transcended rationality, like ghosts and haunting (consider that Mary Shelley wrote *Frankenstein* during the Romantic period). Strawberry Hill and the reconstructed Parliament building (1835) exemplify the Neo-Gothic revival with their soaring spires, crenellated roofs, and pointed arches.

John Nash's Royal Pavilion

The Royal Pavilion in Brighton, England, reflects the influence of Britain's imperialism in India (**CD Fig. 28-1**). Tales of the soldiers involved in skirmishes with native warriors in British East India as well as the behavior of the exotic cultures romanticized India for people throughout Great Britain. John Nash incorporated this interest as the motif for a seaside pleasure palace for King George IV.

Does the Royal Pavilion remind you of a famous building in India? If you said the Taj Mahal, you would be correct. The onion-shaped domes, the minarets, and screens (decorative and used between corridors) exude the influence of the Islamic architecture (see Chapter 11) of India under the Moguls. Architects dubbed the style of the Royal Pavilion **Indian Gothic** because of its combination of Indian-Islamic elements and the pointed arches of the Gothic style. The building also incorporates influences of Greece and Rome as well as motifs from China. Cast-iron columns in the kitchen are shaped like the palm trees of exotic locations. Notice also the symmetrical appearance of the Royal Pavilion. Like Chiswick House and Parliament, it incorporates the rationality and order of classical and Renaissance architecture.

The facade of the Royal Pavilion is made from cast iron, which began to be used in construction in the late eighteenth century. Yet John Nash hides this with exterior decoration. Cast iron was much too utilitarian to fit nineteenth-century tastes in architecture. The Royal Pavilion demonstrates that nineteenth-century architects used older styles (classical and Gothic) and borrowed ideas from exotic lands to mask the structural elements (the supports) of the building. As we will see shortly, architects began to unmask the structural skeletons of their buildings, drawing attention to the new materials of cast iron and steel.

Cast Iron and Steel

Architects first used cast iron as an architectural support in the late eighteenth-century bridge at Coalbrookdale (**CD Fig. 28-2**). Abraham Darby III, who headed his family's cast-iron business in Coalbrookdale, was in the process of investigating other uses for cast iron. After seeing that iron rails and supports were compatible for bridge building, he teamed up with the architect Thomas F. Pritchard to build the bridge. Spanning a distance of 100 feet, the bridge has a cast-iron arch that resembles an arch from a Roman aqueduct. The skeletal framework of the Coalbrookdale Bridge foreshadowed the expanded use of cast-iron in the nineteenth century.

Cast iron opened great possibilities for architecture. Formed from carbon and other elements (iron is found in the earth's crust in combination with other elements), cast iron can support as much weight as masonry (concrete) with much less material. As such, it became a preferred industrial building material. Architects could use cast iron to create larger and stronger structures.

Steel became widely available around 1855, when Henry Bessemer developed an efficient process for converting iron ore into steel. His factory was soon able to smelt a 25-ton load of pig iron into steel in half an hour. Steel is a metal alloy made mostly of iron. But steel also contains a certain amount of carbon and other elements, which prevent the metal alloy from separating under stress and make it stronger than cast iron. Different proportions of carbon and other elements can affect other attributes of steel such as elasticity, flexibility, and tensile strength. These qualities expanded the use of steel in architecture. Architects utilized steel in the construction of train stations such as Saint-Lazare in Paris (recall Monet's rendition shown in Chapter 26) and in great exhibition halls.

Henri Labrouste's Library

Henri Labrouste's Bibliotheque Sainte-Genevieve (1843–1850) is highly recognizable (**CD Fig. 28-3**). It contains a cast-iron skeleton blended with Renaissance style. This library's reading room contains two barrel vaults separated by a central arcade. Cast-iron rounded arches support the barrel vaults, and the arcade comprises cast-iron Corinthian columns and arches. The rounded arches and windows of the upper level also reflect classical and Renaissance building. Henri Labrouste demonstrated the prevailing mentality of most nineteenth-century architects. Despite the creative possibilities that cast-iron created, most architects were hesitant to abandon the architectural vocabulary of past styles.

The Crystal Palace

The year was 1851, and London, the capital of Great Britain, the world's greatest colonial power, was preparing to host a Great Exhibition to present the industries of the world. Prince Albert decided to hold the event in Hyde Park. The problem was that the government had to provide a structure in only six months. The solution was to come not from an architect but a horticulturalist who designed greenhouses. His name was John Paxton. The government granted Paxton the commission because his design could be assembled rapidly.

Similar to his greenhouses, Paxton's exhibition hall included extensive amounts of glass and metal. It was dubbed the Crystal Palace (**CD Fig. 28-4**). The length of the structure stretched one-third of a mile and covered 18 acres of land. It included 18,000 panes of glass and 3, 300 iron pillars. The enormous building housed giant trees, working fountains, and a myriad of machines.

Workers constructed the Crystal Palace so quickly because of the use of prefabricated (already made) and standardized (interchangeable) parts. They disassembled the building with equal speed once the exhibition concluded.

Paxton did include some tradition in his radical structure. The Crystal Palace exhibited the influence of the Christian basilica, with its long and flat-roofed nave, side aisles, and barrel-vaulted transept. Yet the theme of the Great Exhibition of 1851 was progress. What better way to display this progress than through one of the most innovative buildings ever designed? The Crystal Palace was way ahead of its time. It was the first major "undraped" structure. The design did not hide its glass and iron supports, which makes it a precursor to twentieth-century skyscrapers.

Victorian England, however, was not ready to follow Paxton's model. Revival architecture held the day. Yet the people of London admired the Crystal Palace so much that the government reassembled it on the outskirts of the city, where it remained until a fire destroyed it in 1936.

The Eiffel Tower

Gustave Eiffel used wrought iron to create the largest structure in the world in 1889: a tower for the Great Exhibition in Paris in 1889. Before constructing the tower, Eiffel designed bridges (he also designed the interior armature for the Statue of Liberty). It was the centennial of the storming of the Bastille, which France celebrates as its Independence Day. At the hundred-year mark, the Eiffel Tower was to be the symbol for modern nineteenth-century Paris (**CD Fig. 28-5**). After descending the 984-foot tower, one twentieth-century writer compared the experience to flying in an airplane. Like Paxton, Eiffel did not mask his design beneath embellishments (although the rounded arches that make up the tower's skirt obscure the horizontal girders). Art historians view the creation of such a soaring structure as another important step toward the development of the modern skyscraper.

Evolution of the Skyscraper

As the nineteenth century came to a close, in the big cities throughout the United States, property values were climbing and space contracting. Attempting to work within these restrictions, architects began to build upward. Building taller, narrower structures gave owners of the buildings more rental property. Ever-higher floors could command top-dollar rents in the city. Thus, the demand for taller buildings used for commercial purposes increased.

Cast iron played an important role in the evolution of the skyscraper. Before its emergence, masonry (concrete) was the main material. At first, architects embraced cast iron and greatly decreased the amount of masonry they used for building support. After a series of fires revealed the weakness of using cast iron alone, engineers discovered that encasing cast-iron beams in masonry offered the benefits of the increased strength of the former and the fire-resistant qualities of the latter.

As we said at the opening of this chapter, a slide-based short essay on the 2006 AP Art History exam dealt with how a tall building of the nineteenth century, Louis Sullivan's Carson, Pirie, Scott Building, influenced the creation of the modern skyscraper. The important role iron and steel played in the significance of these tall buildings should be clear. We will examine Louis Sullivan's buildings shortly; first, let us look at one of his predecessors.

Henry Hobson Richardson

Henry Hobson Richardson designed tall buildings such as the seven-story Marshall Field Wholesale Store in Chicago (**CD Fig. 28-6**). He chose to use heavy masonry, however, to mask the building's metal infrastructure. One of Richardson's biggest influences was the Romanesque period (see Chapter 13). He designed Trinity Church in Boston with a large stone portal, rough-hewn stone blocks, and windows with rounded arches. Private and public patronage of Richardson resulted in Romanesque revival architecture throughout the New England area.

Richardson's greatest contribution to nineteenth-century architecture stems from the originality of his designs. He did not look to only one style as a reference, and even though his designs bear some resemblance to earlier periods, they are unique. For example, the Marshall Field Wholesale Store has a three-part elevation similar to the Roman Pont-du-Gard aqueduct or the facade of the Rucellai Palace by Alberti. Yet the store lacks classical ornamentation such as vine scrolls (which Labrouste included in the cast-iron transverse arches in his library). The way that the levels of windows interrupt the courses of bricks causes us to focus on the horizontal lines between each level. This gives the effect of weightiness and monumentality (Richardson was a large man himself, with a 350-pound frame). The horizontal lines magnify the length of the building, which occupies a city block. The large amount of window space opens the walls of the building and foreshadows how windows will replace more and more of the wall surface in twentieth-century buildings.

Louis Sullivan: The First Modern Architect

Art historians consider Louis Sullivan to be the first modern architect. His designs revealed the interior structure in combination with decorative elegance. His Guaranty (Prudential) Building in Buffalo, New York, epitomizes his technique (**CD Fig. 28-7**). What do you see? First of all notice that Sullivan's design emphasizes verticality.

Second, the vertical lines that separate the columns of windows are the actual supports, which are made from steel covered in terra-cotta. Louis Sullivan's favorite motto was "form follows function." The Guaranty Building is an office building; its function is to provide commercial space. Therefore, its vertical height reflects its purpose. Its numerous windows allow ample light for the white-collar workers within.

Along with its functionality, Sullivan includes touches of elegance. The entrance resembles a Romanesque portal with a rounded arch, a lintel, and jambs, all of which have relief designs. The columns of windows are capped by rounded arches. Near the roof, Sullivan included circular windows beneath a cornice. The vertical supports and the cornice have sculptural decorations. Sullivan could have done without these designs but desired to demonstrate taste and refinement.

Sullivan's design for the Carson, Pirie, Scott Building demonstrates further progression toward the modern skyscraper (**CD Fig. 28-8**). Built as a department store, it had to have a large amount of window space for displays. Sullivan included a minimal steel skeleton to the building to provide space for displays and shoppers. Decorations cover the lower levels of the building that Sullivan created out of cast iron. These designs acted as picture frames for the displays that people would see from the street. The rest of the building, however, is more abstract, focusing on the function rather than form. At nine stories tall, the Carson, Pirie, Scott Building has verticality. It includes the modern material of steel as well as many glass windows.

Because the Carson, Pirie, Scott Building was the subject of a slide-based question on a recent test, it is unlikely to appear on any tests in the near future. However, no AP Art History test has included Sullivan's Guaranty Building. Therefore, that Sullivan design might be included with a series of multiple-choice questions. You may have to recall that Sullivan also designed the Carson, Pirie, Scott Building. You should also understand that his buildings paved the way for modern skyscrapers and that aesthetic and structural elements interested him.

Sullivan's designs were a watershed for architectural history. He would inspire his pupil, Frank Lloyd Wright, the self-proclaimed greatest architect of the twentieth century. But the majority of the patrons were not ready to accept Sullivan's designs. The public forgot about Sullivan, and he became a poor recluse. Like Paxton with his Crystal Palace, Sullivan was ahead of his time.

Richard Morris Hunt, The Breakers, and Renaissance Revival

Revival styles remained the preferred choice of wealthy patrons. A building that displays this preference is the summer home of Cornelius Vanderbilt II in Newport, Rhode Island. Nicknamed The Breakers because of its vista of the Atlantic Ocean, this opulent residence reflects the influence of Renaissance architecture (**CD Fig. 28-9**). Its architect, Richard Morris Hunt, studied in Paris at the prestigious École des Beaux Arts and brought its classical and Renaissance influences (known as the beaux arts style) into his work. The Breakers resembles a sixteenth-century Italian palazzo. The home is constructed of expensive materials such as marble. Hunt used round arches, arcades, and engaged columns in the design and gave the whole residence a sense of balance and symmetry. The interior of the building contains classical columns, painted ceilings, and sculptured trimmings.

Figure 28-9. Richard Morris Hunt, The Breakers, 1892

America's elite delighted in the designs of Richard Morris Hunt, who used their great wealth to his creative advantage. He designed another home for the Vanderbilt's in Asheville, North Carolina, that cost $4.1 million to build in the 1890s and resembles a French chateau. Hunt also created a chateau for the Astor family.

Conclusion

One key point about nineteenth-century architecture is that America was not yet fully ready for modern designs. The wealthy elite and the government still preferred revival styles such as Neoclassical (known in America as the Federal Style) for government buildings (e.g., the Capitol), Neo-Gothic for churches and college campuses (e.g., Saint Patrick's Cathedral in New York City), and the Renaissance-inspired Beaux Arts Style for the homes of the American aristocracy.

Modernity gradually took hold in public and office buildings. Cast iron and steel became important elements in this evolution. At first, architects were reluctant to reveal how the new materials supported their designs. A few architects blazed a trail toward modernism by creating innovative designs and exposing the underlying structure of their buildings. Louis Sullivan became the first modern architect, and his lessons would be learned and expanded on by the twentieth-century architect Frank Lloyd Wright.

Part 6
Twentieth-Century Art

Chapter 29

Early Twentieth-Century Art

Due to copyright issues, use of 20th-century art images is restricted on our accompanying Art CD. Below is the list of images referred to in this chapter. REA suggests that readers refer to their textbook or use trusted Internet sites to view the images presented in this section's narrative.

Henri Matisse, *Woman with a Hat*, 1905

André Derain, *Big Ben*, 1905

Pablo Picasso, *Gertrude Stein*, 1906–1907

Pablo Picasso, *Les Demoiselles d'Avignon*, 1907

Pablo Picasso, *Brick Factory in Tortosa* (or *Factory in Horta de Ebro*), 1909

Georges Braque, *The Portuguese*, 1911

Robert DeLaunay, *Champ de Mars* (or *The Red Tower*), 1911

Pablo Picasso, *Still Life with Chair Caning*, 1912

Pablo Picasso, *Guernica*, 1937

Pablo Picasso, *maquette for The Guitar*, 1912

Jacques Lipchitz, *Bather*, 1917

Julio Gonzalez, *Woman Combing Her Hair, ca.* 1930–1933

Aleksandr Archipenko, *Woman Combing Her Hair*, 1915

Giacomo Balla, *Dynamism of a Dog on a Leash*, 1912

Eadweard Muybridge, *The Horse in Motion*, 1878

Umberto Boccioni, *Dynamism of a Soccer Player*, 1913

Umberto Boccioni, *Unique Forms of Continuity in Space*, 1913

Gino Severini, *Armored Train in Action*, 1915

Vladimir Tatlin, *Monument to the Third International*, 1919–1920

Vera Mukhina, *The Worker and the Collective Farm Worker*, 1937

Marcel Duchamp, *Nude Descending a Staircase, No.* 2, 1912

Constantin Brancusi, *Mademoiselle Pogany*, 1912

Ernst Ludwig Kirchner, *Street, Dresden*, 1907

Emil Nolde, *Saint Mary of Egypt Among Sinners*, 1912

Vassily Kandinsky, *Improvisation No.* 30 (or *Cannons*), 1913

Franz Marc, *Yellow Cow*, 1911

Franz Marc, *Fate of the Animals*, 1913

Max Beckmann, *Night*, 1918–1919

Max Beckmann, *Departure*, 1932–1933

Introduction and Exam Strategy Overview

Filipo Tomasso Marinetti, an early twentieth-century writer who promoted Futurism, made the following statement: "A roaring racing-car is more beautiful than the *Winged Victory of Samothrace*." Which do you think is more beautiful, the classical sculpture of the goddess Nike or a speeding car at the Talladega 500? If the AP Art History committee had its way, every student taking the exam would answer the *Winged Victory of Samothrace*. But a group of artists led by F. T. Marinetti disagreed. In "The Foundation and Manifesto of Futurism," Marinetti wrote, "The world's magnificence has been enriched by a new beauty, the beauty of speed."

Have you ever wondered why some artists paint human figures in unnatural colors? Or have you ever seen a metallic sculpture comprising cubelike shapes and to your astonishment discovered that it is a portrait of a person? The modern art movements of the early twentieth century marked the full transition of art to Modernism, with artists creating works that express their vision and emphasize that art is a subjective discipline that need not copy the natural world.

Art of the twentieth and twenty-first centuries makes up 10 percent to 15 percent of the points on the AP Art History exam. This chapter prepares you for the various artistic movements that have appeared on past tests by explaining the formal, stylistic tendencies of early modern art as well as relevant contextual information.

Modernist Art

Why did artists begin to change their work to reflect their own vision? Post-Impressionism and Symbolism were influential (see Chapters 26 and 27). Artists also changed their views on art because during the early twentieth century, people began to look at the world differently. Scientists questioned the nature of matter. Physicists such as Max Planck and Niels Bohr wrote about atomic structure. In his theory of relativity, Albert Einstein postulated that space and time were not absolute. He also explained that matter was not solid at all but really another form of energy. Industrial technology also evolved as inventors developed ever-more complex and efficient machines. Planes, trains, automobiles, and electricity became significant parts of everyday life. Chemistry developed newer materials through oil refining, the various qualities of steel, and plastic polymers.

Meanwhile, intellectuals challenged the traditional beliefs of society. Friedrich Nietzsche believed that European civilization had become decadent and that a major factor holding society back was religion. Nietzsche preached "God is dead" and explained that as soon as people realize there is no God, they can begin to follow their passions and truly live. Meanwhile, the Austrian psychologist Sigmund Freud hypothesized that the human repression of unconscious desires affects human behavior. Freud advocated analyzing the dreams and relationships of his patients to discover their repressed desires, which he believed caused their psychoses.

In the 1890s, artists such as Gauguin and the Symbolists began to explore their own artistic vision rather than copying a realistic perception of the natural world. The styles of artists evolved to reflect the changing viewpoints on science, matter, concepts of "reality," and humanity of the early twentieth century.

Henri Matisse

Henri Matisse was one of the most innovative artists of the twentieth century. His dazzling experiments with color marked a turning point in the history of art and formed the basis for most subsequent artistic developments. Matisse came late to painting, having trained to become a lawyer to please his father. While he was recovering from an appendectomy, his mother brought him a box of paints and a how-to book. The world lost an attorney and gained an artist.

The key principles of Matisse's art revolve around his use of color, simple forms, and feel-good paintings. He once said, "When I paint green, it doesn't mean grass; when I paint blue, it doesn't mean sky." In this way, Matisse summed up the essence of his approach to color. He also said, "Color was not given to us so that we should imitate nature, but so that we could express our emotions." Matisse freed color from its literal descriptive role. In other words, Matisse used **nonrepresentational colors**. Observation, feeling, and the nature of each experience guided his use of color. If you recall, Gauguin and Van Gogh were among the first artists to use color to express inner feelings (see Chapter 26). Retrospective exhibitions of the work of these Post-Impressionists influenced Matisse.

Matisse strove to eliminate nonessential details from his art, retaining only his subjects' most fundamental qualities. He ignored the social and political controversies surrounding him, saying that he dreamed of "an art of balance, of purity and serenity devoid of troubling or depressing subject matter."

Matisse and the Fauves

Matisse and a small group of avant-garde artists exhibited their works at the Third Annual Salon d'Automne in 1905. Matisse and his fellow artists used nonrepresentational colors, broad abstract brushstrokes, and simplified figures in their paintings. Critics who viewed the exhibit were aghast at what these artists had created. Some called the exhibit "raving madness." Another critic described the works as "the naive and brutal effects of a child playing with its paint box." It was at the 1905 Salon d'Automne that a critic gave a name to these painters: the Fauves, which is French for "wild beasts."

Fauvism, as the movement came to be known, turned out to be short lived. Matisse and the small group of painters worked together informally and within a few years they went on to develop their own distinctive styles. Nevertheless, the impact of Fauvism on twentieth-century art was tremendous. The Fauves completely liberated color from imitating the natural world

Matisse's *Woman with a Hat*

A fine example of Matisse's use of nonrepresentational color is his painting *Woman with a Hat*, which he displayed in the Salon d'Automne. Matisse used a traditional three-quarter pose for his model, who was his wife, Amelie. He painted her with a huge, decorative hat, gloves, and a dress that make the painting look like traditional bourgeois portraiture. Amelie's facial shape, eyes, fine nose, and lips exude traditional beauty. However, tradition ends at those features.

Matisse painted a green stripe down Amelie's nose as well as a green stripe across her forehead. She has bright orange hair and a patch of orange on her neck. She has yellow, green, and orange highlights on her face. Matisse used loose brushwork for her face, clothing, and hat. The background consists of broad strokes of different colors. Although Matisse's use of color was unusual, it was not thoughtless. Because the colors of the background harmonize with the colors in Amelie's clothing and the highlights on her face, the composition is unified. Rather than modeling fully with chiaroscuro, an important Renaissance technique, Matisse used colors that capture shadows and highlights. He also left parts of the painting without color.

For Matisse, color was subjective, expressing his unique approach to his subject. Matisse also reinforced the two-dimensionality of the painted surface, as evident in parts of Amelie's dress and hair. Some parts of the background appear to be part of another plane, but other parts exist on the same plane as her face. Like Gauguin, Matisse occasionally used **flat planes** of color. *Woman with a Hat* used the tradition of portraiture to express revolutionary ideas.

André Derain

Another exhibitor at the 1905 Salon d'Automne was André Derain. His work displays Fauvist features as well. He created a famous series of paintings of sites in England such as Big Ben and the Charing Cross Bridge in London. The dabs of color that he used resemble Impressionist and Post-Impressionist techniques. However, like Matisse, he used nonrepresentational color, which is why art historians consider him a Fauve at that point in his career.

Pablo Picasso

Picasso is a legendary figure. The most prolific artist of all time, he worked in all mediums and was productive up to the end of his life at the age of 91. His work dominated the avant-garde. As soon as critics would start making sense of his work, Picasso would change his style, always staying on the cutting edge of art.

Art history credits Pablo Picasso with inspiring the advent of Cubism, based on an important revolutionary painting called *Les Demoiselles d'Avignon*. Even before this painting, he created a portrait of a famous female patron named Gertrude Stein (she was one of the greatest avant-garde patrons of the earlier twentieth century, commissioning work from Matisse as well as Picasso) that revealed glimpses of the Cubism to come. Many of the avant-garde artists had grown tired of the traditions of European painting. That is not to say that Picasso did not study the work of famous masters. In fact, some of his favorites included Velazquez (whom he considered the best painter of all time), Manet, and Cézanne.

However, Picasso and other artists began to look beyond the European tradition to other cultures for inspiration. African and Oceanic cultures produced artwork that conveyed meaning through abstract forms. Avant-garde artists admired this trait because it was pure. Instead of trying to imitate the world exactly, which consumed European artists since the Renaissance, tribal artists used simple and decorative forms to express concepts. It was this simplicity and purity that drew Gauguin to Tahiti and early twentieth-century avant-garde artists to the exhibitions of African and Oceanic masks in Paris's anthropological museum.

Picasso's portrait of *Gertrude Stein* displays some tribal features. After Stein had sat for him eighty times, Picasso still could not finish the portrait. Dissatisfied, he left Paris to take a short vacation in Spain. He returned with new vigor and finished the portrait in one sitting. While in Spain, Picasso studied Iberian stone sculpture. These sculptures have block-shaped heads and almond-shaped eyes. Picasso also used African masks as an influence in completing the painting. Picasso captured the powerful, wise, and determined features of one of the twentieth century's most significant patrons. Stein prized the painting and kept it until her death.

The subjects of *Les Demoiselles d'Avignon* (**Fig. 29-1**) are five women and a fruit dish. The painting takes its title from a red-light district in Barcelona, Spain. The women are prostitutes. The fruit in the foreground is most likely a reference to vanitas painting, and the figures demonstrate Picasso's interest in the abstract forms of Iberian and African sculpture. The three figures on the left exhibit the Iberian influence, while the figures on the right illustrate the African influence. The faces of the two women on the right resemble decorative and geometric African masks.

Figure 29-1. Pablo Picasso, *Les Demoiselles d'Avignon*, 1907

Picasso smashed the traditional depiction of the human figure as continuous volumes. Instead, he used fragmented forms to depict the women's bodies, the space around them, drapery, and the still life scene in the foreground. Picasso was trying to find a new way to render figures in space. He displayed the tension of rendering the illusion of space with the two-dimensional qualities of paint. His creation is the way he wanted to see space.

Besides fragmenting the forms, Picasso rendered the figures from multiple angles. For example, the model in the lower-right corner sits with her back to us, but her face is turned forward. This demonstrates the influence of Cézanne's still life paintings, in which he investigated space by illustrating multiple viewpoints (see Chapter 26).

Les Demoiselles d'Avignon is one of the most revolutionary paintings in art history because it was the first work in which an artist presented the human form in this manner. Picasso was hesitant to reveal this painting and at first showed it only to a small group of fellow artists. They were shocked by his depiction of the figures. One artist, Georges Braque, was so moved by the painting, that he began to work with Picasso. Together they developed Cubism.

Analytic Cubism

Cubism received its name when Matisse described a Braque painting as nothing but little cubes. As you will see, however, Cubism is much more. Cubist artists reexamined the shapes and qualities of objects by breaking them apart into their simple geometric components and reconstituting the pieces as the artists saw fit. Artists had to understand what they were dissecting and were not to leave out important parts of the object. One French writer stated, "Everyone must agree that a chair, from whichever side it is viewed, never ceases to have four legs, a seat and a back, and that if robbed of one of these elements, it is robbed of an important part."

Cézanne was a major influence on the Cubist approach to form. He was the first artist to render the basic geometric shapes of objects, painting them in a flat manner, instead of modeling objects, conveying spatial relationships through multiple perspectives.

Art historians refer to the style established by the collaboration between Picasso and Braque as Analytic Cubism, so named because the artists analyzed the forms of objects before reconstituting them.

One good example is Picasso's painting of a factory in the town of Horta de Ebro. We can see the smokestacks that make this a factory, but Picasso reconstituted the factory and the surrounding land into basic, fragmented shapes of his own vision.

Georges Braque's painting *The Portuguese* provides another fine example. Braque fragmented the form so much that you must look hard to find elements of the guitar player (Braque based *The Portuguese* on a musician he once knew). What elements make a guitar player? They are a man and the neck and strings of his guitar. Look closely and find these elements. Braque also layers dark and light paint on the canvas to convey various levels of space and stenciled letters and numbers on the canvas because they are known for their flatness. Braque provides a complex interpretation of not only form but also its relationship to space.

One other significant element of Analytic Cubism is the artists' use of muted colors. Vivid color could distract these artists and the viewer from interpreting the shapes and the surrounding space. Another artist, Robert Delaunay, developed Color Cubism. He created a series of paintings of the Eiffel Tower (see Chapter 28). The combination of his fragmented forms in space with vivid color creating shocking contrasts that influenced the Futurists and German Expressionists.

Synthetic Cubism

Around 1912, Picasso and Braque developed Synthetic Cubism. Synthetic Cubism involves pasting synthetic objects such as pieces of paper, cloth, and other objects to the canvas to create a **collage**. Art historians view Picasso's *Still Life with Chair Caning* as the first work of Synthetic Cubism. Picasso took an oilcloth with the image of a cane chair photo-lithographed onto it, giving this piece a **trompe l'oeil** effect—it looks as if a real chair is in the painting. Rather than a traditional frame, Picasso used rope. Near the oilcloth, he painted Cubist shapes that, although they are painted, are technically more real than the image of the cane chair. Picasso examines shapes, space, materials, and the nature of reality in this piece.

Picasso's Guernica

Unlike Matisse, who avoided troubling social and political events, Picasso took an avid interest in politics. He was a member of the Socialist Party while in France, and engaged in political debate with fellow artists and writers. Politics also motivated Picasso's creativity, as seen in his monumental work titled *Guernica*.

Guernica depicts an event from the Spanish Civil War, which occurred before World War II. Spain's fledgling republic was being threatened by rebel Fascists led by General Francisco Franco. Franco invited the German Luftwaffe, an important part of Hitler's plan for blitzkrieg, to test its fighting techniques by bombing the republican stronghold of Guernica. For forty-five minutes, German planes dropped massive bombs and fired machine guns at the inhabitants. Of Guernica's 7,000 inhabitants, 1,654 were killed and 889 injured.

The Spanish republican government in exile commissioned Picasso to create art in honor of the republic. Picasso was outraged by the bombing of Guernica and developed his monumental painting in recognition of the atrocity. In the Cubist Style, Picasso used fragmented forms with jagged edges to convey the violence of the event. He used black, gray, and white to create a scene dominated by struggle and death. *Guernica* contains deeply meaningful symbols. A bull in the painting represents brutality and darkness.

An anguished horse represents the Spanish people. We can see a mother holding her dead child, a mutilated rider in the foreground, a body reaching upward in agony, and injured and frightened women. The figures are distorted to convey the mutilation and destruction of Guernica. All the figures have their mouths open to let out an enormous collective scream. Picasso's *Guernica* raised public awareness of the horrors of the Spanish Civil War at the Paris International Exposition in Paris in 1937.

Cubist Sculpture

Cubism made an important contribution to modern sculpture. Picasso applied Cubism to sculpture when he created *The Guitar*. Using the three-dimensional medium enabled him to investigate the inner and outer parts of the instrument. To create the guitar's exterior shapes and spaces, he used planar shapes. Picasso explored both three-dimensionality and two-dimensionality by sculpting with flat pieces of cardboard. He also investigated space in the sculpture. For example, the sound hole of *The Guitar* is a prominent formal element of the work, creating a significant space in the composition.

Picasso's Cubist Sculpture influenced other avant-garde artists living in Paris. Jacques Lipchitz, an artist of Jewish origin born in Lithuania, moved to Paris to study art at the École de Beaux Arts and Academie Julian. He began to experiment with Cubist forms while associating with Picasso in Paris's Montmartre and Montparnasse sections. Lipchitz would become one of the most famous modern sculptors of the twentieth century. In *Bather*, he included several elements of the Cubist Vocabulary: fragmented forms, flat planes, and multiple viewpoints.

Picasso's friend Julio Gonzalez extended the application of the Cubist Vocabulary to sculpture even further. His *Woman Combing Her Hair* is almost completely nonrepresentational (although parts of the sculpture do resemble human form: rounded and wavy wires look like hair, and metal plates represent the torso, waist, and a leg). His work inspired sculptors of the latter part of the twentieth century to work with contorted metal wires—for example, Alexander Calder in his mobiles (see Chapter 30) and David Smith in his *Cubi* series (see Chapter 31).

Aleksandr Archipenko, a Russian sculptor, challenged traditional Russian methods of representation when he created his Cubist sculpture titled *Woman Combing Her Hair*. Although we can see an upraised arm, round hips, and almost contrapposto positioning, Archipenko included a **void** (space) in the region of her head. This is a significant formal element not used by previous artists, such as Bernini in his Baroque *David* (see Chapter 20). Yet Archipenko boldly places the void through the center of this sculpture in the round. Archipenko's investigation of space and mass with its intersecting planes, voids, and abstract shapes, makes *Woman Combing Her Hair* a significant twentieth-century sculpture.

Futurism

Color Cubist paintings by Delaunay and Cubist sculpture influenced the form of the next major avant-garde movement, Futurism. Originating in Italy, this movement glorified the technology of the modern world. The founder of Futurism, F. T. Marinetti (discussed earlier), expounded the principles of the movement in the "The Foundation and Manifesto of Futurism," published in 1909. He wrote that artists needed to free the land from the "smelly gangrene" of professors, archaeologists, and antiquarians (people who studied Roman antiquities). Marinetti equated "admiring an old picture" with "pouring our sensibility into a funerary urn." Traditional art forms such as classicism affected European art for hundreds of years, which caused stagnation. Marinetti and other Futurists declared war on the artistic traditions of the past. They wanted to destroy art museums, libraries, and collections of history. Marinetti even recommended having an annual funeral for the *Mona Lisa* to recognize the death of traditional art forms.

In his manifesto, Marinetti advocated celebrating a "new beauty, the beauty of speed." Of particular interest to the Futurists were the speed and dynamism of modern technology. Marinetti insisted that "a speeding automobile . . . is more beautiful than the *Nike of Samothrace*." Futurists used fragmented forms and multiple viewpoints to convey the motion of objects and figures.

Balla's *Dynamism of a Dog on a Leash*

How can an artist portray the sensation of motion? Giacomo Balla's painting *Dynamism of a Dog on a Leash* answers that question. One influence on Balla's painting was the **sequential motion photography** of Eadweard Muybridge. By conducting multiple camera motion studies, Muybridge recorded progressive moments in a single action, such as a person running or a horse galloping. Balla conveys the motion of the dog, the leash, and the owner by painting the images several times. Another influence on Balla was the **simultaneous views** of Analytic Cubism.

Boccioni's *Dynamism of a Soccer Player*

Umberto Boccioni, another leading Futurist, captured simultaneous views of a subject in *Dynamism of Soccer Player*. In traditional art, the subject could be seen in only one time and place. Although the painting is highly abstract with a number of jagged, fragmented forms, on closer inspection, you can see parts of a soccer player. Boccioni shows various parts of the leg, from the muscular thighs, to the knee, and finally to the foot as it makes contact with the ball. Boccioni conveys speed and power as he records the path of a soccer player's leg movement to kick a ball.

Boccioni's *Unique Forms of Continuity in Space*

Boccioni created a sculpture representation of the concept of motion with *Unique Forms of Continuity in Space* (**Fig. 29-2**). In this work, Boccioni was able to transcend the traditional static (motionless) medium of sculpture. How did he do it? Think about viewing objects from the car window as you are driving. The objects become stretched and blurred, do they not? Boccioni's sculpture presents a figure, although it is highly abstracted. We can see a head, shoulders, and legs. Instead of naturalistic curves, we see multiple planes and jagged curves, which convey a body in motion. Jagged shapes flow backward from the legs, giving the effect of a body moving forward. The effect of vitality and motion is somewhat similar to the *Winged Victory of Samothrace*, yet its use of fragmented forms and highly polished bronze convey the modern depictions of motion favored by the Futurists.

Figure 29-2. Umberto Boccioni, *Unique Forms of Continuity in Space*, 1913

Gino Severini's *Armored Train in Action*

The Futurists glorified war. They believed that war would cleanse Europe of its stagnation. Gino Severini's painting *Armored Train in Action* conveys the artist's interest in machines of war. He used jagged shapes and force lines (lines that slash across the painting) to convey the feeling of a speeding train and the concept of aggression. The soldiers appear as automatons; lacking any individual identity, they wear the same plain blue uniforms and point their rifles in the same direction. A rail gun (large cannon) anchored on the train lets forth a huge blast. It is interesting to note that the colors Severini used for the train and the soldiers' uniforms—blues and silver—resemble metal.

By contrast, he uses flashes of yellow and red to represent shots from the rifles. Severini glorifies the technology of modern weapons and mechanized warfare, giving visual representation to the Great War (World War I) that was raging in Europe at that time.

Russian Constructivism

The Russian equivalent of Futurism occurred contemporaneously with the Russian Revolution of 1917. The leading figure of the movement, Vladimir Tatlin, described the Russian avant-garde movement as Constructivism. His aim was to construct a new art rather than compose art according to the traditions of the past. Who dominated the creations of the past? It was the bourgeoisie, the class against whom the Russian proletariat revolted. Therefore, Tatlin argued, artists needed to construct an art that stripped away the symbols and themes of the art of the past. Constructivism used the new industrial materials of the day such as steel (Russia was behind other countries in steel production) and plastic.

Tatlin's most famous work, *Monument to the Third International,* celebrated the Communist Revolution. The monument was intended to provide lecture halls, information centers, and government offices of the Communist Party. Tatlin created an innovative design that cast aside previous architecture. Although the actual structure was never built, the model suggested that it consist of a tilted spiraling cage made of steel and glass—industrial materials that represented the proletariat. Gears would power the various levels, causing them to revolve at various time increments. If completed, the structure would have been twice as tall as the Empire State Building.

Vladimir Lenin tolerated Russian Constructivism. He thought the artists could teach the illiterate public the main concepts of communism. In creating a new social order, a new style of art was appropriate. After Lenin's death and the rise of Stalin, art reverted to representational forms of idealized human figures representing the proletariat. Russian Constructivism was said to represent the bourgeoisie, and some of the Constructivists fled abroad.

A good example of the representational art that emerged after Russia became the Soviet Union is Vera Mukhina's *The Worker and the Collective Farm Worker*. This sculpture with its pedestal was 78 feet tall. Its glorification of the proletariat was easier for the public to comprehend and provided an ideal toward which the public should strive: muscular figures determined to work for the common good.

Armory Show (1913)

In February 1913, the United States had its first taste of modern art. Organizers created the Armory Show, which was held at the National Guard Armory, on Lexington Avenue in New York City. Officially called the International Exhibition of Modern Art, the Armory Show displayed about 1,250 works by more than three hundred avant-garde European and American artists. Featuring the works of Impressionists, Post-Impressionists, Fauves, and Cubists, among others, the show was an important catalyst that inspired American artists and exposed greater numbers of Americans to

Modern art. Yet the works horrified most of the American public. In reaction to the show, Teddy Roosevelt exclaimed, "That's not art!" Critics described the artists as depraved lunatics and bomb throwers. Public officials even debated closing the show because it endangered the public's morals.

Duchamp's *Nude Descending a Staircase*

One of the most controversial paintings of the 1913 Armory Show was Marcel Duchamp's *Nude Descending a Staircase*. The title misled visitors to the exhibition, who probably expected a realistic representation of nudity. However, Duchamp included no detectable body parts that would indicate the gender of this figure. At this stage of his career, Duchamp was examining the fragmented forms of Cubism. Although the flesh-colored body is not completely nonrepresentational, it is abstract and very angular. To depict a body in motion descending a staircase, Duchamp used simultaneous viewpoints; this feature of the painting reveals the influence of Futurism and the sequential motion photography of Eadweard Muybridge.

A *New York Times* critic described *Nude Descending a Staircase* as "an explosion in a shingle factory." Duchamp eventually moved past his Cubist phase toward a new avant-garde movement called Dadaism (see Chapter 30).

Brancusi's *Mademoiselle Pogany*

Constantin Brancusi's *Mademoiselle Pogany* was another revolutionary work that caused a storm among the visitors to the Armory Show. This did not look like a traditional portrait of a woman. One visitor described it as a hard-boiled egg resting on a sugar cube. Influenced by the works of Rodin, Brancusi strove to reduce representational images to elemental forms. Brancusi eliminated the exterior qualities of his sitters and subjects. Instead, focusing on internal qualities, Brancusi produced **abstract, organic** sculpture that captured the **essence** of his subjects.

German Expressionism Before World War I

German Expressionism refers to art that used color, shape, and composition to create works of art (mostly paintings but also woodcuts) that expressed inner feelings and truths over objective representations of reality. Art historians divide pre–World War I German Expressionism into two basic movements: Die Brucke ("The Bridge") and Der Blaue Reiter ("The Blue Rider"). In general, the movements spanned from 1905 to 1913, shortly before the outbreak of World War I. There were also independent German Expressionists, who were not part of either movement, and artists of the postwar German Expressionism movement are examined later in the chapter.

Die Brucke

In 1905, a group of German artists gathered to form the first German Expressionist group led by Ernst Ludwig Kirchner. These artists disliked the effects of industrialization on Germany and sought as a group to react against the social changes caused by industrialization. Various artistic sources inspired these artists. The colors of the Fauves, the paintings of Edvard Munch (see Chapter 27), African and Oceanic masks, and German medieval art influenced their creations. Kirchner and his group called their movement Die Brucke, which in German means "The Bridge." They viewed themselves as the bridge between the past and a better future that they wished to create.

Key stylistic features of Die Brucke include arbitrary and intense use of colors. Like the Fauves, these artists used color to express themselves. The figures of Die Brucke painting are sharply stylized and distorted. The figures have simplified forms that are not realistically modeled with chiaroscuro. They possess flat faces and empty eye sockets resembling African and Oceanic masks. People of the time labeled this characteristic **primitivism** (believing non-European societies to be primitive). Die Brucke paintings often contain steep diagonal compositions that invade the viewer's space. Recall that Van Gogh (Post-Impressionist) and Munch (Symbolist) used some of these same techniques. In *Night Café*, Van Gogh used jarring color juxtapositions and a steep diagonal composition to convey the dangers of frequenting such a place (see Chapter 26). In *The Scream*, Munch painted with violent colors and brushstrokes and a steep diagonal plane to convey the psychological effect of fear (Munch was especially influential because he exhibited in Berlin in 1892). Like Van Gogh and Munch, Die Brucke artists used color, brushstrokes, shapes, and unusual compositions to express their feelings about the world.

Kirchner's *Street Dresden*

When Kirchner and other Die Brucke artists spent time in large German cities such as Berlin and Dresden, they witnessed the effects of industrialization. Industrialization spawned urbanization, which in turn contributed to alienation among people. Think about going to any big city today. Do people stop to talk to you, or do they push past you to carry on with their own lives? Kirchner (and most of us) would choose the latter. He expresses this feeling of alienation and isolation through a series of street paintings. Let us examine *Street, Dresden*.

Notice how he used jarring contrasts of colors: blues and oranges, yellows and purples, greens and reds. Unlike the Impressionists, Kirchner did not use these complementary colors to express the luminosity of natural light. Instead, his intent was to disturb the viewer just as he was disturbed by the street scene. Notice the women in the foreground. They look in our direction, and it feels as if they are coming into our space. Their ghoulish, masklike faces give them a menacing quality. The masks that these women seem to wear express the hypocrisy of modern society. Notice the steep ground plane that accentuates the effect of these women approaching our space. Despite the fine clothing of everyone in the picture, no one seems happy. Kirchner expresses the decadence of the twentieth-century cities.

Emil Nolde

Emil Nolde was an older and well-known German artist who joined Die Brucke for a short time. Being raised in a Protestant household in which he read the Bible a great deal, Nolde produced very expressive paintings of biblical scenes. He used the stylistic elements associated with German Expressionism: jarring color contrasts, abstraction of human forms, faces with masklike qualities (showing the influence of non-European cultures). So expressive are his paintings that they can be disturbing. In *Saint Mary of Egypt Among Sinners*, Nolde depicts Mary Magdalene entertaining a group of perverse-looking men. Before following Christ, Mary Magdalene supposedly had a bad reputation, and Nolde captured this. He painted ugliness in her face with bright red lips and a sinister grin as well as voluptuous curves on her topless body. Meanwhile, the men, with masklike faces and mouths agape, laugh and attempt to grope her. Nolde used shocking color juxtapositions and abstract forms to express his feelings about the story. So violent was he with his application of paint at times that German mothers threatened their naughty children by telling them that Nolde was going to take them and squeeze them onto his canvases.

The Die Brucke group of artists broke up shortly before the outbreak of World War I. Their agitated works and social critique portended the coming of the conflict that would devastate Europe and turn the art world on its head.

Der Blaue Reiter

Der Blaue Reiter was the name chosen by Vassily Kandinsky and Franz Marc for the group they formed in 1911. It reflected their interest in the color blue, which they both felt was spiritual. They also based the name on a statue of Saint George the Dragon Slayer in Moscow. Both artists sought to express inner truths about the world through color and abstraction. Kandinsky used color and line to create the first completely non-representational works of art. Marc chose to focus on animals, which he believed were pure creatures compared to humans.

Vassily Kandinsky

Kandinsky was an intellectual who was well read in various disciplines, including religion, philosophy, music theory, and science. He was one of the first artists to study Einstein's paper on thermodynamics and Bohr's writings on atomic structure. The writings of these scientists convinced Kandinsky that there was no solid, tangible reality. To express his belief, Kandinsky eliminated all recognizable objects from his pictures. Art historians cite Kandinsky's work as the first completely nonrepresentational European art.

In his book *Concerning Spirituality and Art* (1911), Kandinsky stated that color can convey emotion and spirituality irrespective of the content of the painting. He explained that color directly influences the soul. "Color is the keyboard, the eyes are the hammers, the soul is the piano with many strings. The artist is the hand that plays, touching one key or another purposively, to cause vibrations of the soul."

Kandinsky created improvisation paintings, which were the expressions of his own internal nature. He also produced what he called compositions, which were the result of a long process of formulating an inner feeling. *Improvisation No. 30* (also known as *Cannons*) does contain some recognizable forms. For example, the cannon in the right corner fires a blast. Buildings in the background represent churches in Moscow, where Kandinsky was born and attended university. But notice the blocks of color and the extent of abstraction. This painting may represent the Second Coming of Christ. Some Christians believed that Moscow would replace Rome as the spiritual center of the world.

Kandinsky's paintings thus express spirituality through the use of color. The abstract lines, shapes, and colors refer to his interest in atomic structure. The flowing lines and colors also reflect his interest in music, which he used as analogy to explain the interaction between a viewer and a painting.

Franz Marc

Franz Marc started from a profound understanding of the anatomy of animals and then went on to paint them in an unrealistic, abstract manner. Marc chose animals over people because he believed that they had a purer existence in harmony with nature. Like Kandinsky, Marc used color to express his feelings. His painting *Yellow Cow* contains chromatic symbolism. He explained that yellow is "the female principle, gentle, cheerful, and sensual." Blue is "the male principle . . . spiritual and intellectual." Red is "matter . . . heavy." In *Yellow Cow*, the cow, which seems to be floating in harmony within the colorful landscape, represents Marc's bride, Maria, while the blue mountains in the distance symbolize the artist.

In 1913, the threat of an impending war menaced society. Great Britain and Germany competed in an arms race. Inventors developed new and devastating weapons during this modern era. European countries were competing for colonies around the globe, each being spurred on by nationalism. The Futurists embraced the new technologies and the purifying function of war. Franz Marc's painting *Fate of the Animals* exhibited a different opinion regarding the threat of war.

How many animals can you find in the painting? The animals appear trapped in a forest. The entire scene is distorted with slashing red lines of force and fragmented shapes. A blue wolf appears to howl in the center. Green wolves appear to chase each other in the left. Brown animals gather in a pack to the right. The collection of abstract animals, fragmented forms, and slashing lines are disturbing compared with *Yellow Cow*. Marc discovered just how well his painting portended the future when he joined in the fighting on the Western front the following year. In hindsight, he considered *Fate of the Animals* as a premonition of the horrors of war. Marc did not survive the war, dying in 1916.

Postwar German Expressionism

World War I exerted a profound influence on all Europe. Germany experienced some of the most traumatic effects. As one of the main belligerents, it sent many men to the fronts to fight for the fatherland. By the end of the war, Germany was sending boys as young as 14 to fight. Meanwhile, the British navy maintained a blockade of Germany, which included keeping out supplies of food. The German government needed to continue producing weapons and began to use nitrates, usually used for fertilizing crops, for bomb making. Consequently, Germany experienced a famine. Workers and intellectuals revolted against the kaiser in Berlin, and sailors mutinied against the German admiralty. Germany was in chaos.

In November 1918, Germany signed an armistice (cease-fire) with the Allied Powers. As part of the Treaty of Versailles, signed in 1919, the Allies forced Germany to accept a war guilt clause (claiming total responsibility for starting the war) and to pay heavy reparations. The German people thus suffered even more after the war. Hyperinflation, economic depression, and temporary occupation by French troops along the border (a response to Germany's failure to make reparations) humiliated the Germans even more.

German artists found Expressionism to be a good vehicle to convey the mood of the country after the war. Max Beckmann is one of the most famous postwar German Expressionists. He served in the German army during World War I. The mass destruction of the war disillusioned Beckmann. He crowds his paintings with striking colors, exaggerated and distorted human figures, and symbols that reflect his pessimistic view of human nature. In *Night*, we see that three menacing intruders have entered a family's house. A partially nude woman hangs limply by her bound hands. The intruders torture a man, presumably her husband, by choking him and dislocating his arm. One of the intruders, seen on the right, is leaving with an innocent-looking, fair-haired boy under his arm.

Influenced by the effects of World War I and the rising threat of Nazism in 1930s Germany, Beckmann painted a triptych titled *Departure*. The colossal triptych, with its extensive Symbolism, demonstrates the influence of Hieronymous Bosch (see Chapter 19). Beckmann also visited Paris throughout the 1920s and became acquainted with Surrealist works, with their odd juxtapositions of recognizable objects (see Chapter 30).

Beckmann depicted scenes of physical and psychological torture in the left panel. The victims are bound and blindfolded, a man with his hands cut off and his legs spread-eagled and a woman prostrate in the foreground await the actions of a man with a striped shirt in the center. A woman in the right panel tries to find her way in the dark with the aid of a lamp. A dead figure tied to her body represents all the failures and bad memories of life, from which she will not be free during her lifetime. A man in the foreground bangs a drum, perhaps representing the drumbeat of life. The central panel contains brighter colors and images of a king and queen on a boat with their child and an oarsman with a medieval Saxon helmet. This represents the departure from the misery of life. Beckmann believed that even if viewers did not understand every symbol, *Departure* would convey the suffering of human existence.

Several other German Expressionists conveyed the misery and humiliation of World War I. The works of George Grosz, Otto Dix, and Kathe Kollwitz make up only a portion of the intense and poignant postwar Expressionist pieces. Although these and other German Expressionist works deserve closer recognition, the demands of the exam force us to be concise. If the AP Art History test includes a slide and you think it might be German Expressionist, look for scenes of war (German-style helmets, gas masks, explosions) and scenes of misery (a mother holding a dead child, common people being exploited by the warmongers of government).

The Third Reich and German Expressionism

Adolf Hitler became chancellor of Germany in 1933. Because he was an artist in his earlier years (he was rejected from the School of Fine Arts in Vienna twice), he believed himself capable of judging the quality of art. He labeled German avant-garde art as "degenerate" and organized an infamous exhibition called the Degenerate Art Exhibit. Approximately two thousand people visited the exhibit daily. They were encouraged to mock and defile the art.

This exhibition exacted a major toll on the German Expressionists. Ernst Ludwig Kirchner, one of the founders of Die Brucke, burned many of his woodcuts and prints. In 1938, he committed suicide. The day that the exhibit opened, Beckmann and his wife fled to the Netherlands, never returning to Germany. Emil Nolde, an acclaimed German artist nearing his seventies at the time, was the biggest target of all. Because he was a member of the Nazi Party, the Third Reich was hardest on him, confiscating approximately one thousand of his works from museums and displayed twenty-seven works at the Degenerate Art Exhibit.

Conclusion

The early twentieth century (1900–1910s) experienced several major artistic movements. The earliest and most influential were Fauvism and Cubism. Fauvism, epitomized by Matisse and Derain, is known for expanding the use of nonrepresentational colors and gained notoriety at the Salon d'Automne of 1905. Cubism expanded the use of line with the use of fragmented forms and multiple viewpoints. The cofounders of Cubism were Pablo Picasso and Georges Braque. In their Synthetic Cubist phase, they developed the medium of collage, a combination of various materials adhered to a flat surface. Cubist interest in mass and space also infiltrated sculpture in the work of Jacques Lipchitz, Julio Gonzalez, and Aleksandr Archipenko.

Fauvism and Cubism influenced the other major avant-garde movements. Futurism used jarring colors and multiple viewpoints to glorify technology and convey speed. (Futurism has been a very popular topic on past tests.) Russian Constructivism used modern materials and the Cubist and Futurist vocabulary to advance a new social order in the Soviet Union. German Expressionists, both the Die Brucke and Der Blaue Reiter groups, used color and line expressively to criticize modern society and advocate the quest for deeper spirituality. Kandinsky, a member of Der Blaue Reiter, created improvisations and compositions that were the first completely nonrepresentational works in art history. After World War I, from 1920 to the early 1930s, German artists continued to use Expressionism to decry the horrors of war and the rise of Nazism. Because of their influence on all these movement, Matisse and Picasso have been labeled the "Twin Titans of the Twentieth Century."

America received its first taste of the avant-garde at the Armory Show of 1913. Although it shocked the American public, the exhibit influenced American artists and foreshadowed the role of New York City in the future of the avant-garde.

Chapter 30

Twentieth-Century Art Between the World Wars

Due to copyright issues, use of 20th century art images is restricted on our accompanying Art CD. Below is the list of images referred to in this chapter. REA suggests that readers refer to their textbook or use trusted Internet sites to view the images presented in this section's narrative.

Hans (Jean) Arp, *Collage Arranged According to the Laws of Chance*, 1916–1917

Marcel Duchamp, *Fountain*, 1917

Marcel Duchamp, *The Bride Stripped Bare by Her Bachelors, Even* (or *The Large Glass*), 1915–1923

Hannah Hoch, *Cut with the Kitchen Knife Dada Through the Last Weimar Beer Belly Cultural Epoch of German*, 1919–1920

Giorgio de Chirico, *Melancholy and Mystery of a Street*, 1914

Giorgio de Chirico, *The Song of Love*, 1914

Max Ernst, *Two Children Are Threatened by a Nightingale*, 1924

Salvador Dali, *Persistence of Memory*, 1931

René Magritte, *The Treachery* (or *Perfidy*) *of Images*, 1928–1929

Joan Miró, *The Potato*, 1928

Marc Chagall, *I and the Village*, 1911

Meret Oppenheim, *Object* (or *Le Déjeuner en fourrure*), 1936

Frida Kahlo, *The Two Fridas*, 1939

Piet Mondrian, *Composition with Red, Blue, and Yellow*, 1930

Constantin Brancusi, *The Newborn*, 1915

Constantin Brancusi, *Bird in Space*, 1928

Barbara Hepworth, *Oval Sculpture* (*No. 2*), 1943

Henry Moore, *Recumbent Figure*, 1938

Alexander Calder, *Lobster Trap and Fish Tail*, 1939

Introduction and Exam Strategy Overview

What would you do if you were walking through a famous exhibit in a prestigious museum and viewed a urinal turned upside down on display? Most people would probably turn to their friends, laugh, and say, "That's not art." After reading this chapter, you would respond, "That's Duchamp's *Fountain*." If you are confused, this chapter will clarify this and many other key points on art between the two world wars.

Major developments were afoot in European art after World War I. The Great War caused the deaths of two great artists—Umberto Boccioni (a Futurist) and Franz Marc (a member of the Der Blaue Reiter group of German Expressionists)—and affected many others (such as Max Beckmann, a German Expressionist). Because World War I affected art history so dramatically (see also Chapter 29), AP Art History test writers give the period a great deal of attention.

This chapter discusses two major, interrelated artistic movements that developed during the period between the wars: Dadaism and Surrealism. It also explains the evolution of twentieth-century sculpture.

Effects of World War I

World War I had a devastating effect on European life. Europe lost a generation of men through the incredible destruction of new weapons and trench warfare. A current estimate is that nearly 10 million men from the Allies and Central Powers died in combat. Many men who returned experienced "shell shock" from all the bombings and violence, a condition psychologists today refer to as posttraumatic stress disorder. Historians label the generation that lived through the Great War the Lost Generation because of all the death and social trauma caused by the war. People became disillusioned with the concept of humanity because they realized just what "humanity" was capable of doing. Cynicism and nihilism began to replace the progressive spirit of the early 1900s.

What Is Dada?

Let us enter into the history of the Dada artists. Dada artists believed that the traditional supports of society—law, faith, culture, language, economy—failed to prevent the war and its unprecedented effects. Declaring war on tradition, Dadaists often lambasted formal institutions in their art and disdained conventional notions of art as well. Instead, they artistically expressed absurdity, spontaneity, and free will.

They chose the name for their movement, Dada, at random from a French dictionary. *Dada*, the French word for "rocking horse," satisfied the Dadaists' desire for something irrational and nonsensical. Dada artists often incorporated the word into their compositions, like a calling card or a modern-day advertising logo. In addition, many Dadaists incorporated the word into their signatures. For example, Max Ernst sometimes signed his name "Dadamax." *Dada* eventually became part of the world's vocabulary.

The values on which Dadaism was based were entirely unique. In addition to their novel objectives, Dada artists used innovative approaches to creating art, including the use of new materials, methods, and technologies. Dada artists expanded the use of **collage** (see Chapter 29), **photomontage** (cutting parts of pictures and pasting them into artistic compositions), and **assemblage** (similar to collage but using more three-dimensional objects). Dada artists also made sound recordings and short films. These new methods influenced artists throughout the twentieth century, from Romare Bearden (an African American artist famous for collages) to Robert Rauschenberg and Louise Nevelson, who were both famous for assemblages.

Let us meet some of the Dada artists.

Hans (Jean) Arp

Hans (also known as Jean) Arp worked with his wife, who was a textile maker, to create abstract geometric collages that resembled his wife's textiles. In addition, Arp believed in free drawing, in which the body would automatically create a picture. He tried not to control the drawing, because he wanted his creation to be the subject of subconscious forces. You will see how this concept of the subconscious is developed even further when we discuss Surrealism later in the chapter.

Arp relied on chance to create compositions like *Collage Arranged According to the Laws of Chance*. For this piece, Arp ripped paper into square shapes and dropped them onto a sheet of paper on the floor. Afterward he did rearrange them slightly, but nonetheless, his incorporation of chance in the creative process was avant-garde. Also, Arp's work shows the importance of using the subconscious in creating art, which reflected Freud's theories on the unconscious mind (see Chapter 29).

Marcel Duchamp

Marcel Duchamp is perhaps the most famous (some might say notorious) of the Dada artists. Early in his career, he experimented with Impressionism and Cubism. Recall how *Nude Descending a Staircase*, his controversial submission to the Armory Show of 1913, resembled Cubism and sequential motion photography (see Chapter 29). During World War I, Duchamp, most likely influenced by Synthetic Cubism, developed a form of art he called the **ready-made**. He arranged already manufactured parts into innovative compositions that changed their ordinary meanings. For example, he took a bicycle wheel, inverted it, and bolted its shaft into the seat of a wooden stool. He said that he kept this ready-made in his studio and enjoyed looking at it.

His most notorious ready-made was *Fountain* (**Fig. 30-1**). Duchamp inverted a urinal, painted the signature "R. Mutt" on it, and dated it 1917. The signature was a play on the R. Mott plumbing company that manufactured Paris's sewer pipes. It also was a comment on social class: *R* is the initial for "Richard," which is French slang for "moneybags," and the German word *armut* refers to poverty.

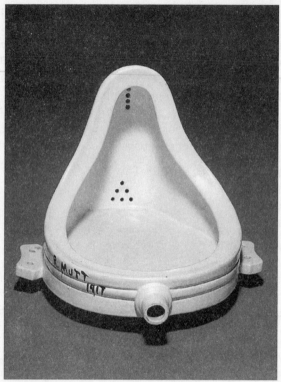

Figure 30-1. Marcel Duchamp, *Fountain*, 1917

How do you think people reacted to *Fountain*? The supposedly avant-garde Society of Independent Artists rejected *Fountain* from a planned exhibit. The group's official response was that the work may be a very useful object in its place, but its place is not in an art exhibition, and it is, by no definition, a work of art. Duchamp, a member of the group, subsequently resigned from its board of directors.

Another famous work by Duchamp is *The Bride Stripped Bare by Her Bachelors, Even* (also known as *The Large Glass*). It is a combination of oil, lead, wire, foil, dust, and varnish inside large panes of glass. Duchamp worked on this piece from 1915 to 1923, when he gave up on finishing the work. Did you notice the cracks in the glass? In 1927, while workers transported it from an exhibit in Brooklyn to Philadelphia, they dropped it. Duchamp did not respond negatively, nor did he replace the glass panes. Instead, he glued the broken pieces of glass back together and said that *The Large Glass* was finished by chance.

Dada Photomontage

Hannah Hoch's *Cut with the Kitchen Knife Dada Through the Last Weimar Beer Belly Cultural Epoch of Germany* exhibits several characteristics of the Dada movement. To an untrained person, it seems **absurd** to refer to this as a work of art, but accentuating the absurd was a Dadaist goal. Typical of the avant-garde, only fellow avant-garde artists appreciated Hoch's work. *Cut with a Kitchen Knife* is a photomontage—a collection of photographs and images cut from newspapers and periodicals, arranged based on the vision of the artist. Prussian war photographers preceded Dadaists in using this technique (they would take pictures of Prussian soldiers, cut the heads from the photos, and replace them with heads of their customers), but Hannah Hoch used it to convey Dada objectives—namely, to tear down the old order and represent the new.

Hoch also integrated images from the world of machines and industry into *Cut with a Kitchen Knife*. This was an innovative method of artistic creation. She used pictures of revolutionary intellectuals such as Karl Marx and Vladimir Lenin. She placed photos of members of the German regime during World War I next to pictures of exotic dancers as a humorous critique. She pasted the word *dada* several times in the piece, propagating the movement. She also included her photo in the lower-right corner and photos of other women to elevate the status of women in this new Dada world.

Dada had a brief but emphatic impact on the history of art. Several Dadaists, influenced by the work of an Italian artist named Giorgio de Chirico, gravitated toward a deeper investigation of the subconscious, which would become known as Surrealism.

Precursor to Surrealism: Giorgio de Chirico

Although Futurism was popular in Italy (see Chapter 29), Giorgio de Chirico developed a style of painting he called the metaphysical style. *Metaphysical* refers to an alternate reality that lies below what we can perceive. He was influenced by the classical architecture and symbols of Italy as well as the writings of Friedrich Nietzsche and the romantic philosophy he became familiar with while visiting Germany. De Chirico synthesizes these eclectic influences into his metaphysical paintings. Let us examine *Melancholy and Mystery of a Street*.

De Chirico used steep diagonals to create the feeling of an alternate dimension. His firmly outlined and solid forms recede toward multiple vanishing points, conveying the feeling of a skewed reality. As he did in many of his metaphysical paintings, De Chirico set figures and objects in an Italian piazza (town square) surrounded by arcaded Italian architecture. *Mystery and Melancholy of a Street* contains a girl playing with a hoop and moving toward an opened van. She appears alone, but is she really? We see a long shadow looming in the distance. Is it a man approaching or a statue in the piazza? Is the girl in danger? Will she get locked in the van? These characteristics as well as the darkened arcades and windows make us feel uneasy. De Chirico gave no explanation of these incongruous elements.

De Chirico's *The Song of Love* (**Fig. 30-2**) may not leave us with the same feeling of foreboding as *Mystery and Melancholy of a Street*, but it does contain elements of the metaphysical. He painted the head of a Classical Greek statue prominently in the center of the piazza (De Chirico was born in Greece and studied in Athens). A large rubber glove is nailed to a wall near the classical statue. De Chirico painted a green ball in the foreground and a steam locomotive in the background. As in *Mystery and Melancholy of a Street*, he included similar vacuous (empty) architecture. Although the items seem incongruous and unrelated, De Chirico used them to suggest the human presence in his metaphysical world. The glove has the shape of a hand, yet it is not; it is a limp piece of rubber. The ball and train suggest a human presence, yet we see no one in the piazza.

Figure 30-2. Giorgio de Chirico, *The Song of Love*, 1914

Here are a few useful phrases to recall the work of Giorgio de Chirico: vacuous (empty) Italian architecture, fragments of classical statuary, multiple vanishing points to create an unusual perspective, steep diagonal compositions, unusual juxtapositions of recognizable objects, and a metaphysical world. These elements of De Chirico's work inspired the Surrealists during the 1920s.

What Is Surrealism?

So far, we have examined four worlds in the history of art. The world of **reality** focused on painting nature and creating the illusion of the real world. This was the world of artists from the Renaissance through Impressionism. The world of **feelings** included artists who painted to express their emotions in art, such as the Romantics, Van Gogh and Gauguin, Fauvists, and Expressionists. The world of **form** captured the underlying geometry and structure of the world, as evident in the work of Cezanne, the Cubists, and the Futurists. Finally, there is the world of the **subconscious mind**, art that captured inner visions, fantasies, dreams, and nightmares. The Romantics, Symbolists, and to some extent the Dadaists did this. The group that focused solely on this fourth world was the Surrealists.

Surrealism drew inspiration from various sources. The enigmatic symbols and fantasy of the sixteenth-century painter Hieronymous Bosch (see Chapter 19) influenced the pictorial language of the Surrealists. They also drew from Symbolists' emphasis on the inner world of fantasy. The Dadaists' sense of the absurd opened the unconscious mind as a relevant subject area. Freud's *Interpretation of Dreams* and exploration of the unconscious mind provided another influence. The last and greatest artistic influence was the metaphysical painting of De Chirico. One Surrealist, Yves Tanguy, said that on seeing the work of De Chirico, he was determined to become a painter, even though he had never picked up a paintbrush.

In his *Manifesto of Surrealism*, André Breton discussed the need for new techniques of pictorial construction because Surrealism transcended the real world. Some key characteristics of the Surrealist style include giving the unconscious visual form, juxtaposing familiar objects and unfamiliar contexts, and depicting irrational and bizarre scenes that defy common sense. This style of art was popular from the 1920s through the 1930s.

Max Ernst

Originally a Dadaist, Max Ernst moved toward Surrealism as the Dada movement waned. In *Two Children Are Threatened by a Nightingale*, Ernst demonstrated the pictorial construction for which Surrealism would become famous. Ernst included a representational landscape with a wall in the distant background, a tiny flying bird, two girls, and a house. Yet the picture resembles a dream world. A girl brandishes a knife while the second girl faints. A man carrying a baby balances on the roof of a hut. Ernst constructed a small wooden gate, little wooden hut, and a small doorknob to the painting and frame, thereby accentuating the illusion of depth. The man on the roof of the hut is trying to press the doorknob, which resembles a doorbell. Along the wooden frame, Ernst wrote the title of the piece in French. The hut and the wooden gate are a reddish-orange, while the sky and the grass vary from aquamarine and yellow to green.

Ernst used odd juxtapositions of familiar objects, colors, and words in *Two Children Are Threatened by a Nightingale*. This piece can have many meanings or none at all. It is the odd juxtapositions and eerie world Ernst creates that makes this piece Surrealist.

Salvador Dali

When you think of Surrealism, whose name comes to mind first? Most people immediately think of Salvador Dali, partly because he was such an innovative artist and partly because he had such a flamboyant and attention-grabbing personality. Dali was terrified of insects, crossing streets, and traveling by train, boat, and airplane. He carried a piece of driftwood with him at all times to ward off evil spirits. One of his most famous attributes was his long, handlebar mustache, through which, he claimed, aliens would communicate with him. He once said, "My mental windows have been opened really wide." Dali represented his hallucinogenic visions with meticulous realism.

Dali's *Persistence of Memory* is a stark and oddly illuminated landscape. We see a strange, melted figure on the ground, apparently either sleeping or dead. Surrounding the figure are three melting clocks and one solid timepiece. Dali placed one melting clock on the figure, another, which has a fly on it, on a boxlike platform to the left, and the third on a dead tree planted in the platform. Ants crawl on the fourth timepiece, which is closed. The land is barren and vacuous (reminiscent of De Chirico's settings). Dali painted steep, craggy cliffs, a rectangular metallic plate lying flat in the far left, and smooth blue water in the distance.

What do all these symbols mean? The cliffs may reflect the Mediterranean coast of Spain, Dali's homeland. The figure's physical attributes resemble a profile of Dali. Given Dali's fear of insects, the ants and the fly may represent his own apprehension, or they might symbolize decay, because both the fly and the ant are associated with decomposition. We cannot fully understand the connection between all the symbols in Dali's *Persistence of Memory*. He altered familiar objects and arranged them in a strange context. But he painted the objects so realistically that his surreal world looks real.

René Magritte

René Magritte was a Belgian painter who became acquainted with the Surrealists in France. Magritte developed his own style of combining realistically painted images in unfamiliar contexts. Like Dali, he used the trompe l'oeil painting technique, as we can see in *The Treachery of Images*. The combination of the picture and words confounds people who lack a background in the fundamental concepts of Surrealism. We see a very realistically painted smoking pipe. It is so realistic that it is almost photographic. Below the pipe, Magritte wrote "This is not a pipe" in French. Why did Magritte write that, when the picture clearly is a pipe? The answer becomes obvious when we realize that he created the image of a pipe, not an actual pipe. We have to look twice at *The Treachery of Images*, because the statement appears incongruous, yet it expresses a truth.

On a past AP Art History exam, a long-essay question asked students to give examples of artwork that incorporated the use of words and to discuss how the words reflect the goals of the artistic style. Magritte's *The Treachery of Images* would work well for that type of question.

Joan Miró

Unlike the works of Dali and Magritte, Joan Miró's art is almost completely nonrepresentational. Yet most of his pieces include forms that are somewhat identifiable, like naturalistic curves and objects that represent abstract creatures. Art historians refer to these naturalistic figures as **biomorphic shapes**. Because Miró's paintings lack definitive shape, they represent his own unconscious world. He said his source for these paintings was hallucinations caused by starvation and staring at cracks in his ceiling. Although

Miró eschewed inclusion with the Surrealists, the writer André Breton described Miró as "the most Surrealist of us all."

Marc Chagall

Another artist who created works with elements of Surrealism but was not affiliated with the group was Marc Chagall. He actually preceded the Surrealists with *I and the Village*, painted in 1911. Notice in the painting the fragmented forms of Cubism and the incorporation of nonrepresentational color similar to Fauvism. Yet his placement of figures and the creation of his own inner fantasy share an affinity with later Surrealist paintings.

Chagall grew up in a Jewish community in Vitebsk, Russia. Although he left his homeland for the cosmopolitan Paris, Chagall drew on childhood experiences for creative inspiration. In *I and the Village*, for instance, a green-faced peasant is locked in a staring contest with a cow. The peasant wears a cross and carries a strange flowering plant. We can see inside the cow's head a vision of the cow being milked. In the distance, a male peasant and female peasant walk through a town with a Russian Orthodox cathedral. The only catch is that Chagall paints the peasant woman upside down. This is not a real scene but the work of Chagall's memory. Despite living in the hub of the avant-garde art scene, Chagall used the familiar imagery of his village in Russia.

Meret Oppenheim

Meret Oppenheim was one of the few women officially associated with the Surrealists. On one occasion, Picasso, admiring Oppenheim's fur-covered bracelet, commented that it would be interesting if everything were covered in fur. Inspired by his remarks, Oppenheim covered a teacup, saucer, and spoon and entitled her creation *Object* (also known as *Le Déjeuner en fourrure*, which is a witty reference to Manet's *Le Déjeuner sur l'Herbe*). Why is this a Surrealist piece? It looks nothing like the work of Dali, Magritte, or Miró, or does it? Consider one of the hallmark characteristics of Surrealism: odd juxtapositions of familiar items. Oppenheim combined recognizable animal fur (from an unusual animal, a Chinese gazelle) with commonplace items you might have in your home or see in any eating establishment. The unexpected combination of everyday objects creates an unfamiliar context. The thought of drinking from such a teacup repulses many viewers. Others look on the work with great curiosity. Either way, in a poll of visitors to the Museum of Modern Art in New York, *Object* was considered one of the most revolutionary works of the twentieth century.

Frida Kahlo

Frida Kahlo was not a member of the Surrealists. In fact, she disavowed them. Yet Kahlo's paintings contain similarities with the work of the Surrealists. Let us examine *The Two Fridas*.

In this painting, we see some very unusual juxtapositions that create a Surreal realm. Kahlo painted two self-portraits. The one on the left represents the Frida influenced by European culture. She wears a lacy white dress that suggests European aristocracy. The Frida on the right is wearing a traditional dress from her native region of Zapotec, Mexico. The exposed hearts of the two Fridas, which she renders somewhat realistically, are connected by a long artery. The artery originates at a miniscule baby picture of her husband, Diego Rivera, the famous Mexican muralist. It terminates at the surgical forceps in the hand of the European Frida. Behind the Fridas, the deep blue sky with its stormy white clouds gives the painting an otherworldly feel.

If Kahlo denied being a Surrealist, what can this painting mean? Does it mean anything? Let us examine her influences. The daughter of a German Jewish father and Mexican mother, Kahlo worshipped her father but was extremely proud of her Mexican heritage. Despite her middle-class upbringing, she identified with the struggles of the *mestizos* (Mexicans of mixed Spanish and Native American ancestry), who worked hard at farming and were exploited by Mexico's landed elite. Kahlo fell in love with Diego Rivera, who shared these interests. Both of them joined the Communist Party and even entertained Leon Trotsky when he visited Mexico while in exile from the Soviet Union.

Kahlo's life was dramatically affected by what she described as the two accidents: her meeting Diego Rivera while she was a student at a preparatory school and a bus accident in which she sustained serious injuries. Diego Rivera was unfaithful through-out their marriage, leading to a divorce, eventual remarriage, and a second separation. Their relationship was the cause of much emotional duress (and artistic inspiration) to Kahlo. At the age of 18, not long after her first meeting the much-older Rivera, Kahlo experienced a traumatic accident in which a tram crashed into the bus she was riding. Seriously injured by the incident, Kahlo was left unable to bear children and in lifelong physical pain. Another significant influence on Frida was a European tour she took at the pinnacle of her career and during which she met many avant-garde celebrities.

The Two Fridas reveals these various influences. Despite its odd juxtapositions, which are normally associated with Surrealism, Frida Kahlo's style is distinctly her own, reflecting her life experiences and innovative pictorial imagination.

Neoplasticism and Mondrian

Not all avant-garde artists responded to the effects of World War I by joining the Dadaist or Surrealist movements. In Germany, Expressionism was still popular, exemplified by artists like Max Beckmann, Otto Dix, and Kathe Kollwitz. Picasso con-tinued to revise his style, transcending dogmatic Cubism to express his views of life, and Matisse continued to create happy art with free use of color and simplified forms (see Chapter 29).

Piet Mondrian was a Dutch artist who believed that art should express the universal reality that lay beneath everything in the world. In his opinion, for example, all objects in the universe could be reduced to basic geometric shapes and colors. This may sound similar to Cubism, but it is quite different. Mondrian believed that Cubism was on the right path but did not reach the evolution of Neoplasticism, an artistic concept that would reveal universal themes that existed below conscious reality.

Mondrian worked with other Dutch writers, artists, and architects to further develop Neoplasticism. They believed that their art style would become the only art style, and that all art would eventually arrive at their conclusion. Therefore, Mondrian and his compatriots called their movement **De Stijl**, or "The Style."

Mondrian reduced his compositions to the primary colors (red, blue, and yellow) and primary values (white, black, and gray) and used only vertical and horizontal lines to convey the basic visual elements of the universe. Although all his paintings share these features, no two are identical. Mondrian sought to express the individuality of each composition, even the individuality of each line and panel of pure color. For example, the lines often vary in thickness.

Mondrian's approach to art influenced the architecture of Gerrit Rietveld (see Chapter 32), also affiliated with De Stijl, and the mobiles of the Modernist sculptor Alexander Calder (discussed in the next section).

Modernist Sculpture

Between the wars, sculptors began to move increasingly toward abstraction of form. The work of Rodin influenced these sculptors (see Chapter 27). In their sculptures, the Modernists tried to capture the inner essence of the subject material. Like other Modernists, the sculptors also prized the values of "primitive" sculpture from non-European cultures. Therefore, these sculptors simplified figural and natural forms to capture the monumentality of certain concepts, such as nature or femininity.

Like the Cubist sculptors Aleksandr Archipenko and Julio Gonzalez, for example, Modernist sculptors explored the use of holes to create negative space in their creations. Modernist sculptors established that the voids of their creations were just as important as the masses, a revolutionary concept that proved to be their legacy. The Modernists for the most part eschewed the geometric configurations of the Cubist sculptors. Because Modernist sculptors often looked to landscape and nature as inspirations, their works often contain **organic** or natural contours.

Constantin Brancusi

The last time we discussed Brancusi, it was when his *Mademoiselle Pogany* appeared in the controversial Armory Show of 1913 (see Chapter 29). Brancusi became one of the most influential Modernist sculptors because he served as the bridge between Rodin and the twentieth century. Born in Romania and educated in Bucharest, Brancusi traveled to Munich and eventually to Paris, where he studied at the École des Beaux Arts. Brancusi served as an assistant to Rodin for two months before moving on to develop his own style.

Brancusi's *The Newborn* is an abstract sculpture that typifies his Modernist style. He shaped the creation like an egg, which is symbolic of life. The egg shape also resembles a head. Brancusi carved a portion of it to suggest the mouth of a crying baby. Abstract slits resemble a baby's eyes, and the area at which the slits meet the mouth resembles the nose. Brancusi stripped away external details to reach an internal truth. To heighten the effect of a newborn, Brancusi told the curators to place the piece on a lower platform so that viewers would have to lean over it, just as adults lean over a baby's crib.

Brancusi developed a series based on the bird and the concept of flight. Influenced partly by a mythical bird from Romanian folklore and partly by nature, Brancusi created a highly abstract design called *Bird in Space*. He created several versions of this piece. It was the subject of significant controversy when a U.S. customs official, inspecting a version of the work being imported by an American patron, refused to recognize it as a work of art. As a result, the patron had to pay an import duty on the piece.

A highly publicized trial ensued, delving into the meaning of art. Each side relied on testimony from art historians: the patron (who was the plaintiff) used art historians with avant-garde sympathies, while the defendant (the U.S. government) relied on academic art historians. The conservative art historians said that *Bird in Space* had none of the main features associated with birds—no visible wings, feathers, or a beak. With its tapered design and smooth finish, the piece almost resembles an enormous paperweight or fountain pen. But let us analyze this piece for "birdiness."

Bird in Space possesses a vertical orientation. In addition, Brancusi usually advised placing his works in positions that would accentuate their meaning. Thus, *Bird in Space* is usually placed on an elevated platform. The vertical orientation and placement remind the viewer of where birds spend their time—in the sky. Notice that *Bird in Space* is streamlined and aerodynamic. It reminds the viewer of a bird that has just flapped its wings and now has its wings flush with its sides. The point on the top of the piece resembles a beak. Although highly abstract, *Bird in Space* has an organic quality. Can you observe these features?

The Modernist art historians must have presented a persuasive analysis of the work because the plaintiff eventually won the case and received his money back from the government.

Barbara Hepworth

Barbara Hepworth was a Modernist English artist who revolutionized sculpture by including significant open spaces in her creations. Although this had been done before (recall Archipenko's *Woman Combing Her Hair*, shown in Chapter 29), Hepworth included more space so that its value became the same as the sculpture's mass. Art historians credit her as being the first artist to introduce the concept of *negative space*—a space inside a creation that has no significant meaning other than as an aesthetic device. From this point on, spaces and voids became important components of Modernist sculpture.

Hepworth's work also contains organic qualities. She often used the oval as a component in her designs. The natural landscape of England was one of her influences. At the outbreak of World War II, Hepworth moved to the southwestern coast of England to distance herself from the conflict. The rounded curves and holes in her designs resemble the curving hills of the English landscape and the rock formations of the English coast.

Henry Moore

Sir Henry Moore is one of the most important Modernist sculptors of the twentieth century. He often carved abstract reclining figures based on pre-Columbian figures (Native American art before the arrival of Christopher Columbus). Although his pieces seem highly abstract, closer inspection reveals body parts such as heads, shoulders, hips, and legs. Moore is famous for his series of reclining female figures. Carved out of stone or wood, the figures and the material blend together. Often the natural cracks in the stone or the wood grain move harmoniously with the contours of the figure.

Moore's *Recumbent Figure* has this quality. The female form blends with the stone medium and resembles the curves found in landscapes and rock formations by the sea. An important element of *Recumbent Figure* is the use of voids. The spaces reflect the caves and crevices found in nature. Moore was a friend of Barbara Hepworth, and his inclusion of space reflects, to some degree, her influence. The spaces, the curvilinear shapes, and the use of natural materials give Henry Moore's creations an organic quality.

Alexander Calder

Alexander Calder was a third-generation sculptor born in Philadelphia. When he went to Paris to study in 1926, avant-garde artists such as Duchamp and Miró influenced him. Calder was interested in incorporating mechanics and movement into his sculptures. His first mechanical assemblage included miniature metallic circus performers that moved when he cranked gears. Duchamp labeled Calder's sculptures **mobiles** because of their movement. Calder continued to revise his ideas for mobiles, using simpler organic forms, space, and basic colors. He designed them so, when suspended from a ceiling, the pieces would catch small air currents and perpetually move.

Calder's mobile titled *Lobster Trap and Fish Tail* appeared on the 2006 AP Art History test as a slide with accompanying multiple-choice questions. Perhaps, despite the abstract nature of the metal plates, you can observe qualities that befit the title. For example, the black metal plates resemble fish tails and as a group are similar to a school of fish. The red-striped metal plate at the top resembles a lobster tail, and the wire contraption below resembles a trap. So simplified are the shapes of the mobile that you can compare them to the Neoplastic paintings of Mondrian and the biomorphic shapes of Miró, who became one of Calder's friends.

Conclusion

World War I affected artists differently. Dada artists expressed the absurdity of life in their works. To accomplish this goal, the Dadaists used media ranging from collage to photomontage to Duchamp's ready-mades. Several Dada artists evolved into Surrealists, who sought to convey the unconscious that existed below reality. They developed their own pictorial language that included the placement of familiar objects in odd contexts. Dali and Magritte tended to use the tromp l'oeil painting technique to convey the unconscious, while Miró used biomorphic shapes.

Mondrian and other Dutch artists responded to the effects of World War I by developing De Stijl. Following the twentieth-century trend toward abstraction, Modernist sculptors such as Brancusi, Hepworth, Moore, and Calder stripped away unessential superficial details to capture the essence of life.

Chapter 31

Twentieth-Century Art After World War II

Due to copyright issues, use of 20th-century art images is restricted on our accompanying Art CD. Below is the list of images referred to in this chapter. REA suggests that readers refer to their textbook or use trusted Internet sites to view the images presented in this section's narrative.

Jackson Pollock, *Autumn Rhythm (Number 30)*, 1950

Willem de Kooning, *Woman I*, 1950–1952

Mark Rothko, *No. 61 (Rust and Blue)*, 1953

Barnett Newman, *Vir Heroicus Sublimus*, 1950–1951

Helen Frankenthaler, *Mountains and Sea*, 1952

David Smith, *Cubi XIX*, 1964

Louise Nevelson, *Sky Cathedral*, 1958

Frank Stella, *Mas o Menos*, 1964

Donald Judd, *Untitled*, 1969

Maya Ying Lin, Vietnam Veterans Memorial, 1981–1983

Richard Hamilton, *Just What Is It That Makes Today's Homes So Different, So Appealing?* 1956

Jasper Johns, *Flag*, 1954–1955

Robert Rauschenberg, *Canyon*, 1959

Roy Lichtenstein, *Drowning Girl*, 1963

Andy Warhol, *Marilyn Diptych*, 1962

Claes Oldenberg, *Lipstick (Ascending) on Caterpillar Tracks*, 1969

Audrey Flack, *Marilyn*, 1977

Chuck Close, *Big Self-Portrait*, 1967–1968

Duane Hanson, *Tourists*

Judy Chicago, *The Dinner Party*, 1974–1979

Robert Smithson, *Spiral Jetty*, 1970

Nancy Holt, *Sun Tunnels*, 1976

Introduction and Exam Strategy Overview

The devastation and annihilation of World War II and the Holocaust had a significant impact on the art world. The center of the art world shifted from Paris to New York City. This was a major change, considering that Paris had been the focal point of art since the eighteenth century and the reign of Louis XIV. Avant-garde European artists immigrated to New York City, and American artists developed their own avant-garde spirit. The concentration of artists in New York City became known as the New York School.

New York School artists created works that questioned the human existence and the presence of a divine, omnipotent power. Building on trends established by earlier avant-garde movements, painters expressed their unconscious mind and universal themes of life in a style known as Abstract Expressionism. Sculptors of the New York School used metal and wood to create Abstract Expressionist pieces in basic geometric shapes. In some cases, sculptors even stopped sculpting their own works, opting instead to send measurements out to metal workers who would create the pieces.

Other artists reacted against Abstract Expressionism, focusing instead on the basic elements of color and line, creating a painting style named Hard Edge. Still other artists explored twentieth-century consumerism, concentrated on everyday imagery, and used art to make political statements.

After World War II, many artistic movements emerged. AP Art History tests usually contain four or five multiple-choice questions related to the artistic movements of this period of the twentieth century. This chapter explains the diverse appearances of and meanings behind the postwar movements.

Abstract Expressionism

Abstract Expressionism is an artistic movement of the late 1940s and early 1950s in which artists expressed their inner feelings through abstract paintings with few identifiable objects. The center of the movement was New York City.

Art historians divide Abstract Expressionism into two varieties: gestural abstraction and chromatic abstraction. **Gestural abstraction** refers to the expressive application of paint leaving visible and often chaotic brushstrokes. It is also called **action painting**. Jackson Pollock and Willem de Kooning are the most famous action painters. **Chromatic abstraction** lacks the energetic application of painting but uses blocks and lines of color to express complex feelings about the universe. Mark Rothko and Barnett Newman are famous chromatic Abstract Expressionists. Art historians sometimes refer to their canvases as **color field paintings**. Despite their idiosyncrasies, all these artists were part of the Abstract Expressionist movement in New York City. As a result, art historians also refer to the movement as the **New York School**.

Jackson Pollock

With a raw, unprimed canvas spread out on the floor, Jackson Pollock created his art by dripping, flinging, splashing, and pouring paint (**Fig. 31-1**). Pollock also used sticks, dried paintbrushes, industrial cans of paint (rather than paint tubes), sand, and glass to create his expressive paintings. He walked around the canvas and even stepped on the paintings. He liked to work this way because it gave him the feeling of actually being in the painting. In 1951, *Time* referred to Jackson Pollock as "Jack the Dripper," a witticism that compared his radical effect on the art world to the infamous Jack the Ripper, the serial killer who terrorized nineteenth-century London.

Figure 31-1. Jackson Pollock, *Autumn Rhythm* (*Number 30*), 1950

Pollock's action paintings contain no hidden meanings or symbols. They are records of his body movements and gestures at specific points in time. When you look at a Pollock painting, you should try to follow the swirls of line and consider his movements. What was he using to create those lines? How did he make those drips of paint? Did he flick paint from the brush or hold the brush and allow the paint to drip? Did he use both techniques? An action painting by Pollock is the physical manifestation of feelings deep in his subconscious, a concept he became familiar with through the writings of the twentieth-century psychologist Carl Jung. Pollock referred to his technique as psychic automatism.

Because Pollock's action paintings are **nonrepresentational**, they resemble the works of the German Expressionist Vassily Kandinsky (see Chapter 29). Both artists **did not include spatial recession** (depth), naturalism, or realism in their works. Instead, Kandinsky expressed spirituality, and Pollock expressed his subconscious.

Willem de Kooning

A Dutch painter who immigrated to the United States early in the twentieth century, Willem de Kooning was also a member of the New York School. Like Pollock, De Kooning created action paintings. He expressed his inner thoughts and emotions through highly visible brush and knife strokes (he used a painter's knife). De Kooning often reworked his canvases, wiping off previous layers of paint and replacing them.

Other times, he just painted over previous layers. Although this technique was part of his attempt to express his personal vision, he sometimes overworked the canvas. One of his art dealers complained that some of his canvases were worked clean through, leaving little holes.

Woman I is one of De Kooning's most famous paintings and is part of a series of colossal female images he created. Although the figure's feminine features are recognizable as is her toothy grin (he based her smile on toothpaste and cigarette advertisements), De Kooning's abstraction of her form and energetic application of paint epitomize action painting.

Mark Rothko

Art students find Rothko's paintings highly recognizable because of their huge blocks of color placed on large canvases. Typically, Rothko created two or three large, rectangular fields of color against a single background color. Some of the paintings incorporate light hues while others contain muted or dark shades.

The seemingly simplistic color fields belie a much deeper expression of feeling. Rothko once said that if you only observed the colors of his paintings, you were missing the deep "religious" experience he had while creating them. Art historians refer to Rothko as a chromatic Abstract Expressionist because his paintings lack any identifiable imagery and he uses color to express his vision.

Rothko saw life as a cycle of tragic times and happy times. His fields of color express this cycle. Ultimately, Rothko observed that all life was doomed by mortality. Afflicted by a terminal heart condition, Rothko used his abstract blocks of colors to express deep feelings about life.

Barnett Newman

Barnett Newman used color to express his complex feelings about humanity and its relationship to the universe. Newman usually painted a large canvas one color and included a few stripes of paint running vertically through the canvas's height. Newman referred to the stripes as **zips**. He likened the large monochromatic canvas to the infinite universe and the zips to the finite. One interpretation of his paintings is that they express the finite existence of human beings in an infinite universe. Because Newman used color to express concepts in a nonrepresentational way, he is considered a chromatic Abstract Expressionist.

Helen Frankenthaler's Color Stains

The paintings of Helen Frankenthaler combine Abstract Expressionism and a style referred to as **Post-Painterly Abstraction**. Although her work lacks the intentional subconscious expressiveness of action painting, Frankenthaler used Pollock's method of laying canvas on the ground to do her work. She diluted her oil paints with turpentine and her watercolors with water until the paint was very thin. Then she poured the paint onto raw, unprimed canvas, letting the colors soak into the material, much as spilled juice is soaked up by a paper towel. Art historians refer to this technique as **color stains**.

New York School Sculpture

The New York School artists also produced sculptures. These sculptures resemble Abstract Expressionist paintings because they are primarily nonrepresentational and express the subjectivity of the artists that created them. New York School sculptors were drawn to working with industrial materials such as metal and wood. Despite being linked by time (1950s) and location, the New York School artists and sculptors displayed different objectives in their creations.

David Smith's *Cubi* Series

David Smith welded pieces of metal together in abstract compositions. In his early work, he used thin pieces of steel welded together with large open spaces. The spaces between the lines of welded metal bear an interesting resemblance to the action paintings of Pollock. But David Smith's influences included other artists as well, especially the cubist sculptures of Picasso and Julio Gonzalez (*The Guitar and Woman Combing Her Hair*, respectively; see Chapter 29).

As Smith's career progressed, his style evolved. Perhaps his most famous work, the *Cubi* series, came out in the early 1960s. The *Cubi* sculptures consist of basic geometric shapes such as squares, rectangles, and circles. Smith welded them together in such a way that some of the shapes appear to be in a precarious balance, as if they will fall from the sculpture. They are cantilevered in space, a technique that Frank Lloyd Wright implemented in his architectural designs (see Chapter 32). Almost all the sculptures are made from stainless steel. Smith also used machines with wire brushes to burnish (make markings) the sides of the pieces of metal to give them various textures. Some appear rough while others are smooth.

Art historians view David Smith's *Cubi* sculptures as having some **human characteristics**. For example, the precarious balance in which he places them can represent the precariousness of human life. Just the cubes appear as if on the brink of tumbling down at any moment, life has its own impermanent qualities. Some critics also note *Cubi*'s resemblance to Native American totem poles in their size and the way they are stacked. This is plausible given Smith's interests in **spirituality** and Existential philosophy.

It is best to observe the *Cubi* sculptures outdoors. The geometric metal shapes and the organic environment provide an interesting contrast. In addition, the textured surfaces of the *Cubi* often catch rays of the sun that enhance their formal elements.

Louise Nevelson's Assemblages

Louise Nevelson created assemblage sculpture out of wood and welded metal. Russian born and raised in Maine, she became acquainted with wood at the lumberyard her father owned. She eventually became a part of the New York School. Although

Nevelson shaped the wood or metal in various ways, she unified her compositions through repeating shapes and color. Nevelson's sculptures often consist of stacked, boxlike compartments with various shapes inside them. She repeated some shapes but did so according to her own unique vision. Nevelson's preoccupation appears to be with shape and line, so she often painted her sculpture one color so as not to distract the viewer.

Hard Edge: A Departure from Abstract Expressionism

It would seem as though the Abstract Expressionists dominated the 1950s, and to some extent they did. Yet just as Abstract Expressionism was beginning to be accepted by the mainstream, it declined as the main avant-garde movement. A new movement that evolved during the late 1950s and 1960s focused purely on the expression of color and line. The critique of Abstract Expressionism was that in attempting to express personal feelings about the world, the artist deemphasized (probably inadvertently) the basic components of art. The new movement, which art historians refer to as Hard Edge (or Post-Painterly Abstraction), sought to extract all the Expressionistic qualities of the action painting while creating abstract canvases of crisp lines and solid colors.

Frank Stella's Pinstripe Paintings

Frank Stella is the one of the most famous Hard Edge artists. Past AP Art History tests have included an internal multiple-choice question about one of his "pinstripe paintings." Stella developed canvases of solid color separated by areas of bare canvas. The canvases emphasize flatness with no sense of recessional space whatsoever. From a distance it appears that his canvases actually have pinstripes, like the uniforms of the New York Yankees (although the stripes are usually light against a dark background). When asked about the meaning of his style, Stella responded, "What you see is what you see." Stella used canvases of different sizes and shapes for variation. Some of the canvases are shaped like the protractors you used in elementary math to measure angles. Nonetheless, he maintained his pinstripe motif.

Why do art historians consider Stella's work part of the Hard Edge movement? Unlike the action paintings of Pollock and De Kooning, Stella's work emphasizes straight lines and monochromatic schemes. Unlike the chromatic Abstract Expressionism of Rothko and Newman, whose canvases also include a few basic colors and zips, Stella's work is not steeped in expressing existential concepts about the universe.

Minimalism: Hard Edge's Sculptural Equivalent

Minimalism was an American art movement of the 1960s and 1970s. Like the Hard Edge painters, Minimalists sought to emphasize the shapes and straight edges of their creations. In doing so, Minimalist sculptors included no surface decoration, narrative elements, figures, or other imagery in their works. Donald Judd, a leading Minimalist, described the ideal as "getting rid of the things that people used to think were essential to art." These artists did not seek to create abstractions of figures but, like Frank Stella, created basic geometric sculptures so that what a viewer saw is what the viewer saw. Minimalist sculptures are also typically large and made from metal. Like the artists of the Hard Edge movement, the Minimalist sculptors sought to remove any visible signs of themselves in the work. Some Minimalist artists did not even create the finished products but rather sent blueprints to artisans who then welded the metal sculptures for them.

Donald Judd's Boxes

Among Minimalist works, one of the most recognizable is Donald Judd's series of boxes called *Untitled*. The sculpture consists of several metal boxes arranged in a vertical composition and attached to the wall by steel brackets. The boxes are evenly spaced and prefabricated. Judd did not try to hide the material of his work. Each box is highly polished brass without any exterior paint. He also allowed the viewer to see inside the boxes by making the top and bottom of each from pieces of colored Plexiglas. Several museums have Donald Judd sculptures in their twentieth-century art collections because they epitomize the Minimalist movement.

Vietnam Veterans Memorial: Maya Ying Lin's Minimalist Masterpiece

While still a college student, Maya Ying Lin won the commission to design the Vietnam Veterans Memorial in Washington, D.C. She designed the monument as an angled, black wall that slowly increases to ten feet tall at the corner and then gradually recedes back into the ground. "The Wall" (as it is commonly known) is geometric and simple in appearance. It is made of black granite that is reflective and incised with the names of the approximately 58,000 casualties and missing American soldiers of the Vietnam War.

Some Vietnam veterans criticized Lin's simple design as a critique of American involvement in the war. But Lin said that she deeply pondered the effects of war on a nation. She wanted the memorial to cut into the ground, and as the grass grew back, the memorial would be like a scar, similar to the way the Vietnam War made a permanent mark on American society.

By its simplicity, the monument was intended not to distract viewers with fancy embellishments but rather cause them to ponder the Vietnam War. To enhance that effect, the shiny granite allows viewers to see their reflections in the wall as they look at the names of the veterans. Lin wanted viewers to have a personal experience with her Minimalist design. It is effective. People usually react to the monument with solemnity and emotion, leaving flowers and personal mementos at the base of the wall. Family members of the veterans often make graphite rubbings of the names of their lost loved ones.

Pop Art

Another reaction to Abstract Expressionism was the Pop Art movement. Most of the public could not comprehend the arcane concepts of Abstract Expressionism. Pop Artists attempted to meet people's demand for more recognizable art.

Pop Art became popular in the early 1960s. It was based on **recognizable imagery** drawn from popular ("pop") culture such as advertising, consumer products, comic books, and celebrities. During the 1950s, the U.S. economy became increasingly consumer based. Historians even refer to 1950s America as the "throw-away culture" because most people chose to discard outdated appliances in exchange for the newest products. Pop Artists viewed art in a similar manner—as a commodity to be sold.

To create their pieces based on consumerism, Pop Artists used efficient methods to produce their artwork. Thus, their production methods also reflected the consumerism of American society. Pop Artists used graphic art techniques like photographic transfer to create images, supplying color by using benday dots and silkscreens.

However, Pop Art was not a unique phenomenon of the 1960s. Recall that Dada art incorporated imagery from the 1910s culture with photomontages and ready-mades (see Chapter 30). Also, a few artists in the 1950s used imagery from popular culture in their works.

Richard Hamilton

The British artist Richard Hamilton first expressed himself by including images of pop culture in his work. The role and meanings of symbols from mass culture and advertising media interested him. He created a work titled *Just What Is It That Makes Today's Homes So Different, So Appealing*? It is a small collage with many pop culture references. He expressed mass media by including a television, a newspaper, and a theater marquee outside the window. He referred to advertising by including images of Hoover vacuums, Ford cars, Hormel Canned Ham, and Tootsie Pops. To express the pop culture, Hamilton included images of a famous bodybuilder named Charles Atlas and an image from an erotic magazine. Viewers feel as if they are stepping into a display of a 1950s department store, but with a twist. On the ceiling, Hamilton included an image of the earth, and the rug on the floor is the cover of a notebook used by students.

Because Richard Hamilton created this work in 1956, *Just What Is It* functions as a precursor to Pop Art, just as the work of Giotto was a precursor to the Renaissance. The expression of the mundane elements of pop culture became the new avant-garde.

Jasper Johns

When Richard Hamilton created *Just What Is It*, Pop Art was confined to the British and European popular cultures. Jasper Johns was one artist who influenced the development of Pop Art in the United States. His works contain objects that people recognize but look at twice to consider the meaning and relationships of the objects.

Johns created a famous series of bull's-eye paintings. In *Target with Four Faces*, he included painted plaster casts of four faces from the nose down with a target painted below. Although the viewer can recognize all the objects, Johns presents only parts of the faces, and their juxtaposition with the target encourages the viewer to ponder the work.

Johns incorporated recognizable imagery in *Flag*, an encaustic painting of an American flag measuring 3 feet 6 inches by 5 feet 5/8 inch. The American flag is a commonplace image in the United States, but Johns places it within an unusual context. Underneath the painted flag are newspaper clippings. Because parts of the encaustic are translucent, viewers can spot the newspaper clippings beneath the colored wax. It is also interesting that Johns chose encaustic as a medium for an "iconic" symbol such as the American flag (recall that Byzantine painters used encaustic for their icons; see Chapter 10).

Robert Rauschenberg

Robert Rauschenberg used a technique similar to that of his friend Jasper Johns in gathering scraps of newspaper, photographs, and discarded materials to make his assemblages. Rauschenberg collected his materials from the environment around him: New York City. He stated, "Painting relates to both art and life. Neither can be made. (I try to act in the gap between the two)." Rauschenberg combed the streets of New York City for materials to use in his assemblage paintings, which he called **combines**.

Although Rauschenberg's combines have single-word titles such as *Odalisk* and *Canyon*, his creations do not necessarily possess a single unifying meaning. Instead, his combines have multiple meanings. The recognizable objects and images of objects may seem odd when juxtaposed, but on closer examination, Rauschenberg's arrangements have connections. For example, in *Canyon*, a stuffed eagle placed on a pedestal shares a connection with the pillow suspended by fabric from the pedestal: the eagle is covered with feathers while the pillow is stuffed with them. A photograph with a young boy with his hand raised echoes the pose of a postcard of the Statue of Liberty holding the torch aloft.

Roy Lichtenstein's Comic Paintings

Roy Lichtenstein is famous for his comic-strip-style paintings. He began to paint in this manner after being challenged by one of his children to produce a drawing of Mickey Mouse (the child claimed that Lichtenstein could not draw as well as the comic artist). Afterward, Lichtenstein frequently used images from romantic comic strips and war comics in his paintings. He usually re-created a melodramatic moment in his paintings, such as a plane dogfight or a girl drowning, but on a more monumental scale than that of a comic book. The paintings contain flat areas of color surrounded by heavy black lines.

One of Lichtenstein's trademarks was to use **benday dots**. The name derives from the printer Benjamin Day, who used a method of dots for printing color on cheap paper. Benday dots are usually solid dots of color that when seen from a distance, give the viewer the perception of a solid block of color. Red benday dots on a white background give the impression of flesh tones, while blue benday dots on white give the impression of a light blue sky or water. Comic books used this printing method extensively, and Lichtenstein included it in his paintings to give them an authentic comic book feel.

Andy Warhol

Perhaps no name is more synonymous with Pop Art than Andy Warhol. Warhol went to art school and worked designing newspaper advertisements for consumer goods such as shoes. This influenced him to develop an art of commodities—objects that are bought and sold. Warhol used efficient graphic arts production methods such as photographic transfer (rather than drawing objects by hand) and silkscreen, a method of printing colors onto a silkscreen using premade shapes. These methods allowed Warhol and his assistants to make multiple copies of consumer items such as Campbell's Soup cans, Coca-Cola bottles, and Brillo Pad boxes. Warhol even named his studio The Factory, an appropriate name considering the efficient, machine like methods of production. Warhol also produced images of 1960s pop icons such as Marilyn Monroe and Elvis Presley (**Fig. 31-2.**)

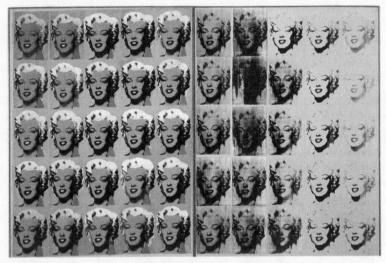

Figure 31-2. Andy Warhol, *Marilyn Diptych*, 1962

Pop Sculptor: Claes Oldenburg

Pop Art had its sculptural representation in the work of Claes Oldenburg. Using consumer items such as polyester fibers, vinyl, and canvas, Oldenburg created large, soft sculptures of everyday food items such as pistachio ice cream and pieces of cake. He even made a soft toilet! Oldenburg also made hard, painted sculptures of food out of plaster. Sculptures such as these included hot dogs and hamburgers. Why do art historians consider Oldenburg's sculptures part of Pop Art? These sculptures reflected the foods seen in diners, which were popular in American culture during the 1960s. As the United States became increasingly industrialized, the use of automobiles increased and so did fast food. Oldenburg represented this with his work.

Later in Oldenburg's career, wealthy patrons commissioned him to create large outdoor sculptures. For a courtyard in Yale University, Oldenburg created *Lipstick* (*Ascending*) *on Caterpillar Tracks*, which resembles a tank topped by an enormous red lipstick. In the 1980s, Oldenburg began collaborating with his wife, Coosje van Brug-gen. For the sculpture garden of the Walker Art Center in Minneapolis, they designed *Spoonbridge with a Cherry*. In 2001, Oldenburg and Van Bruggen created *Dropped Cone* for the roof of Neumarkt Galerie in Cologne, Germany; it looks like a large vanilla ice cream cone that has been dropped and is melting on the corner of the building. Despite transitioning to larger works and collaborative efforts, Oldenburg created designs that retained their popular subject matter.

Superrealism

Superrealist artists created still-life paintings or portraits with photographic accuracy during the 1960s and 1970s. Their works are often based on photographs and employ airbrush, which is used to retouch photographs, and grid lines on canvas, meticulously recording every realistic detail. Art historians also describe these artists as Photorealists. Like Pop Artists, Superrealists used everyday recognizable imagery and average people presented in ordinary poses. Good examples of Superrealism are the works of Audrey Flack and Chuck Close.

Audrey Flack

Audrey Flack focused on realistic still-life paintings that resemble seventeenth-century Dutch vanitas paintings in both their tromp l'oeil technique and Symbolism (see Chapter 21). Flack created a famous painting titled *Marilyn*, referring to Marilyn Monroe. A past AP Art History exam included a slide-based short essay comparing Flack's treatment of still life to a still-life painting by Paul Cézanne. Let us examine the important qualities of Flack's painting.

Marilyn Monroe was the quintessential 1960s icon, famous for her physical beauty and seductive persona. As mentioned earlier, Warhol created many silkscreens of her image. But Marilyn did not always exhibit the superficial qualities for which she would become famous. Her original name was Norma Jean. Flack's painting contains symbolism that tells the story of Marilyn's life from a childhood photograph of her and another photograph in an opened biography, as well as references to a life tragically cut short at the age of 36.

Flack included fruit, symbolizing life, some of which has been partially peeled. Dutch vanitas paintings often contained opened or peeled fruit to show how life is slowly being peeled away. An hourglass and pocket watch also symbolize the passage of time. Behind the opened biography, Flack painted a calendar page for August, the month in which Marilyn died. The red lipstick, perfume, and pearls were trademarks of Marilyn's image. The glass and small Dutch porcelain cup are more references to Dutch vanitas still-life paintings.

Audrey Flack commented once that when she studied art history, the images she saw were almost exclusively photographic in quality. She remarked that much of how humans see the world is through photographs. Flack thus chose Superrealism

(Photorealism) as a method to express her vision. Adding to the photographic quality of the painting, Flack used airbrush to blend away any trace of brushstrokes.

Chuck Close

Chuck Close created large realistic portraits of average people, usually his friends and family. When Close developed this style of painting, other artists were still creating abstract works of art. Abstract Expressionism was waning and Hard Edge and Minimalism were in vogue. Some critics felt that portraiture was dead, but Close revived it. His first portrait in this style was *Big Self-Portrait*, based on a photograph he took of himself on the spur of the moment. Every piece of hair—from the stubble on his chin to his nose hair and disheveled pate—appears in this self-portrait. Close created a grid on a copy of the photograph as well as on the canvas and captured details of the image in each square. Then he used an airbrush to create a photographic quality. His realistically painted portraits are very distinct and easily recognizable, even for people outside the domain of art history.

Duane Hanson

A sculptor of the Superrealist style whose work reflects American popular culture is Duane Hanson. Hanson created sculptures of average Americans during the 1960s and 1970s. His work titled *Tourists* depicts a man and woman, probably husband and wife, in gaudy attire. The man is balding and overweight, and wears a garish Hawaiian shirt. The woman dons similar attire but is slightly taller and heavier than the man and wears thick lipstick and sunglasses. Both figures are tan, have wrinkled skin, and appear beyond middle age. A first impression is that this is a retired husband and wife visiting a tropical location.

What was Hanson saying about Americans? U.S. society has a large middle-to-upper class that can afford to travel. Yet because many Americans do not follow international news and have limited cultural awareness, their physical appearance lacks acculturation (blending gracefully with other cultures). Hanson presents a stereotype of American tourists.

Hanson created many other Realistic sculptures, including a boxer, a weightlifter, a supermarket shopper, and a sunbather. He took casts of the bodies of real people and made either bronze or polyester resin sculptures of their forms. Hanson often included real hair and real clothing on his sculpted figures. His figures are so realistic that people who see them in museums often mistake them for real people. In one instance, an elderly woman asked a "museum guard" for directions to an exhibit. When the figure did not respond (because it was really a Hanson sculpture of a museum guard), she stomped off indignantly, remarking how rude he was.

Art and Politics

The next two examples of art styles, Feminist Art and Earth Art, exemplify the politically charged climate of America during the 1960s and 1970s. It was the era of the Cold War and the Vietnam War. Peace protests criticized America's military involvement in Vietnam. Meanwhile, rock music proliferated, and social mores became more relaxed as the younger generation experimented with sexuality and narcotics. America was also forced to come to grips with racial and gender inequality, which caused a slew of protests and even riots. Amidst this political turmoil, many American artists sought unique ways to express their reactions.

Feminist Art and Judy Chicago

During the 1960s, female artists began to use their work to address issues of sexual discrimination and subjugation of women. Not only do the works critique the gender gap in American society, but they also raise awareness of the significant accomplishments of women. Judy Chicago's *The Dinner Party* is one such work. *The Dinner Party* is an **installation**, which is an artwork that creates an environment of its own in a section of a museum or gallery. *The Dinner Party* alludes to thirty-nine famous women that Judy Chicago believed should be recognized by having a seat at "the table."

The Dinner Party includes symbolism on a variety of levels. Originally, Chicago wanted the party to comprise thirteen women, the number in a witches' coven. As she continued her work, the original number became inadequate, and Chicago eventually tripled it so that thirty-nine famous women are convened at the table. The table consists of a large equilateral triangle with each side measuring 48 feet. The triangular shape is an ancient symbol for the Sacred Feminine or Mother Goddess. To further emphasize femininity, Chicago incorporated traditional women's art mediums, such as ceramics and embroidery for the plates and placemats at the table. Each setting has a distinct design with abstract organic imagery resembling the female reproductive organs. Despite the differences among the thirty-nine place settings, Chicago achieved unity of composition by using the same goblets and utensils for each setting, which also refers to equality. The names of additional famous women are incised into the platform surrounding the table.

Environmentalism and Earth Art

During the 1960s and 1970s, the environmental movement emerged in America. Concerned citizens began efforts to preserve nature in the face of increasing industrialization and the proliferation of automobiles. Following the trend in politics, artists began to create works that incorporated natural materials and were placed in outdoor locations. These artists sought to move art from the museum and the sculpture garden into new contexts in which their creations would have a dialogue with the site itself. Much of the art coming out of this movement, which is called Environmental Art or Earth Art, is **site specific**. Also, many examples of Earth Art are in remote locations such as deserts.

Robert Smithson's *Spiral Jetty*

Robert Smithson disliked the idea of turning natural sites into photographs and paintings. He believed that an artist or photographer could not truly capture the beauty of the earth by transforming it into a two-dimensional work. Instead, Smithson created most of his **earthworks** outdoors. When he created a work indoors, it involved taking pieces from an outdoor site, such as sand and rocks, and bringing them into the museum. He also disliked trapping nature into a rectangular, finite format. Even Smithson's indoor works incorporate the use of space and mirrors, thereby eliminating the fixed viewpoint that is characteristic of most art but is difficult to narrow down in the outdoors.

The best known of Robert Smithson's work is *Spiral Jetty* at the Great Salt Lake, Utah (**Fig. 31-3**). Smithson would drive around a remote location until he was inspired by the site. He would continue his search, which he called **low-level scanning**, until something about the site conveyed a shape or design in his mind. At the Great Salt Lake, he visualized a spiraling shape. Smithson also discovered that the salt crystals in the lake have a spiral. With this concept in mind, Smithson moved tons of sand and stone into a spiral formation 1,500 feet long. *Spiral Jetty* is thus site specific; the design has a dialogue with the site.

Figure 31-3. Robert Smithson, *Spiral Jetty*, 1970

Smithson drew on diverse influences for the artistic vocabulary for *Spiral Jetty*. Neolithic stone structures in Great Britain, such as Stonehenge, influenced Smithson, as did prehistoric earth mounds in the United States, such as the Great Serpent Mound in Ohio. Smithson also looked to the Minimalist sculptural vocabulary to achieve the simplicity and clarity of his design for *Spiral Jetty*.

Nancy Holt's *Sun Tunnels*

Nancy Holt, Robert Smithson's wife, also created earthworks. Her most famous creation is *Sun Tunnels*, which is located in Utah not far from *Spiral Jetty. Sun Tunnels* consists of concrete pipes that are 18 feet long and have an internal diameter of 8 feet, anchored into place by concrete bases. Holt drilled a series of circles of varying sizes through the walls of the pipes so that they align with four constellations: Draco, Columbia, Perseus, and Capricorn. Holt also arranged the pipes so that the sun appears in the center of the pipes when it is on the horizon during the summer and winter solstices. A past AP Art History test included *Sun Tunnels* juxtaposed with Stonehenge for slide-based multiple-choice questions. Authorities believe that Stonehenge was used as an astronomical observatory, and its stones are aligned with the sun during the summer solstice.

What would happen if someone or something moved *Sun Tunnels*? The work would lose its meaning. Like Smithson's *Spiral Jetty*, Holt's work interacts and draws its meaning from the site.

Conclusion

The art world underwent a variety of movements and changes after World War II. By 1945 (the end of the war), the center of the art world was moving to New York City. Here are the main points of art movements that emerged after World War II:

- **Abstract Expressionism** arose in the 1940s and early 1950s. **Gestural abstraction**, which is also called **action painting**, contains visible and chaotic brush strokes and swirls of paint expressing the artists' subconscious; examples are the works of Jackson Pollock and Willem de Kooning. **Chromatic abstraction** painters used blocks of color to convey complex concepts about life and the universe; examples are Mark Rothko and Barnett Newman. Barnett Newman is famous for his **zips**.

- **Helen Frankenthaler** is famous for **color stains**.

- **New York School** was the group of Abstract Expressionists and associated artists living in New York City during the 1940s and 1950s.

- **David Smith** created the *Cubi* series, which are metallic sculptures cantilevered in space. Each piece in the series has human and totemlike features.

- **Louise Nevelson** is famous for assemblages composed of boxes with repeating patterns.

- **Hard Edge** is a style of painting that emerged in the 1950s. The works comprise abstract shapes with clear lines and flat planes of color. The paintings lack any narrative meaning. Frank Stella, who created a series of pinstripe paintings, voiced the motto of the movement: "What you see is what you see."

- **Minimalism** emerged in the 1960s as the sculptural form of Hard Edge. Minimalists created solid shapes out of metal or stone; examples are Donald Judd's boxes and Maya Ying Lin's Vietnam Veterans Memorial.

- **Pop Art** started in the 1960s. Artists used everyday, recognizable imagery and subject matter taken from popular culture to comment on consumerism and art as a commodity; examples are Roy Lichtenstein's comic paintings with benday dots, Andy Warhol's repeating images and silkscreens, and Claes Oldenburg's sculptures.

- **Superrealism** (or **Photorealism**) of the 1960s is characterized by everyday, recognizable imagery and people painted or sculpted with tremendous detail and lifelike accuracy; examples are Audrey Flack's still-life paintings with vanitas references, Chuck Close's large portraits, and Duane Hanson's sculptures of average Americans.

- **Judy Chicago** created an **installation** glorifying the achievement of women titled *The Dinner Table*.

- **Earth Art**, a movement of the 1960s and 1970s, was influenced by environmentalism. Also called **environmental art** or **earthworks**, works of art from this movement are site specific, usually in remote locations. The works have a dialogue with the site; examples are Robert Smithson's *Spiral Jetty* and Nancy Holt's *Sun Tunnels*.

Chapter 32

Twentieth-Century Architecture

Introduction and Exam Strategy Overview

In 2006, Angelina Jolie took Brad Pitt on a trip to Bear Run, Pennsylvania, for his birthday. What were two of Hollywood's hottest stars doing at Bear Run? The town is home to one of Frank Lloyd Wright's most significant designs, Fallingwater. Brad is an architecture buff, and Angelina knew he would enjoy a trip to such an architectural landmark. Following their private two-hour tour of the home, Brad described the experience as amazing. But why is Fallingwater such an important site for twentieth-century architecture? Could Angelina and Brad have known that the AP Art History test writers included it on several past exams?

This chapter discusses Frank Lloyd Wright's Fallingwater as well as some of his other designs. It also summarizes the important architects and architectural movements of the twentieth century. Recall that 25 percent of the points on the exam are drawn from questions related to architecture. The AP Art History exam of 2000 included a slide-based short essay on twentieth-century architecture. Since it has been seven years since then, some test in the near future is likely to contain a slide-based short essay on the topic. Multiple-choice questions on twentieth-century architecture usually number two or three per test.

Frank Lloyd Wright

Early in his career, Frank Lloyd Wright worked with Louis Sullivan. Recall that Louis Sullivan was the first modern architect of the nineteenth century and that his designs were precursors to modern skyscrapers (see Chapter 28). But Wright was determined to become famous in his own right and went to work independently. He became the self-proclaimed best architect in the world. On the witness stand, testifying at his divorce proceeding (he left his wife and six children for an affair with the wife of one of his clients in Europe), Wright testified to being the world's best architect. Realizing that such testimony would probably result in awarding more of the assets to his ex-wife, reporters asked Wright after he gave testimony why he testified in this manner. His reply was, "I was under oath, wasn't I?"

Frank Lloyd Wright believed in incorporating a few key concepts into his designs: a design should blend with its surroundings, architecture should reinforce democratic ideals, and the hearth (fireplace) is the traditional center of the home. Let us examine these concepts more closely. First, good design should blend organically with its surroundings, leaving the surrounding landscape looking more beautiful than it was originally. Consider the example of his design for Frederick C. Robie's house. Wright designed the Robie House in 1908, and workers completed its construction in 1910. The Robie House **(CD Fig. 32-1)** has a long, low, rectangular design.

Figure 32-1. Frank Lloyd Wright, Robie House, 1907–1909

The Robie House has large open rooms with uninterrupted spaces and stained-glass windows with modern designs. Wright believed that architecture should reinforce concepts of democracy and freedom of movement. Therefore, rooms should lack impediments to movement. The windows of the Robie House allow an unobstructed view of the outside gardens. Despite the open spaces, the focal point of the home is its hearth.

The roofs of the building extend as overhangs on the side of the house, using cantilevered construction. **Cantilevers** are beams that extend from a structure and are anchored only at one side **(CD Fig. 32-2)**. Wright is famous for incorporating cantilevers into his designs. Recall that David Smith used cantilevers for his *Cubi* series (see Chapter 31).

Why did Wright design Robie House to be long, low, and flat? The answer lies in the landscape of the Midwest (the Robie House is in Chicago, Illinois). That part of the country is prairie land, known for its flat landscape. Thus, Wright's design blends harmoniously with its surroundings. The Robie House exemplifies Wright's **prairie style**. Today the house is part of the campus of the University of Chicago.

In 1935, Wright designed a weekend home for Edgar Kaufmann Sr., the wealthy owner of the Kaufmann Department Stores. The owners of several cabins in the forest of Bear Run, Pennsylvania, the Kaufmann family decided to build a full-size house there. The Kaufmanns asked Wright to design a house overlooking a waterfall that was on the property. They never expected that he would design the home over the waterfall. Because of this, the Kaufmann home at Bear Run is called **Fallingwater (CD Fig. 32-3)**. It served as the weekend home for the family from 1937 to 1963. Fallingwater opened to the public in 1964, and millions of visitors have toured it.

Wright wanted the Kaufmann home to blend organically with its environment. He constructed the living room using stones gathered from the site. As in other Wright designs, the center of Fallingwater is the hearth. The building has two cantilevered terraces that extend over the waterfall. The cantilevered terraces resemble nearby rock formations in both their shape and coloration. A staircase extends from the upper floors all the way down to the stream, and broad expanses of windows provide the Kaufmanns a view of the surroundings. Not since the pueblos of the Native Americans of the Southwest had construction sought to make people such a part of the land.

De Stijl

A new style of architecture developed in Holland that completely abandoned the features of previous architectural styles. The movement also embraced art and became known as de Stijl (the Style). Recall that Piet Mondrian adopted De Stijl using only primary colors, basic shades, and horizontal and vertical lines in his paintings (see Chapter 30). Although the style began in Holland, it became the avant-garde architectural movement of the continent in the 1920s. Art historians refer to the transformation of de Stijl into an international phenomenon as the **International Style**.

Gerrit Thomas Rietveld's design for the Schröder House exemplifies De Stijl. Built between 1923 and 1924, the Schröder House **(CD Fig. 32-4)** contains flat, rectangular planes and straight lines. No Classical columns, arches, or flying buttresses are included. It looks like the embodiment of a Mondrian painting. The interior of the home contains movable, sliding glass doors. Red, blue, and yellow as well as white and black are the only colors used for the décor of the Schröder House. The house is an expression of Rietveld's belief that architecture can be reduced to basic geometric shapes and colors similar to Mondrian's painting style.

Walter Gropius and the Bauhaus School of Design

The Bauhaus was a school of design in Germany dedicated to teaching the International Style. The founder of the Bauhaus, Walter Gropius, established the school to unite fine and applied arts in a "new architecture." Students would learn about not only designing buildings and works of art but also painting in oil, making lithographs, weaving, making stained-glass windows, binding books, and even creating tapestries. Gropius directed the Bauhaus from 1919 through 1928.

He banished the study of architectural history. Why would he institute such a revolutionary policy? For millennia, architects from Ancient Egypt through the Neoclassical period studied the works of past architects. Gropius sought to omit architectural history because it would stifle the creativity of the students. According to Gropius, architecture should *avoid embellishments* of any earlier style.

Figure 32-5. Walter Gropius, Shop Block, Bauhaus School of Design, 1925–1926

Construction workers built the Bauhaus School of Design from basic materials: glass, steel, and concrete. The Shop Block **(CD Fig. 32-5)**, which was one of the main wings of the Bauhaus building, exemplifies the architecture advocated by Gropius. It contained no exterior ornamentation or decoration. Instead, the wing had straight lines, right angles, and flat roofs. It resembled a glass box. The interior of the Shop Block lacked permanent walls. Gropius thought walls would interfere with sharing ideas of the various creative disciplines. Gropius envisioned an egalitarian style of architecture in which buildings and residences could be produced efficiently and affordably for humanity.

Hitler and the Bauhaus

Adolf Hitler gained power over Germany in 1933. As one of his first acts, Hitler closed and later demolished the Shop Block of the Bauhaus. Recall that Hitler attempted to become an artist earlier in life and during his regime called for the Degenerate Art Exhibit, a mockery of modern art (see Chapter 29). He viewed the lessons being learned at the Bauhaus as degenerate. Gropius and other Bauhaus teachers (Josef Albers, a famous precursor to the Hard Edge style of the 1950s) left Germany and came to America.

International Style

The International Style refers to the architecture of the 1920s through the 1950s that is geometrically simple and devoid of exterior ornamentation. (Do not confuse this movement with the International Gothic Style of painting, popular in Europe during the fourteenth and fifteenth centuries.) Instead, International Style architects focused on straight lines and sleek designs that used materials such as glass and steel.

The International Style advocated the creation of functional buildings that would use space, materials, and financial resources in the most efficient manner. For example, extensive use of glass allowed natural light to penetrate the building. Aesthetically, the glass reflected light as well, giving the building a sense of life and movement. Ludwig Mies van der Rohe's model of a glass skyscraper **(CD Fig. 32-6)** exhibited at the Bauhaus in 1921 presaged the proliferation of such designs later in twentieth century. Mies van der Rohe would become one of the leading proponents of the International Style.

Ludwig Mies van der Rohe

Mies van der Rohe became the new director of the Bauhaus when Walter Gropius left. He extended the International Style, and his designs influenced the development of modern architecture. Mies van der Rohe reduced architecture to pure rectilinear forms and eschewed external decorations. He believed that "less is more." He once said, "For me, novelty has no interest, none whatsoever. I don't want to be interesting, I want to be good." His "less is more" philosophy extended to all aspects of design, from the exterior to the interior. When the German government commissioned him to design the German Pavilion **(CD Fig. 32-7)** for the Barcelona World Arts Fair in 1929, he also designed a specific style of chair for royal visitors to the pavilion.

The German Pavilion exemplifies Mies van der Rohe's philosophy. First, notice that the building **lacks exterior ornamentation**. No cornices, pediments, or revivalist elements, which were popular during the nineteenth century, were used. Instead, the building exhibits **basic geometric shapes**. Its materials include glass, steel, and marble. The interior of the building incorporates open space, also with minimal ornamentation. Instead of being distracted by embellishments—as a person would be in a Gothic, Baroque, or Rococo design—visitors to the German Pavilion would stand in awe of the progress architecture had made toward the future. By presenting less distraction, Mies van der Rohe enabled viewers to admire the sleek, straight lines of the structure and the modern use of building materials such as steel and glass.

Mies van der Rohe designed the Barcelona Chair **(CD Fig. 32-8)** for the pavilion. He anticipated that the king and queen of Spain would sit in the chair while visiting the German Pavilion. It incorporates a sleek design with some comfort and functionality. The chair does not contain embellished features. It is a metal chair with thick leather cushioning for comfort. Because it lacks decorative elements as part of its structure, it is not too heavy to move. Yet the chair is strong enough to support a person's weight. The combination of sleek design and functionality typify the International Style.

Later in his career, Mies van der Rohe worked with an American architect, Philip Johnson, to create the Seagram Building **(CD Fig. 32-9)** in midtown Manhattan for the famous Canadian distillery, Seagram Brothers. What stands out most is the building's pronounced verticality. Recall that the space in cities was limited and expensive (see Chapter 28). The Seagram Building stands 515 feet tall, making it a skyscraper (which usually has a minimum height of 490 feet). It appears to be made of glass and contains thin strips of bronze that hold the numerous panes of glass in place.

In keeping with the International Style, the Seagram Building is sleek, lacks exterior ornamentation, and contains regularity (a repeating pattern of glass windows and vertical bronze beams). To reinforce regularity, Mies van der Rohe designed window shades that functioned in only three ways: fully open, half open, and fully closed. He did not want the possibility of shades being opened differently to disrupt his design.

The regularity of the Seagram Building resembles the Shop Block of the Bauhaus. Other influences for the building include Mies van der Rohe's model for a glass skyscraper (discussed earlier) and Louis Sullivan's tall buildings of the nineteenth century (see Chapter 28).

On the 2000 AP Art History exam, a slide-based short-essay question showed students a picture of the Seagram Building and asked students to discuss the structural innovations that enabled the construction of skyscrapers. It also asked students to discuss the building as an example of the International Style. We have addressed the latter part of the question. Let us now consider the first part.

Skyscrapers such as the Seagram Building contain **steel frames**, which are a series of vertical steel columns in the center of the building. The steel columns can be composed of I-beams (I-shaped metal beams) **(CD Fig. 32-10)** or circular or square columns **reinforced with concrete**. The properties of steel make its inner structure strong enough to support a building. Steel beams extend from the vertical steel supports and are attached by threaded bolts and rivets. The floors consist of **steel bedding** (flat plates), supported by the horizontal steel beams and coated in **ferroconcrete** (concrete with embedded steel bars).

Unfortunately for Mies van der Rohe, American building codes required that fire-resistant materials coat the steel infrastructure (steel melts in intense heat). With his international-style aesthetic, he preferred to reveal the inner structure, similar to his model of a glass skyscraper. He resolved this issue by including the bronze I-beams running vertically on the exterior of the building. This conveyed the sense of revealing the inner supports. Because of such strong supports, Mies van der Rohe and Johnson could cover most of the exterior in glass.

Le Corbusier

The Swiss architect Charles-Edouard Jeanneret, also known as Le Corbusier, was another champion of the International Style. His designs for buildings include basic geometric shapes, maximum use of space, and lack of ornamentation. Le Corbusier referred to his style as **Purism** because it relied on pure geometric shapes. He created maximum space by eliminating load-bearing walls. Instead, he used steel beams to support the floors.

Le Corbusier's Villa Savoye **(CD Fig. 32-11)** demonstrates the International Style. The Villa Savoye is a country house. Notice that the house lacks exterior ornamentation.

It consists of flat planes and a boxy, geometric shape. The building makes maximum use of space. Le Corbusier believed that a home should not include load-bearing walls; the steel beams would support the structure. Therefore, the lower level is fairly open. The enclosed part of the lower level contains a three-car garage, bedrooms, a bathroom, and stairs to the upper levels. Thin steel columns support the second level, which consists of a living space (the focal point of the home) partially open to the air. The Villa Savoye also contains a third-level roof garden. Le Corbusier believed that a good building should be a functional living space and fulfill the basic human needs of air, space, and vegetation. His design for the Villa Savoye is consistent with his beliefs.

Modernist Architecture

The International Style became part of Modernist architecture. Modernist-style buildings contain sleek designs with little exterior ornamentation. Mies van der Rohe's "less is more" philosophy was upheld by Modernist architects. Yet Modernist architecture extended beyond the values of the International Style to include buildings that curve organically into their surroundings.

Frank Lloyd Wright's design for the Solomon R. Guggenheim Museum in Manhattan **(CD Fig. 32-12)** fits into the Modernist style. Designed as an ascending spiral, the building has a smooth exterior shell and ascends gracefully. When he was commissioned to design it late in his career, Wright wanted to create a design that would be a temple for Modern Art. In the chaos and noise of the city, the interior of the spiral building contains a large central space from floor to ceiling. The ceiling incorporates panes of glass reminiscent of the clerestory windows of Gothic churches. The effect of light pouring through the ceiling resembles the divine light of the windows of the Hagia Sophia. The effect of the museum's interior is that of a sanctuary. Wright's design lacks the spartan geometric designs of Mies van der Rohe or Le Corbusier. Nonetheless, it is Modernist because it has smooth lines and the design fulfills its function.

Le Corbusier's design for Notre-Dame-du-Haut in France **(CD Fig. 32-13)** is another example of Modernist architecture. Recognizing that he needed to take a different approach in designing a church, Le Corbusier departed from the earlier geometric arrangement of the Villa Savoye. From the outside, the building has an organic shape resembling hands folded in prayer or a dove representing the Holy Spirit. The inside is small and dark, reminiscent of mystical Christian structures like medieval monasteries. Such a reference was appropriate for Notre-Dame-du-Haut because it was located on a pilgrimage route (see Chapter 13). Small stained-glass windows resembling Mondrian paintings pierce the thick walls. Despite these unusual features, the building is consistent with Modernist architecture because it is streamlined, lacks unnecessary sculptural embellishments (consider Gothic tracery or ornate Baroque architecture), and is functional.

Post-Modern Architecture: Less Is a Bore

In the late twentieth century, some architects challenged the hegemony of Modern-ism and developed a more inclusive style of architecture, which architectural historians called Post-Modernism. Whereas Mies van der Rohe propagated "less is more," a Post-Modern architect would be apt to say "less is a bore." Post-Modern architects relied on an expansive architectural vocabulary incorporating pediments, arches, pilasters, and columns into highly original and eclectic designs.

Why did architectural tastes change? Actually, it did not change for all architects. Modernism was a firmly entrenched movement, and ironically, Modernist architects became the reactionaries (conservatives) criticizing the Post-Modernists. The architects who became Post-Modernists criticized the sterility (plainness) and anonymity of Mod-ernist architecture, especially the skyscrapers in cities. In the pursuit of pure shapes and lines, most Modernists did not consider the history and culture of the neighborhoods and regions of their buildings.

Philip Johnson's AT&T Building

Recall that Philip Johnson helped Mies van der Rohe design the International Style Seagram Building in the late 1950s. In the 1970s, Johnson did an about-face with his design for the AT&T Building, also in New York City (CD Fig. 32-14). Why is it dif-ferent? It is tall (660 feet) and therefore a skyscraper. Yet unlike the Seagram Building, which emphasized glass and metal with its sleek, rectangular exterior, the AT&T Build-ing is predominantly masonry (only 30 percent of the building's surface area consists of glass) and revives a classical architectural vocabulary.

Notice that Johnson and his associates divided the building into three parts, reminiscent of the three-part elevation of a Greek temple with its base, column, and pediment. The AT&T Building includes a massive round arch at the entrance, similar to a triumphal arch or a Romanesque portal. The thin strips of masonry that extend the height of the center of the building resemble the fluting of columns. At the top, the roof slopes downward from the center like a pediment. However, the building is eclectic, incorporating more than just classical features. A similar three-part elevation existed during the Renaissance in designs such as Alberti's Palazzo Rucellai (see Chapter 16). Also, the center of the roof contains a space known as an **orbiculum**, which gives the building the look of eighteenth-century clothing dressers. Bold for its time, Johnson's design was roundly criticized by staunch Modernists. Yet it played a major role in the development of Post-Modern architecture.

Michael Graves

Examine Michael Graves's Portland Public Services Building (CD Fig. 32-15). The structure is multicolored, quite different from the uniformity of the Seagram Building. Graves used the square as the basis for his design. The building has a box shape, and the square windows reinforce that theme. But that is where the simplicity ends. Graves included reddish-brown seven-story pilasters on the side of the building, incorporating capitals that extend far beyond the building like sculpture. Above the pilasters, Graves included an inverted reddish trapezoidal design. On the other side of the building, he used light blue roundels with ribbons, similar to Baroque architecture. The top of the building contains a light blue penthouse area offset from the rest of the building's facade. The colors derive from nature. The building's eclectic mix of architectural vocabulary and color demonstrates a striking contrast from buildings such as the Shop Block and Villa Savoye.

Pompidou National Centre of Art and Culture

The Pompidou Centre **(CD Fig. 32-16)** is a multipurpose structure. It contains a public library, France's National Museum of Modern Art, a theater, and numerous halls. In addition, it contains an open plaza that is abuzz with people at all hours. Because the building is in the Beaubourg section of Paris, guides also call the building the Beaubourg. It opened in 1977 and was named the Pompidou Centre after the French president Georges Pompidou.

The Pompidou Centre contains very interesting features. First, the building appears to be turned inside out. All its pipes are exposed, and no "skin" covers the building as glass covers Modernist skyscrapers. Several architects collaborated on the project, the main two being Richard Rodgers and Renzo Piano. They drew on the architecture of industry, such as metal pipes. The use of colors to indicate the various functions of the pipes gave rationality to the structure. Green indicates water, blue indicates air conditioning, yellow indicates electricity, red indicates elevators and escalators, and white indicates air shafts. Interestingly, the building demonstrates Modernist architecture by exposing its steel support beams, its functionality, and inclusion of vast areas of interior space (one of the advantages of a building turned inside out). But in contrast to Modernist architecture, which reduces architecture to bare essentials, the Pompidou Centre embraces a mixture of influences, making it an extremely popular tourist destination.

Guggenheim Museum in Bilbao, Spain

Frank Gehry's design for the Guggenheim Museum in Bilbao, Spain **(CD Fig. 32-17)**, differs dramatically from Frank Lloyd Wright's design for the Guggenheim Museum in New York City. Whereas Wright's design contains smooth edges and simple spiral shapes, Gehry's design has sloping surfaces juxtaposed with jagged edges. Architectural historians label the Spanish Guggenheim's style as **Deconstructivist** architecture. Deconstructivism is a Post-Modern movement that eliminates continuous lines and incorporates unusual shapes. Unlike the inclusive mentality of Post-Modernist architects, Deconstructivists sought to destroy normal lines and shapes. How does this apply to the Guggenheim? Just as you begin to follow a wall of the Guggenheim in Bilbao, it stops and turns away at a sharp angle. The building's exterior resembles the twists and turns of a roller coaster. When the museum opened in 1997, supporters claimed that its unique design helped put Bilbao on the map.

Figure 32-17. Frank Gehry, Guggenheim Bilbao Museo, 1997

It is rare for such a building to shimmer the way the Guggenheim Museum does. Gehry intended his design to represent fish scales because fishing was part of Bilbao's economy. Gehry used titanium panels to convey this effect. Titanium is a lightweight metal known for its strength. This aspect of the design was a sore point for some nearby residents, who complained that the highly reflective titanium sent blinding rays of sunlight through their windows.

Conclusion

Frank Lloyd Wright ushered in the innovations of architecture early in the twentieth century. He departed from revivalist styles and sought to organically connect his designs with their surroundings. The Robie House in Chicago, Illinois, had a long, flat roof resembling the grasslands of the Midwest. Art historians call it Wright's prairie style. His cantilevered designs for the terraces of Fallingwater were revolutionary. Remember that the hearth was the center of Wright's home designs.

Modernist architecture began with De Stijl, a movement in Holland exemplified by the Gerrit Rietveld's Schröder House. De Stijl grew so much in popularity that it became the International Style. The Bauhaus School of Design in Germany inculcated the values of the International Style—sleek lines, basic geometric shapes, good use of interior space, and lack of ornamentation—to a new generation of architects, until Hitler's regime closed it. The Bauhaus's Shop Block (which the German government demolished) epitomized the International Style.

Ludwig Mies van der Rohe was an important proponent of Modernist architecture. He coined the phrase "less is more" and used the philosophy in his designs for the German Pavilion of the Barcelona World Arts Fair, the Barcelona Chair, and the Seagram Building.

The Seagram Building is a skyscraper that implements the advancements of twentieth-century building materials. Skyscrapers have vertical steel frames reinforced by masonry. The floors comprise horizontal steel beams as well as steel plates. The steel is layered in ferroconcrete (concrete embedded with additional steel bars). Skyscrapers like the Seagram Building include a glass "skin." They are Modernist in that they are sleek and functional, made good use of space, and lack exterior ornamentation.

Post-Modernist architecture is more inclusive than modernist architecture. Remember that the Post-Modernist dictum is "less is a bore." Post-Modernist architects combined past architectural styles with new materials to create unique structures. Philip Johnson's design for the AT&T Building is a good example of this style.

Although Frank Gehry designed the Guggenheim Museum in Bilbao, Spain, during the Post-Modern architectural era, the building is an example of the Deconstructivist style. The primary features of deconstructivism are the lack of continuous lines and the use of unusual shapes. Gehry used titanium for the exterior of the museum.

Part 7

Key Points You Absolutely, Positively Have to Know

Chapter 33

Key Female Artists and Patrons

The AP Art History committee strives to construct exams that represent the contributions of prominent female artists and patrons. Most tests have included two or three multiple-choice questions on female artists and patrons. In addition, exams have almost always contained at least one slide-based multiple-choice question or short essay devoted to the work of a female artist. The following list briefly identifies the most important female artists and patrons from Ancient Egypt to the present.

1. Hatshepsut (ruler of Egypt from 1473–1458 BCE)

   - First great female ruler whose name has been recorded

   - Built a famous mortuary temple at Deir el-Bahri

   - Painted reliefs in Hatshepsut's mortuary temple constitute the first great tribute to a woman's achievements in history or art

2. Nefertiti (queen from approximately 1348–1336 BCE)

   - Akhenaton's queen

   - Reigned during the New Kingdom

   - Famous painted limestone bust is a good example of the naturalistic Amarna style

3. Theodora (500–548 CE)

   - Justinian's empress

   - One of the most remarkable women of the Middle Ages

   - Portrayed leading a procession in a famous mosaic in San Vitale, Ravenna

4. Isabella d'Este (1479–1539)

   - Daughter of the duke of Ferrara and wife of Francesco Gonzaga, marquis of Mantua

   - Most important female patron during the Renaissance

   - Subject of a famous portrait by Titian

5. Sofonisba Anguissola (1527–1625)

   • Renowned for painting informal and charming group portraits

   • Court painter to Philip II of Spain

6. Caterina van Hemessen (1528–1587)

   • Flemish artist

   • Painted the first known northern European self-portrait by a woman

7. Lavina Teerling (1515–1576)

   • Flemish artist

   • Best known for her life-size portrait of Queen Elizabeth I

8. Artemisia Gentileschi (1593–1653)

   • Baroque artist

   • A Caravaggista, or follower of Caravaggio

   • Best known for painting several versions of Judith slaying the Assyrian general Holofernes

9. Marie de' Medici (1573–1642)

   • Wife of Henry IV, the first of the Bourbon kings of France

   • Commissioned Rubens to paint a series of monumental paintings glorifying her career

10. Judith Leyster (1609–1660)

    • Dutch Baroque artist who developed a thriving career as a portraitist

    • Influenced by Hals

    • Her famous *Self-Portrait* demonstrates her skill and status

11. Rachel Ruysch (1663–1750)

    • Dutch Baroque artist

    • Renowned for her detailed floral paintings

12. Élisabeth Vigée-Lebrun (1755–1842)

    • Famous for her portraits of Marie Antoinette

    • One of the few women admitted into the French Royal Academy

    • Contemporary of Adélaïde Labille-Guiard

13. Adélaïde Labille-Guiard (1749–1803)

    - Famous for her portraits of French aristocrats

    - One of the few women admitted into the French Royal Academy

    - Contemporary of Élisabeth Vigée-Lebrun

14. Angelica Kauffmann (1741–1807)

    - Neoclassical artist

    - Best known for her painting titled *Cornelia, Mother of the Gracchi* (or *Cornelia Presenting Her Children as Her Treasures*)

15. Edmonia Lewis (1845–1909)

    - African American Neoclassical sculptor

    - Best known for her sculpture *Forever Free*, depicting freed African American slaves

16. Julia Margaret Cameron (1815–1879)

    - One of the most famous portrait photographers in Victorian England

    - Known for images with a slightly blurred focus

17. Rosa Bonheur (1822–1899)

    - The most celebrated woman artist of the nineteenth century

    - Famous for her realistic paintings of animals

    - *The Horse Fair* is her most famous work

18. Gertrude Kasebier (1852–1934)

    - American photographer

    - Famous for photographs with symbolic themes

    - *Blessed Art Thou Among Women* is her most famous photograph

19. Berthe Morisot (1841–1895)

    - Impressionist artist

    - Married Manet's brother and often posed for Manet

    - Praised for the grace and delicacy of her work

20. Mary Cassatt (1844–1926)

    • American Impressionist

    • Exhibited regularly with the Impressionists

    • Best known for her portraits showing the relationship between mother and child

    • Influenced by Degas and Japanese woodblock prints

21. Gertrude Stein (1874–1946)

    • Important patron of Picasso, Matisse, and other avant-garde artists living in Paris

    • Subject of an important portrait by Picasso

22. Hannah Hoch (1889–1978)

    • Dada artist

    • Known for her photomontages

23. Georgia O'Keeffe (1887–1986)

    • American Precisionist

    • Best known for her detailed paintings of flowers and bones

    • O'Keeffe simplified her subjects almost to the point of complete abstraction

24. Kathe Kollwitz (1867–1945)

    • German Expressionist

    • Best known for her poignant depictions of grief and loss

    • Worked in a variety of printmaking techniques, including woodcut, lithography, and etching

25. Meret Oppenheim (1913–1985)

    • Surrealist artist

    • Best known for *Object* (or *Le Déjeuner en fourrure*), a fur-lined teacup inspired by a conversation with Picasso

26. Frida Kahlo (1907–1954)

    • Mexican Surrealist artist

    • Married to muralist Diego Rivera

    • Best known for her series of self-portraits

27. Barbara Hepworth (1903–1975)

   • Influenced by Brancusi's dictum that sculptors should strive to represent the essence of things

   • *Oval Sculpture* is her most famous work

28. Dorothea Lange (1895–1965)

   • Preeminent American photographer of the Great Depression

   • Most famous picture is *Migrant Mother*

29. Helen Frankenthaler (1928–present)

   • A Post-Painterly Abstractionist

   • Best known for her color field paintings

30. Maya Ying Lin (1960–present)

   • Minimalist sculptor

   • Best known for designing the Vietnam Veterans Memorial in Washington, D.C.

31. Louise Nevelson (1899–1988)

   • American sculptor

   • Best known for creating assemblages—artworks constructed from existing objects

32. Audrey Flack (1931–present)

   • American Superrealist

   • Most famous work is *Marilyn*

   • *Marilyn* can be compared with Dutch vanitas paintings

Chapter 34

Key Figures in American Art

Beginning with the Neoclassical architecture of Thomas Jefferson, American artists, sculptors, and architects have played a prominent role in most artistic styles. This has been particularly true in architecture and in twentieth-century art. Indeed, American artists have played a dominant role in artistic trends since the advent of Abstract Expressionism in 1950.

Most AP Art History exams now have five to six multiple-choice questions devoted to American artists. In addition, there have been seven slide-based multiple-choice questions and five short essay questions since 1999. Our list briefly identifies key figures in American art from Thomas Jefferson to the present.

1. Thomas Jefferson (1743–1826)

   • Spearheaded movement to adopt Neoclassicism as a national architecture

   • Designed Monticello, influenced by the Villa Rotunda and Chiswick House

   • Designed the Virginia State Capitol, influenced by a Roman temple in Nimes in southern France

   • Designed the rotunda at the University of Virginia, influenced by the Pantheon in Rome

2. Edmonia Lewis (1845–1909)

   • African American Neoclassical sculptor

   • Best known for *Forever Free,* depicting freed African American slaves

3. Thomas Cole (1801–1848)

   • Leader of the Hudson River School

   • Famous for his landscape paintings featuring the unspoiled woods and valleys of the Hudson River

   • Best known for *The Oxbow*

4. Winslow Homer (1836–1910)

   •American Realist

   •Best known for his drawings of the Civil War and paintings of the sea

5. Thomas Eakins (1844–1916)

   • Preeminent American Realist

   • Famous for his portraits and genre paintings

   • Best known for *The Gross Clinic*

6. Eadweard Muybridge (1830–1904)

   • Realist photographer

   • Best known for his photographic studies of sequential motion

7. John Singer Sargent (1856–1925)

   • American Realist

   • Best known for his fashionable portraits of leading figures in Europe and America

8. Henry Osswa Tanner (1859–1937)

   • Realist artist who studied with Eakins

   • First important African American artist

   • Works feature dignified portraits of ordinary people

9. Mary Cassatt (1844–1926)

   • American Impressionist

   • Exhibited regularly with the Impressionists

   • Best known for her portraits showing the relationship between a mother and her children

   • Influenced by Degas and Japanese prints

10. Louis Henry Sullivan (1856–1924)

   • Called the first truly modern architect

   • Renowned for his dictum that "form follows function"

   • His synthesis of industrial structure and ornamentation perfectly expressed the spirit of late nineteenth-century commerce

- Best known for designing the Guaranty (Prudential) Building in Buffalo, New York, and the Carson, Pirie, Scott Building in Chicago, Illinois

11. John Sloan (1871–1951)

    - Leading member of the Ashcan School

    - Captured the social realities of American urban life in the early 1900s

12. Alfred Stieglitz (1864–1946)

    - Established the "291" Gallery to promote avant-garde art

    - Renowned photographer and organizer of photographic exhibits

    - Best known for *The Steerage,* a work showing immigrants returning to Europe in the second-class lower decks of a luxury liner

13. Georgia O'Keeffe (1887–1986)

    - American Precisionist

    - Best known for her detailed paintings of flowers

    - O'Keeffe simplified the form of her flowers almost to the point of complete abstraction

14. Aaron Douglas (1898–1979)

    - Leading artist in the Harlem Renaissance

    - Influenced by Synthetic Cubism

15. Frank Lloyd Wright (1867–1959)

    - Considered by many America's greatest architect

    - Believed there should be an organic or harmonious relationship between a building and its site

    - Incorporated concrete cantilevers into his homes

    - Believed that the hearth should be the core of a home

    - Best-known works include the Robie House in Chicago as well as Fallingwater in Bear Run, Pennsylvania

16. Alexander Calder (1898–1976)

    - Fascinated by motion

    - Invented mobiles—delicately balanced sculpture with movable parts set in motion by air currents

17. Dorothea Lange (1895–1965)

   • Preeminent American photographer of the Great Depression

   • Most famous picture is *Migrant Mother*

18. Edward Hopper (1882–1967)

   • Paintings portray the loneliness and isolation of life in the United States

   • Best known for *Nighthawks*, a haunting portrait of urban alienation

19. Jacob Lawrence (1917–2000)

   • Works focus on the culture and history of African Americans

   • Best known for *The Migration of the Negro*, a sixty-painting series depicting the exodus of black labor from the southern United States

20. Grant Wood (1891–1942)

   • American Regionalist

   • Works focus on rural scenes in Iowa

   • Best known for *American Gothic*

21. Thomas Hart Benton (1889–1975)

   • American Regionalist

   • Works focus on life in Missouri

22. Jackson Pollock (1912–1956)

   • Leading Abstract Expressionist artist

   • Works exemplify gestural abstraction

   • Best-known action paintings include *Lavender Mist* and *Autumn Rhythm: Number 30*

23. Barnett Newman (1905–1970)

   • Work exemplifies chromatic abstraction

   • Works often include narrow bands called **zips**

   • Best known for *Vir Heroicus Sublimis* (*Heroic Sublime Man*)

   • Newman used abstraction to convey metaphorical meaning

24. Mark Rothko (1903–1970)

   • Work exemplifies chromatic abstraction

   • Best known for creating works with two or three large rectangles of pure color that seem to float on the canvas

   • Used abstraction to convey metaphorical meaning

25. Ellsworth Kelly (1923–Present)

   • Hard Edge artist

   • Works feature clearly delineated shapes with razor-sharp edges

26. Frank Stella (1936–Present)

   • Hard Edge artist

   • Images often include evenly spaced pinstripes

27. Helen Frankenthaler (1928–Present)

   • A Post-Painterly Abstractionist artist

   • Best known for her color field paintings

28. David Smith (1906–1965)

   • Best known for his *Cubi* series of balanced stainless steel cubes and cylinders

   • Although cantilevered into space, the squares and rectangles convey a sense of poised balance

   • Smith's work had a strong influence on the Minimalists

29. Donald Judd (1928–1994)

   • Minimalist sculptor

   • Best known for machine-made stainless steel, Plexiglas, and plywood boxes arranged in horizontal or vertical rows on walls

30. Maya Ying Lin (1960–Present)

   • Minimalist sculptor

   • Best known for designing the Vietnam Veterans Memorial in Washington, D.C.

31. Louise Nevelson (1899–1988)

   - Known for creating assemblages—artworks constructed from existing objects

   - Best known assemblages include *Sky Cathedral* and *Tropical Garden*

32. Romare Bearden (1911–1988)

   - Influenced by Cubism

   - Best known for photocollages that depict aspects of the African American experience

33. Jasper Johns (1930–Present)

   - Leading Pop artist

   - Works such as *Flag* have highly textured surfaces resulting from John's use of encaustic

34. Roy Lichtenstein (1923–1997)

   - Leading Pop artist

   - Selected many scenes from romance comic books

   - Works often include benday dots—a printing technique that involves the modulation of color through the placement of individual colored dots

35. Andy Warhol (1928–1987)

   - Leading Pop artist

   - Renowned for Pop Art images of consumer goods such as Coke bottles and celebrities such as Marilyn Monroe

36. Claes Oldenburg (1929–Present)

   - Pop sculptor

   - Known for large works of ordinary objects such as spoons, clothespins, and baseball bats

37. Audrey Flack (1931–Present)

   - Leading Superrealist

   - Most famous work is *Marilyn*

   - *Marilyn* can be compared with Dutch vanitas paintings

38. Duane Hanson (1925–1996)

    • Superrealist sculptor

    • Known for sculptures that depict stereotypical average Americans

39. Robert Smithson (1938–1973)

    • Leading Environmental or Earth artist

    • Best known for *Spiral Jetty*, a mammoth coil of black basalt, limestone rocks, and earth that extends into the Great Salt Lake in Utah

40. Frank Gehry (1929–Present)

    • Deconstructivist architect

    • Designed the Guggenheim Museum in Bilbao, Spain, which is renowned for its dramatic titanium-clad exterior

Chapter 35

Key Points About Art Beyond the European Tradition

It is very important to understand what the AP Art History committee means by "art beyond the European tradition." According to the Art History Course Description booklet, artworks from the ancient Near East, Egypt, and Middle East are considered to be beyond the European tradition. This test review book provides comprehensive chapters on each of those topics.

Not covered by this book are Africa (other than Egypt), the Americas, and Asia as the remaining areas that are beyond the European tradition. These cultures created a vast amount of art that could easily generate a full exam, but so far, have not. Previous AP Art History exams have typically included just three to five multiple-choice questions on these three cultural areas. In addition, students must use an example of art from beyond the European tradition to illustrate one of the 25-point essay questions. It is important to remember that you can use examples from the ancient Near East, Egypt, and Middle East to illustrate your answer to that question.

From a purely pragmatic point of view, we recommend that you spend only a modest amount of time reviewing art from Africa (other than Egypt), the Americas, and Asia. Five multiple-choice questions are only worth 3.5 of the 200 points on your exam. The following list of key points is *not* intended to be a comprehensive review of art beyond the European tradition. It is, however, a reasonably complete list of key points asked on recent exams.

Native Arts of the Americas before 1500

1. The Olmecs are best known for carving colossal basalt heads of their rulers.

2. Codices and large narrative murals are the most important forms of painting found in ancient Mesoamerica.

3. The Toltecs erected colossal atlantids. An **atlantid** is a male statue-column.

4. The Mississippians constructed effigy mounds built in the form of animals and birds. The Serpent Mound is an effigy mound located in Ohio.

5. The Anasazi constructed impressive pueblos in the Chaco Canyon and at Mesa Verde. A **pueblo** is a communal multistoried dwelling made of stone or adobe brick.

6. At their height in 1500, the Aztec and Incan empires were contemporary to Renaissance Europe.

Mexican Muralists (Twentieth Century)

1. José Clemente Orozco (1883–1949) painted public murals that depicted scenes from Mexican history. One of his finest mural cycles, *The Epic of American Civilization: Hispano-American,* is located in the Baker Library at Dartmouth College.

2. Diego Rivera (1886–1957) also achieved great renown for painting large public murals depicting scenes from Mexican history.

Benin Art (Africa)

1. Located in what is now Nigeria, the Benin Kingdom thrived between 1400 and 1897. A long line of **Obas**, or kings, decorated their palace columns with bronze plaques and commemorative busts.

2. Cast in bronze, commemorative busts adorned shrines dedicated to the Obas' ancestors. The heads are idealized representations of Benin rulers rather than idealized portraits of the deceased.

3. The Obas sometimes wore ivory pendant masks. One famous example is believed to represent the queen mother. The oba may have worn the mask at rites commemorating his mother.

Buddhist and Hindu Art

1. When the Hindu god Shiva appears in human form, he frequently has four arms. The Dancing Shiva is the most widely known sculpted image of Shiva.

2. A **stupa** is a large, mound-shaped Buddhist reliquary shrine.

3. In Buddhist and Hindu iconography, a **mudra** is a stylized and symbolic hand gesture.

Chinese Art

1. A **pagoda** is a Chinese tower, usually associated with a Buddhist temple. It has a multiplicity of winged eaves, thought to be derived from the Indian stupa.

2. Ink was the favorite medium used to paint Chinese hand scrolls.

3. **Calligraphy**, or the art of writing, was (and still is) highly esteemed in China.

Japanese Art

1. Katsushika Hokusai (1760–1849) and Utagawa Hiroshige (1797–1858) were Japan's greatest woodblock artists.

2. *The Great Wave off Kanagawa* by Hokusai is a woodblock print.

3. Japanese woodblock prints featured areas of flat color and cropped edges.

4. Japanese woodblock prints influenced Impressionists such as Manet and Cassatt and Post-Impressionists such as Van Gogh and Gauguin.

Chapter 36

Fifty Terms You Absolutely, Positively Have to Know

Art historians use a large number of terms to describe works of art. The glossaries of most art history texts contain between seven hundred and eight hundred terms. Fortunately, the AP Art History exam will not cover all those terms. This chapter provides you with a list of the fifty terms that are most frequently included on exams and therefore most important for you to know. Because these terms are used in multiple-choice questions, you do not have to memorize the definitions. Instead, read over the list, and *familiarize* yourself with each term. Once again, remember: **Familiarize, Don't Memorize!**

1. **Pylon:** A pair of truncated, pyramidal towers flanking the entrance to an Egyptian temple. The Temple of Horus at Edfu has a particularly well-preserved pylon entrance.

2. **Hypostyle:** A hall with a roof supported by rows of columns. The Temple of Amon-Re at Karnak has an enormous hypostyle hall.

3. **Hierarchical scale:** The representation of more important figures as larger than less important ones. The sculptor who carved the *Victory Stele of Narim-Sin* used hierarchical scale to indicate Narim-Sin's lofty status.

4. **Register:** One of a series of rows in a pictorial narrative. For excellent examples of registers, see the *Standard of Ur* and the *Palette of King Narmer.*

5. **Repoussé:** A technique in which a relief is formed on the front by hammering a metal plate from the back. The funerary masks discovered at Mycenae were created using the repoussé technique.

6. **Corbelled vault:** A vault formed by the piling of stone blocks in horizontal courses, cantilevered inward until the two walls meet in an arch. The Lion's Gate at Mycenae provides an excellent example of a corbelled vault and a relieving triangle.

7. **Kouros:** An Archaic Greek statue of a standing nude male.

8. **Kore:** An Archaic Greek statue of a standing, draped female.

9. **Caryatid:** A column carved to represent a woman. The Erechtheum is famous for its porch of caryatids.

10. **Pediment:** In Classical architecture, the triangular section of a temple roof often decorated with sculpture.

11. **Entablature:** In Classical architecture, the part of a building above the columns and below the roof. The entablature of a Classical temple includes the architrave, frieze, and cornice.

12. **Contrapposto:** The relaxed natural pose, or "weight shift," first introduced in Greek sculpture in 480 BCE. First used in *Kritios Boy*, contrapposto separates Classical from Archaic Greek statuary.

13. **Frieze:** In Classical architecture, a frieze is a continuous horizontal band of sculptural decoration. The Ionic frieze in the Parthenon depicts the Panathenaic Procession.

14. **Mosaic:** Images composed of small pieces of colored glass or stone. The *Alexander Mosaic* shows Alexander the Great pursuing Darius III at the Battle of Issus. The Romans often used mosaics to decorate their floors.

15. **Voussoir:** A wedge-shaped block used in the construction of a true arch. The central voussoir, which sets the arch, is called the keystone.

16. **Pendentive:** The concave triangular section of a vault that forms the transition between a square or polygonal space and the circular base of a dome. Pendentives, or dome supports, enabled Byzantine architects to construct the dome for Hagia Sophia.

17. **Iconoclasm:** A movement in the Byzantine Empire that favored banning and destroying images. The destroyers of images were known as iconoclasts.

18. **Encaustic:** A painting technique in which pigment is mixed with wax and applied to the surface while hot. Sixth- and seventh-century Byzantine artists used encaustic to create panel paintings. Interestingly, Jasper Johns used encaustic in his famous painting titled *Flag*.

19. **Enamel:** A technique in which powdered glass is applied to a metal surface in a decorative design.

20. **Mihrab:** A semicircular niche set into the qibla wall of a mosque.

21. **Westwork:** The facade and towers at the western end of a medieval church, principally in Germany.

22. **Ambulatory:** The passageway around the apse and choir of a church. The ambulatory was originally a feature of Romanesque churches that developed in connection with their use as pilgrimage centers.

23. **Tympanum:** The lunette-shaped space above the portals of Romanesque and Gothic churches.

24. **Clerestory:** A row of windows in the upper part of a wall.

25. **Barrel vault:** A vault is a roof or ceiling. A barrel vault is, in effect, a deep arch or an uninterrupted series of arches. Roman architects used barrel vaults in the construction of the Colosseum and the Baths of Caracalla. Barrel vaults are one of the characteristic features of Romanesque churches.

26. **Groin vault:** Vault formed at the point at which two barrel vaults intersect at right angles. Groin vaults are one of the characteristic features of Gothic cathedrals.

27. **Crypt:** A vaulted space usually located under the apse of a church. Because a crypt is wholly or partly underground, it is not found in the nave elevation of a church.

28. **Vellum:** Calfskin prepared as a surface for writing or painting. The *Lindisfarne Gospels* use tempera on vellum, and the calendar pictures of *Les Trés Riches Heures* use ink on vellum.

29. **Diptych:** A two-paneled painting or altarpiece. The *Melun Diptych* by Jean Fouquet is a famous example of a diptych.

30. **Triptych:** A three-paneled painting or altarpiece. Famous examples of triptychs include the *Garden of Earthly Delights* by Hieronymous Bosch, the *Merode Altarpiece* by Robert Campin, and the *Portinari Altarpiece* by Hugo van der Goes.

31. **Predella:** The painted or sculpted lower portion of an altarpiece that relates to the subjects of the upper portion.

32. **Chiaroscuro:** In drawing or painting, the treatment and use of light and dark, especially by gradations of light that produce the effect of mottling. Masaccio demonstrated his mastery of chiaroscuro in the *Tribute Money*.

33. **Cartoon:** In painting, a full-size preliminary drawing from which a painting is made. Da Vinci's *Virgin and Child with Saint Anne and the Infant Saint John* is a famous example of a cartoon.

34. **Ecorche:** A figure painted or sculpted to show the muscles of the body as if without skin. Pollaiuolo's *Battle of the Ten Nudes* is a famous example of an engraving that uses ecorche.

35. **Orthogonal:** A line imagined to be behind and perpendicular to the picture plane. The orthogonals in a painting appear to recede toward a vanishing point. The orthogonals can be clearly seen in Perugino's *Christ Delivering the Keys of the Kingdom*.

36. **Intaglio:** A graphic technique in which the design is incised, or scratched, on a metal plate, either manually (*engraving*) or chemically (*etching*). The incised lines of the design take the ink, making this the reverse of the woodcut technique.

37. **Impasto:** Technique in which the artist applies thick layers of oil paint. Both Rembrandt and Van Gogh used impasto in their works.

38. **Japonisme:** The French fascination with all things Japanese. Japonisme emerged in the second half of the nineteenth century. The Impressionists and Post-Impressionists were particularly impressed with the use of bold contour lines, flat areas of color, and cropped edges in Japanese woodblock prints.

39. **Avant-garde:** Late nineteenth- and twentieth-century artists whose work emphasized innovation and challenged established conventions.

40. **Bauhaus:** A school of architecture in Germany in the 1920s under the leadership of Walter Gropius.

41. **Ready-made:** An ordinary object that, when an artist gives it a new context and title, is transformed into an art object. Ready-mades were important features of the Dada and Surrealism movements of the early twentieth century. Marcel Duchamp's *Fountain* is a famous example of a ready-made.

42. **Cantilever:** A beam or structure that is anchored at one end and projects horizontally beyond its vertical support. In Fallingwater, Frank Lloyd Wright made a particularly dramatic use of cantilevers.

43. **Biomorphic:** An adjective used to describe forms that resemble or suggest shapes found in nature. Biomorphs are therefore not abstract shapes. An excellent example of a work that uses biomorphs is *Painting* and *Composition* by Joan Miró.

44. **Assemblage:** An artwork constructed from existing objects. Louise Nevelson is famous for creating assemblages such as *Sky Tower* and *Tropical Garden*.

45. **Photomontage:** A composition made by pasting together pictures or parts of pictures, especially photographs. Also called a photocollage. Hannah Hoch and Romare Bearden created noteworthy examples of photomontages.

46. **Stupa:** A large, mound-shaped Buddhist shrine.

47. **Pagoda:** A multistoried Chinese tower, usually associated with a Buddhist temple, having a multiplicity of projecting eaves.

48. **Pueblo:** A communal multistoried dwelling made of stone or adobe brick by the Native Americans of the Southwest. The Cliff Palace at Mesa Verde is an excellent example of a pueblo.

49. **Mudrah:** In Buddhist and Hindu iconography, a stylized and symbolic hand gesture.

50. **Ukiyo-e:** Japanese for "pictures of the floating world." A style of Japanese genre painting that influenced nineteenth-century Western art.

Chapter 37

Our Top Picks

Art history textbooks are usually more than a thousand pages long. Theoretically, any image or fact could be on the AP Art History exam. Fortunately, the exam committee focuses on key facts and works of art. Here are the key facts and works of art that are our top picks. Good luck!

Our Top Ten Sculptures

1. *Bust of Nefertiti*

   - A painted limestone bust

   - Carved in the Amarna style

   - Created during the New Kingdom of Egypt

   - Nefertiti was one of Akhenaton's queens

2. *Doryphoros*

   - Carved by Polykleitos

   - Best described as depicting an ideal athlete or warrior

   - Originally known as the *Canon* because it epitomized the ideal proportions of Classical Greek sculpture

   - Excellent example of contrapposto

   - Dates to between 450 and 440 BCE

3. *Statue of Augustus from Primaporta*

   - Pose is based on the *Doryphoros*

   - Illustrates Roman use of art as propaganda

   - Presents the image of a godlike leader who never aged

   - Breastplate depicts the return of a Roman military standard

   - Cupid reminds us of Augustus's divine ancestors

4. *Tetrarchs*

   • Originally in Constantinople, now in Saint Mark's, Venice

   • Portrays the four Roman rulers of the tetrarchy

   • Drapery is schematic, and bodies are shapeless

   • Faces are emotionless masks

5. *Gero Crucifix*

   • Commissioned by Archbishop Gero

   • Style is Ottonian

   • Carved in oak and then painted and gilded

   • Six-foot-tall image of Christ nailed to the cross is both a statue and a reliquary

   • Powerful image that emphasizes Christ's suffering

6. *Nymph and Satyr*

   • Carved by Clodion

   • Style is Rococo

   • Standing just under 2 feet high, illustrates the Rococo penchant for small works

7. *Forever Free*

   • Carved by Edmonia Lewis

   • Style is Neoclassic

   • Depicts freed African American slaves

8. *George Washington*

   • Carved by Jean-Antoine Houdon

   • Style is Neoclassic

   • Natural contrapposto pose

   • Washington wears a general's uniform, but the sword, no longer needed in peacetime, is suspended from a bundle of thirteen rods, one for each of the original states

   • Plow behind his feet symbolizes peace

9. *Jaguar Devouring a Hare*

   - Sculpted by Antoine-Louis Barye

   - Style is Romantic

   - Demonstrates the Romantic interest in strong emotion and untamed nature

10. Ivory Belt Mask of a Queen Mother

   - Commissioned by Oba Esigie, the Benin king who ruled from 1504 to 1550

   - The mask probably represents the queen mother, Idia

   - Made of ivory

   - Heads are symbolic references to Benin's trade and diplomatic relations with the Portuguese

   - The mudfish are symbolic references to Olokun, god of the sea, wealth, and creativity

Our Top Ten Works of Architecture

1. Stepped Pyramid of King Djoser

   - Designed by Imhotep

   - Imhotep is the first named artist in recorded history

   - Built during the Old Kingdom

   - Located at Saqqara

   - Composed of a series of mastabas of diminishing size

   - A tomb, *not* a temple platform

   - Designed to protect Djoser's mummy and symbolize his power

   - All columns in the Saqqara complex are engaged or attached. Still, this marks the first appearance of columns in the history of architecture.

2. Parthenon

   - Commissioned by Pericles

   - Centerpiece of a massive building project on the Acropolis

   - Doric temple designed by Iktinos and Kallikrates

   - Sculptural program designed and supervised by Phidias

- Temple dedicated to Athena and celebrates wisdom

- Contains Doric metopes and an Ionic frieze depicting the Panathenaic Procession

3. Arch of Titus

- Product of imperial Rome

- Relief sculptures celebrate Roman military victories

- Shows Romans carrying the seven-branched menorah from the Temple in Jerusalem

- Spandrels contain figures representing Victory, known in Greek as *Nike*

- Arch was placed on the Sacred Way into the Forum Romana

- Admired by Napoleon, who used it as the model for the Arc de Triomphe in Paris

4. Pantheon

- Temple dedicated to all the gods

- One of the best-preserved buildings of antiquity

- Traditional front portico

- Rotunda consisting of a drum and a dome

- Dome is a huge hemisphere 142 feet high and 142 feet in diameter

- Dome's weight was lessened through the use of coffers, or sunken decorative panels

- Round opening or oculus allows light to enter the building

- Influenced Palladio's design for the Villa Rotunda

5. San Vitale, Ravenna

- Built during the reign of Justinian

- Plan is best described as centralized

- Odd angle of the narthex has never been explained

- Contains the most complete collection of surviving Byzantine mosaics, including mosaics depicting Justinian and Theodora

- Design of San Vitale influenced the design of the Palatine Chapel of Charlemagne

6. Palazzo Pubblico, Siena

   - Style is Late Gothic

   - Served as Siena's town hall and thus the city's secular center

   - Tower served as a fortified lookout

7. Sant' Andrea, Mantua

   - Commissioned by Ludovico Gonzaga

   - Designed by Alberti

   - Facade pilasters run uninterrupted through three stories in an early application of the colossal or giant order later used by Michelangelo

   - Facade also includes a triumphal arch derived from Roman arches

   - Pilasters and an arch support a classically inspired pediment

   - Facade's height and width are equal

   - Interior barrel vault may have been inspired by the ruined Basilica Nova of Constantine

8. Villa Rotunda

   - Designed by Palladio

   - A country villa

   - Had a significant influence on Neoclassical architects

   - Strongly influenced the design of Chiswick House

9. Casa Mila, Barcelona

   - Designed by Antonio Gaudi

   - Style is Art Nouveau

   - Building is an apartment house

   - Rough surface of the stone walls suggests naturally worn rock

   - Gaudi's passionate naturalism inspired Expressionist painting and sculpture

10. Robie House, Chicago

   - Designed by Frank Lloyd Wright

   - Fulfills Wright's dictum that a building should be an organic part of its environment

- Uses dramatic cantilevers

- Rooms are grouped around a huge central fireplace

- Illustrates Wright's naturalism—his adjustment of a building to its site

Our Top Ten Paintings and Engravings

1. Carpet Page from the *Lindisfarne Gospels*

   - Style is Hiberno-Saxon

   - Work is tempera on vellum

   - Produced by monks for devotional worship

   - Called a carpet page because it resembles a beautiful carpet

   - Features intricate interlace patterns

   - The interlaced patterns are based on earlier Celtic metalwork

2. Merode Altarpiece

   - Painted by Robert Campin, the Master of Flemalle, during Flemish Renaissance

   - Work is a triptych

   - Subject is the Annunciation

   - Campin makes extensive use of disguised symbols

   - During the time in which the Merode Altarpiece was painted, patronage shifted from ecclesiastical patrons to private donors

   - The couple portrayed on the left wing are the donors

3. *Battle of the Ten Nudes*

   - Pollaiuolo is the graphic artist

   - Medium is engraving

   - Focus is on the human figure in action

   - Pollaiuolo's figures are so lean and muscular that they appear ecorche—as if without skin

4. *The Fetus and Lining of the Uterus*

   - Drawn by Leonardo da Vinci

   - Demonstrates Leonardo's interest in the scientific study of anatomy

   - Drawing is from Leonardo's extensive collection of notebooks

5. *School of Athens*

   - Commissioned by Pope Julius II

   - Painted by Raphael

   - Work is a fresco

   - Raphael was trained by Perugino

   - Work expresses Neoplatonic ideas

   - Work includes a self-portrait

6. *The Fall of Man*

   - Dürer is the graphic artist

   - Work is an engraving

   - Engraving enabled artists to create multiple copies of a work

   - Dürer was a German

   - Dürer was the first Northern Renaissance artist to fully absorb the innovations of the Italian Renaissance

   - Ideal human forms of Adam and Eve are based on Classical models Dürer studied during his trips to Italy

   - Dürer's distinctive signature is a Renaissance trademark

   - Detailed forest is clearly Northern Renaissance

7. *Arrival of Marie de' Medici at Marseilles*

   - Commissioned by Marie de' Medici

   - Painted by Rubens

   - Part of a series of twenty-one huge historical-allegorical paintings

   - Style is Flemish Baroque

   - Rubens also painted landscapes, portraits, and ceiling paintings

8. *The Nightmare*

   - Painting is by Henri Fuseli

   - Style is Romantic

   - Artist is interested in human psychology

9. *The Great Wave off Kanagawa*

   - Graphic artist is Katsushika Hokusai

   - Work is a woodblock print

   - Created during the Edo period

   - Part of a series of thirty-six prints

10. *The Migration of the Negro*

    - Part of a series of sixty paintings by Jacob Lawrence

    - Paintings in this series show the influence of Cubism

    - Artist uses expressive colors and rhythmic patterns

    - Paintings depict the northward migration of African Americans after World War I

    - Lawrence's interest in social justice for everyday people places him in the tradition of artists such as Honoré Daumier

Our Top Ten Key Facts

1. Early Christian figures are usually carved from ivory.

2. Pietro Cavallini's *Seated Apostles* influenced Giotto.

3. Louis Le Nain's paintings of peasants are most similar to those of Breugel the Elder.

4. A cartoon is a full-scale sketch.

5. Michelangelo's *Moses* was intended to be part of the tomb of Pope Julius II.

6. Annibale Carracci's ceiling fresco titled *Loves of the Gods* was influenced by Michelangelo's Sistine Chapel ceiling.

7. Antonio Canova was a Neoclassical sculptor who was especially popular during the early 1800s.

8. The Pre-Raphaelites worked in England during the second half of the nineteenth century.

9. Chemist Michel-Eugene Chevreul's color theories had an important influence on the work of Seurat and other Post-Impressionists.

10. The *Dinner Party* by Judy Chicago is a multimedia work designed to educate viewers about women's role in history.

Our Top Five Topics for the Free-Response Question Requiring Students to Incorporate at Least One Example of Art Beyond the European Tradition

1. Works of art that have a healing function:

   • Matthias Grunewald, Isenheim Altarpiece

   • Nail Figure, *Nkisi Nkonde*, Kongo

2. Sculptures that depict ordinary people in genre scenes:

   • Hellenistic, *Old Market Woman*

   • Duane Hanson, *Tourists*

3. Landscapes based on views of mountains:

   • Cezanne, *Mont Sainte-Victoire*

   • Hokusai, *The Great Wave off Kanagawa*

4. Monuments that are funerary works of art:

   • Maya Lin, Vietnam Veterans Memorial

   • Mortuary Temple of Hatshepsut

5. Works of art that express war in a highly expressive, symbolic way:

   • Picasso, *Guernica*

   • *Victory Stele of Naram-Sin*

PRACTICE EXAMS

AP Art History

PRACTICE EXAM 1

This exam is also on CD-ROM in our
special interactive AP Art History TEST*ware*®

AP Art History

Slide-Based Multiple-Choice and Free-Response Questions

Section I, Part A

TIME: 16 minutes
32 questions

DIRECTIONS: Questions 1–32 are divided into sets of questions based
on slides. In these sets, each question or incomplete statement is followed
by four suggested answers or completions. Select the one that is best for
each question, and then fill in the corresponding oval on the answer sheet.
The slide or slides for each group of questions will appear on the screen
for 4 minutes.

Note: This exam uses BCE (before the common era) and CE (common era) as chronological labels rather than BC (before Christ) and AD (anno Domini).

**Questions 1–8 are based on the slides you see on the screen. The slides will
be shown for 4 minutes only.**

1.   The image on the left dates from the

   (A)   eighth century BCE

   (B)   sixth century BCE

   (C)   fifth century BCE

   (D)   third century BCE

2.   The image on the left

   (A)   commemorated a historical event

   (B)   decorated an Assyrian palace

   (C)   adorned the Altar of Zeus at Pergamon

   (D)   marked the grave of a Greek male

3.   The stylistic qualities of the image on the right could best be described as

   (A)   Orientalizing

   (B)   white figure

   (C)   Hellenistic

   (D)   Byzantine

4.   The image on the right can be dated to a later period than the image on the left because of

   (A)   the medium used

   (B)   its highly developed naturalism

   (C)   the inclusion of drapery

   (D)   its intended purpose

5.   The pose of the image on the left shows the influence of art from

   (A)   Sumerian cities

   (B)   ancient Egypt

   (C)   the Roman Republic

   (D)   the Benin Kingdom

6. Sculptures that were contemporary with the image on the right are best known for

   (A) expressive and veristic qualities

   (B) their glorification of youthful males

   (C) a high degree of figural abstraction

   (D) aloofness and pious reserve

7. The work most similar in subject matter to the image on the right is the

   (A) *Doryphoros*

   (B) *Kritios Boy*

   (C) *Seated Boxer*

   (D) *Aphrodite of Knidos*

8. The most significant city, culturally and politically, during the period in which the image on the right was produced was

   (A) Athens

   (B) Nineveh

   (C) Karnak

   (D) Pergamon

Questions 9–17 are based on the slides you see on the screen. The slides will be shown for 4 minutes only.

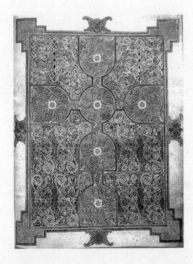

9.   The image on the left dates from approximately

(A)   500 CE

(B)   700 CE

(C)   900 CE

(D)   1100 CE

10.   The image on the left is a page from the

(A)   *Akbarnama*

(B)   *Tale of Genji*

(C)   *Last Judgment of Hu-Nefer*

(D)   *Lindisfarne Gospels*

11.   The image on the left is painted on

(A)   papyrus

(B)   paper

(C)   vellum

(D)   silk

12.   Which of the following characteristics does NOT apply to the image on the left?

(A)   It is referred to as a carpet page.

(B)   It is from the Carolingian Renaissance.

(C)   It contains a Celtic cross.

(D)   It contains designs known as interlace.

13.   The image on the right is an example of

(A)   Gestural abstraction

(B)   Chromatic abstraction

(C)   Minimalism

(D)   German Expressionism

14.   The artist who produced the image on the right is most likely

(A)   Barnett Newman

(B)   Emile Nolde

(C)   Mark Rothko

(D)   Jackson Pollock

15. The city that was most prominent in the art world during the time in which the image on the right was created was

    (A) New York City

    (B) Dresden

    (C) Paris

    (D) Rome

16. The image on the right was painted in the

    (A) 1910s

    (B) 1930s

    (C) 1950s

    (D) 1970s

17. Both the image on the right and image on the left

    (A) use sensuous color

    (B) lack spatial recession

    (C) contain a narrative

    (D) have abstract figural elements

Questions 18–25 are based on the slides you see on the screen. The slides will be shown for 4 minutes only.

18. The image on the left is generally referred to as

    (A) a *fête galante*

    (B) a genre scene

    (C) a historical narrative

    (D) propagandistic

19. The painter of the image on the left is considered the first great painter of the

    (A) Baroque period

    (B) Rococo period

    (C) Neoclassical style

    (D) Impressionist style

20. The use of color in the image on the left was most likely influenced by

    (A) Poussin

    (B) Le Nain

    (C) Chardin

    (D) Rubens

21. The image on the right is an example of the work of a

    (A) Pre-Raphaelite

    (B) Classicist

    (C) Realist

    (D) Symbolist

22. The painter of the image on the right also painted

    (A) *The Stonebreakers*

    (B) *The Angelus*

    (C) *Mother of the Gracchi*

    (D) *Jupiter and Semele*

23. The image on the right was criticized for its

    (A) lack of attention to naturalism

    (B) coarse depiction of the subject matter

    (C) use of a somber palette of color

    (D) affiliation with Romanticism

24. Images such as that on the left were denounced by

    (A) Fragonard

    (B) Boucher

    (C) David

    (D) Rigaud

25. An artist with similar interests to the artist of the image on the right was

    (A) Millet

    (B) Delacroix

    (C) Ingres

    (D) Bouguereau

Questions 26–32 are based on the slides you see on the screen. The slides will be shown for 4 minutes only.

26. The medium of the image on the left is

    (A) encaustic   (C) oil on panel

    (B) egg tempera   (D) fresco buon

27. The misty quality of the image on the left is known as

    (A) cross-hatching

    (B) sfumato

    (C) divisionism

    (D) color patches

28. The artist of the image on the left is also known for his

    (A) numerous finished paintings

    (B) monumental ceiling frescoes

    (C) design for the Campidoglio

    (D) detailed anatomical drawings

29. The artist of the image on the right is

    (A) Seurat

    (B) Munch

    (C) Matisse

    (D) Kandinsky

30. The style of the image on the right is referred to as

    (A) Expressionism

    (B) Fauvism

    (C) Postpainterly Abstraction

    (D) Symbolism

31. Paintings such as the one in the image on the right were first exhibited publicly at the

    (A) Salon Universelle, 1855

    (B) Salon des Refuses, 1863

    (C) Salon d' Automne, 1905

    (D) Armory Show, 1913

32. Both images share all the following characteristics EXCEPT

    (A) the arbitrary use of color

    (B) use of three-quarter pose

    (C) interest in portraiture

    (D) the female as objet d'art

Section I, Part B

TIME: 44 minutes
      83 questions

DIRECTIONS: Each question or incomplete statement in this section is followed by four suggested answers or completions. Select the one that is best in each case and then fill in the corresponding oval on the answer sheet.

---

33. Isabella d'Este was a

    (A) well-known Caravaggista

    (B) leading patron of Renaissance art

    (C) subject of one of Verrochio's portraits

    (D) Spanish queen who sponsored Velazquez

34. Diego Rivera and José Orozco are best known for

    (A) painting mural cycles designed to dramatize Mexican history

    (B) sculpting public statues commemorating key heroes from the Mexican Revolution

    (C) supporting avant-garde Mexican artists

    (D) designing Mexico's first skyscrapers

35. Which of the following structures use groin vaults?

    (A) The Parthenon

    (B) The Baths of Caracalla

    (C) The Eiffel Tower

    (D) The Seagram Building

36. All of the following architects were influenced by classical Roman buildings EXCEPT

    (A) Leon Battista Alberti

    (B) Andrea Palladio

    (C) Jacques-Germain Soufflot

    (D) Gerrit Rietveld

37. Which of the following is one part of the entablature of a classical temple?

    (A) Capital

    (B) Pediment

    (C) Architrave

    (D) Cult statue

38. The semicircular niche set into the qibla wall of an Islamic mosque is called a

    (A) metope

    (B) mihrab

    (C) tympanum

    (D) minaret

Questions 39–42 refer to the following illustration.

39. The artist of the work is

    (A) Alfred Stieglitz   (C) Marcel Duchamp

    (B) Aaron Douglas   (D) Georges Braque

40. The work created a sensation when it was displayed at the

    (A) Salon des Refusés, 1863

    (B) Columbian Exposition, 1893

    (C) Salon d'Automne, 1905

    (D) Armory Show, 1913

41. The artist's fragmented presentation of the human form was influenced by

    (A) Analytic Cubism

    (B) Surrealism

    (C) German Expressionism

    (D) Fauvism

42. The work's sense of sequential motion shows the influence of

    (A) Thomas Eakins   (C) Claude Monet

    (B) Eadweard Muybridge   (D) Henri Matisse

43. Which of the following would have been most likely to purchase a work by Frans Hals?

    (A) An English duke

    (B) An Italian cardinal

    (C) A Spanish king

    (D) A Dutch shopkeeper

44. Renaissance humanists revived all of the following Roman artistic forms EXCEPT

    (A) still lifes

    (B) equestrian statues

    (C) sculptured busts

    (D) free-standing nude statues

45. Helen Frankenthaler is best known for her

    (A) stain paintings   (C) mobiles

    (B) assemblages   (D) hard-edge paintings

46. Louis Le Nain and Pieter Bruegel the Elder are both known for paintings

    (A) satirizing middle-class foibles

    (B) dramatizing biblical stories

    (C) celebrating the charms of aristocratic life

    (D) depicting the hardships of peasant life

47. The *Bayeux Tapestry* provides a pictorial narrative of the

    (A) destruction of the Temple in Jerusalem

    (B) construction of the Versailles Palace

    (C) Roman victory over the Dacians

    (D) Norman conquest of England

Questions 48–50 refer to the following illustration.

48. The work was commissioned by

    (A) Bishop Bernward

    (B) Archbishop Gero

    (C) Abbot Suger

    (D) Pope Julius II

49. Because it contains sacred religious objects, the work is both a statue and a

    (A) sarcophagus

    (B) reliquary

    (C) triptych

    (D) predella

50. The emotional power of the work suggests that its style is

    (A) Late Roman

    (B) Early Christian

    (C) Hiberno-Saxon

    (D) Ottonian

51. Which of the following is NOT a true statement about the *Palette of Narmer*?

    (A) It is divided into horizontal registers.

    (B) It commemorates the political unification of Upper and Lower Egypt.

    (C) It uses hierarchical scale to show rank.

    (D) It uses high relief to enhance the visibility of its central figures.

52. All the following Greek sculptors are correctly paired with the statues they created EXCEPT

    (A) Polykleitos and the *Doryphoros*

    (B) Praxiteles and *Aphrodite of Knidos*

    (C) Lysippos and *Kritios Boy*

    (D) Phidias and *Athena Parthenos*

Questions 53–55 refer to the following illustration.

53. This scene is part of a continuous band of sculptural decoration known as

    (A) an archivolt

    (B) a pediment

    (C) a frieze

    (D) an entablature

54. The figures were originally part of the

    (A) library in Alexandria

    (B) Parthenon in Athens

    (C) Pantheon in Rome

    (D) Altar of Zeus in Pergamon

55. The violent movement, swirling draperies, and emotional intensity indicate that the work is from the

    (A) Geometric period

    (B) Archaic period

    (C) Classical period

    (D) Hellenistic period

56. Which city and artistic style are NOT correctly paired?

    (A) New York City and Abstract Expressionism

    (B) Paris and Impressionism

    (C) Moscow and Constructionism

    (D) London and de Stijl

57. Which historic figure was most often portrayed by Neoclassical artists?

    (A) Napoleon

    (B) Saint Francis

    (C) Alexander the Great

    (D) Charlemagne

58. All of the following artists produced important works in the graphic arts EXCEPT

    (A) Titian   (C) Goya

    (B) Dürer   (D) Rembrandt

59. Which of the following is NOT true of the Crystal Palace?

    (A) It was built to house the Grand Exhibition of 1851.

    (B) It was built with prefabricated parts.

    (C) It was constructed out of cast iron and glass.

    (D) It was inspired by "Indian Gothic" features such as domes, minarets, and screens.

60. Which of the following artists is most closely associated with the Northern Renaissance?

   (A) Petrus Christus   (C) Masaccio

   (B) Raphael   (D) Titian

61. Élisabeth Vigée-Lebrun and Adélaïde Labille-Guiard were both leading portraitists during the

   (A) late sixteenth century

   (B) late seventeenth century

   (C) late eighteenth century

   (D) late nineteenth century

Questions 62–65 refer to the following illustration.

62. The artist of the work is

   (A) Sandro Botticelli

   (B) Donatello

   (C) Masaccio

   (D) Antonio Pollaiuolo

63. The work exemplifies the artist's interest in

   (A) depicting a contemporary event

   (B) decrying the rivalry between Florence and Siena

   (C) depicting the male body reacting under tension

   (D) commenting on a controversial religious issue

64. The medium of the work is

    (A) engraving

    (B) watercolor

    (C) oil painting

    (D) repoussé

65. The figures in the work were clearly influenced by

    (A) Classical sources

    (B) Early Christian sources

    (C) Byzantine sources

    (D) Carolingian sources

66. Robert Smithson's *Spiral Jetty* is an example of

    (A) Environmental Art

    (B) Pop Art

    (C) Minimalism

    (D) Superrealism

67. A symbolic hand gesture used in representations of the Buddha is called a(n)

    (A) nemes

    (B) mudra

    (C) minbar

    (D) orant

68. Which city was Florence's chief rival during the early Renaissance?

    (A) Rome   (C) Naples

    (B) Siena   (D) Milan

69. Thomas Eakins was committed to portraying

    (A) the realities of the human experience

    (B) the workings of the subconscious mind

    (C) the fantasies of wealthy patrons

    (D) the fleeting effects of light and atmosphere

70. When did Canova create his most important works?

    (A) early seventeenth century

    (B) early eighteenth century

    (C) early nineteenth century

    (D) early twentieth century

Questions 71–72 refer to the following illustration.

71. The work was sculpted by

    (A) Edmonia Lewis

    (B) Francois Rude

    (C) Antoine-Louis Barye

    (D) Camille Claudel

72. The male figure's heroic contrapposto stance is reminiscent of

    (A) Armarna statues

    (B) Classical statues

    (C) High Gothic statues

    (D) Mannerist statues

Questions 73–75 refer to the following illustration.

73. The work is an early example of

   (A) Pop Art

   (B) Abstract expressionism

   (C) Superrealism

   (D) Postmodernism

74. The work is a

   (A) fresco   (C) collage

   (B) mosaic   (D) limestone relief

75. The work includes references to all of the following EXCEPT

   (A) religious symbols

   (B) popular culture

   (C) advertising

   (D) mass media

76. Jean-Antoine Houdon is best known for carving individualized portrait sculptures in the

   (A) Baroque style   (C) Neoclassical style

   (B) Rococo style   (D) Romantic style

77. Which of the following is a characteristic of Roman architecture?

    (A) Corbelled vaulting

    (B) Cantilevers

    (C) Arches and columns

    (D) Flying buttresses

78. The term *encaustic* refers to a

    (A) painting technique in which pigment is mixed with wax and applied to a surface while hot

    (B) kind of engraving in which the design is incised in a layer of wax on a metal plate

    (C) painting technique in which pigments are mixed with water and applied to a wet plaster surface

    (D) drawing technique in which fine lines are drawn close together to achieve the effect of shading

79. All the following artists created collages EXCEPT

    (A) Romare Bearden   (C) Pablo Picasso

    (B) Henri Matisse   (D) Mark Rothko

80. A voussoir would be found in

    (A) a Greek temple   (C) a Sumerian ziggurat

    (B) a Roman aqueduct   (D) an Egyptian temple

Questions 81–83 refer to the following illustration.

81. The building in the foreground was designed by

    (A) Victor Horta and Antonio Gaudi

    (B) Louis Sullivan and Frank Lloyd Wright

    (C) Gerrit Rietveld and Piet Mondrian

    (D) Ludwig Mies van der Rohe and Philip Johnson

82. The sleek, rectilinear form of the building embodies the

    (A) Baroque style   (C) International style

    (B) Neo-Gothic style   (D) Postmodern style

83. The building is notable for its

    (A) revolutionary use of cantilevers

    (B) eclectic combination of styles

    (C) lack of architectural ornamentation

    (D) use of organic forms

84. All the following are associated with Neoclassicism EXCEPT

    (A) Antonio Canova

    (B) Jacques-Louis David

    (C) Eugène Delacroix

    (D) Thomas Jefferson

85. Which of the following was a Romantic sculptor who specialized in scenes of violent animal behavior?

    (A) Francois Rude

    (B) Antoine-Louis Barye

    (C) Rosa Bonheur

    (D) Jean-Antoine Houdon

86. All of the following are characteristics of Mannerist paintings EXCEPT

    (A) staged, contrived imagery

    (B) elongated figures in twisted poses

    (C) crowded compositions with asymmetrical groups of figures

    (D) beams of light that highlight key figures and actions

87. The Serpent Mound is located in

    (A) Ohio

    (B) New Mexico

    (C) Mexico

    (D) Guatemala

88. The Vietnam Veterans Memorial by Maya Ying Lin is best described as an example of

    (A) Performance Art   (C) Pop Art

    (B) Conceptual Art   (D) Minimalist Art

89. Which Dutch artist is best known for painting a series of insightful self-portraits?

    (A) Frans Hals

    (B) Jan Vermeer

    (C) Rembrandt van Rijn

    (D) Jacob van Ruisdael

90. The work of Umberto Boccioni exemplifies

    (A) Symbolism

    (B) Futurism

    (C) Suprematism

    (D) Constructivism

Questions 91–93 refer to the following illustration.

91. The Stepped Pyramid of Djoser was constructed during the

    (A) Old Kingdom

    (B) Middle Kingdom

    (C) New Kingdom

    (D) Late Kingdom

92. It is believed to have been designed by

    (A) Senmut

    (B) Khafre

    (C) Imhotep

    (D) Akhenaton

93. Which of the following statements about the Stepped Pyramid is NOT accurate?

    (A) It is composed of a series of mastabas of diminishing size.

    (B) It is part of a mortuary precinct.

    (C) It was built at approximately the same time as the Sumerian Royal Cemetery at Ur.

    (D) It is both a tomb and a temple platform.

94. Which of the following northern Renaissance painters was most directly influenced by Italian art of the fifteenth and early sixteenth centuries?

    (A) Jan van Eyck

    (B) Albrecht Dürer

    (C) Pieter Bruegel the Elder

    (D) Rogier van der Weyden

95. Which of the following Roman monuments contains a relief panel depicting Roman soldiers carrying spoils from the Temple in Jerusalem?

    (A) Arch of Titus

    (B) Trajan's Column

    (C) Pantheon

    (D) Ara Pacis

Questions 96–99 refer to the following illustration.

96. This work was created by

(A) Nadar

(B) Honoré Daumier

(C) Jean-Francois Millet

(D) Caspar David Friedrich

97. The medium of the work is

(A) oil on canvas

(B) collage

(C) lithograph

(D) fresco

98. The work depicts

(A) a dream or fantasy

(B) an outcry against conformity

(C) an idealized image of contemporary life

(D) the aftermath of an atrocity

99. The medium enabled the artist to

(A) create an unprecedented number of copies

(B) explore the transient effect of atmosphere and color

(C) use the new pointillist technique

(D) advertise his skills to important patrons

100. Which of the following artists was NOT influenced by Caravaggio?

    (A) Titian

    (B) Artemisia Gentileschi

    (C) Francisco de Zurbarán

    (D) Rembrandt

101. Late nineteenth- and twentieth-century avant-garde artists are best described as

    (A) innovators who challenged established conventions

    (B) traditionalists who opposed Modernism

    (C) Regionalists who want to portray rural life in a clearly readable, Realist style

    (D) Romantics who emphasized feeling and imagination over reason and thought

102. The tympanum in a Romanesque church often depicts Christ as

    (A) a good shepherd   (C) a stern judge

    (B) an aloof philosopher   (D) an omnipotent Pantocrator

103. Which of the following was NOT associated with creating the gardens and palace of Versailles?

    (A) Claude Lorraine

    (B) Andre Le Notre

    (C) Jules Hardouin-Mansart

    (D) Louis Le Vau

104. Which of the following nineteenth-century English artists made a significant impact on the development of modern art because of his innovations with color?

    (A) J. M. W. Turner   (C) John Constable

    (B) William Hogarth   (D) John Singer Sargent

105. Which of the following artists is most closely associated with the International Gothic style?

    (A) Ghiberti   (C) Gentile da Fabriano

    (B) Masaccio   (D) Donatello

106. Who commissioned the Limbourg brothers to illustrate *Les Tres Riches Heures*?

    (A) Bishop Bernward

    (B) Louis IX

    (C) The city council of Siena

    (D) Jean, the duke of Berry

107. All the following archaeologists are correctly paired with their most famous discoveries EXCEPT

    (A) Howard Carter and the Tomb of Tutankhamen

    (B) Heinrich Schliemann and the Treasury of Atreus

    (C) Sir Arthur Evans and Knossos

    (D) Leonard Woolley and the Tomb of Alexander the Great

Questions 108–111 refer to the following illustration.

108. The statue is a portrait of

    (A) Augustus as a victorious athlete

    (B) Augustus as a celebrated author

    (C) Augustus as a devout priest

    (D) Augustus as a victorious general

109. Like other Roman statues and relief sculpture, this work is primarily intended to

    (A) mold public opinion

    (B) honor the gods

    (C) promote artistic creativity

    (D) provide a realistic portrait of the emperor

110. The figure of Cupid at Augustus's foot is intended to proclaim his

    (A) love of classical mythology

    (B) divine lineage

    (C) victory over Antony and Cleopatra

    (D) hope for a large family

111. The statue is based closely on

    (A) Polyeuktos's *Demosthenes*

    (B) Polykleitos's *Doryphoros*

    (C) Lysippos's *Weary Herakles*

    (D) Praxiteles's *Hermes and the Infant Dionysos*

112. Which of the following was the first building to include a clerestory?

    (A) A New Kingdom Egyptian temple

    (B) A Roman basilica

    (C) An early Christian church

    (D) A Romanesque cathedral

113. Color and sensuality are characteristic of

    (A) Analytic Cubism   (C) Venetian art

    (B) Futurism   (D) Hiberno-Saxon art

114. Brunelleschi was renowned for

    (A) studying the treatise of Vitruvius and writing his own text on architecture

    (B) introducing parallel hatching and oil paints to Italy

    (C) reinventing the classical nude and casting the first equestrian statue

    (D) developing a system of linear perspective and designing the dome over Florence Cathedral

115. Which of the following was a Roman architect whose work was rediscovered during the Renaissance?

    (A) Vasari

    (B) Polykleitos

    (C) Vitruvius

    (D) Alberti

STOP

This is the end of Section I, Part B.
If time still remains, you may check your work only in this section.
Do not begin Section II until instructed to do so.

Section II

Time: 120 minutes
   9 questions

This section of the exam contains the following types of essay questions:

- **Question 1** is a 30-minute essay question that is *not* based on slides.

- **Questions 2–8** are short-essay questions based on slides and/or quotations from primary sources or documents.

- **Question 9** is a 30-minute essay question that is *not* based on slides.

Note: This exam uses the chronological designations BCE (before the common era) and CE (common era). These labels correspond to BC (before Christ) and AD (anno Domini), which are used in some art history textbooks.

Directions for Question 1: You have 30 minutes to answer question 1. Read the question and take a moment to think about what it asks. You can receive full credit only by answering the question asked. Therefore, spend a few minutes organizing or outlining your response in the blank space provided above the question. Notes in the blank space will not be graded. Be sure to analyze the question carefully and choose appropriate examples as fully as possible.

---

1.   Although the world is filled with diverse cultural traditions, there exist certain similarities in purpose among the buildings of each culture.

Choose and fully identify two buildings that have similar functions. Each building must be from a different culture. One of your choices must be from beyond the European tradition. Identify and describe the specific purpose of each building. Discuss the manner in which they reflect their respective cultures.

STOP

If you finish before time is called, you may check your work on question 1.

Do not go on to question 2 until you are told to do so.

Directions for Questions 2–8: The following seven short-essay questions are based on slides and/or text. Each question is separately timed, and each slide or set of slides will be shown only for the length of time indicated after the question. You are to answer each question in the space provided.

Read the question and take a moment to think about what the question asks. Formulate your answer before you begin to write. You can receive full credit only by answering the question asked.

Note: For any question based on two slides, when you are not asked specifically to name the artists and/or titles of the works, you may refer to the work on the left as (L) and the work on the right as (R).

2. Identify the culture that produced this piece and describe the sculpture's function. Discuss the characteristics that place the work in its culture. (5 minutes)

3.   How do these paintings, *Luncheon of the Boating Party* and *Madame Charpentier with Her Children*, exemplify the thematic and formal concerns of Impressionism? (5 minutes)

4.   Both images refer to the same structure. What technological innovations enabled the construction of cathedrals such as this one? Discuss this building as an example of the Gothic style in architecture. (10 minutes)

 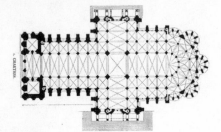

5. The painting on the left is *The Rocky Mountains, Lander's Peak* by Albert Bierstadt. The painting on the right is *Mont Sainte-Victoire* by Paul Cézanne. Both are landscapes, but they have very different objectives and methods of representation. Identify and discuss the differences between these two paintings. (10 minutes)

6. Identify the building or its architect. Discuss the ways in which the building exemplifies the ideals of the period in which it was created. How did this building influence architectural styles in America? (10 minutes)

7. Describe the stylistic and iconographic features of this ivory relief that recall its classical heritage as well as those features that identify it as early Christian. (10 minutes)

Note: Question 8 is based on the following quotation. There are no slides with this question.

This excerpt comes from F. T. Marinetti's "The Foundation and Manifesto of Futurism," from 1908.

> We declare our primary intentions to all living men of the earth.
>
> We declare that the splendor of the world has been enriched with a new form of beauty, the beauty of speed. A race-automobile adorned with great pipes like serpents with explosive breath a race-automobile which seems to rush over exploding powder is more beautiful than the *Victory of Samothrace.*
>
> We will destroy museums, libraries, and fight against moralism.

8.   With what conventions of art does Marinetti take issue? What new approach to art is he advocating? Your essay must identify one work of art from 1900 to 1950 CE and discuss how that work exemplifies the change that Marinetti is advocating. (10 minutes)

End of short-essay questions.

Directions for Question 9: You have 30 minutes to answer question 9. Read the question and take a moment to think about what it asks. You can receive full credit only by answering the question asked. Therefore, spend a few minutes organizing or outlining your response in the blank space provided above the question. Notes in the blank space will not be graded. Be sure to analyze each question carefully and choose appropriate examples. Identify your examples as fully as possible.

---

9.   Artists have presented peasants and laborers in various ways. Select and fully identify two specific paintings. Your choices must be from different periods in art history. Discuss the similarities and differences in the ways the artists present peasants and/or laborers. (30 minutes)

END OF EXAM

PRACTICE EXAM 1

AP Art History

Answer Key

1.	(B)	31.	(C)	61.	(C)	91.	(A)
2.	(D)	32.	(A)	62.	(D)	92.	(C)
3.	(C)	33.	(B)	63.	(C)	93.	(D)
4.	(B)	34.	(A)	64.	(A)	94.	(B)
5.	(B)	35.	(B)	65.	(A)	95.	(A)
6.	(A)	36.	(D)	66.	(A)	96.	(B)
7.	(C)	37.	(C)	67.	(B)	97.	(C)
8.	(D)	38.	(B)	68.	(B)	98.	(D)
9.	(B)	39.	(C)	69.	(A)	99.	(A)
10.	(D)	40.	(D)	70.	(C)	100.	(A)
11.	(C)	41.	(A)	71.	(A)	101.	(A)
12.	(B)	42.	(B)	72.	(B)	102.	(C)
13.	(A)	43.	(D)	73.	(A)	103.	(A)
14.	(D)	44.	(A)	74.	(C)	104.	(A)
15.	(A)	45.	(A)	75.	(A)	105.	(C)
16.	(C)	46.	(D)	76.	(C)	106.	(D)
17.	(B)	47.	(D)	77.	(C)	107.	(D)
18.	(A)	48.	(B)	78.	(A)	108.	(D)
19.	(B)	49.	(B)	79.	(D)	109.	(A)
20.	(D)	50.	(D)	80.	(B)	110.	(B)
21.	(C)	51.	(D)	81.	(D)	111.	(B)
22.	(A)	52.	(C)	82.	(C)	112.	(A)
23.	(B)	53.	(C)	83.	(C)	113.	(C)
24.	(C)	54.	(D)	84.	(C)	114.	(D)
25.	(A)	55.	(D)	85.	(B)	115.	(C)
26.	(C)	56.	(D)	86.	(D)		
27.	(B)	57.	(A)	87.	(A)		
28.	(D)	58.	(A)	88.	(D)		
29.	(C)	59.	(D)	89.	(C)		
30.	(B)	60.	(A)	90.	(B)		

PRACTICE EXAM 1

AP Art History

Detailed Explanations of Answers

Section I

Note: Even the incorrect choices are meant to be instructive. As you review the answers to the multiple-choice questions in this practice test, try to mentally connect the incorrect choices to their appropriate styles or periods of art. Often the answer explanations reveal the origins of the incorrect choices and enable you to continue reviewing other information that you have been studying.

Section I, Part A

1. **(B)**

The *New York Kouros* is an example of Archaic sculpture. The Archaic period in Greek art falls within the sixth century BCE (700–500 BCE). It preceded the most famous Greek artistic period, the Classical period of the fifth century BCE, choice C. Choice A, the eighth century BCE, is the Greek Geometric period. Choice D, the third century BCE, is the Hellenistic period of Greek art, in which the image on the right was produced.

2. **(D)**

The kouros usually marked the grave of a young Greek. That is why the kouros is nude and appears as a youthful male figure. Choice A, which states that the object commemorates a historical event, is incorrect because this is a statue, not a frieze, which the Greeks used for historical narration. Choice B is incorrect because the Assyrians would not show a figure such as this in the nude. Choice C is incorrect because the Altar of Zeus in Pergamon was not created until the Hellenistic period.

3. **(C)**

The object on the right is known as the *Market Woman* and is Hellenistic. Hellenistic statues often show ordinary people without idealizing their features, a typical characteristic of the Greek Classical period. This reflects the growing interest of artists in the suffering of humanity. Choice A is incorrect because the statue lacks Orientalizing features. Orientalizing features on Greek statues show the influence of Near Eastern cultures and date to the seventh century BCE, which is too old for this piece. Choice B is incorrect because *white figure* is a term applied to Greek vase painting. Choice D is incorrect because Byzantine art begins to be seen in approximately the fifth century CE and focuses predominantly on Christian figures and themes.

4. **(B)**

By comparing the two images, you can see a clear difference in their formal elements. The image on the right looks much more lifelike and naturalistic than the image on the left. Choice A is incorrect because they are both sculpted in marble. Choice C is incorrect because although the kouros is naked, the Archaic period did have female statues known as korai (*kore* is the singular term), which were clothed. Choice D is incorrect because the purposes of the statues are difficult to ascertain and are not a clear indicator of why the images are from different periods.

5. **(B)**

The positioning of the kouros reveals the influence of Egyptian statues. The arms are close to the body, the body is rigid and upright, and one leg of the statue is shown striding forward. Egyptian funerary statues preceded the archaic period in Greece and had all these elements. The Egyptians and Greeks most likely had contact with each other, and some similarity among their respective art styles was not uncommon in the ancient Mediterranean. Choice A is incorrect because the kouros has little in common with Sumerian art. Choice C is incorrect because the Roman Republican period came significantly later than the Archaic period. Choice D is incorrect because it bears no significant similarities to the sculpture of the Benin Kingdom.

6. **(A)**

Notice the fatigued expression and wrinkles on the *Market Woman's* face. Always pay attention to the wording used in the choices to see if they fit with the work of art being discussed. *Expressive* refers to the facial expression and body language of sculpture. *Veristic* refers to the very realistic features that are shown as opposed to idealizing her physiognomy.

7. **(C)**

The *Seated Boxer* is an important Hellenistic work of art that illustrates expressive and veristic qualities. He is seated and slouches forward as if defeated. His muscles are sagging, showing the onset of aging, and his face, besides looking older, has gashes and displays an expression that elicits pity from the viewer. Choice A, the *Doryphoros*, and choice D, *Aphrodite of Knidos*, are Classical works of art. Choice B, the *Kritios Boy* is from the Early Classical period.

8. **(D)**

Pergamon was a famous Greek city in the Hellenistic world. It replaced Athens in the extent of its influence, so choice A is incorrect. Choice B, Nineveh, was the capital of the Assyrian Empire, and choice C, Karnak, was an important Egyptian city.

9. **(B)**

The date of about 700 CE is the correct answer. The work on the left is a carpet page from the *Lindisfarne Gospels*. This work is best described as Hiberno-Saxon art because it was produced on the British Isles or Ireland circa 700 CE. The other choices correspond to other artistic periods. Choice A, 500 CE, corresponds to the Early Christian/Byzantine period. Choice C, 900 CE, refers to the Ottonian revival in Europe. Choice D, 1100 CE, was the time of the Romanesque period in which many European Christians were making pilgrimages.

10. **(D)**

This page is from the *Lindisfarne Gospels*, a famous Hiberno-Saxon illuminated manuscript. Notice the Celtic cross and the interlace pattern, which are hallmark features of Hiberno-Saxon art. Choice A, *Akbarnama*, was an Indian illuminated manuscript that tells the story of a Mogul king named Akbar. Choice B, *Tale of Genji*, is a famous Japanese story and series of paintings telling of lives and loves of a Japanese prince and his descendants. Choice C, *Last Judgment of Hu-Nefer*, is a page from an Egyptian book of the dead showing the weighing of Hu-Nefer's heart before Osiris.

11. **(C)**

Vellum is calfskin (the skin of young cattle) that is dried and prepared for writing and painting. It was a popular material for Hiberno-Saxon illuminated manuscripts. Choice A, papyrus, was popular in Ancient Egypt. Choice B, paper, which is made from trees, was popular in modern Europe. Choice D, silk, was popular in China.

12. **(B)**

The Carolingian Renaissance was a period of art during the reign of Charlemagne, circa 800 CE. Carolingian art tends to be less abstract and more naturalistic than the *Lindisfarne Gospels* carpet page. Notice the Celtic cross, the interlace pattern, and its resemblance to a Near Eastern carpet.

13. **(A)**

Gestural abstraction refers to action painting, a type of Abstract Expressionism, which became prominent in the United States during the 1950s. Choice B, chromatic abstraction, is another type of Abstract Expressionism that focuses on the use of blocks of color to express the artist's inner feelings as opposed to the visible brushstrokes of gestural abstraction. Choice C, Minimalism is a sculptural movement of the 1960s. Choice D, German Expressionism, was a painting movement spanning from 1910 through the 1930s.

14. **(D)**

Jackson Pollock is the name most often associated with gestural abstraction (action painting), and his painting is titled *Autumn Rhythm*. Both Barnett Newman and Mark Rothko, choices A and C, respectively, are associated with chromatic abstraction (using blocks of color to express abstract concepts). Choice B, Emil Nolde, was a German Expressionist painter of the first half of the twentieth century.

15. (A)

New York City became the capital of the art world by the 1950s because of the devastation of Europe by World War II. New York City became the haven for artists associated with Abstract Expressionism. Dresden, Paris, and Rome, choices B, C, and D, respectively, are European cities that had been too beleaguered by war to serve as artistic capitals.

16. (C)

Abstract Expressionism became a prominent artistic movement in the 1950s.

17. (B)

"Lacking spatial recession" is another way of saying that both paintings appear two-dimensional and lack the illusion of depth. It is important to notice the wording of the question: the word "both" is a signal that the answer applies to both paintings. Neither the *Lindisfarne Gospels* carpet page nor Pollock's *Autumn Rhythm* reveal the use of linear perspective, atmospheric (aerial) perspective, or modeling of figures or objects with light and shadow (in fact, the Pollock painting has no figural elements, making choice D incorrect). All these features are associated with creating a sense of spatial recession. Choice A is incorrect because neither painting has sensuous color (rich reds and golds), which is typical of the Venetian style of Renaissance painting. Choice C is incorrect because neither work attempts to tell a story.

18. (A)

The image on the left is called a *fête galante*, a style that became popular in the early eighteenth-century period of French painting known as Rococo. Notice the delicate application of paint (parts of the painting look fuzzy and indistinct) and the use of pastel colors. These characteristics typify the Rococo period. *Fête galante* paintings of the Rococo period typically show gatherings of aristocrats enjoying outdoor amusements. Remember, Rococo paintings often show nobles at play and are thus considered frivolous (interested in fun and lacking moralistic meaning).

19. (B)

The painter of the image on the left is Antoine Watteau. He is considered the first great painter of the Rococo period and a significant influence on other Rococo painters such as Francois Boucher, his student. Choice A is incorrect because the painting lacks the typical Baroque features, such as a single light source that leaves much of the rest of the painting dark and a focus on a dramatic moment in a narrative. Rococo succeeded the Baroque period in France. The painting lacks the basic elements of Neoclassical painting and Impressionism, so choices C and D are incorrect. In addition, the Neoclassical period came after and is considered a reaction to the frivolity of the Rococo period. Impressionism also came about much later (1870s).

20. **(D)**

Peter Paul Rubens, a Flemish Baroque painter, is considered a champion of the emphasis of color over the intricate use of line by other artists. Visible brushstrokes, vagueness of some details, and emphasis of color are evident in the later-style Rubens paintings. Choice A, Poussin, is incorrect because Poussin is seen as an artist who stressed precise drawing and line in his paintings.

21. **(C)**

The image on the right is a painting in the Realist style of the mid-nineteenth century. Notice the use of muted colors and the gathering of common people at a funeral. Its theme and method of painting are key characteristics of the Realist style. Choice A is incorrect because the Pre-Raphaelite paintings, which were inspired by English literature, show scenes from medieval folklore, not common people. Choice B is incorrect because a Classicist depicts Greco-Roman styles of art. Choice D is incorrect because the Symbolists of the 1890s depict fantasy scenes in an attempt to record the workings of the inner mind.

22. **(A)**

The artist Gustave Courbet, who painted the work on the right, *Burial at Ornans*, also painted *The Stonebreakers*. Courbet is considered the founder of Realism. Similarities between the two paintings can be seen in both theme (common people, the working class) and formal elements (use of color, painting technique). Choice B, *The Angelus*, is an attractive option because it is also considered a Realist painting. However, the theme of *The Angelus* has more to do with agriculture. Millet, who painted *The Angelus*, focused on the lives of farmers in the countryside rather than on common people in towns.

23. **(B)**

Courbet was criticized for his coarse depiction of subject matter. The focus on common people and the use of somber colors are seen in the works of earlier painters such as Chardin and Grueze, who were accepted. However, unlike these artists, Courbet used an earthier painting technique to visually express the qualities of the working class. Notice that although some spatial recession is present, Courbet was not as concerned with illusionism as he was with the people themselves. Visible brushstrokes and the rough application of paint (Courbet sometimes used a palette knife) were among the reasons this painting was rejected by the 1855 Salon Universelle. Choice A is incorrect because the painting does show a concern for naturalism in the details in the people, their surroundings, and the dog in the foreground. Choice C is incorrect because that was not the reason the painting was criticized. Choice D is incorrect because this painting does not exhibit the themes of Romanticism.

24. **(C)**

Jacques-Louis David criticized the Rococo style because of its frivolous themes. He is associated with Neoclassicism, an art style that, among other qualities, strove to depict a higher sense of morality and duty. Choices A and B are incorrect because Fragonard and Boucher are considered Rococo painters. Choice D is incorrect because Rigaud was a Baroque painter best known for portraits glorifying Louis XIV of France.

25. **(A)**

Jean-Francois Millet was another Realist artist with interests similar to Courbet's. Unlike Courbet, however, Millet moved to the village of Barbizon in the French countryside and focused on the work of peasants. Millet and a small group of painters who followed him are called the Barbizon School because their themes revolved around life near the Barbizon village.

26. **(C)**

The *Mona Lisa* was painted in oil on a wooden panel. Oil became the favored medium of High Renaissance painters such as Leonardo da Vinci. If paintings were done on a smaller scale, such as portraits, they were usually painted on wooden panels. Choice A, encaustic, was popular in Byzantine icon paintings. Choice B, egg tempera, was popular in various periods, from later Byzantine icons through Early Renaissance paintings (Botticelli's *Birth of Venus* is tempera on canvas). Choice D, *fresco buon*, refers to painting on wet plaster and was popular for large-scale paintings done on walls.

27. **(B)**

The term used to describe the misty quality of the *Mona Lisa* is *sfumato*, which means "smoky" in Italian. Da Vinci used several layers of thin oil paint to blur the contour lines of the *Mona Lisa* as well as to make details in the surrounding landscape hazier.

28. **(D)**

Leonardo da Vinci is also known for his detailed anatomical drawings. It is popularly known that he dissected human cadavers to understand the workings of the body. He used this knowledge to enhance the naturalism of the subjects of his paintings. Choice A is an attractive possible answer because Da Vinci is such a famous painter. However, it is well known among art historians that he did a *small number* of finished paintings.

29. **(C)**

Henri Matisse painted the image on the right. The clearest clue is the nonrepresentational use of color. *Nonrepresentational* color means that Matisse did not use traditional colors to depict the woman's flesh, her hair, and other parts of the painting. Choice A is incorrect because Seurat's style is known as pointillism or divisionism, which is based on small dots of pigment. Choice B is incorrect because Munch, who is famous for painting *The Scream*, used swirls of color that are for the most part representative of natural life. Choice D is incorrect because Kandinsky painted in almost a completely nonrepresentational style, meaning that his paintings have very few or no figures or objects.

30. **(B)**

Fauvism is correct because this was the name critics gave to the works of Matisse and fellow painters who used nonrepresentational colors. The term *fauve* means "wild beast" in French and was used as an insult to these artists when their work was exhibited at the Salon d'Automne in 1905. Choice A is incorrect because Expressionism refers to a style of art from 1910 through the 1930s. Choice C is incorrect because Postpainterly Abstraction refers to paintings of the 1950s and 1960s that have blocks of color with *no figural elements* and lack any meaning other than being pure color and line. Choice D, Symbolism, is incorrect because paintings in that style often appear to express fantastic visions from the artist's inner mind or mythology.

31. **(C)**

Salon d'Automne of 1905 was the first show in which works of the Fauves appeared. At first, it is difficult to differentiate between the artistic shows or salons in which famous artists and artistic styles were born. They are nonetheless important to the history of art. With practice and review of the periods (the dates after each show often correspond to the emergence of a stylistic period), it will become easier.

32. **(A)**

The paintings do not use color in the same way. Matisse used color arbitrarily. Da Vinci strove to be faithful to nature in his use of color. The other characteristics—the three-quarter pose, interest in portraiture, and using a female as an objet d'art (art object)—apply to both paintings.

Section I, Part B

33. **(B)**

   As the daughter of the duke of Ferrara and the wife of Francesco Gonzaga, Isabella d'Este was a leading patron of Renaissance art. However, Isabella was not a Caravaggista or follower of Caravaggio. Aremisia Gentileschi is the best known Caravaggista. Verrochio is best known as the master who trained Da Vinci and sculpted a realistic David. The Spanish king Philip IV sponsored Velazquez.

34. **(A)**

   Diego Rivera and José Orozco are renowned for painting mural cycles that dramatize Mexican history. These two artists did not sculpt public statues, support avant-garde artists, or design Mexico's first skyscrapers.

35. **(B)**

   Also known as a cross vault, a groin vault is formed at the perpendicular intersection of two barrel vaults. Like other major Roman structures, the Baths of Caracalla use groin vaults. The Parthenon is a Greek temple that uses post-and-lintel construction. Neither the Eiffel Tower nor the Seagram Building use groin vaults; both buildings use steel frames.

36. **(D)**

   Alberti, Palladio, and Soufflot were all influenced by classical Roman buildings. In contrast, Rietveld was a de Stijl architect whose homes use plain geometric shapes both inside and outside.

37. **(C)**

   In classical architecture, the entablature consists of three parts: the architrave (which rests immediately on the column), the frieze, and the cornice. The capital is the top part of a column or pilaster. The pediment is the triangular space above the entablature. Cult statues of gods and goddesses were placed in an inner room called a cella.

38. **(B)**

   The mihrab is the semicircular niche set into the qibla wall of an Islamic mosque. It ensures that worshippers pray in the direction of Mecca. A metope is the panel between triglyphs in a Doric frieze. A tympanum is a lunette-shaped space above the portal in Romanesque and Gothic churches. A minaret is a tower from which the faithful are called to prayer.

39. **(C)**

   Nude Descending a Staircase was painted by Marcel Duchamp. Alfred Stieglitz is best known for his work as a photographer. Aaron Douglas was a leading artist in the Harlem Renaissance. Georges Braque helped Picasso create Cubism.

40. **(D)**

The Armory Show was a pivotal event in the history of American art. With more than 1,600 works on display, it provided many Americans with their first exposure to European avant-garde art. *Nude Descending a Staircase* was the exhibit's most controversial work. The Salon des Refuses featured works rejected by the official French salon. Located in Chicago, the Columbian Exposition celebrated the four hundredth anniversary of Columbus's discovery of America and featured Neoclassical architecture. The Salon d'Automne featured works by Matisse and other Fauvists.

41. **(A)**

Duchamp's fragmented presentation of the human form was influenced by Analytic Cubism, pioneered by Picasso and Braque. Surrealists focus on the unconscious while both German Expressionists and Fauves make expressive use of color.

42. **(B)**

The sense of sequential motion in *Nude Descending a Staircase* shows the influence of the pioneering motion photography by Eadweard Muybridge. Thomas Eakins was an American artist best known for his Realistic paintings. Claude Monet was one of the foremost French Impressionists. Henri Matisse is best known for his innovative use of colors and collages.

43. **(D)**

Frans Hals was a Dutch artist who excelled in painting both individual and group portraits. He and other Dutch artists created art that appealed to the taste of middle-class Protestant citizens, such as shopkeepers. English dukes would have preferred aristocratic subjects. Italian cardinals and Spanish kings would have preferred religious art.

44. **(A)**

Renaissance humanists revived equestrian statues, sculptured busts, and free-standing nude statues. However, they did not revive the painting of still lifes. One explanation is that the only still lifes to survive the fall of the Roman Empire were buried in Pompeii and not discovered until the eighteenth century.

45. **(A)**

Helen Frankenthaler is best known for her stain paintings. Louise Nevelson is best known for her assemblages. Alexander Calder is best known for his mobiles. Josef Albers and Ellsworth Kelly are best known for their hard-edge paintings.

46. **(D)**

Louis Le Nain and Pieter Bruegel the Elder were among the first artists to depict the hardships of peasant life. Other artists celebrated the privileges and charms of aristocratic life or the pious deeds of religious leaders and saints.

47. **(D)**

The *Bayeux Tapestry* provides a pictorial narrative of the Norman conquest of England in 1066. The Arch of Titus contains a relief depicting the destruction of the Temple in Jerusalem. Numerous paintings depict the construction of the Versailles Palace. The Roman conquest of the Dacians is graphically depicted on Trajan's Column.

48. **(B)**

The crucifix was commissioned by Archbishop Gero. Bishop Bernward commissioned the bronze doors at Hildesheim. Abbot Suger's innovations helped create the Gothic style of church architecture. Pope Julius commissioned the Sistine Chapel ceiling painting by Michelangelo and a number of paintings by Raphael.

49. **(B)**

The *Gero Crucifix* is a reliquary because it contained sacred relics. A sarcophagus is a coffin usually made of stone. A triptych is a three-paneled painting. A predella is the narrow ledge on which an altarpiece rests. It usually contained a number of small paintings.

50. **(D)**

During the Middle Ages, German religious art exhibited an emotional power that exceeded the more classically inspired works in the rest of Europe. The style of the *Gero Crucifix* is Ottonian.

51. **(D)**

Choices A, B, and C are accurate. The Palette of Narmer is carved in low relief.

52. **(C)**

Choices A, B, and D are correctly paired. *Kritios* Boy was carved by an unknown sculptor. Lysippos is best known for carving the *Weary Hercules* and the *Scraper*.

53. **(C)**

A frieze is a continuous band of sculptural decoration. An archivolt is one of the series of concentric bands framing a tympanum. A pediment is the triangular space above an entablature. An entablature is the horizontal beam that includes an architrave, frieze, and cornice.

54. **(D)**

The figures were originally part of a huge frieze depicting the gigantomachy, the battle between the gods and the giants. The frieze was part of the Altar of Zeus in Pergamon. The Parthenon in Athens contains a famous frieze depicting the Panathenaic Procession.

55. **(D)**

Violent movement, swirling draperies and emotional intensity are characteristics of Hellenistic art.

56. **(D)**

Choices A, B, and C are correctly paired. De Stijl is associated with the work of Gerrit Rietveld in Utrecht, the Netherlands.

57. **(A)**

David, Ingres, Gros, and other leading Neoclassical artists created portraits depicting Napoleon's heroic deeds and military victories.

58. **(A)**

Dürer, Goya, and Rembrandt produced graphic art. Although Titian is considered a giant among the High Renaissance artists, he did not produce important works in the graphic arts.

59. **(D)**

Choices A, B, and C are characteristics of the Crystal Palace. The Royal Pavilion in Brighton, England, is know for "Indian Gothic" features like domes, minarets, and screens.

60. **(A)**

Raphael, Masaccio, and Titian are closely associated with the Italian Renaissance. Petrus Christus was associated with the Northern Renaissance.

61. **(C)**

Élisabeth Vigée-Lebrun and Adélaïde Labille-Guiard were leading portraitists during the late eighteenth century. Vigée-Lebrun is well known for her portraits of Marie Antoinette.

62. **(D)**

The Battle of the Ten Nudes was created by Antonio Pollaiuolo. Botticelli is celebrated for his *Birth of Venus*. Donatello is remembered for his nude *Statue of David* and his equestrian statue called the *Gattamelata*. Masaccio is renowned for his pioneering use of linear perspective in the *Holy Trinity*.

63. **(C)**

The Battle of the Ten Nudes exemplifies the artist's interest in depicting the male body reacting under tension.

64. **(A)**

The Battle of the Ten Nudes is one of the first engravings created in Italy.

65. **(A)**

The figures in *The Battle of the Ten Nudes* were influenced by Classical sources. There were no nudes in early Christian, Byzantine, or Carolingian art.

66. **(A)**

Spiral Jetty is an example of Environmental or Earth Art. Environmental artists often use the land itself to construct monuments of great scale and minimal form. Pop Art uses images drawn from popular culture. Minimalism is a predominantly American sculptural movement comprising works characterized by a severe reduction of form. Superrealism is a school of painting and sculpture that emphasizes producing artworks based on scrupulous fidelity to optical fact.

67. **(B)**

A mudra is a symbolic hand gesture used in representations of the Buddha. A nemes is the linen headdress worn by ancient Egyptian pharaohs. In a mosque, the minbar is the pulpit on which the iman stands. In early Christian art, an orant is a figure with both arms raised in the ancient gesture of prayer.

68. **(B)**

Siena was Florence's chief rival during the Early Renaissance. Rome eventually supplanted Florence as the leading city of the High Renaissance. Naples and Milan were secondary centers of Renaissance art.

69. **(A)**

Thomas Eakins was an uncompromising realist. His first concern, whether painting a religious picture or, more commonly, portraits and Philadelphia scenes, was to represent human anatomy accurately. To learn anatomy, he dissected cadavers and became so knowledgeable on the subject he lectured to medical students.

70. **(C)**

Antonio Canova was born in 1757 and died in 1822. While he did produce important works during the 1790s, he created *Pauline Borghese as Venus* and other key works during the early nineteenth century.

71. **(A)**

Forever Free was sculpted by Edmonia Lewis. It is a marble sculpture depicting freed African-American slaves.

72. **(B)**

In *Forever Free*, the man stands heroically in a contrapposto stance reminiscent of classical statues. Amarna statues were created in ancient Egypt and usually depict the pharaoh Akhenaton and his family. High Gothic statues have a Gothic S curve but do not use contrapposto. Mannerist statues are meant to be viewed from multiple angles and feature deliberately elongated forms.

73. **(A)**

Just What Is It is an early example of Pop Art. Notice the references to mass media, advertising, and popular culture.

74. **(C)**

Just What Is It is a collage consisting of images from popular culture. A fresco would be painted on a wet surface. A mosaic consists of small pieces of stone or glass. A limestone relief would be a sculpture.

75. **(A)**

The work includes a number references to popular culture (Charles Atlas, romance comic books, and girlie magazines); advertising (Ford cars, Tootsie Pops, and Hoover vacuums); and mass media (television, theater marquee outside the window, and the newspaper). The work contains no religious symbols.

76. **(C)**

Jean-Antoine Houdon is best known for carving individualized portrait sculptures in the Neoclassical style. He made more than 150 portrait busts of the great men and women of his age. For example, he portrayed Voltaire, George Washington, Thomas Jefferson, and Robert Fulton.

77. **(C)**

Arches and columns are distinctive features of Roman architecture. They can be clearly seen in the Colosseum. Corbelled vaulting was used in Mycenaean citadels and tombs. Cantilevers are horizontal beams supported only at one end. Fallingwater by Frank Lloyd Wright features cantilevers. Flying buttresses are one of the distinctive characteristics of Gothic cathedrals.

78. **(A)**

Encaustic is a painting technique in which pigment is mixed with wax and applied to a surface while hot. Intaglio is a kind of engraving in which the design is incised in a layer of wax on a metal plate. Fresco is a painting technique in which pigments are mixed with water and applied to a wet plaster surface. In cross-hatching, fine lines are drawn close together to achieve the effect of shading.

79. **(D)**

Romare Bearden, Henri Matisse, and Pablo Picasso all created collages. Mark Rothko did not.

80. **(B)**

A voussoir is a wedge-shaped block used in the construction of a true arch. A voussoir would therefore be part of a Roman aqueduct. A voussoir would not be found in a Greek temple, Sumerian ziggurat, or Egyptian temple because these structures did not incorporate true arches.

81. **(D)**

The Seagram Building was designed by Ludwig Mies van der Rohe and Philip Johnson. Victor Horta and Antonio Gaudi are known for their Art Nouveau buildings in Brussels and Barcelona. Louis Sullivan is known for designing early skyscrapers, and Frank Lloyd Wright is known for his Organic style of architecture that can be seen in Fallingwater and the Prairie Houses. Gerrit Rietveld and Piet Mondrian created works in the de Stilj style.

82. **(C)**

The Seagram Building's sleek, rectilinear form embodies the International Style. A Baroque building would be very ornate and have extensive exterior decoration. A Neo-Gothic building would have picturesque towers and other features associated with Gothic architecture. A Postmodern building would use an eclectic mix of architectural styles.

83. **(C)**

The Seagram Building is notable for its lack of architectural ornamentation. For example, there are no exterior statues or designs of any type.

84. **(C)**

Antonio Canova, Jacques-Louis David, and Thomas Jefferson are associated with the Neoclassical style. Canova was a sculptor, David was a painter, and Jefferson was an architect. Delacroix was one of the foremost Romantic artists and is not associated with Neoclassicism.

85. **(B)**

Antoine-Louis Barye was a Romantic sculptor who specialized in scenes of violent animal behavior. Francois Rude was a Romantic sculptor who is best known for sculpting *La Marseillaise* on the Arc de Triomphe. Rosa Bonheur is best known for her paintings of animals. Jean-Antione Houdon is best known for his busts of contemporary writers, inventors and statesmen.

86. **(D)**

Choices A, B, and C are characteristics of Mannerist paintings. Beams of light that highlight key figures and actions is a characteristic of Baroque art.

87. **(A)**

The Serpent Mound is located in Ohio.

88. **(D)**

The Vietnam Veterans Memorial is best described as an example of Minimalist Art because it is a simple geometric form. The *V*-shaped wall is constructed of polished black granite panels. The panels begin at ground level at each end and gradually ascend to a height of 10 feet at the center of the *V*. The names of the 57,939 casualties of the Vietnam War (and those still missing) are incised on the wall in the order of their deaths.

89. **(C)**

Rembrandt van Rijn recorded his own likeness in at least 75 paintings, drawings, and prints that date from his earliest years in Leyden to the last year of his life in Amsterdam. The dozens of painted examples had many purposes ranging from theatrical displays of emotional expression in the youthful works, to the most candid self-scrutiny in some of the later works. Hals is best known for his individual and group portraits of everyday Dutch citizens. Vermeer is best known for his domestic scenes featuring solitary figures. Ruisdael is best known for his landscapes.

90. **(B)**

Umberto Boccioni was the leading Futurist artist. His paintings portray the dynamism of modern life.

91. **(A)**

The Stepped Pyramid was constructed during the reign of King Djoser (2630–2611 BCE) during the period known as the Old Kingdom.

92. **(C)**

According to tradition, the Stepped Pyramid was designed by Imhotep, the first artist in recorded history. Senmut was the architect who designed Hatshepsut's mortuary temple. Khafre was a powerful Old Kingdom pharaoh. Akhenaton was the iconoclastic pharaoh of the Eighteenth Dynasty who sponsored the Amarna style of Egyptian art.

93. **(D)**

Choices A, B, and C are true statements. Although the Stepped Pyramid was a tomb, it was not a temple platform.

94. **(B)**

Albrecht Dürer was one of the first northern artists to travel to Italy expressly to study Italian art and its underlying theories at their source.

95. **(A)**

The Arch of Titus contains a relief panel depicting Roman soldiers carrying spoils, including the sacred seven-branched candelabrum, the menorah, from the Temple in Jerusalem. Trajan's Column contains relief panels depicting Trajan's victory over the Dacians. The Pantheon is known for its portico and rotunda. The Ara Pacis contains relief panels depicting an imperial procession.

96. **(B)**

Rue Transnonain was created by Honoré Daumier.

97. **(C)**

The work is a lithograph.

98. **(D)**

Rue Transnonain depicts an atrocity. The title refers to a street in Lyon where an unknown sniper killed a civil guard, part of a government force trying to repress a worker demonstration. Because the fatal shot had come from a workers' housing block, the French National Guard stormed the building and killed fourteen unarmed citizens. Daumier depicted the incident's terrible aftermath.

99. **(A)**

Because he used a lithograph, Daumier could print an unprecedented number of copies.

100. **(A)**

Artemisia Gentileschi, Francisco de Zurbarán, and Rembrandt were influenced by Caravaggio's revolutionary use of light. Titian was a High Renaissance master who died in 1576, almost a quarter century before Caravaggio painted his most important works.

101. **(A)**

Avant-garde artists of the late nineteenth and twentieth centuries were by definition innovators who challenged established artistic conventions.

102. **(C)**

Romanesque tympanums often depict Christ as a stern judge. Many Early Christian mosaics and paintings depict Christ as a good shepherd. Byzantine mosaics typically depict Christ as the Pantocrator, or almighty.

103. **(A)**

Claude Lorraine was known for his classically inspired landscapes. However, he had no role in creating the gardens or palace at Versailles. Andre Le Notre, Jules Hardouin-Mansart, and Louis Le Vau all played important roles in the creation of the gardens and palace of Versailles.

104. **(A)**

J. M. W. Turner's innovations with the use of pure color had a significant impact on the development of modern art. Hogarth is best known for his paintings and prints satirizing English society. Constable is best known for his romantic landscapes of the English countryside. Sargent is best known for his portraits of wealthy English and American families.

105. **(C)**

Ghiberti, Masaccio, and Donatello are early Renaissance masters. Da Fabriano was most closely associated with the International Gothic style.

106. **(D)**

Jean, the duke of Berry, commissioned the Limbourg brothers to illustrate *Les Trés Riches Heures*. Bishop Bernward commissioned the famous bronze doors at Hildesheim. Louis IX commissioned the building of Sainte-Chapelle. The city council of Siena commissioned the Ambroglio Lorenzetti to paint *The Effects of Good Government in the City and in the Country*.

107. **(D)**

Choices A, B, and C are correct pairings. Leonard Woolley discovered the Royal Cemetery at Ur. The tomb of Alexander the Great has yet to be discovered.

108. **(D)**

The statue depicts Augustus as a victorious general. A relief on his breastplate shows the Parthians returning a Roman legionary standard.

109. **(A)**

The primary purpose of Roman public statues and relief sculpture was to mold public opinion. These works of art thus functioned as propaganda, showing the rulers as invincible leaders supported by the gods.

110. **(B)**

The figure of Cupid proclaims Augustus's divine lineage. Caesar's family, the Julians, traced their ancestry back to Venus. Cupid was the goddess's son.

111. **(B)**

The *Statue of Augustus from Primaporta* is clearly based on Polykleitos's *Doryphoros*. For example, in both statues, the figures have a tight cap of layered hair and an almost identical contrapposto stance.

112. **(A)**

Egyptian temples of the New Kingdom period were the first buildings to include a clerestory, a row of windows near the ceiling.

113. **(C)**

Color and sensuality are the key characteristics of Venetian art. Analytic Cubism features fractured forms and does not use bright colors. Futurism is concerned with portraying dynamic motion. Hiberno-Saxon art features dense intertwined designs.

114. **(D)**

Brunelleschi was renowned for developing a system of linear perspective and designing the dome over Florence Cathedral. Palladio was renowned for studying the treatise of Vitruvius and writing his own text on architecture. Parallel hatching and oil paints were introduced by Northern Renaissance artists. Donatello reinvented the classical nude and cast the first equestrian statue since antiquity.

115. **(C)**

Vitruvius was the famous Roman architect whose work was rediscovered during the Renaissance. Vasari wrote a famous history of art and is often called the Father of Art History. Polykleitos is the famous Greek sculptor best known for the *Doryphoros*. Alberti was a famous Renaissance architect and writer.

Section II

1. Question 1 asks you to identify two buildings with similar purposes. One building must be from beyond the European tradition. One main purpose would be for fulfilling religious requirements; this is a characteristic many cultures share. After identifying two buildings, their respective cultures, and their similar purposes, you should include four characteristics about each building that express how the buildings reflect their respective cultures.

You must specifically identify these buildings. Simply using the generic name for structures such as "a Romanesque church" or "a mosque" will cost you points. If you blank out on the question and can only think of generic labels, use them. It is better to do this than to receive a 1 or 0 on the essay. But if you want to score higher than 5 on the essay, you must give the specific name of each building.

The following examples of buildings intended for fulfilling religious purposes could work well for this question. The building's religious affiliation and purpose are included for each example.

Non-European Tradition

- The Great Mosque in Kairouan, Tunisia (Islam, communal prayer, and hearing passages from the Koran)

- The Great Stupa in Sanchi, India (Buddhism, pilgrimage site for venerating relics of Buddha)

- Ziggurat of Ur (ancient Near East building that served as a bridge between heaven and earth for the Sumerians and included a temple on top)

- Dome of the Rock in Jerusalem (Islam, pilgrimage site for Muslims, site from which Muhammad ascended to meet Allah)

European Tradition

- Parthenon in ancient Athens (Greek religion, dedicated to the goddess Athena, a place to bring offerings to Athena and honor her for blessing Athens)

- Saint Sernin in Toulouse, France (Christianity, Romanesque pilgrimage church dedicated to Saint Saturninus, an early Christian missionary who was martyred in France)

- Chartres Cathedral in Chartres, France (Christianity, Gothic church that held the Virgin Mary's veil as a sacred relic)

- New Saint Peter's in Vatican City, Rome, Italy (Christianity, shows the power of the Catholic church, built during the High Renaissance through the baroque periods)

There are other examples of buildings and purposes that would work for this question. The buildings that are listed lend themselves well to analysis and explanation of how they reflect their respective cultures. As far as function is concerned, it is more difficult to name structures from different cultures that have functions other than fulfilling religious requirements. Governmental functions or historical monuments are other viable choices, but finding examples of buildings is more challenging. The concept of religion and deities is a notable similarity among most world cultures.

2. The image shown is the funerary statue of Menkaure and Khamerernebty from the Old Kingdom of Egypt. Important points to make revolve around the purpose of the sculpture: It is the alternate dwelling place for the kas of the pharaoh and his queen should their mummies deteriorate and become uninhabitable. Ancient Egyptian religion believed that humans possessed a ka, or soul. Depending on your actions in life, your ka could continue living in the afterlife or be devoured as a punishment. Pharaohs as well as other Egyptians made extensive preparations so that their kas would have all the materials they would need for eternity.

The statue of Menkaure and Khamerernebty reflects the purpose of housing the ka for eternity. Notice the hard black stone from which it is made. Known as diorite, this durable material will decrease the chance of damage over eternity so that the kas of the king and queen will have complete bodies. The positioning of the king and queen also protects the statues. The bodies are compact, with all appendages enclosed within a fixed space. The statue is not completely in the round but more like high relief. Notice how the figures are still attached to the backing. Finally, the fact that Menkaure and Khamerernebty are placed together indicates that their kas will remain joined through eternity. In a pose conventional in Old Kingdom Egypt, she places her arm around her king and stands one step behind him, indicating her dedication to him for eternity.

3. Both the *Luncheon of the Boating Party* and *Madame Charpentier with Her Children* reflect the Impressionist movement in art. Although it is difficult to precisely pinpoint what made an impressionist an impressionist, certain basic characteristics narrow their work into a specific style. These paintings attempt to capture a specific moment in time and are interested in the effects of light at that moment. The painting on the left is painted outdoors and illustrates a vast array of colors caused by natural light. Although the painting on the right has less natural light (maybe some from a window), it too demonstrates an interest in light based on the pale skin of the children, highlights in the sitters' hair, and other highlighted objects in the room. Impressionists often used short, choppy brushstrokes because they did not want to lose the moment that they were trying to capture. Both paintings have this element. Although the painting on the right is obviously posed, it would have been difficult for the children and the dog to hold this position for any length of time. Finally, the Impressionists were interested in the lives of bourgeois Parisian society. Although Madame Charpentier appears to belong to a higher social class than the members of the boating party, the interest in a pleasant slice of life such as people enjoying a lunch and fellowship in a café on the Seine reflects the leisure of the Parisian middle class.

4. This building, Chartres Cathedral in France, is an example of Gothic architecture. Gothic architecture became prevalent in the thirteenth century in France because of the architectural writings of Abbot Suger, who was in charge of the remodeling of

Saint Denis's Cathedral. He advocated building churches with greater interior height that would encourage people to contemplate heaven. In addition, he advocated the inclusion of large amounts of multicolored, stained-glass windows. A light poured through the windows, the filtered light would make people consider the beauty of the "heavenly Jerusalem" that would be established after the Apocalypse. Chartres Cathedral has both of these important Gothic features: height and light.

One architectural innovation that made achieving these goals feasible was the inclusion of ribbed vaults. Ribbed vaults allowed the weight of the roof to be transferred more directly into the compound piers in the nave arcade. In addition, Gothic architects began to use pointed arches. Pointed arches transfer the weight of the roof more directly to the piers than do the rounded arches typically used during the Romanesque period that came after the Gothic period. Thus, Gothic architects could build taller structures. Pointed arches also give the illusion of greater height and actually provide more space for stained-glass windows. Flying buttresses also allowed for the building of taller churches. Flying buttresses are vertical supports with horizontal support arms that are used outside of the church to hold up the nave walls. Without these supports, the taller nave walls would be in danger of collapsing as a result of the outward thrust caused by the weight of the roof and the walls. All these support structures allowed for less actual material in the walls and more open spaces for stained-glass windows.

5.   The Bierstadt painting on the left reflects the Hudson River School of American painting in the second half of the nineteenth century. Painters of the Hudson River School, such as Thomas Cole, Frederick Edwin Church, and Albert Bierstadt, captured the pristine beauty of the American landscape that had yet to be touched by industrialization and civilization. The paintings are very realistic. Despite their grand scale (some paintings are almost seven feet across), the paintings include minute details. Bierstadt captured all the crevices in the Rocky Mountains; the details in the tree branches, leaves, and bark; the details in the teepees of the natives; as well as the details of Native American life, with various activities proceeding in the small camp on the lower right. To some extent, the Hudson River School advocated the American concept of Manifest Destiny: that God intended the United States to have all the land of North America that was yet unclaimed. The Hudson River School painters reflect this divine providence by showing the vastness of nature, its peacefulness and tranquility, and usually powerful sunlight falling on part of the scene in an almost symbolic indication of God's will for Americans to possess the land.

Cézanne's *Mont Sainte-Victoire* shows the artist's interest in the shapes and colors that exist in nature. Unlike Bierstadt, who attempts to capture every detail realistically, Cézanne breaks the landscape into elemental shapes such as rectangles and cones. He also uses patches of color and varies them to portray distance accordingly. Stronger and warmer colors are used in the foreground—greens, browns, and yellows. Lighter paint application and cooler colors such as blues and violets are used for the mountain in the background. Cézanne is usually categorized as a Post-Impressionist, although he did exhibit with the Impressionists earlier in his career. As a Post-Impressionist, he was more interested in investigating the shapes and colors that exist in nature and in art in general. By the 1890s, which was the approximate time of Post-Impressionism, photography could capture nature more realistically and with greater efficiency than painting. Only an artist like Cézanne could examine the formal elements of art that exist in nature and capture them on canvas.

6.   This is Chiswick House by Richard Boyle and William Kent. It was built in the eighteenth century and reflects the renewed interest that Europeans had in Classical-style architecture. With the excavation of and tourism to Pompeii and Herculaneaum in the eighteenth century, there was a revival in interest in the classical world that was reflected in the architecture. Notice the dome, rotunda, pediment, portico, and Corinthian columns. Besides reflecting this movement, which would come to be described as Neo-classicism, Chiswick House also reflects an interest in the work of Palladio, the Venetian Renaissance architect. Palladio was famous for creating villas or country houses on the Venetian mainland. Intellectuals of the eighteenth century such as Thomas Jefferson owned translations of Palladio's books and created designs that clearly show his influence, such as Monticello, Jefferson's home in Virginia. Chiswick House in England is reminiscent of the Villa Rotunda designed by Palladio two centuries earlier.

Thomas Jefferson advocated the use of Neoclassical architecture in the newly formed United States. The United States needed a fresh break from the Georgian architecture of its former oppressor, Great Britain. The Neoclassical architecture, which came to be known as the Federal style in the United States, would be used on various government buildings from the Virginia capitol building in Richmond to various buildings in Washington, D.C. The choice of using architecture from Classical culture was appropriate because the fledgling American government was to some extent influenced by the democracy of ancient Athens and the senate of Republican Rome.

7.   This panel demonstrates the influence of classical art and its interest in illusionism and symbolism. The figure in the center, most likely Constantine the Great, protrudes from the panel in high relief to give the panel a sense of spatial recession that was seen in the marble panels of the Romans and Greeks. Constantine the Great is also shown triumphantly riding a horse in the tradition of the equestrian statues of the great Roman emperors such as Trajan and Marcus Aurelius. This symbolism equates him with the good emperors and conveys his power. Another classical symbol can be seen in the hands of the figure on the left. The figure is offering Constantine a statue of Athena Nike lifting a laurel crown to place on Constantine's head. This was the classical symbol for victory and triumph.

The Early Christian elements of this work are evident in its emphasis on telling a message about Constantine rather than achieving any kind of naturalism. Notice the decreased realism in the human proportions. There is some remaining interest in classical realism with the attention to drapery and musculature, but the work lacks the realism and naturalism of Roman Republican and Early Imperial sculpture. Heads are more rounded and figures overlap each other unrealistically. Important Christian symbolism can be seen on the top, where either Jesus or God the Father makes a gesture of blessing over Constantine. You can tell this figure is a Christian deity because of the cross in his hands. The message being told about Constantine is that he is a powerful and respected leader given the divine right to rule by God. Notice the figures in the register below bringing grain and animals before Constantine, and an angelic figure serving as an intermediary between them and their magnificent leader.

8. F. T. Marinetti is taking issue with the standards of art that had been influenced by the Classical world and Renaissance period. Most art sought to imitate nature and, to some extent, idealize it. Whether it was the human form, landscapes, or still life, artists seemed to be slaves to nature. Marinetti is advocating the abandonment of the old standards of acceptability, such as the Hellenistic *Victory of Samothrace*, which most art historians of Marinetti's time would have seen as the pinnacle of artistic excellence. Instead, Marinetti states that art should be based on the machines of the new age, on speed, and on the technology of the future. He explains these ideas in his statement about how a race car is more beautiful than the *Victory of Samothrace*. Marinetti published these ideas in his "The Foundation and Manifesto of Futurism," and he developed the movement known as Futurism.

Umberto Boccioni's *Unique Forms of Continuity in Space* exemplifies Marinetti's opinions about art. It is considered a Futurist work of art. Made of metal, it is an abstract human form striding forward. It has a head, arms, and legs. But that is where the naturalism ends. Instead of a well-developed musculature, the legs, arms, and torso have jagged pieces of metal flaring out from them. These pieces of metal make the sculpture appear futuristic and enhance the sense of motion begun by the foot striding forward. It is like a visual representation of the "great pipes like serpents with explosive breath" in Marinetti's race car. This sculpture deviated from the norms of the art establishment, which by this time were just beginning to accept the works of Rodin from the 1890s. This is what Marinetti meant when he said that museums based on classical standards of beauty should be destroyed. *Unique Forms of Continuity in Space* created a new standard in art that was in line with the ideas of Marinetti.

9. This essay question asks for examples of two paintings that demonstrate an interest in the lives of peasants or laborers. You must choose paintings from two different periods of art history to receive full credit. Both paintings can be from the European tradition. Following are some appropriate examples:

*   *Hunters in the Snow*, Northern Renaissance, Pieter Bruegel the Elder

*   *The Harvesters*, Northern Renaissance, Pieter Bruegel the Elder

*   *Water Carrier of Seville*, Spanish Baroque, Diego Velazquez

*   *Family of Country People*, seventeenth-century French genre painting, Louis Le Nain

*   *The Village Bride*, eighteenth-century French genre painting, Jean-Baptiste Greuze

*   *Adoration of the Shepherds*, eighteenth-century French religious painting, Georges de La Tour (although this is a Christian nativity scene, Georges de La Tour focuses on the humble appearance of the shepherds so much that it appears to be a genre scene)

- *The Stonebreakers*, nineteenth-century French Realism, Gustave Courbet

- *The Gleaners*, nineteenth-century French Realism, Jean-Francois Millet

- *The Third-Class Carriage*, nineteenth-century French Realism, Honoré Daumier

- *The Thankful Poor*, nineteenth-century American Realism, Henry Ossawa Tanner

- *The Vision after the Sermon* (also know as *Jacob Wrestling with the Angel*), Post Impressionism, Paul Gauguin

- *American Gothic*, twentieth-century American Regionalism, Grant Wood

PRACTICE EXAM 2

This exam is also on CD-ROM in our
special interactive AP Art History TEST*ware*®

AP Art History

Slide-Based Multiple-Choice and Free-Response Questions

Section I, Part A

TIME: 16 minutes
    32 questions

DIRECTIONS: Questions 1–32 are divided into sets of questions based on slides. In these sets, each question or incomplete statement is followed by four suggested answers or completions. Select the one that is best for each question, and then fill in the corresponding oval on the answer sheet. The slide or slides for each group of questions will appear on the screen for 4 minutes.

Note: This exam uses BCE (before the common era) and CE (common era) as chronological labels rather than BC (before Christ) and AD (anno Domini).
Questions 1–8 are based on the slides you see on the screen. The slides will be shown for 4 minutes only.

1. The image on the left was sculpted by

    (A)   Antonio Canova

    (B)   Antoine-Louis Barye

    (C)   Jean-Antoine Houdon

    (D)   Francois Rude

2. The image on the left dates from the

    (A)   eighth century CE

    (B)   fourteenth century CE

    (C)   sixteenth century CE

    (D)   eighteenth century CE

3. The figure depicted in the image on the left was an important figure of

    (A)   the Carolingian Renaissance

    (B)   Romanticism

    (C)   the Enlightenment

    (D)   the Italian Renaissance

4. The work on the left shares notable similarities with the sculptures of

    (A)   ancient Rome

    (B)   Early Christianity

    (C)   the Romanesque period

    (D)   Mannerism

5. The person shown in the image on the right is

    (A)   Philip IV

    (B)   Thomas Jefferson

    (C)   Napoleon

    (D)   Louis XIV

6. Based on its stylistic elements and subject matter, the image on the right is from the

    (A)   late Roman period

    (B)   Renaissance

    (C)   Baroque period

    (D)   Ottonian revival

7. The artist who created the image on the right is most likely

    (A) Giovanni da Bologna

    (B) Gianlorenzo Bernini

    (C) Umberto Boccioni

    (D) Andrea del Verrochio

8. Both images have all of the following in common EXCEPT

    (A) realistic qualities while elevating the appearance of the sitter

    (B) an interest in conveying the character of the sitter

    (C) using symbols that are allusions to classical antiquity

    (D) characterizing the period in which each was produced

Questions 9–17 are based on the slides you see on the screen. The slides will be shown for 4 minutes only.

9. The image on the left uses the medium of

    (A) egg tempera

    (B) *fresco buon*

    (C) encaustic

    (D) oil on panel

10. The image on the left is part of a fresco cycle that is in the

    (A) Arena Chapel in Padua

    (B) Palazzo Pubblico in Siena

    (C) Palazzo Ducale in Mantua

    (D) Piazza San Marco in Venice

11. The image on the left is noteworthy for all of the following reasons EXCEPT

    (A) the sculptural mass of its figures

    (B) its depiction of spatial depth

    (C) its secular subject matter

    (D) its interest in human emotion

12. The image on the left was created in the

    (A) 1200s

    (B) 1300s

    (C) 1400s

    (D) 1500s

13. Which of the following artists was NOT a contemporary of the artist who produced the work on the left?

    (A) Masaccio

    (B) Duccio di Buoninsegna

    (C) Simone Martini

    (D) Lippo Memmi

14. The style of the image on the right is best described as

    (A) Renaissance

    (B) Mannerist

    (C) International Style

    (D) Proto-Renaissance

15. A distinguishing stylistic element of the image on the right is its

    (A) elongated figures

    (B) clarity of composition

    (C) uniform light source

    (D) sensuous colors

16. Which of the following artists was NOT associated with the style of work on the right?

    (A) Parmigianino

    (B) Bronzino

    (C) Pontormo

    (D) Andrea del Castagno

17. Both images are similar in their

    (A) composition

    (B) religious narrative

    (C) modulation of light

    (D) medium

Questions 18–25 are based on the slides you see on the screen. The slides will be shown for 4 minutes only.

18. The image on the left dates from the

    (A) Neo-Babylonian period

    (B) Golden Age of Ur

    (C) late Minoan period

    (D) Egyptian New Kingdom

19. The sculpted head on the left depicts a(n)

    (A) aristocrat

    (B) queen

    (C) pagan seer

    (D) snake goddess

20. The sculpted head is in an art historical style called

    (A) Amarna

    (B) Minoan

    (C) Sasanian

    (D) Sumerian

21. Which of the following works was NOT produced contemporaneously with the image on the left?

    (A) Sculpture of Akhenaton

    (B) *Palette of Narmer*

    (C) *Miniature Head of Tiye*

    (D) Relief of Nefertiti and three daughters

22. Which of the following choices best describes the formal relationship being examined by the work on the right?

    (A) Line and color

    (B) Perspective and foreshortening

    (C) Mass and space

    (D) Modulation of light and shadow

23. The sculpture on the right is best categorized as

    (A) Minimalist

    (B) assemblage

    (C) Pop Art

    (D) Cubist

24. Both sculptures are examples of

    (A) bas relief

    (B) high relief

    (C) sculpture in the round

    (D) additive method

25. Both sculptures are similar in that they

  (A) challenged traditional methods of representation

  (B) have a highly developed sense of naturalism

  (C) are both cast using the lost-wax process

  (D) incorporate color using encaustic

Questions 26–32 are based on the slides you see on the screen. The slides will be shown for 4 minutes only.

26. The structure on the left is a

  (A) gymnasium

  (B) stadium

  (C) theater

  (D) basilica

27. The circular part of the structure on the left is called the

  (A) orchestra

  (B) choir

  (C) arena

  (D) skene

28. The structure on the left is best known for its

  (A) use of concrete and stone

  (B) harmonious proportions

  (C) barrel-vaulted passages

  (D) walls with frescoes

29. The structure on the left was used for

    (A) public elections

    (B) sacred plays

    (C) athletic events

    (D) chariot races

30. The purpose of the structure on the right was to

    (A) hold legislative proceedings

    (B) allow public bathing

    (C) serve as an emperor's home

    (D) display public spectacles

31. The structure on the right makes extensive use of

    (A) round arches and engaged columns

    (B) broken pediments and the giant order

    (C) cyclopean stones and corbelled arches

    (D) columns in its hypostyle

32. The original name for the structure on the right was the

    (A) Forum Augustae

    (B) Baths of Caracalla

    (C) Circus Maximus

    (D) Flavian Amphitheater

Section I, Part B

Time: 44 minutes
83 questions

> **DIRECTIONS:** Each question or incomplete statement in this section is followed by four suggested answers or completions. Select the one that is best in each case, and then fill in the corresponding oval on the answer sheet.

33. Which of the following artists was the leader of the nineteenth-century French realists?

    (A) Jacques-Louis David

    (B) Gustave Courbet

    (C) Eugène Delacroix

    (D) Theodore Gericault

34. Impressionists attempted to

    (A) depict the inner world of fantasy

    (B) convey a sense of the dynamism of speed and industry

    (C) capture the fleeting qualities of light and atmosphere

    (D) analyze the form of objects by shattering them into fragments

35. All the following are Neoclassical works EXCEPT

    (A) *Oath of the Horatii*

    (B) *Pauline Borghese as Venus*

    (C) Chiswick House

    (D) *Raft of the Medusa*

36. Which artist attempted to "reproduce nature in terms of the cylinder and sphere and the cone"?

    (A) Gustave Courbet

    (B) Edouard Manet

    (C) Mary Cassatt

    (D) Paul Cézanne

37. A female figure that functions as a supporting column is called a

    (A) caryatid

    (B) kore

    (C) kouros

    (D) cella

38. The design of the Roman Pantheon influenced all of the following EXCEPT

    (A) Villa Rotunda

    (B) Palazzo Rucellai

    (C) Chiswick House

    (D) Monticello

Questions 39–42 refer to the following illustration.

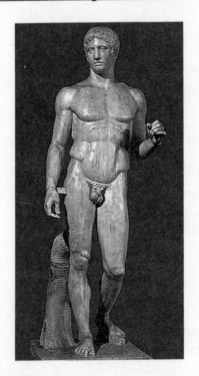

39. The work was sculpted by

    (A) Myron

    (B) Polykleitos

    (C) Phidias

    (D) Praxiteles

40. Which of the following statements about the statue is NOT accurate?

    (A) It was originally called the *Canon*.

    (B) The statue was created during the Archaic period of Greek art.

    (C) The statue was intended to illustrate the ideal male body.

    (D) The original statue was cast in bronze.

41. The influence of this statue can clearly be seen in which of the following works?

    (A) The *Statue of Augustus from Primaporta*

    (B) The *Colossal Head of Constantine the Great*

    (C) The *Equestrian Statue of Charlemagne*

    (D) *Moses* by Michelangelo

42. The statue uses a relaxed natural stance called

    (A) chiaroscuro

    (B) contrapposto

    (C) chakra

    (D) canonization

43. Which of the following is NOT true of San Vitale in Ravenna?

    (A) It is a centrally planned church that influenced Charlemagne's Palatine Chapel in Aachen.

    (B) It contains an extensive set of mosaics that proclaim the triumph of Justinian and the Orthodox faith.

    (C) It contains a narthex whose odd angle and unsymmetrical placement have never been fully explained.

    (D) It depicts royal processions that are stylistically similar to the procession of Augustus on the Ara Pacis.

44. Hatshepsut's mortuary temple did NOT contain

    (A) painted reliefs depicting her achievements

    (B) colonnaded terraces connected by ramps

    (C) gardens with trees and rare plants

    (D) stone pyramids for the royal family

45. Hogarth is best known for

  (A) narrative paintings and prints that satirize English society

  (B) landscape paintings that depict the pastoral beauty of the English country-side

  (C) lithographs that lampoon politicians and call attention to atrocities

  (D) etchings that portray darkly emotional images

46. Which of the following photographers is most closely associated with the development of sequential motion studies?

  (A) Eadweard Muybridge

  (B) Jacob Riis

  (C) Dorothea Lange

  (D) Félix Nadar

47. A full-size preliminary drawing from which a painting is made is called a

  (A) cartoon

  (B) canon

  (C) cloison

  (D) codex

48. All of the following are artists associated with Abstract Expressionism EXCEPT

  (A) Willem de Kooning

  (B) Barnett Newman

  (C) Jackson Pollock

  (D) Claes Oldenburg

49. Which of the following is NOT true about Jan Vermeer?

  (A) He used a *camera obscura* to help render space.

  (B) He was a master of depicting pictorial light.

  (C) He painted domestic interior scenes, often featuring a solitary woman.

  (D) He painted innovative landscapes.

50. Which of the following was a prominent patron of avant-garde artists during the early twentieth century?

   (A) Gertrude Stein

   (B) Charles Baudelaire

   (C) Michel-Eugène Chevreul

   (D) Madame de Pompadour

Questions 51–52 refer to the following illustration.

51. The structure is part of a lunette-shaped part of a cathedral portal called a(n)

   (A) trumeau

   (B) archivolt

   (C) pediment

   (D) tympanum

52. The composition's anguished figures and passionate drama are characteristic of

   (A) Romanesque Spain

   (B) Romanesque France

   (C) Gothic Germany

   (D) Gothic France

Questions 53–55 refer to the following illustration.

53. The architect who designed this country house was

    (A) Vitruvius

    (B) Palladio

    (C) Bernini

    (D) Maderno

54. The use of a temple porch in front of a dome-covered interior shows the influence of

    (A) Hagia Sophia

    (B) the Pantheon

    (C) an Egyptian pylon temple

    (D) the Temple of Athena Nike

55. Which of the following homes was influenced by this building?

    (A) Chiswick House

    (B) Fallingwater

    (C) Villa Savoye

    (D) Strawberry Hill

56. Which of the following is an important characteristic of the work of Italian Futurists?

    (A) love of nature

    (B) use of biblical references

    (C) use of classical references

    (D) love of speed and industry

57. Which of the following is an example of a nonrepresentational work created in the early twentieth century?

    (A) Ernst Ludwig Kirchner's *Street, Dresden*

    (B) Andre Derain's *London Bridge*

    (C) Paul Cézanne's *Mont Sainte Victoire*

    (D) Vassily Kandinsky's *Improvisation 28*

58. Which of the following works of art was NOT made using the repoussé method?

    (A) The death mask of Tutankhamen

    (B) The head of the Sasanian king Shapur II

    (C) The funerary masks found in the Treasury of Atreus

    (D) The two warriors of Riace

59. Which of the following most directly caused the construction of Romanesque churches?

    (A) The revival of learning during the Carolingian Renaissance

    (B) The popularity of pilgrimages to see holy relics

    (C) The spiritual needs of Protestant churches

    (D) The architectural innovations advocated by Abbot Suger

60. A pylon is the entrance to

    (A) an Egyptian temple

    (B) a Sumerian ziggurat

    (C) an Assyrian palace

    (D) a Mycenaean tomb

61. All of the following works of art and architecture were created during Nebuchadnezzar's reign in Babylon EXCEPT the

   (A) Ishtar Gate

   (B) Marduk Ziggurat

   (C) Hanging Gardens

   (D) White Temple

Questions 62–65 refer to the following illustration.

62. *Spiral Jetty* is best described as an example of

   (A) Pop Art

   (B) Earth Art

   (C) Op Art

   (D) Performance Art

63. *Spiral Jetty* was influenced by all the following EXCEPT

   (A) Neolithic stone structures in Great Britain

   (B) prehistoric earth mounds in the United States

   (C) Analytic Cubism

   (D) Minimalist sculptures

64. *Spiral Jetty* was created by

   (A) Robert Smithson   (C) Christo

   (B) Nancy Holt   (D) Andy Goldsworthy

65. The artistic movement represented by *Spiral Jetty* became prominent during the

   (A)   1940s and 1950s

   (B)   1960s and 1970s

   (C)   1980s and 1990s

   (D)   first decade of the twenty-first century

Questions 66–68 refer to the following illustration.

66. The church shown above was designed by

   (A)   Brunelleschi

   (B)   Alberti

   (C)   Borromini

   (D)   Bramante

67. The architect of the building is associated with the period style known as

   (A)   High Gothic

   (B)   Renaissance

   (C)   Baroque

   (D)   Rococo

68. The church facade contains all of the following EXCEPT

(A) a triumphal arch

(B) a pediment

(C) pilasters

(D) decorative figural sculptures

69. The *Standard of Ur* is

(A) inscribed on a tall black-basalt stele

(B) divided into horizontal bands called registers

(C) a milestone in legal history

(D) carved in high relief

70. Which of the following Roman structures was NOT built to glorify the achievements of an emperor?

(A) Ara Pacis

(B) Trajan's Column

(C) the catacombs

(D) Arch of Constantine

71. The Archaic period of Greek art is contemporary with the

(A) Armarna statues in Ancient Egypt

(B) Fourth Style wall paintings in Pompeii

(C) Etruscan temples in Italy

(D) Minoan frescoes in Crete

72. Which of the following artists was a leader in the Harlem Renaissance?

(A) Aaron Douglas

(B) Charles Demuth

(C) Georgia O'Keeffe

(D) Romare Bearden

73. Which of the following is NOT true of the bronze doors at Saint Michael's, Hildesheim?

    (A)   The doors were commissioned by Bishop Bernward.

    (B)   The doors are an example of Romanesque art.

    (C)   The doors pair narrative scenes from the Old and New Testaments.

    (D)   The doors contain panels with scenes influenced by Carolingian manuscript illuminations.

74. Which of the following were located at the EAST end of a medieval church?

    (A)   Clerestory and transept

    (B)   Narthex and nave

    (C)   Crypt and side aisle

    (D)   Choir and apse

75. The term *orthogonal* refers to

    (A)   imaginary visions portrayed by early Symbolists

    (B)   imaginary symbols used by German Expressionists

    (C)   imaginary conversations among saints from various epochs

    (D)   imaginary lines that appear to recede toward the vanishing point on the horizon

76. The Surrealists' fascination with the unconscious and dreams had precedents in the works of

    (A)   Van Gogh

    (B)   Pollock

    (C)   Bosch

    (D)   Grunewald

77. Which of the following was a renowned Caravaggista?

    (A)   Annibale Carracci

    (B)   Artemisia Gentileschi

    (C)   Sofinisba Anguisola

    (D)   Angelica Kauffmann

Questions 78–80 refer to the following illustration.

78.   The figures represent

(A)   apostles

(B)   popes

(C)   tetrarchs

(D)   martyrs

79.   Which of the following best describes the figures?

(A)   They wear flowing drapery that emphasizes their natural appearance.

(B)   They are highly individualized and unique.

(C)   They are idealized but recognizable individuals.

(D)   They are anonymous but equal partners.

80.   Based on their appearance, the group can be dated to the

(A)   early Roman Empire under Augustus

(B)   late Roman Empire under Diocletian

(C)   Byzantine Empire under Justinian

(D)   Carolingian Empire under Charlemagne

Questions 81–84 refer to the following illustration.

81. The work was painted by

    (A) Caspar David Friedrich

    (B) Thomas Cole

    (C) John Constable

    (D) Frederick Edwin Church

82. The work is best described as a

    (A) Romantic landscape painting

    (B) Dutch genre painting

    (C) Dutch still life

    (D) French Realist painting

83. The painting contains or expresses all of the following EXCEPT

    (A) relaxed figures who blend into the scene

    (B) a placid, picturesque portrait of the countryside

    (C) angry farmers displaced by the Industrial Revolution

    (D) a sense of the texture of atmospheric conditions

84. Which of the following was a contemporary and rival artist whose works were deeply rooted in the emotive power of pure color?

    (A) J. M. W. Turner

    (B) Edouard Manet

    (C) Rosa Bonheur

    (D) Winslow Homer

85. The term *predella* refers to the

    (A) painted base of an altarpiece

    (B) horizontal band in a pictorial narrative

    (C) wedge-shaped blocks used in the construction of a true arch

    (D) passageway around the apse and choir of a church

86. The Cathedra Petri (Throne of Saint Peter) and the bronze baldacchino in Saint Peter's Cathedral are both intended to

    (A) symbolize the unification of the Roman Catholic and the Greek Orthodox faiths

    (B) symbolize a new spirit of reconciliation between Catholics and Protestants

    (C) symbolize the welcoming arms of the Church

    (D) symbolize the triumph of Christianity and the papal doctrine of supremacy

87. All of the following artists are correctly paired with a prominent patron who was associated with their work EXCEPT

    (A) Élisabeth Vigée-Lebrun and Marie Antionette

    (B) Diego Velazquez and Philip IV

    (C) Peter Paul Rubens and Marie de' Medici

    (D) Leonardo da Vinci and Pope Julius II

88. Louise Nevelson is best known for her

    (A) stain paintings

    (B) assemblages

    (C) mobiles

    (D) *Cubi* series

89. Paul Gauguin is known for all of the following EXCEPT

  (A) rejecting Western culture to live in Tahiti

  (B) influencing the Symbolists

  (C) attempting to paint nature in terms of its underlying structure

  (D) using flat planes of unmodulated color

90. Which of the following is NOT characteristic of the Pre-Raphaelite brother-hood?

  (A) They worked in England in the second half of the nineteenth century.

  (B) They incorporated references to literary sources.

  (C) They used Realist techniques but rejected Realist subjects.

  (D) They had a significant influence on the Futurists.

91. Which of the following is NOT a characteristic of the plaques created by Benin artists in the sixteenth and seventeenth centuries?

  (A) They use hierarchical scale to show rank.

  (B) The use low relief figures.

  (C) They include symbols of royal power.

  (D) They are made out of bronze.

92. Marc Chagall's works include all the following EXCEPT

  (A) Fauve colors

  (B) Cubist fragmented space

  (C) themes from his childhood

  (D) biomorphic forms

93. The decline of Florence at the end of the fifteenth century is related to the rise of

  (A) Paris

  (B) Rome

  (C) Sienna

  (D) Venice

94. Which of the following artists created cycles that focus on African American history and culture?

    (A) Thomas Cole

    (B) Winslow Homer

    (C) Jacob Lawrence

    (D) Edmonia Lewis

95. *The Great Wave off Kanagawa* by Katsushika Hokusai is

    (A) a woodblock print

    (B) a diorite sculpture

    (C) an ivory statuette

    (D) an enamel plaque

Questions 96–98 refer to the following illustration.

96. This painting by Henri Fuseli is best classified as

    (A) Rococo

    (B) Romantic

    (C) Realist

    (D) Impressionist

97. Fuseli was one of the first artists to depict

(A) the mentally insane

(B) Roman legends and myths

(C) the problems caused by rapid industrialization

(D) the human subconscious

98. Like other artists in this style, Fuseli was influenced by

(A) Baroque dynamism

(B) Neoclassical rationality

(C) Rococo frivolity

(D) Realist outrage

99. Which of the following is NOT a characteristic of nineteenth-century Japanese prints?

(A) Flat planes of solid color

(B) Cropped edges

(C) Intimate moments of daily life

(D) One-point perspective

100. Which of the following does NOT correctly pair a Renaissance master with his apprentice?

(A) Verrocchio and Leonardo

(B) Duccio and Giotto

(C) Ghirlandaio and Michelangelo

(D) Perugino and Raphael

101. Which of the following are characteristics of Islamic art?

(A) Ionic and Corinthian columns

(B) Painted portraits and landscapes

(C) Sculpted busts and herms

(D) Arabesques and calligraphy

Questions 102–105 refer to the following illustration.

102. The medium of the work is

    (A) tempera

    (B) oil

    (C) fresco

    (D) mosaic

103. The work once decorated the

    (A) Altar of Zeus in Pergamon

    (B) walls of the Colosseum in Rome

    (C) Lighthouse in Alexandria

    (D) floor of a Roman villa in Pompeii

104. It is widely believed that this work is

    (A) a reasonably faithful copy of a Hellenistic panel painting

    (B) derived from an Etruscan sarcophagus

    (C) based upon a now lost painting on a Greek vase

    (D) based on an image from an embroidered Persian carpet

105. The subject of the work is

    (A) a battle between Augustus and Mark Antony

    (B) the assassination of Julius Caesar

    (C) a battle between Alexander the Great and Darius III

    (D) the gigantomachy between Zeus and the giants

106. Which of the following is NOT true of the Guggenheim Museum in Bilbao?

    (A) It was designed by Frank Gehry.

    (B) It has a titanium-clad exterior.

    (C) It is asymmetrical.

    (D) It uses pendentives to support a Postmodern dome.

107. Picasso and Georges Braque collaborated

    (A) to organize the Armory Show

    (B) to create the Cubist style

    (C) to form the Blue Riders

    (D) to write the "The Foundation and Manifesto of Futurism"

108. Which of the following is NOT a feature of Fallingwater by Frank Lloyd Wright?

    (A) The hearth is the core room of the house.

    (B) The design incorporates concrete cantilevers.

    (C) The home is an "organic" part of the natural setting.

    (D) The home is designed to be a "machine for living."

109. Which of the following is NOT a feature of the Cycladic figures of the third millennium BCE?

    (A) They mainly represent women.

    (B) They closely resemble Sumerian votive statues.

    (C) They have strikingly abstract forms.

    (D) They are carved out of marble.

110. Communal multistoried dwellings built of stone or adobe brick by the Native Americans of the Southwest are called

    (A) pueblos

    (B) porticoes

    (C) parapets

    (D) pylons

111. Michelangelo's *Moses* was intended to be part of

    (A)   Bramante's Tempietto

    (B)   Pope Julius II's tomb

    (C)   St. Mark's Square in Venice

    (D)   Mantegna's Camera Picta

112. The Bauhaus was a school of design and architecture that helped create the

    (A)   International Style

    (B)   Postmodernist Style

    (C)   Photorealist Style

    (D)   Futurist Style

Questions 113–115 refer to the following illustration.

113. This work was designed by

    (A)   Maya Ying Lin

    (B)   Louise Nevelson

    (C)   Donald Judd

    (D)   Robert Smithson

114. The work is a(n)

    (A)   theater set

    (B)   ready-made piece

    (C)   assemblage

    (D)   war memorial

115. The work is often described as an example of

    (A)   Futurist Art

    (B)   Dadaist Art

    (C)   Earth Art

    (D)   Minimalist Art

STOP

This is the end of Section I, Part B.
If time still remains, you may check your work only in this section.
Do not begin Section II until instructed to do so.

Section II

Time: 120 minutes
   9 Questions

This section of the exam contains the following types of essay questions:

- **Question 1** is a 30-minute essay question that is not based on slides.

- **Questions 2–8** are short-essay questions based on slides and/or quotations from primary sources or documents.

- **Question 9** is a 30-minute essay question that is not based on slides.

Note: This exam uses the chronological designations BCE (before the common era) and CE (common era). These labels correspond to BC (before Christ) and AD (anno Domini), which are used in some art history textbooks.

Directions for Question 1: You have 30 minutes to answer question 1. Read the question and take a moment to think about what it asks. You can receive full credit only by answering the question asked. Therefore, spend a few minutes organizing or outlining your response in the blank space provided. Notes in the blank space will not be graded. Be sure to analyze each question carefully and choose appropriate examples as fully as possible.

---

1.   Many works of art have represented important political and religious leaders.

   Select and fully identify two works of art, each from a different culture. At least one culture must be non-European or non-European based. Describe the ways in which each work portrays the leader and visually represents his or her roles, achievements, and beliefs.

STOP

If you finish before time is called, you may check your work on question 1.
Do not go on to question 2 until you are told to do so.

Read the question and take a moment to think about what it asks. Formulate your answer before you begin to write. You can receive full credit only by answering the question asked.

Note: For any question based on two slides, when you are not asked specifically to name the artists and/or titles of the works, you may refer to the work on the left as (L) and the work on the right as (R).

2. Identify the period in Greek art that this work exemplifies. Describe the main elements of the work that place it in its period and differentiate it from the preceding periods of Greek art. (10 minutes)

3. The exterior of this building contains elements from various earlier architectural styles. Describe three of these elements, and identify the styles from which they came. (5 minutes)

4.   Discuss the elements of the work that define it as Byzantine. (5 minutes)

5.   Name the artist who painted these two works, and identify the art historical style with which they are most often affiliated. Using elements from these works, discuss the artist's innovations in both treatment of subject matter and composition.

6. These two statues depict similar subjects. Which work is earlier? Explain your choice, comparing and contrasting the two images. (10 minutes)

7.   Very different approaches have been used by Andrea del Castagno and Dirk Bouts in their treatment of the common subject, the Last Supper. Discuss the stylistic differences between these two works with reference to the contrasting art historical contexts in which they were created. (10 minutes)

Note: Question 8 is based on the following quotation. There are no slides with this question.

This excerpt comes from J. J. Winckelmann's "Thoughts on the Imitation of Greek Works in Painting and Sculpture," published in 1755.

> To take the ancients for models is our only way to become great…
>
> Their masterpieces reveal not only nature in its greatest beauty, but… certain ideal beauties of nature which… exist only in the intellect.
>
> These frequent opportunities for observing nature caused the Greek artists to go even further; they began to form general concepts of beauty for the individual parts of the body as well as for its proportions; concepts that were meant to rise above nature, being taken from a spiritual realm that existed only in the mind.

8. What approach does Winckelmann suggest eighteenth-century artists should take to produce great art? Your response should include and discuss one work of art from the mid-eighteenth to early nineteenth centuries that reflects Winckelmann's ideas. (10 minutes)

End of short-essay questions.

Directions for Question 9: You have 30 minutes to answer question 9. Read the question and take a moment to think about what it asks. You can receive full credit only by answering the question asked. Therefore, spend a few minutes organizing or outlining your response in the blank space provided above the question. Notes in the blank space will not be graded. Be sure to analyze each question carefully and choose appropriate examples. Identify your examples as fully as possible.

---

9. The visual effect of light is a very important element in some paintings. Choose and fully identify two paintings—one from before and the other from after 1800 CE—in which light and its effects are an important element. Compare and contrast the role played by light in each painting. (30 minutes)

END OF EXAM

PRACTICE EXAM 2

AP Art History

Answer Key

1.	(C)	31.	(A)	61.	(D)	91.	(B)
2.	(D)	32.	(D)	62.	(B)	92.	(D)
3.	(C)	33.	(B)	63.	(C)	93.	(B)
4.	(A)	34.	(C)	64.	(A)	94.	(C)
5.	(D)	35.	(D)	65.	(B)	95.	(A)
6.	(C)	36.	(D)	66.	(B)	96.	(B)
7.	(B)	37.	(A)	67.	(B)	97.	(D)
8.	(C)	38.	(B)	68.	(D)	98.	(A)
9.	(B)	39.	(B)	69.	(B)	99.	(D)
10.	(A)	40.	(B)	70.	(C)	100.	(B)
11.	(C)	41.	(A)	71.	(C)	101.	(D)
12.	(B)	42.	(B)	72.	(A)	102.	(D)
13.	(A)	43.	(D)	73.	(B)	103.	(D)
14.	(B)	44.	(D)	74.	(D)	104.	(A)
15.	(A)	45.	(A)	75.	(D)	105.	(C)
16.	(D)	46.	(A)	76.	(C)	106.	(D)
17.	(B)	47.	(A)	77.	(B)	107.	(B)
18.	(D)	48.	(D)	78.	(C)	108.	(D)
19.	(B)	49.	(D)	79.	(D)	109.	(B)
20.	(A)	50.	(A)	80.	(B)	110.	(A)
21.	(B)	51.	(D)	81.	(C)	111.	(B)
22.	(C)	52.	(C)	82.	(A)	112.	(A)
23.	(D)	53.	(B)	83.	(C)	113.	(A)
24.	(C)	54.	(B)	84.	(A)	114.	(D)
25.	(A)	55.	(A)	85.	(A)	115.	(D)
26.	(C)	56.	(D)	86.	(D)		
27.	(A)	57.	(D)	87.	(D)		
28.	(B)	58.	(D)	88.	(B)		
29.	(B)	59.	(B)	89.	(C)		
30.	(D)	60.	(A)	90.	(D)		

PRACTICE EXAM 2

AP Art History

Detailed Explanations of Answers

Section I

Note: Even the incorrect choices are meant to be instructive. As you review the answers to the multiple-choice questions in this practice test, try to mentally connect the incorrect choices to their appropriate styles or periods of art. Often the answer explanations reveal the origins of the incorrect choices and enable you to continue reviewing other information that you have been studying.

Section I, Part A

Questions 1–8

The image on the left is Jean-Antoine Houdon's *Bust of Voltaire*, which is considered Neoclassical and dates to the late eighteenth century. The image on the right is Gianlorenzo Bernini's *Bust of Louis XIV* from the seventeenth-century Baroque tradition.

1. **(C)**

Jean-Antoine Houdon was a sculptor famous for his portraits of prominent eighteenth-century figures such as George Washington, Thomas Jefferson, Benjamin Franklin, and Voltaire. He is considered a Neoclassical sculptor because most of his portraits include Classical references. Most of the contemporary figures he portrayed were connected with the eighteenth-century period known as the Enlightenment.

2. **(D)**

The *Bust of Voltaire* dates to the eighteenth century. Voltaire was a famous figure of the French Enlightenment period, which occurred during the eighteenth century.

3. **(C)**

Voltaire was a famous figure of the Enlightenment—a time when intellectuals promoted the use of the scientific method and the use of reason to explain events occurring in the world around them. Enlightenment figures also championed the concept of liberty and the right to express ideas. Voltaire once said, "I may disagree with what you say, but I will fight to the death for your right to say it."

4. **(A)**

The *Bust of Voltaire* is similar to Roman portrait busts. The wrinkles in his face convey wisdom and experience, similar to the veristic qualities of Roman portrait busts. Yet Houdon also idealizes Voltaire's appearance with stylish eighteenth century clothing and a facial expression conveying Voltaire's wit and intelligence. This quality of representing nature and at the same time idealizing it was one of the hallmarks of Greco-Roman Classical Art.

5. **(D)**

The image on the right is a portrait of Louis XIV of France. Louis XIV was known as the Sun King, reigning from the second half of the seventeenth century through the early eighteenth century. He was one of the most powerful patrons of the time and helped to make France the center of the art world in the eighteenth century.

6. **(C)**

Notice how the hair and robes of Louis XIV flow dramatically. This is the style of seventeenth-century Baroque art. Baroque art tends to be very dramatic and ornate, both of which can be seen in the *Bust of Louis XIV.* Bernini uses these elements to convey Louis's power and majesty, idealizing the Sun King.

7. **(B)**

Gianlorenzo Bernini was one of the most famous artists of the Baroque period. He was multitalented and well known for his work for the Catholic Church in Rome during the Counter-Reformation. Louis XIV was so powerful that some of Europe's greatest artists, including Bernini, traveled to Paris to work for him.

8. **(C)**

Both works of art do not allude to classical antiquity; only Houdon's *Bust of Voltaire* has classical symbols. Both works have realistic details in the faces, hair, and garments of the sitters, and they attempt to elevate their statuses; therefore, choice A applies to both. Choice B also applies to both because the portraits do attempt to capture the personalities of their subjects. Both works also characterize the periods in which they were produced: the *Bust of Voltaire* has the classical symbolism characteristic of the Neoclassical period, and the *Bust of Louis XIV* has the flowing drapery and dramatic qualities of the Baroque.

Questions 9–17

The image on the left is *The Lamentation,* from a fresco cycle painted by Giotto in the Arena Chapel. The image on the right is Pontormo's *Descent from the Cross.*

9. **(B)**

Giotto's painting uses the technique of *fresco buon*, which is painting on wet plaster. He was the first artist since the ancient Romans to use this technique. With the Arena Chapel fresco cycle—a group of several frescoes linked by a common themes—Giotto established *fresco buon* as a medium that would be used frequently throughout the Italian Renaissance. That the image is a fresco is also evident by the lines in the plaster, which show that the plaster was applied each day as Giotto would paint.

10. **(A)**

This painting is in the Arena Chapel in Padua. The Arena Chapel was built by Enrico Scrovegni, a member of one of Padua's wealthiest families. His father, Fermo Scrovegni, was a very avaricious man, and greed is considered sinful in Christianity. Enrico had this chapel built to atone for his father's avarice. The chapel's name reflects that the site on which it was built was a Roman arena (used for gladiator fights and spectacles). Giotto was commissioned to decorate the interior of the chapel.

11. **(C)**

The subject of this painting definitely is not secular. The term *secular* is commonly used to describe art considered worldly. This painting is religious art, the opposite of secular. The image tells a story from the final days of Jesus Christ. The scene is known as the Lamentation because all the followers of Christ and even the angels are crying as a result of his death. Choice A does apply to the painting because all the figures appear to have body mass. This is significant because Giotto displays his interest in trying to show the human form naturalistically as opposed to the symbolic use of the body in art of the Middle Ages. Choice B applies because the overlapping of characters, the varying positions, and the background convey spatial depth. Choice D can also be seen in the painting because Giotto captures human emotions through the agonizing expressions of Christ's mourners. The key phrase for Giotto's Arena Chapel fresco cycle is "real people (they have body mass), occupying real space (they are firmly on the ground and overlap each other realistically), and showing real human emotion."

12. **(B)**

Giotto painted his fresco cycle in the Arena Chapel in the early 1300s. This is noteworthy because he preceded the famous Italian Renaissance painters by more than 100 years. In fact, Renaissance painters would go to the Arena Chapel and study Giotto's work. Because of his achievement, Giotto is often considered a precursor to the Renaissance, and his work is considered Proto-Renaissance.

13. **(A)**

Masaccio is not a contemporary of Giotto. Masaccio became famous as an early Renaissance painter in the 1420s. Even though this seems like a challenging list of names, the object of the question is to recognize that Masaccio painted during the Renaissance, not during the early 1300s. Choice B, Duccio di Buoninsegna is a famous contemporary of Giotto. While Giotto was painting the Arena Chapel, Di Buoninsegna was painting *La Maesta*, a famous altarpiece dedicated to the Virgin Mary, for the city of Siena. Choices C and D, Simone Martini and Lippo Memmi, respectively, were also contemporaries of Giotto. However, unlike Giotto, they painted in the more traditional International Gothic style.

14. **(B)**

The style of the painting on the right is Mannerist. Mannerism became popular in Italy from the 1530s through the 1590s, until the emergence of the Baroque period in the seventeenth century. The painting shown here has several elements of Mannerism. First, notice the elongated human figures, a hallmark of the Mannerist style. For example, the torso of Christ, the deceased figure in the center, is too long for his lower half. A second characteristic identifying this painting as Mannerist is the unusual multiple light sources. This departs from the use of light by Renaissance painters, who attempted to imitate light as they observed it in nature. One more characteristic that helps to identify this as Mannerist is the unusual composition of the painting. The painting has a space in the center, and all the figures are crowded together and swirl around that space. A Renaissance painting would not have a composition like this. Most Renaissance paintings were organized in a pyramidal, balanced composition.

15. **(A)**

As explained in the answer for question 14, elongated figures and body proportions are important stylistic elements of Mannerism. Choice B is incorrect because the painting lacks clarity of composition, which usually refers to a simpler organization in which there is an identifiable order and rationality. Choice C is incorrect because the painting lacks a uniform light source. A uniform light source means that you can usually spot the direction of the light source and trace its effects on the human figures depicted. Using a uniform light source is part of chiaroscuro (light and shading), which was developed during the Renaissance.

16. **(D)**

Andrea del Castagno was a Renaissance painter. The other three choices were Mannerists. Choice A, Parmigianino is famous for his painting *Madonna of the Long Neck*. Choice B, Bronzino, is known for including elongated features on his human figures, whether the paintings are allegorical (symbolic) or portraits. Choice C, Pontormo, is the artist of the painting on the right known as the *Descent from the Cross*.

17. **(B)**

Both paintings are similar in their religious narrative because they tell the story of what happened when Christ was taken down from the cross. Choice A is incorrect because the compositions are different. Choice C is incorrect because Giotto's *The Lamentation* attempts to modulate light naturalistically, while Pontormo uses multiple light sources. The mediums are also different: Giotto's painting is *fresco buon* and Pontormo's is oil on wood.

Questions 18–25

The image on the left is the *Bust of Nefertiti,* from the New Kingdom period in Egypt. The image on the right is *Woman Combing Her Hair* by Aleksandr Archipenko, an example of Cubist sculpture.

18. **(D)**

The image on the left is from the Egyptian New Kingdom. The pectoral, the eyes with their ceremonial makeup, and the crown with the remnants of intertwined snakes help to identify this as Egyptian.

19. **(B)**

The image depicts a queen, who is identified as Nefertiti, one of the wives of Akhenaton. The crown is too regal for an aristocrat or pagan seer (fortune teller), so choices A and C are incorrect. Choice D is a distracter because remnants of serpentine decorations can be seen on Nefertiti's headdress, but the *Snake Goddess* is a famous sculpture in Minoan art.

20. **(A)**

The sculpture is in a style known as Amarna. Nefertiti's husband, Akhenaton, was an iconoclastic pharaoh who implemented significant changes in Egypt. Akhenaton changed Egypt's religion from polytheism (worshipping many gods) to monotheism (worshipping only one god), focusing on the worship of Aton, who was represented as a sun disk. Akhenaton then moved his capital downriver from Thebes to a place he named Akhenaton. Today the site is known as el-Amarna. Because much New Kingdom art was discovered in this area, the art of Akenaton's reign is known as the Amarna style.

21. **(B)**

The *Palette of Narmer* was produced during the Predynastic period in Egyptian history and tells of the unification of Upper and Lower Egypt. The other choices are considered part of the Amarna style of New Kingdom Egyptian art.

22. **(C)**

Aleksandr Archipenko's *Woman Combing Her Hair* is a Cubist sculpture that analyzes the relationship of mass and space. Notice that some parts of the sculpture are bulky while others are tapered and that a space defines the head of the woman. Choice A is incorrect because although the sculpture reveals an interest in line and shape, it does not show an interest in color. Choice B is incorrect because there is no interest in the illusionist techniques of perspective and foreshortening. Choice D is incorrect because the focus of the sculpture is not on the modulation of light and shadow, which is usually observed in painting.

23. **(D)**

Woman Combing Her Hair is considered Cubist because of its geometric shapes and intersecting planes. Although the sculpture is somewhat representational (notice the woman's hair, abdomen, and legs and the curves in her hips), it fragments and abstracts her form into basic shapes. Archipenko was not concerned with depicting her underlying musculature and form as much as examining the use of shape and space. Choice A,

Minimalist, usually focuses on basic metal shapes that have representation other than what they are. Many Minimalist sculptures consist of a few large metal boxes. Choice B, Assemblage, refers to combining different materials to make a sculpture. This is usually obvious when you look at the sculpture. Archipenko's woman appears to be made entirely from one material (bronze). Choice C, Pop Art, would have recognizable and not abstract images drawn from American or British popular culture from the 1960s.

24. **(C)**
Both sculptures are examples of sculpture in the round. It is not choice A, bas relief, because bas relief barely projects from its background material. Bas relief often appears to be carved onto a flat space. Choice B, high relief, describes sculpture that projects significantly from its backing, but the backing still remains. If you were to walk around a high relief, you would still see its original material. Choice D, additive method, refers to sculpture that is made by adding materials. An example of this would be using clay to make a sculpture. Additive sculpture is different from sculpture made through the subtractive method, which means to carve away material from an object. Stone sculptures are usually made through subtractive means. The *Bust of Nefertiti* was made through subtractive means.

25. **(A)**
Both the *Bust of Nefertiti* and *Woman Combing Her Hair* challenged conventional methods of representation. The conventions for royal sculpture in ancient Egypt depicted the human form as rigid, compact, with little space within the human form, and expressionless. In contrast, the *Bust of Nefertiti* has a contoured, flowing appearance, space around her long graceful neck, and an expression that conveys her personality. This beautiful sculpture helps to explain how she received the name Nefertiti, which means "Beautiful One of the Palace." Archipenko also challenged conventional depictions of women because of his abstract depiction of the female form, which includes a void in the area of her head.

Questions 26–32

The image on the left is the Theater of Epidauros in Greece. The image on the right is the Flavian Amphitheater, also known as the Colosseum.

26. **(C)**
The image on the left is a Greek theater. The Greeks used gymnasiums for athletic purposes, and these structures look different than theaters; therefore, choice A is incorrect. Choice B is also incorrect because stadiums were more oblong and were used for running a stade—a 200-yard race. Choice D, basilica, refers to a Roman courthouse and is more rectangular. The basilica form was used for Christian churches after Constantine legalized the religion.

27. **(A)**
The circular space in which a play would be performed is called the orchestra. Greek plays usually were performed by no more than two actors, accompanied in music and song

by a chorus. Choice B, choir, does not apply to the Greek theater. Choice C, arena, refers to the sandy floor on which Roman gladiatorial combat would take place. Choice D, skene, was a building in which actors dressed and served as a backdrop for the plays.

28. **(B)**

This Greek theater is best known for its harmonious proportions. Greek art, architecture, and music are renowned for their balance and mathematical bases. "Harmonious proportions" is a common expression when referring to Classical Greek structures. Choice A, concrete and stone, were common materials in Roman construction. The Ancient Greeks did not use concrete but precisely cut blocks of stone, usually marble, locked together with pins. Choice C is incorrect because the Ancient Greeks did not use barrel vaults, which are tunnels with rounded ceilings. Choice D is incorrect because there are no surviving examples of Greek frescoes. Greek painting survives mainly through vases.

29. **(B)**

Greek theaters were used to perform plays on holidays dedicated to the various Greek deities. They were not used for public elections, athletic events, or chariot races.

30. **(D)**

The structure on the right, the Colosseum, was used to display spectacles such as gladiator contests. Spectacles also included mock naval battles, reenactments of the eruption of Mount Vesuvius, men fighting wild animals, and performances of plays in which the characters, usually criminals, were really executed. Choice A is incorrect because legislative proceedings were held in the Roman senate building. Choice B is incorrect because Romans did not bathe in the Colosseum but in the numerous bathhouses built for that purpose. Choice D is incorrect because although the Roman emperor had special seating in the Coliseum, it did not serve as his home.

31. **(A)**

The Colosseum's facade is composed of many round arches and engaged columns. Romans were the first civilization known to make extensive use of round arches. Before round arches, the main method of support was post-and-lintel construction. Engaged columns are columns that protrude but are still attached to the facade. Choice B refers to construction methods first used in tandem by Renaissance architects. A broken pediment is one pediment resting on top of another, and a giant order is a type of column that vertically spans several stories. Choice C is incorrect because cyclopean stones and corbelled arches were older construction methods used by the ancient Mycenaean civilization. The Colosseum does not have a hypostyle, so choice D is incorrect as well.

32. **(D)**

The Colosseum was originally known as the Flavian Amphitheater. Roman amphitheaters completely enclose spectators, whereas Greek theaters are open. It is important to recognize some of the differences in purpose, design, and materials between a Greek theater and a Roman amphitheater. A Roman forum, which was used as a gathering place and a place of civic activities, looks nothing like an amphitheater. Choice A, Forum Augustae is thus incorrect. Choice B is incorrect because the Baths of Caracalla, the largest bathing facility in the Roman Empire, also looks nothing like the amphitheater. Choice C, Circus Maximus, is an attractive distracter because, like the Coliseum, it was enclosed and used for chariot racing. However, the Circus Maximus was much longer in its appearance, similar to a modern-day racetrack.

Section I, Part B

33. **(B)**

Gustave Courbet was the leading figure of the Realist movement in nineteenth-century French art. David was the leading figure of the Neoclassical movement. Delacroix and Gericault were the leading figures in the Romantic movement.

34. **(C)**

Impressionists sought to capture the fleeting qualities of light and atmosphere, thereby conveying the illusiveness and impermanence of images and conditions. The Symbolists attempted to depict the inner world of fantasy. The Futurists attempted to convey a sense of the dynamism of speed and industry. The Cubists attempted to analyze the form of objects by shattering them into fragments.

35. **(D)**

Oath of the Horatii by David, *Pauline Borghese as Venus* by Canova, and Chiswick House by Richard Boyle and William Kent are renowned works in the Neoclassical style. In contrast, *Raft of the Medusa* by Gericault helped launch the Romantic movement in art.

36. **(D)**

Cézanne believed that Impressionism lacked form and structure. He is well known for saying that he wanted to "reproduce nature in terms of the cylinder and sphere and the cone," expressing his goal of focusing on the underlying geometric structures of the scenes and objects he was painted. In contrast, Courbet is remembered as one of the leading figures of the Realist movement, Manet produced works in both the Realist and Impressionist styles, and Mary Cassatt was the leading female Impressionist artist.

37. **(A)**

A caryatid is a female figure that functions as a supporting column. The best-known caryatids are found on the south porch of the Erechtheion on the Acropolis in Athens. A kore is a freestanding, draped, female figure sculpted during the Archaic period of ancient Greek art. A kouros is a freestanding, nude figure sculpted during the Archaic period of ancient Greek art. A cella is a room built at the center of a classical temple and containing a cult statue.

38. **(B)**

The Pantheon boasts one of the most influential designs in architectural history. Its key features include a traditional rectangular portico supported by Corinthian columns and a huge concrete rotunda. These features can be clearly seen in the Villa Rotunda, Chiswick House, and Monticello. In contrast, Alberti modeled the facade of the Palazzo Rucellai after the facade of the Colosseum.

39. **(B)**

The *Doryphoros* was sculpted by Polykleitos. Myron is best known for sculpting the *Diskobolos*, Phidias is best known for sculpting the *Statue of Athena Parthenos* in the Parthenon, and Praxiteles is best known for sculpting the *Aphrodite of Knidos*.

40. **(B)**

Choices A, C, and D are true statements. The *Doryphoros* was *not* created during the Archaic period of Greek art. Its idealized proportions and use of contrapposto make it an excellent example of the Classical style of Greek art.

41. **(A)**

Compare and contrast pictures of the *Doryphoros* and the *Statue of Augustus from Primaporta*. Augustus's tight cap of layered hair, his overall shape, and especially his contrapposto clearly emulate the *Doryphoros*. In contrast, the *Colossal Head of Constantine the Great* is from a huge statue that does not use Polykleitos's system of ideal proportions. The *Equestrian Statue of Charlemagne* is a miniature version of the *Equestrian Statue of Marcus Aurelius*. Michelangelo's *Moses* displays a pent-up emotional and physical energy that was influenced by Hellenistic statuary.

42. **(B)**

Contrapposto refers to the relaxed natural stance first used during the Classical period of Greek art. Chiaroscuro refers to the use of light and dark, especially the gradations of light that produce the effect of modeling. Chiaroscuro was first used during the Early Renaissance. Chakra is the Buddha's wheel, set in motions at Sarnath. Canonization refers to the process by which a revered deceased person is declared a saint by the pope.

43. **(D)**

The procession at San Vitale recalls the procession of Augustus and his entourage on the Ara Pacis. However, the two works are stylistically very different. In the Ara Pacis, the fully modeled marble figures have their feet planted firmly on the ground. In contrast, the figures in San Vitale are flat and frontal. They seem to hover before viewers, weightless and speechless. Choices A, B, and C are true statements.

44. **(D)**

Choices A, B, and C are true statements. Hatshepsut's mortuary temple does *not* include stone pyramids for the royal family. Stone pyramids are a feature of Old Kingdom mortuary complexes.

45. **(A)**

Hogarth is best known for narrative paintings and prints such as the *Marriage a la Mode* series that satirizes English society. Constable is best known for landscape paintings that depict the pastoral beauty of the English countryside. Daumier is best known for lithographs that lampoon politicians and call attention to atrocities. Goya created etchings that portray darkly emotional images.

46. (A)

Eadweard Muybridge is most closely associated with the development of sequential motion photography. His sequential motion studies influenced Edgar Degas and Marcel Duchamp. Jacob Riis is best known for his photographs of the deplorable living conditions endured by immigrants living in Manhattan's Lower East Side. Dorothea Lange is best known for her poignant photographs of migrant workers taken during the Great Depression. Félix Nadar was a pioneering and innovative French photographer who was among the first to use electric light for photographs and invented aerial photography, hovering above Paris in a hot air balloon.

47. (A)

A cartoon is a full-size preliminary drawing from which a painting is made. Leonardo da Vinci and Michelangelo created much-admired cartoons for the east wall of the Grand Council Hall in Florence's Palazzo Vecchio. A canon is a system of proportions. For example, Polykleitos used a canon to create the *Doryphoros*. A cloison is a cell made of metal wire or a narrow metal strip soldered edge-up to a metal base to hold enamel or other decorative materials. The purse cover discovered at Sutton Hoo provides a good example of the cloison technique. A codex consists of pages of vellum or parchment bound together at one side and is thus the predecessor of the modern book.

48. (D)

De Kooning, Newman, and Pollock are associated with Abstract Expressionism. Claes Oldenburg is a Pop artist best known for creating huge outdoor sculptures of everyday objects such as spoons, peeled bananas, and clothespins.

49. (D)

Choices A, B, and C are true statements. Vermeer did not paint innovative landscapes. Jacob van Ruisdael is the Dutch artist best known for painting innovative landscapes.

50. (A)

Gertrude Stein supported a number of avant-garde artists, including Picasso, Matisse, and Duchamp. Baudelaire was a French poet and essayist whose writings influenced both the Realists and the Impressionists. Baudelaire urged artists to focus on the "heroism of modern life." Chevreul was a chemist whose work on color influenced Seurat. Madame de Pompadour was Louis XV's official mistress. She was an important patron of Rococo artists such as Francois Boucher.

51. (D)

A tympanum is a lunette-shaped space above a cathedral portal. Do not confuse a tympanum with a pediment. A pediment is triangular-shaped space above the entrance to a classical temple. In church architecture, the trumeau is the pillar or center post supporting the lintel in the middle of a doorway. In Gothic architecture, an archivolt is one of a series of concentric bands framing the tympanum.

52. (C)

The Death of the Virgin, from a tympanum at Strasbourg Cathedral, illustrates how Gothic German artists emphasized passionate drama. For example, Mary Magdalene crouches beside the deathbed wringing her hands in despair. In addition, each of the apostles expresses the grief and anguish they feel as a result of Mary's death.

53. (B)

Palladio is one of history's most admired and copied architects. He is best known for designing country villas. The Villa Rotunda is his universally acclaimed masterpiece. Vitruvius was a Roman architect whose treatise was rediscovered in 1414. Bernini was the greatest Baroque sculptor. Maderno was an architect best known for completing the facade of St. Peter's Cathedral.

54. (B)

The Villa Rotunda's temple porch and dome-covered rotunda clearly show the influence of the Pantheon. Hagia Sophia, an Egyptian pylon temple, and the temple of Athena Nike all lack these distinctive features.

55. (A)

Located outside of London, Chiswick House was strongly influenced by the Villa Rotunda. For example, both homes have a classical portico and rooms that radiate from a central rotunda. Designed by Frank Lloyd Wright, Fallingwater is an example of organic architecture. The Villa Savoye illustrates the International Style of architecture. Strawberry Hill helped popularize the Gothic Revival style.

56. (D)

Futurism began in 1909 when the Italian poet F. T. Marinetti issued "The Foundation and Manifesto of Futurism." Marinetti urged painters to show "courage and audacity" by rejecting nature as well as biblical and classical references. He encouraged artists to instead celebrate "a new beauty, the beauty of speed."

57. (D)

The paintings in choices A, B, and C contain some representational elements. In contrast, Kandinsky was the first artist to abandon all reference to recognizable reality.

58. (D)

Repoussé is a technique in which reliefs are formed by beating a metal plate from the back, leaving a metal impression on the face. The repoussé technique was used to create the death mask of Tutankhamen, the head of Shapur II, and the funerary masks from the Treasury of Atreus. The two warriors of Riace are free-standing bronze statues that were cast using the lost wax process.

59. **(B)**

The Crusaders brought back sacred bones, garments, and even splinters from the True Cross. As peace and prosperity spread across western Europe, pilgrims traveled to see the shrines containing these sacred relics. The popularity of pilgrimages played a key role in the construction of Romanesque cathedrals. Note that the architectural innovations advocated by Abbot Suger played a pivotal role in the development of Gothic architecture.

60. **(A)**

A pylon is the slanting towerlike gate at the entrance to an Egyptian temple. Note that Mycenaean tombs used corbelled arches.

61. **(D)**

The Ishtar Gate, Marduk Ziggurat, and Hanging Gardens were built during the reign of Nebuchadnezzar. The White Temple was a ziggurat built in the Sumerian city-state of Uruk in about 3000 BCE.

62. **(B)**

Spiral Jetty is an example of Earth Art. Also called Environmental Art, this American art form first emerged during the 1960s. Earth artists often use the land itself to construct monuments of great scale and minimal form. Pop Art first appeared during the 1950s. It uses images drawn from popular culture. Developed by the English painter Bridget Riley in the mid-1960s, Op Art combines color and abstract patterns to produce optical illusions of pulsating movement. As the name implies, Performance Art involves the artist talking, singing, or dancing. Performance Art requires the artists to use their bodies in front of an audience.

63. **(C)**

Spiral Jetty was influenced by Neolithic stone structures such as Stonehenge, by prehistoric earth mounds in the United States, and by Minimalist sculptures. *Spiral Jetty* was *not* influenced by Analytic Cubism.

64. **(A)**

Spiral Jetty was created by Robert Smithson. Nancy Holt, Christo, and Andy Goldsworthy are also notable Earth artists.

65. **(B)**

Earth Art became prominent during the 1960s and 1970s.

66. **(B)**

Sant' Andrea was designed by Alberti. Brunelleschi, Borromini, and Bramante were also important Italian architects. Brunelleschi is best known for designing the dome of Florence Cathedral. Borromini is best known for the undulating facade of San Carlo alle Quattro Fontane. Bramante is best known for designing the Tempietto in Rome.

67. **(B)**

Sant' Andrea is an excellent example of Renaissance architecture. Notice how it incorporates elements of classical architecture, such as the triumphal arch and pediment, into a church facade. Also note the facade's perfect symmetry. A High Gothic facade would have elaborate portals, a tympanum, and stained-glass windows. Both Baroque and Rococo facades would be far more ornamental.

68. **(D)**

The facade does include a triumphal arch, a pediment, and pilasters. It does *not* include decorative figural sculptures.

69. **(B)**

The *Standard of Ur* is one of the oldest works of art to tell a narrative story. Each of its two sides is divided into three horizontal bands or registers. *Hammurabi's Code* was inscribed on a tall black-basalt stele. The 282 laws carved onto the stele are a milestone in legal history. The figures on the *Standard of Ur* are in very low relief. In contrast, Hammurabi and the god Shamash are carved in high relief.

70. **(C)**

The Ara Pacis, Trajan's Column, and the Arch of Constantine were built to glorify the achievements of Roman emperors. In contrast, the catacombs were subterranean networks of rock-cut galleries and chambers designed as cemeteries for the burial of early Christians.

71. **(C)**

The Archaic period of Greek art is contemporary with sixth-century BCE Etruscan temples. The Armarna statues in ancient Egypt were carved in the mid-fourteenth century BCE. The Fourth-Style wall paintings in Pompeii were drawn in the mid-first century CE. The Minoan frescoes in Crete date to the mid-fifteenth century BCE.

72. **(A)**

Aaron Douglas was an African-American artist who played a prominent role in the Harlem Renaissance, a movement that spanned the 1920s and 1930s. Romare Bearden, often described as America's greatest black artist, began his work in the 1940s. He achieved his greatest acclaim by creating vivid photocollages depicting the African-American experience. Charles Demuth and Georgia O'Keeffe were both noteworthy Precisionists.

73. **(B)**

Choices A, C, and D are accurate statements. The bronze doors at Saint Michael's, Hildesheim, are examples of Ottonian art that were created in 1015, almost a century before the beginning of Romanesque art.

74. **(D)**

The choir and apse are traditionally located at the east end of a medieval church. The clerestory refers to a row of windows located at the upper part of a church nave. The narthex, or porch, is located at the western entrance of a church. The crypt is located below the nave.

75. **(D)**

Orthogonals are imaginary lines that appear to recede toward the vanishing point on the horizon. They are part of a system of linear perspective created during the Early Renaissance. An imaginary conversation among saints from different epochs is called a *sacra conversazione*.

76. **(C)**

Bosch's wildly imaginative settings, fanciful figures and unusual animals are often cited as inspirations for the work of Surrealists such as Salvador Dali.

77. **(B)**

A Caravaggista was a follower of the renowned Baroque artist Caravaggio. Artemisia Gentileschi is one of the best known of the Caravaggista. Annibale Carracci was both a contemporary and rival of Caravaggio. Sofinisba Anguisola was a northern Italian artist who moved to Spain in 1559. She is known for portraits featuring relaxed poses and a graceful treatment of forms. Angelica Kauffmann was an eighteenth-century artist whose works were inspired by classical themes.

78. **(C)**

The tetrarchy (rule by four) was created by Emperor Diocletian to divide power and restore order in the Roman Empire. The figures in this statue represent the four tetrarchs.

79. **(D)**

The artist did not try to portray four unique individuals. Instead, we see four anonymous but equal partners who share power collectively.

80. **(B)**

The tetrarchy was created by Emperor Diocletian in 305 CE. It would therefore date to the late Roman Empire.

81. **(C)**

The Haywain was painted by the English artist John Constable. The German artist Caspar David Friedrich and the American artists Thomas Cole and Frederick Edwin Church are also know for their landscape paintings.

82. **(A)**

The Haywain is best described as a Romantic landscape painting. It was painted during a period when England was being rapidly transformed by the Industrial Revolution. *The Haywain* captures the widespread nostalgia for a lifestyle that was being rapidly lost.

83. **(C)**

The Haywain clearly expresses choices A, B, and D. It does *not* portray angry farmers displaced by the Industrial Revolution.

84. **(A)**

Turner and Constable were contemporaries and rivals. Turner's experiments with pure color foreshadowed the work of modern twentieth-century artists.

85. **(A)**

The predella is the painted base of an altarpiece. The horizontal band in a pictorial narrative is called a register. The wedge-shaped blocks used in the construction of a true arch are called voussoirs. The passageway around the apse and choir of a church is called an ambulatory.

86. **(D)**

Both the Cathedra Petri and the bronze baldacchino in Saint Peter's Cathedral are intended to symbolize the triumph of Christianity and the papal doctrine of supremacy. Choices A and B are historically inaccurate. The Roman Catholic and Greek Orthodox faiths did not become unified, and the Reformation sparked a long series of wars between Catholics and Protestants. Designed by Bernini, the colonnade of the cathedral does symbolize the welcoming arms of the church.

87. **(D)**

Choices A, B, and C are correct pairings. Although Pope Julius II was an important patron of the arts, he did not offer Da Vinci any commissions. Da Vinci's most important patron was Ludovico Sforza, the duke of Milan.

88. **(B)**

Louise Nevelson is best known for her assemblages. Helen Frankenthaler is known for stain paintings, Alexander Calder is known for mobiles, and David Smith is known for his *Cubi* series.

89. **(C)**

Choices A, B, and D are true statements. Cézanne is best known for attempting to paint nature in terms of its underlying structure.

90. **(D)**

Choices A, B, and C are true statements. The Pre-Raphaelite Brotherhood had no influence on the Futurists. The Futurists were influenced by modern technology and a desire to convey an impression of speed and motion.

91. **(B)**

Choices A, C, and D are accurate descriptions of the plaques created by Benin artists. Choice B is an incorrect statement because the plaques use high relief.

92. **(D)**

Choices A, B, and C are accurate descriptions of characteristic features of Chagall's paintings. Chagall did not use biomorphic forms, which are associated with the work of Joan Miro.

93. **(B)**

The decline of Florence at the end of the fifteenth century is related to the growing power, prestige, and patronage of the popes in Rome. For example, Pope Julius II encouraged both Raphael and Michelangelo to come to Rome. Sienna was Florence's rival when the Renaissance began in the early 1300s. Paris became the center of Western art in the early 1700s. Although Venice was an important artistic center, it did not cause the decline of Florence at the end of the fifteenth century.

94. **(C)**

Jacob Lawrence is best known for creating cycles that focus on African American history. For example, *The Migration of the Negro* is a 60-painting series that depicts the historic migration of African Americans from the South to the big cities of the North and West. Thomas Cole was the founder of the Hudson River School. Winslow Homer is best known for his paintings of the sea. Edmonia Lewis was an American Neoclassical sculptor best known for carving *Forever Free*.

95. **(A)**

The Great Wave off Kanagawa is a woodblock print. The Old Kingdom *Statue of Khafre* is made out of diorite. The *Harbaville Triptych* contains ivory statuettes. The Klosterneuburg Altar by Nicholas of Verdun contains a number of enamel plaques.

96. **(B)**

The Nightmare by Henri Fuseli is best classified as an early example of a Romantic painting. Fuseli was among the first to attempt to depict the dark terrain of the human subconscious that became an important theme for Romantic artists.

97. **(D)**

Fuseli was one of the first artists to depict the human subconscious.

98. **(A)**

Fuseli's images of the sublime and the terrible were influenced by Baroque dynamism. This Baroque influence can also be seen in *The Raft of the Medusa* by Gericault.

99. **(D)**

Choices A, B, and C describe important characteristics of Japanese prints. The correct answer is D because Japanese prints did *not* use one-point perspective.

100. **(B)**

Choices A, C, and D are correct pairs linking a Renaissance master with his apprentice. Choice B is incorrect because Duccio di Buoninsegna and Giotto were both Early Renaissance masters. Giotto worked in Florence and Padua, while Di Buoninsegna worked in Sienna.

101. **(D)**

Arabesques (flowing intricate patterns) and calligraphy (ornamental writing) are key characteristics of Islamic art. Ionic and Corinthian columns are elements of Classical architecture. Since the Koran forbids graven images, Islamic artists avoid painting portraits or sculpting busts.

102. **(D)**

The *Alexander Mosaic* incorporates hundreds of thousands of *tesserae,* or tiny stones.

103. **(D)**

The *Alexander Mosaic* once decorated the floor of a Roman villa, now known as the House of the Faun, in Pompeii.

104. **(A)**

The *Alexander Mosaic* is believed to be a copy of a Hellenistic painting.

105. **(C)**

The *Alexander Mosaic* depicts the climactic moment in the Battle of Issus between Alexander the Great and Darius III.

106. **(D)**

Choices A, B, and C are accurate descriptions of the Guggenheim Museum in Bilbao. Choice D is incorrect because the Guggenheim Museum does *not* use pendentives. Pendentives were first used to support the dome of Hagia Sophia in Constantinople.

107. **(B)**

Picasso and Georges Braque collaborated to create the Cubist style. The Armory Show was a pivotal exhibit of modern art held in New York City in 1913. The Blue Riders (Der Blaue Reiter) were a group of German Expressionists cofounded by Vassily Kandinsky and Franz Marc. "The Foundation and Manifesto of Futurism" was written by F. T. Marinetti.

108. **(D)**

Choices A, B, and C are characteristic features of Fallingwater. Choice D is a characteristic of the works of International Style architects such as Le Corbusier.

109. **(B)**

Choices A, C, and D are characteristic features of Cycladic figures. Choice B is not a feature of Cycladic figures. The Cycladic figures are abstract, whereas the Sumerian votive statues are designed to represent their donors.

110. **(A)**

Pueblos are multistoried communal dwellings made of stone or adobe brick built by Native Americans living in the Southwest. A portico is an entrance porch. A parapet is a low, protective wall along the edge of a balcony or roof. A pylon is a massive gateway, with sloping walls, characteristic of Egyptian temples.

111. **(B)**

Michelangelo's *Moses* was intended to be part of Pope Julius II's tomb. The image of the great Old Testament lawgiver is thought to be a portrait of the pope.

112. **(A)**

Founded by Walter Gropius, the Bauhaus was a school of design and architecture that helped create the International Style.

113. **(A)**

The Vietnam Veterans Memorial was designed by Maya Ying Lin. Louise Nevelson is best known for her assemblages. Donald Judd is best known for his minimalist sculptures of geometric forms. Robert Smithson was an Earth artist best known for creating *Spiral Jetty*.

114. **(D)**

The Vietnam Veterans Memorial is a war memorial dedicated to American men and women who died fighting in the Vietnam War. The names of the 57,939 casualties of the war (and those still missing) are incised on the wall in the order of their deaths.

115. **(D)**

The Vietnam Veterans Memorial is a particularly moving example of Minimalist Art. It uses an austere, simple geometric form to convey a powerful emotional message.

Section II

1. Question 1 asks you to identify two works of art that portray important political or religious leaders. Your choices may include leaders who held both political and religious power. You must also include one example from beyond the European tradition. The first part of answering this question successfully is to make appropriate choices in the works of art that you discuss. The figures that you discuss must have been important leaders in their cultures. Another part to answering the question successfully is to be as specific as possible with your examples. For instance, you will receive more credit by referring to the Portrait of Pope Julius II rather than "the portrait of a Renaissance pope." If you can only think of a generic label, it is better to write that than nothing at all. After identifying two appropriate works of art, you should discuss four characteristics of each work that visually explain the leaders' roles, achievements, and/or beliefs. You must convey to the reader that the elements of each work demonstrate the importance of the depicted leader.

The examples listed here could easily apply to this question. This is not an exhaustive list. You and your teacher may be able to think of other appropriate choices.

Non-European Tradition

- *Stele of Naram-Sin* (Sumerian)
- *Stele of Hammurabi*, also known as *Hammurabi's Code* (Babylonian)
- *Seated Statue of Gudea* (Neo-Sumerian)
- *Seated Statue of Khafre* (Old Kingdom, Ancient Egyptian)
- *Hatshepsut with Offering Jars* (New Kingdom, Ancient Egyptian)
- *Statue of Akhenaton* (New Kingdom, Ancient Egyptian)

European Tradition

- *Statue of Augustus from Primaporta* (Imperial Roman)
- *Colossal Head of Constantine the Great* (Late Imperial Roman, Early Christian)
- *Equestrian Statue of Charlemagne* (Carolingian)
- *Bayeaux Tapestry* (William the Conqueror's invasion and conquest of England, Romanesque period)
- *Portrait of Pope Julius II* (Raphael, High Renaissance)
- *King Philip IV of Spain,* also known as *Fraga Philip* (Diego Velazquez, Baroque)
- *Portrait of Henry VIII* (Hans Holbein the Younger, Northern Renaissance)
- *Portrait of Louis XIV* (Hyacinthe Rigaud, Baroque)
- *Bust of Louis XIV* (Gianlorenzo Bernini, Baroque)
- *The Coronation of Napoleon* (Jacques-Louis David, Neoclassical)

2. This image is known as the *Seated Boxer*. It is from the Hellenistic period of Greek art. The style of Hellenistic art departed from the qualities valued in Classical Greek art. For the Classical period, remember the acronym HAIR: classical statues were **h**eroic, **a**loof, **i**dealized, and **r**estrained. The statues usually depicted heroic figures and gods with youthful idealized bodies. The statues were aloof with restrained emotions, often looking off from the viewer.

During the Hellenistic period, artists instead focused on the four *E*'s: everyday people, emotional, expressionistic, and sometimes erotic. The *Seated Boxer* looks past his prime. His muscles are starting to sag, and he hunches over as if he is tired and defeated. On his face, you can see evidence of gashes and scars, trademarks of his violent sport. His face looks up pathetically and causes the viewer to feel sympathy for this defeated figure. Hellenistic artists drew their inspiration from everyday figures like the *Seated Boxer*. The posture and facial expression used by the artist make the work very expressionistic, which means that it conveys emotion and feeling to the viewer.

3. This building is called the Royal Pavilion. It was built as a summer home for the prince regent of England, who would become King George IV. John Nash, who was the architect, drew from Islamic sources in India when he designed it. The building has minarets, which function as embellishments for the design. In authentic Islamic architecture, minarets function as towers from which the calls to daily prayers are announced. The building also incorporates onion-shaped domes reminiscent of the Taj Majal in India. The British practiced colonialism in India, and certain parts of Indian culture were alluring to the British, including the exotic architecture. The building also incorporates screens and pointed arches from Islamic architecture. The pointed arches were also used in Europe during the Gothic period of the thirteenth and fourteenth centuries. In the nineteenth century, there was a revival of Gothic architecture in England. Synthesizing the Gothic revival with the influence of Islamic architecture that the British observed in India, the Royal Pavilion is described by art historians as "Indian Gothic."

Looking at the facade of the Royal Pavilion, you can see the influence of Greek architecture as well. Nash made extensive use of columns in the exterior. The building also has a symmetrical, balanced composition, which shows the influence of Classical-Style architecture. This makes sense because Nash was famous for his Neoclassical designs before designing the Royal Pavilion.

4. This is an apse mosaic in the church in the Monastery of Saint Catherine in Sinai, Egypt. It contains several elements that identify it as Byzantine art. For Byzantine art, remember 3 *F*'s and a *G*: flat, floating, frontal, and golden. Byzantine art does not contain realistic modulations of light and shadow. Although artists do incorporate highlights and shadow in the figures and their clothing, people and objects look somewhat flat and two-dimensional. The figures in Byzantine art usually seem to hover above the ground with their feet pointed downward in an unrealistic manner; the figures appear to be floating. The figures are often arranged frontally in a linear manner with very little overlapping, giving most scenes a planar or flat-looking composition. Finally, Byzantine artists usually use golden backgrounds. All these features are known as the Byzantine aesthetic. Because Byzantine art revolved around Christianity, capturing

nature in a realistic manner and using pictorial illusionism with spatial recession were not important. Byzantine art was supposed to convey spirituality (this may be why the figures hover above the ground). Once you understand these concepts, Byzantine art is usually easy to recognize.

5.   The artist who painted these works is Giorgio de Chirico. The style of art with which his work is associated is Surrealism. Surrealism, which became prominent in the late 1910s and 1920s, is known for its odd juxtapositions of recognizable objects to create mysterious, dreamlike scenes. The image on the left, *Melancholy and Mystery of a Street,* shows a girl rolling a wheel down an apparently empty street with Roman and Italian Renaissance architecture on the sides. She is moving toward an empty van, and an ominous shadow is shown down the street from her. You may ask yourself: Where is this girl going? What is the meaning of that shadow? Is something going to happen to the girl? The odd juxtaposition of these objects makes the viewer ask these questions. The image on the right incorporates similar incongruous imagery. The large head and hands of a classical sculpture peer out from the building on the right. Another statue of a recumbent nude woman is shown in the center. In the background, two small men shake hands. A small locomotive passes a central-plan, domical building in the distance. All these odd juxtapositions and the questions with which they leave the viewer are hallmarks of Surrealism.

6.   Both images depict the Virgin Mary and Jesus Christ as a child. The image on the left dates from an earlier period, the Romanesque of the eleventh and twelfth centuries (note that you do not have to say this and if you are not sure of the period, leave it out because the question does not ask for this information). The image on the right, known as the *Virgin of Paris*, is French Gothic sculpture from the early fourteenth century. The image on the left has much less naturalism. The Virgin sits rigidly with the Christ child on her lap. The composition is frontal and somewhat simplistic. Objects such as this were venerated by pilgrims en route to various important churches throughout Europe. It simply conveys the idea of the Virgin and Christ. In the image on the right, the artist is attempting to show more naturalism. The body positioning is called the Gothic *S* curve. The human proportions in the image on the right are less realistic than in the image on the left. Notice how the arms of the Christ child in the image on the left are too small for his head and the rest of his body. In the image on the right, the sculpture's human proportions are becoming more realistic. During the Gothic period, sculpture was slowly returning to the naturalism of classical antiquity. This movement would come to fruition during the Early Renaissance, which came just after the Gothic period.

7.   Andrea del Castagno's *Last Supper* on the left reflects the Italian Renaissance (notice his Italian name). The work of Dirk Bouts on the right reflects the artistic developments of the Northern Renaissance in Flanders. Castagno's *Last Supper* shows a greater interest in human proportions. Italian Renaissance artists had greater access to classical sculpture than did other artists of the time and modeled the proportions of their human figures on those statues. Notice the highly developed naturalism in the bodies of

the figures, which is revealed underneath their robes. The room in which Castagno's *Last Supper* is set is reminiscent of Italian architecture and incorporates marble panels in the walls. Castagno is also experimenting with linear perspective, which also fascinated the great Italian artists of the *Quattrocento* (1400s). Notice how Castagno attempts to use orthogonal lines and creates a recessional space, although his attempt falls a little short of accurate linear perspective (for example, you can see the orange tiles of the roof and the ceiling of the room simultaneously, which is an inaccurate perspective).

Dirk Bouts's *Last Supper* reflects the characteristics of Northern Renaissance painters. His scene has tremendous detail from the folds in the robes, to the panels on the floor, the chandelier above the table, to the buildings that are visible through the window. You can also see precise detail in the faces and hair of Christ and his apostles. In addition to including details in the features, Northern Renaissance compositions tended to be more complex than those of the Italian Renaissance. Dirk Bouts's painting also makes attempts to use linear perspective within the main room, in the room in the back right, and outside the window on the left. Like Castagno's, Bouts's attempt falls short because his vanishing points do not fall on the horizon line. Finally, notice how the human proportions are slightly off on the figures. This lack of proportionality reflects Northern Renaissance artists' having less access to classical sculptures than the Italians and their lack of interest in reviving classical standards of proportion in the way that the Italian artists did.

8.   J. J. Winckelmann states that eighteenth-century artists should model their works on the art of classical antiquity. In his mind, the ancient artists achieved the pinnacle in imitating the natural world while striving to reveal it in its most perfect form. Winckelmann discusses how the Greeks established a standard of proportions that revealed the perfection of the human form. This perfection was good for the mind because it caused civilization to strive for perfection in its spirit as well. As the fall of the Roman Empire gave way to the Dark Ages and Middle Ages, these standards in art were overlooked because art was used to teach Christian stories and did not necessarily reflect the natural world. In addition, the perfection of the nude human form was proscribed (forbidden) because the naked form was associated with lust and sinfulness. Renaissance artists did revive interest in the art of the ancients. Winckelmann is reinforcing the value of emulating art of the antiquity for his generation and beyond in the eighteenth century. This was spurred on by the excavations happening in Pompeii and Herculaneum, two ancient Roman cities, during the mid-eighteenth century.

David's *Death of Socrates* is a good example of returning to these classical values. It tells the story of how Socrates chose a death sentence over exile from Athens. Because the Athenian Assembly voted democratically to sentence him to death, he agreed to obey the law even if it meant his death. This can be seen by the symbolism of the open shackle by the foot of Socrates in the painting. Yet, Socrates has no thought of fleeing. Socrates instead points his finger upward, teaching one final lesson to his students as he reaches for the hemlock with his other hand. This reflects the higher spirituality to which Winckelmann refers. In addition, Socrates's body as well as the bodies of his students are both very naturalistic and idealized. Socrates does not have the body of an old philosopher but the build of a youthful athlete similar to the *Doryphoros* by Polykleitos.

The whole scene imitates the natural world realistically while idealizing it. David uses accurate chiaroscuro from the figures themselves to the classical architecture that surrounds them. David's *Death of Socrates* is considered Neoclassical art and emulates the pictorial elements as well as the moralistic elements of self-sacrifice for higher ideals of the classical antiquity. This is the type of art that Winckelmann would consider great based on his quotation.

9.   This question asks you to identify two paintings in which light plays an important role. One painting must be from before 1800 CE, and one must be from after 1800 CE. Then you should come up with four characteristics that compare and contrast the two paintings. Both paintings can come from the European tradition. It is important to choose examples in which light clearly plays an important role. If light is not a significant aspect in the painting, this essay will be difficult to write. Then discuss how light is used in each painting. Did the artist use light in a symbolic manner? Did the artist incorporate light to dramatize a significant event or place? Was the artist interested in the effects of light on color? These are questions that should be addressed as you are discussing your choices.

Certain styles of art lend themselves well to this discussion. Before 1800 CE, light was noticeable and significant in Mannerism in the sixteenth century and the Baroque period of the seventeenth century. In certain Renaissance paintings, light is an important stylistic element, usually because Renaissance artists were trying to perfect the effects of light on objects in their paintings. Capturing the effect of light realistically was a goal for Renaissance painters such as Masaccio and Leonardo da Vinci. After 1800 CE, the Romantic artists, Hudson River School painters, and Impressionists often made light a prominent part of their works. If you understand the use of light by the aforementioned styles, you can choose a painting with which you feel comfortable for each period and explain it as well as the overall goals of the movement with which it is associated. Of course, there are paintings outside these traditions in which the use of light is significant. The following paintings, which include but are not limited to these styles, could work well for this question.

Pre-1800 CE

- *Still Life with Peaches* (Herculaneaum, Roman art)
- *Last Supper* (Tintoretto, Mannerism)
- *Burial of Count Orgaz* (El Greco, usually associated with Mannerism)
- *The Calling of Saint Matthew* (Caravaggio, Italian Baroque)
- *The Conversion of Saint Paul* (Caravaggio, Italian Baroque)
- *The Supper at Emmaus* (Caravaggio, Italian Baroque)
- *Return of the Prodigal Son* (Rembrandt, Dutch Baroque)
- *The Love Letter* (Vermeer, Dutch Baroque)
- *Penitent Magdalene* (George de La Tour, French Baroque)

Note: Baroque art makes great use of theatrical lighting. This is fairly consistent throughout the various European countries during the seventeenth-century Baroque period.

Post-1800 CE

- *Raft of the Medusa* (Theodore Gericault, Romanticism)

- *Abbey in the Oak Forest* (Caspar David Friedrich, Romanticism)

- *View from Mount Holyoke, Northampton, Massachusetts, after a Thunderstorm*; also known as *The Oxbox* (Thomas Cole, Hudson River School)

- *Among the Sierra Nevada Mountains, California* (Albert Bierstadt, Hudson River School)

- *Twilight in the Wilderness* (Frederic Edwin Church, Hudson River School)

- *The Angelus* (Jean-Francois Millet, Realism)

- *The Gross Clinic* (Thomas Eakins, American Realism)

- *Impression Sunrise* (Claude Monet, Impressionism)

- *Rouen Cathedral: The Portal (in Sun)* (Claude Monet, Impressionism)

- *Le Moulin de la Galette* (Pierre-August Renoir, Impressionism)

- *At the Moulin Rouge* (Henri de Toulouse-Lautrec, Impressionist era, interested in the effects of gaslight on people's complexions in interior scenes)

PRACTICE EXAM 1

AP Art History

Answer Sheet

1. Ⓐ Ⓑ Ⓒ Ⓓ	28. Ⓐ Ⓑ Ⓒ Ⓓ	55. Ⓐ Ⓑ Ⓒ Ⓓ
2. Ⓐ Ⓑ Ⓒ Ⓓ	29. Ⓐ Ⓑ Ⓒ Ⓓ	56. Ⓐ Ⓑ Ⓒ Ⓓ
3. Ⓐ Ⓑ Ⓒ Ⓓ	30. Ⓐ Ⓑ Ⓒ Ⓓ	57. Ⓐ Ⓑ Ⓒ Ⓓ
4. Ⓐ Ⓑ Ⓒ Ⓓ	31. Ⓐ Ⓑ Ⓒ Ⓓ	58. Ⓐ Ⓑ Ⓒ Ⓓ
5. Ⓐ Ⓑ Ⓒ Ⓓ	32. Ⓐ Ⓑ Ⓒ Ⓓ	59. Ⓐ Ⓑ Ⓒ Ⓓ
6. Ⓐ Ⓑ Ⓒ Ⓓ	33. Ⓐ Ⓑ Ⓒ Ⓓ	60. Ⓐ Ⓑ Ⓒ Ⓓ
7. Ⓐ Ⓑ Ⓒ Ⓓ	34. Ⓐ Ⓑ Ⓒ Ⓓ	61. Ⓐ Ⓑ Ⓒ Ⓓ
8. Ⓐ Ⓑ Ⓒ Ⓓ	35. Ⓐ Ⓑ Ⓒ Ⓓ	62. Ⓐ Ⓑ Ⓒ Ⓓ
9. Ⓐ Ⓑ Ⓒ Ⓓ	36. Ⓐ Ⓑ Ⓒ Ⓓ	63. Ⓐ Ⓑ Ⓒ Ⓓ
10. Ⓐ Ⓑ Ⓒ Ⓓ	37. Ⓐ Ⓑ Ⓒ Ⓓ	64. Ⓐ Ⓑ Ⓒ Ⓓ
11. Ⓐ Ⓑ Ⓒ Ⓓ	38. Ⓐ Ⓑ Ⓒ Ⓓ	65. Ⓐ Ⓑ Ⓒ Ⓓ
12. Ⓐ Ⓑ Ⓒ Ⓓ	39. Ⓐ Ⓑ Ⓒ Ⓓ	66. Ⓐ Ⓑ Ⓒ Ⓓ
13. Ⓐ Ⓑ Ⓒ Ⓓ	40. Ⓐ Ⓑ Ⓒ Ⓓ	67. Ⓐ Ⓑ Ⓒ Ⓓ
14. Ⓐ Ⓑ Ⓒ Ⓓ	41. Ⓐ Ⓑ Ⓒ Ⓓ	68. Ⓐ Ⓑ Ⓒ Ⓓ
15. Ⓐ Ⓑ Ⓒ Ⓓ	42. Ⓐ Ⓑ Ⓒ Ⓓ	69. Ⓐ Ⓑ Ⓒ Ⓓ
16. Ⓐ Ⓑ Ⓒ Ⓓ	43. Ⓐ Ⓑ Ⓒ Ⓓ	70. Ⓐ Ⓑ Ⓒ Ⓓ
17. Ⓐ Ⓑ Ⓒ Ⓓ	44. Ⓐ Ⓑ Ⓒ Ⓓ	71. Ⓐ Ⓑ Ⓒ Ⓓ
18. Ⓐ Ⓑ Ⓒ Ⓓ	45. Ⓐ Ⓑ Ⓒ Ⓓ	72. Ⓐ Ⓑ Ⓒ Ⓓ
19. Ⓐ Ⓑ Ⓒ Ⓓ	46. Ⓐ Ⓑ Ⓒ Ⓓ	73. Ⓐ Ⓑ Ⓒ Ⓓ
20. Ⓐ Ⓑ Ⓒ Ⓓ	47. Ⓐ Ⓑ Ⓒ Ⓓ	74. Ⓐ Ⓑ Ⓒ Ⓓ
21. Ⓐ Ⓑ Ⓒ Ⓓ	48. Ⓐ Ⓑ Ⓒ Ⓓ	75. Ⓐ Ⓑ Ⓒ Ⓓ
22. Ⓐ Ⓑ Ⓒ Ⓓ	49. Ⓐ Ⓑ Ⓒ Ⓓ	76. Ⓐ Ⓑ Ⓒ Ⓓ
23. Ⓐ Ⓑ Ⓒ Ⓓ	50. Ⓐ Ⓑ Ⓒ Ⓓ	77. Ⓐ Ⓑ Ⓒ Ⓓ
24. Ⓐ Ⓑ Ⓒ Ⓓ	51. Ⓐ Ⓑ Ⓒ Ⓓ	78. Ⓐ Ⓑ Ⓒ Ⓓ
25. Ⓐ Ⓑ Ⓒ Ⓓ	52. Ⓐ Ⓑ Ⓒ Ⓓ	79. Ⓐ Ⓑ Ⓒ Ⓓ
26. Ⓐ Ⓑ Ⓒ Ⓓ	53. Ⓐ Ⓑ Ⓒ Ⓓ	80. Ⓐ Ⓑ Ⓒ Ⓓ
27. Ⓐ Ⓑ Ⓒ Ⓓ	54. Ⓐ Ⓑ Ⓒ Ⓓ	81. Ⓐ Ⓑ Ⓒ Ⓓ

82. Ⓐ Ⓑ Ⓒ Ⓓ	94. Ⓐ Ⓑ Ⓒ Ⓓ	106. Ⓐ Ⓑ Ⓒ Ⓓ
83. Ⓐ Ⓑ Ⓒ Ⓓ	95. Ⓐ Ⓑ Ⓒ Ⓓ	107. Ⓐ Ⓑ Ⓒ Ⓓ
84. Ⓐ Ⓑ Ⓒ Ⓓ	96. Ⓐ Ⓑ Ⓒ Ⓓ	108. Ⓐ Ⓑ Ⓒ Ⓓ
85. Ⓐ Ⓑ Ⓒ Ⓓ	97. Ⓐ Ⓑ Ⓒ Ⓓ	109. Ⓐ Ⓑ Ⓒ Ⓓ
86. Ⓐ Ⓑ Ⓒ Ⓓ	98. Ⓐ Ⓑ Ⓒ Ⓓ	110. Ⓐ Ⓑ Ⓒ Ⓓ
87. Ⓐ Ⓑ Ⓒ Ⓓ	99. Ⓐ Ⓑ Ⓒ Ⓓ	111. Ⓐ Ⓑ Ⓒ Ⓓ
88. Ⓐ Ⓑ Ⓒ Ⓓ	100. Ⓐ Ⓑ Ⓒ Ⓓ	112. Ⓐ Ⓑ Ⓒ Ⓓ
89. Ⓐ Ⓑ Ⓒ Ⓓ	101. Ⓐ Ⓑ Ⓒ Ⓓ	113. Ⓐ Ⓑ Ⓒ Ⓓ
90. Ⓐ Ⓑ Ⓒ Ⓓ	102. Ⓐ Ⓑ Ⓒ Ⓓ	114. Ⓐ Ⓑ Ⓒ Ⓓ
91. Ⓐ Ⓑ Ⓒ Ⓓ	103. Ⓐ Ⓑ Ⓒ Ⓓ	115. Ⓐ Ⓑ Ⓒ Ⓓ
92. Ⓐ Ⓑ Ⓒ Ⓓ	104. Ⓐ Ⓑ Ⓒ Ⓓ	
93. Ⓐ Ⓑ Ⓒ Ⓓ	105. Ⓐ Ⓑ Ⓒ Ⓓ	

Section II

Use the following pages to prepare your essays.

PRACTICE EXAM 2

AP Art History

Answer Sheet

1. Ⓐ Ⓑ Ⓒ Ⓓ	28. Ⓐ Ⓑ Ⓒ Ⓓ	55. Ⓐ Ⓑ Ⓒ Ⓓ
2. Ⓐ Ⓑ Ⓒ Ⓓ	29. Ⓐ Ⓑ Ⓒ Ⓓ	56. Ⓐ Ⓑ Ⓒ Ⓓ
3. Ⓐ Ⓑ Ⓒ Ⓓ	30. Ⓐ Ⓑ Ⓒ Ⓓ	57. Ⓐ Ⓑ Ⓒ Ⓓ
4. Ⓐ Ⓑ Ⓒ Ⓓ	31. Ⓐ Ⓑ Ⓒ Ⓓ	58. Ⓐ Ⓑ Ⓒ Ⓓ
5. Ⓐ Ⓑ Ⓒ Ⓓ	32. Ⓐ Ⓑ Ⓒ Ⓓ	59. Ⓐ Ⓑ Ⓒ Ⓓ
6. Ⓐ Ⓑ Ⓒ Ⓓ	33. Ⓐ Ⓑ Ⓒ Ⓓ	60. Ⓐ Ⓑ Ⓒ Ⓓ
7. Ⓐ Ⓑ Ⓒ Ⓓ	34. Ⓐ Ⓑ Ⓒ Ⓓ	61. Ⓐ Ⓑ Ⓒ Ⓓ
8. Ⓐ Ⓑ Ⓒ Ⓓ	35. Ⓐ Ⓑ Ⓒ Ⓓ	62. Ⓐ Ⓑ Ⓒ Ⓓ
9. Ⓐ Ⓑ Ⓒ Ⓓ	36. Ⓐ Ⓑ Ⓒ Ⓓ	63. Ⓐ Ⓑ Ⓒ Ⓓ
10. Ⓐ Ⓑ Ⓒ Ⓓ	37. Ⓐ Ⓑ Ⓒ Ⓓ	64. Ⓐ Ⓑ Ⓒ Ⓓ
11. Ⓐ Ⓑ Ⓒ Ⓓ	38. Ⓐ Ⓑ Ⓒ Ⓓ	65. Ⓐ Ⓑ Ⓒ Ⓓ
12. Ⓐ Ⓑ Ⓒ Ⓓ	39. Ⓐ Ⓑ Ⓒ Ⓓ	66. Ⓐ Ⓑ Ⓒ Ⓓ
13. Ⓐ Ⓑ Ⓒ Ⓓ	40. Ⓐ Ⓑ Ⓒ Ⓓ	67. Ⓐ Ⓑ Ⓒ Ⓓ
14. Ⓐ Ⓑ Ⓒ Ⓓ	41. Ⓐ Ⓑ Ⓒ Ⓓ	68. Ⓐ Ⓑ Ⓒ Ⓓ
15. Ⓐ Ⓑ Ⓒ Ⓓ	42. Ⓐ Ⓑ Ⓒ Ⓓ	69. Ⓐ Ⓑ Ⓒ Ⓓ
16. Ⓐ Ⓑ Ⓒ Ⓓ	43. Ⓐ Ⓑ Ⓒ Ⓓ	70. Ⓐ Ⓑ Ⓒ Ⓓ
17. Ⓐ Ⓑ Ⓒ Ⓓ	44. Ⓐ Ⓑ Ⓒ Ⓓ	71. Ⓐ Ⓑ Ⓒ Ⓓ
18. Ⓐ Ⓑ Ⓒ Ⓓ	45. Ⓐ Ⓑ Ⓒ Ⓓ	72. Ⓐ Ⓑ Ⓒ Ⓓ
19. Ⓐ Ⓑ Ⓒ Ⓓ	46. Ⓐ Ⓑ Ⓒ Ⓓ	73. Ⓐ Ⓑ Ⓒ Ⓓ
20. Ⓐ Ⓑ Ⓒ Ⓓ	47. Ⓐ Ⓑ Ⓒ Ⓓ	74. Ⓐ Ⓑ Ⓒ Ⓓ
21. Ⓐ Ⓑ Ⓒ Ⓓ	48. Ⓐ Ⓑ Ⓒ Ⓓ	75. Ⓐ Ⓑ Ⓒ Ⓓ
22. Ⓐ Ⓑ Ⓒ Ⓓ	49. Ⓐ Ⓑ Ⓒ Ⓓ	76. Ⓐ Ⓑ Ⓒ Ⓓ
23. Ⓐ Ⓑ Ⓒ Ⓓ	50. Ⓐ Ⓑ Ⓒ Ⓓ	77. Ⓐ Ⓑ Ⓒ Ⓓ
24. Ⓐ Ⓑ Ⓒ Ⓓ	51. Ⓐ Ⓑ Ⓒ Ⓓ	78. Ⓐ Ⓑ Ⓒ Ⓓ
25. Ⓐ Ⓑ Ⓒ Ⓓ	52. Ⓐ Ⓑ Ⓒ Ⓓ	79. Ⓐ Ⓑ Ⓒ Ⓓ
26. Ⓐ Ⓑ Ⓒ Ⓓ	53. Ⓐ Ⓑ Ⓒ Ⓓ	80. Ⓐ Ⓑ Ⓒ Ⓓ
27. Ⓐ Ⓑ Ⓒ Ⓓ	54. Ⓐ Ⓑ Ⓒ Ⓓ	81. Ⓐ Ⓑ Ⓒ Ⓓ

82. Ⓐ Ⓑ Ⓒ Ⓓ	94. Ⓐ Ⓑ Ⓒ Ⓓ	106. Ⓐ Ⓑ Ⓒ Ⓓ
83. Ⓐ Ⓑ Ⓒ Ⓓ	95. Ⓐ Ⓑ Ⓒ Ⓓ	107. Ⓐ Ⓑ Ⓒ Ⓓ
84. Ⓐ Ⓑ Ⓒ Ⓓ	96. Ⓐ Ⓑ Ⓒ Ⓓ	108. Ⓐ Ⓑ Ⓒ Ⓓ
85. Ⓐ Ⓑ Ⓒ Ⓓ	97. Ⓐ Ⓑ Ⓒ Ⓓ	109. Ⓐ Ⓑ Ⓒ Ⓓ
86. Ⓐ Ⓑ Ⓒ Ⓓ	98. Ⓐ Ⓑ Ⓒ Ⓓ	110. Ⓐ Ⓑ Ⓒ Ⓓ
87. Ⓐ Ⓑ Ⓒ Ⓓ	99. Ⓐ Ⓑ Ⓒ Ⓓ	111. Ⓐ Ⓑ Ⓒ Ⓓ
88. Ⓐ Ⓑ Ⓒ Ⓓ	100. Ⓐ Ⓑ Ⓒ Ⓓ	112. Ⓐ Ⓑ Ⓒ Ⓓ
89. Ⓐ Ⓑ Ⓒ Ⓓ	101. Ⓐ Ⓑ Ⓒ Ⓓ	113. Ⓐ Ⓑ Ⓒ Ⓓ
90. Ⓐ Ⓑ Ⓒ Ⓓ	102. Ⓐ Ⓑ Ⓒ Ⓓ	114. Ⓐ Ⓑ Ⓒ Ⓓ
91. Ⓐ Ⓑ Ⓒ Ⓓ	103. Ⓐ Ⓑ Ⓒ Ⓓ	115. Ⓐ Ⓑ Ⓒ Ⓓ
92. Ⓐ Ⓑ Ⓒ Ⓓ	104. Ⓐ Ⓑ Ⓒ Ⓓ	
93. Ⓐ Ⓑ Ⓒ Ⓓ	105. Ⓐ Ⓑ Ⓒ Ⓓ	

Section II

Use the following pages to prepare your essays.

Image Acknowledgments:

Page 14, Hall of Bulls, Lascaux Cave, France, photo by Anya

Page 20, Lammasu, photo by Johnny Felker

Page 26, Statue of Khafre, photo by Frank P. Roy

Page 28, Bust of Nefertiti, photo by Arkadiy Etumyan (sic)

Page 82, Dome of the Rock, photo by Gary Bedrosian

Page 110, Chartres Cathedral, photo by Ken and Janet Fries

Page 217, *Tiger Devouring a Gavial Crocodile of the Ganges,* photo by Jeffery Howe

Page 277, Pablo Picasso, *Les Demoiselles d'Avignon,* The Museum of Modern Art/ Licensed by SCALA/Art Resource, NY

Page 294, Marcel Duchamp, *Fountain,* Tate Gallery, London/Art Resource, NY

Page 296, Giorgio de Chirico, *The Song of Love,* The Museum of Modern Art/ Licensed by SCALA/Art Resource, NY

Page 307, Jackson Pollock, *Autumn Rhythm,* The Metropolitan Museum of Art/Art Resource, NY

Page 314, Andy Warhol, *Marilyn Diptych,* Tate Gallery, London/Art Resource, NY

INSTALLING REA's TESTware®

SYSTEM REQUIREMENTS

Pentium 75 MHz (300 MHz recommended) or a higher or compatible processor; Microsoft Windows 98 or later; 64 MB available RAM; Internet Explorer 5.5 or higher

INSTALLATION

1. Insert the AP Art History TESTware® CD-ROM into the CD-ROM drive.
2. If the installation doesn't begin automatically, from the Start Menu choose the RUN command. When the RUN dialog box appears, type d:\setup (where d is the letter of your CD-ROM drive) at the prompt and click OK.
3. The installation process will begin. A dialog box proposing the directory "Program Files\REA\AP_Art_History" will appear. If the name and location are suitable, click OK. If you wish to specify a different name or location, type it in and click OK.
4. Start the AP Art History TESTware® application by double-clicking on the icon.

REA's AP Art History TESTware® is **EASY** to **LEARN AND USE**. To achieve maximum benefits, we recommend that you take a few minutes to go through the on-screen tutorial on your computer.

SSD ACCOMMODATIONS FOR STUDENTS WITH DISABILITIES

Many students qualify for extra time to take the AP exams, and our TESTware® can be adapted to accommodate your time extension. This allows you to practice under the same extended-time accommodations that you will receive on the actual test day. To customize your TESTware® to suit the most common extensions, visit our website at *www.rea.com/ssd*.

TECHNICAL SUPPORT

REA's TESTware® is backed by customer and technical support. For questions about **installation or operation of your software**, contact us at:

Research & Education Association
Phone: (732) 819-8880 (9 a.m. to 5 p.m. ET, Monday–Friday)
Fax: (732) 819-8808
Website: http://www.rea.com
E-mail: info@rea.com

Note to Windows XP Users: In order for the TESTware® to function properly, please install and run the application under the same computer administrator-level user account. Installing the TESTware® as one user and running it as another could cause file-access path conflicts.